A Casebook on Corporate Renewal

A Casebook on
Corporate Renewal

EDITED BY
HARLAN D. PLATT AND MARJORIE B. PLATT

THE UNIVERSITY OF MICHIGAN PRESS
Ann Arbor

Copyright © by the University of Michigan 2004
All rights reserved
Published in the United States of America by
The University of Michigan Press
Manufactured in the United States of America
∞ Printed on acid-free paper

2007   2006   2005   2004   4   3   2   1

A CIP catalog record for this book is available from the British Library.

Library of Congress Cataloging-in-Publication Data applied for
ISBN 0-472-11369-0

Dedicated to our children—
Leah, Sarah, and Jesse

Contents

Investigation Phase

Strategic Issues

Financial Issues

Operating Issues

Preface

Since 1993 corporate renewal has gone from being an unknown and little used skill to being a full-fledged business discipline widely practiced and trusted by managers. Much of that growth and development resulted from the confluence of two events: (1) the professionalization of the field that in large measure is due to the creation of the Turnaround Management Association and the seemingly endless energy of its leadership and (2) a calamitous economic recession starting in late 2000 and officially ending in 2001 but whose lingering effect continued to afflict countless American firms through mid-2003. During these troubled times corporate renewal practitioners have helped many companies experiencing difficulties and in so doing have proved the value of their profession.

Harlan Platt published the first textbook in corporate renewal in 1998, *Principles of Corporate Renewal*. Since then it has been widely used in graduate and undergraduate business programs and in training programs at corporate renewal firms. An updated second edition was released in 2004. This corporate renewal casebook accompanies that textbook, though it can easily be adopted separately or with other textbooks. The availability of both a text and a casebook on corporate renewal should greatly increase the number of business schools teaching the topic to an ever growing number of interested students.

Howard Brownstein provides a cogent introduction to the corporate renewal field. Following this, the casebook is partitioned into six sections that epitomize the principal topics arising during a typical corporate renewal engagement. The first topic is Ethical and Legal Issues. Bankruptcy is a stressful time for managers. Ethical considerations become even more important during such times. The "Harry

Lewis: Ethical Manager" case recounts the experience of a manager of a firm on the brink of failure, the "Shrink, Inc." case focuses on the difference between malfeasance and bad judgment, and the "Corbesco" case looks at accountability in a troubled situation. The next three cases, "Toys and More, Inc." "Clark Automotive Parts, Inc.," and "The Creation of First City Financial Corporation: A Clinical Study of the Bankruptcy Process," involve the creation of bankruptcy plans of reorganization. The issue of valuation is relevant in these three cases, although it appears again in a later section.

The next section, Investigation Phase, studies several issues that predate the occurrence of bankruptcy. "Enron Red Flags Case" and "AOL Latin America (B)" look at companies not yet in bankruptcy but with different perspectives. The first inquires whether the Enron fraud could have been detected; the second asks whether analysis from an early warning system model (the Altman Z score) provides investment advice about a company not yet in bankruptcy. "Periwinkle Software, Inc." looks at a company on the verge of bankruptcy and asks what should be done. "Manchester Wholesale Distributors (A)" introduces operating considerations before failure and also asks, "Who should be in charge?" The last two cases in this section, "Clean Harbors" and "NextCard," concern industry analyses conducted to assess the likelihood that a troubled firm, if renewed, could survive in an industry.

The book then takes a strategic turn. We begin with two articles (not cases per se) that both deal with the software industry. McKinsey & Company provided the first, "A Hard Turnaround for Software." It considers issues arising in the turnaround of a company with limited fixed assets and low variable costs. The second, "Symantec's Strategy-Based Transformation," comes from *strategy+business,* published by Booz Allen Hamilton Inc. In a fashion similar to the *Principles of Corporate Renewal* book, it considers how renewal can affect a healthy company doing a transformation. Also contained within this section are two cases. The first, "Global Foods, Inc.: A Corporate Renewal Engagement," describes a once healthy company with too many products and markets. The second, "American Motors Corporation (B)," illustrates the limitations for strategic change in a company overwhelmed by competitors.

Cases in the Financial Issues section cover a wide range of topics. These include two financial restructuring cases, "RCN: How to Invest in a Turnaround" and "Ajax Electronics," involving companies of vastly different sizes. Since most financial renewal efforts involve substantial negotiations, two cases, "Jet Interiors Company Inc.: Negotiating to Restructure a Convertible Note" and "We Hear a Symphony . . . Or Do We?" bring the problem forward from the perspective of a public company and a not-for-profit company. The next issue concerns the need for cash, which is illustrated with the "P. A. Bergner & Co." case. Finally, probably the most critical need in any renewal effort is to assess and bring a firm to breakeven. The "Investing in BN.com: Can Breakeven Be Achieved?" case uses a well-known company to address this topic.

Operating Issues define the next group of cases. The first topic is bank/lender liability, which is presented in the "Crane Manufacturing Company" case. This topic arises frequently and may affect future operations. Then an activity based costing case, "Turning around the South Dakota Microbrewery," discusses how a company may incorrectly drop products if it fails to correctly allocate its overhead expenses. What to do when too many employees are on the payroll is addressed in the "Intelligent Signals, Inc." case. How to incentivize employees is such an important renewal task that three cases, "Berkshire Industries PLC," "Titeflex Corporation: The Turnaround Challenge," and "Gillette Metal Fabrication," are included. Each discusses the related question of how output and productivity can be influenced by employee performance. "Bouvet Springs, Inc." concerns how price levels are the easiest change to make that influences cash flow. "CUP Corp.: Measuring the Customer Care Center" discusses ways to improve productivity within a plant, while "Lucent Technologies: Shared Financial Services—Balanced Scorecard Implementation" discusses how employee changes affect processes and thereby cost structures.

The final section, Special Topics, considers a number of critical issues not easily classified elsewhere. For example, "Cabriole" and "Sidethrusters, Inc. (A)" discuss topics more common among small business renewals such as fraud and limited funding. The "National Financial Planners Association (A)" case looks at the renewal of a nonprofit enterprise. Last, "U.S. Auto Parts Inc.: Insolvency Simulation Exercise" is a case in which students participate in a role-playing exercise. It provides students the opportunity to practice some of the skills and techniques required for success in corporate renewal.

It is our hope that this volume will spur on the rapid growth and market acceptance of corporate renewal. To enable that, we have prepared with our authors a series of teaching notes that are available upon request to instructors who adopt the book for classroom use. Please send request on department or corporate letterhead to Professor Harlan Platt, Northeastern University, 413 Hayden Hall, Boston, MA 02115.

Acknowledgments

We thank our editor, Ellen McCarthy, and the staff at the University of Michigan Press for their continued encouragement, advice, and support. We also acknowledge the responsiveness of the many contributors to our many requests for documents, permissions, and other material without which this volume would not have come to be.

Grateful acknowledgment is made to the following authors, publishers, and journals for permission to reprint previously published materials.

Journal of Financial Education for "Investing in BN.com: Can Breakeven Be Achieved?" by Harlan D. Platt and Marjorie B. Platt. Copyright © 2002. All rights reserved. "Enron Red Flags Case" by Hugh Grove, Tom Cook, and Jon Goodwin. Copyright © 2003. All rights reserved.

McKinsey & Company, Inc., for "A Hard Turnaround for Software" by Mark Blumling, Kevin A. Frick, and William F. Meehan III. Copyright © 2002. All rights reserved.

North American Case Research Association for the following cases. "Cabriole" by Ray Kinnunen and James Molloy. Reprinted by permission from the *Case Research Journal.* Copyright © 1994 by Ray Kinnunen and James Molloy and the North American Case Research Association. All rights reserved. "The National Financial Planners Association (A)" by Ray Kinnunen, James Molloy, and John Seeger. Reprinted by permission from the *Case Research Journal.* Copyright © 1994 by Ray Kinnunen, James Molloy, and John Seeger and the North American Case Research Association. All rights reserved. "Sidethrusters, Inc. (A)" by Ray Kinnunen, John Seeger, and Robert Goldberg. Reprinted by permission from the *Case Research Journal.* Copyright © 1994 by Ray Kinnunen, John Seeger, and Robert Goldberg and the North American Case Research Association. All rights reserved. "Titeflex Corporation: The Turnaround Challenge" by Ravi Ramamurti. Reprinted by permission from the *Case Research Journal.* Copyright © 1994 by Ravi Ramamurti and the North American Case Research Association. All rights reserved.

Richard Ivey School of Business, the University of Western Ontario, for the following cases. "AOL Latin America (B)" by David Wesley and Harlan D. Platt. Copyright © 2003 by Northeastern University, College of Business Administration. "Clean Harbors" by David Wesley and Daniel McCarthy. Copyright © 2002 by Northeastern University, College of Business Administration. "Manchester Wholesale Distributors (A)" by David Wesley, Paul Croke, and Henry W. Lane. Copyright © 2002 by Northeastern University, College of Business Administration. "P. A. Bergner & Co." by Will Matthews, Chris Lane, Mark Griffiths, and Robert W. White. Copyright © 1996 by Ivey Management Services.

strategy+business for "Symantec's Strategy-Based Transformation" by Lawrence M. Fisher. Reprinted with permission from *strategy+business,* no. 30 (spring 2003), the award-winning quarterly management magazine published by Booz Allen Hamilton. www.strategy-business.com.

Every effort has been made to trace the ownership of all copyrighted material in this book and to obtain permission for its use.

Introduction

1. Turnaround Management:
The Past as Prologue

When I was an MBA student in the 1970s, no one talked about "turnaround management." The hottest career path was investment banking, followed closely by real estate development and venture capital. The notion that businesses could fail—companies of the sort that recruited among the top MBA programs—was completely out of the question. Any suggestion that business school students should bother to learn about corporate renewal, turnaround management, restructuring, and the like—let alone bankruptcy—would have been greeted with disbelief, if not derision.

At law school, which I also attended during those years, bankruptcy law was not a popular course (if it was taught at all—I truly do not remember!). The course on secured transactions and creditors' rights was taught primarily from the viewpoint of lenders and attended, of course, by students who planned to become attorneys for lenders. A law course in business planning was widely regarded as the only course offering at the time truly dealing with the typical American business enterprise, which was a small, closely held company, and that course covered many real-world aspects of the law but little about turnarounds or bankruptcy. In fact, bankruptcy was not a highly regarded field of law practice, with most white-shoe law firms that recruited at the top law schools listing bankruptcy, domestic relations, and criminal law as the areas in which they did *not* practice.

Bankruptcy was virtually unheard of among respected business

This chapter was prepared by Howard Brownstein.

enterprises. In fact, the landmark failure of the Penn Central Railroad in the early 1970s shocked American industry with the realization that a pillar of the economy could actually fail. Still, that was just a *railroad:* a common carrier, a quasi-public monopoly, heavily regulated, a vestige of the 1800s. No multibillion dollar company—let alone an industry leader—could ever fail!

Fast-forward to the present day: business bankruptcies are at an all-time high. Any lingering public squeamishness about bankruptcy has been benumbed by the failures of Enron, Global Crossing, Kmart, several major airlines, and many other once-prominent companies. We have been too distracted by headline-topping controversies about corporate governance and excessive compensation to think about the *real* upheaval in our economy—the fact that virtually *every* company, regardless of its size or ephemeral dominance, will likely go through one or more periods of serious jeopardy to its existence during its business lifetime. It is probable that every business will be in need of a turnaround effort at some point if it is to survive (and many will not survive). Indeed, bankruptcy has become a business-planning tool, with the prepackaged bankruptcy, or "prepack," an often-considered exit strategy and a sale pursuant to §363 of the Bankruptcy Code a familiar method of "cleansing the assets."

PriceWaterhouseCoopers[1] has predicted that bankruptcy filings by public companies in 2003 will stay at close to the pace of 2002, for another near-record year. Assets involved in such filings are forecast to drop only slightly, from over one-third trillion dollars in 2002 to just under one-quarter trillion dollars in 2003.

It is therefore crucial that today's business school students learn turnaround skills as a central part of the curriculum, since it's likely that these will come in handy sooner than the graduate realizes. Such skills will not only help one weather a turnaround during one's career but could be leveraged to seek and obtain a position in a company in turnaround mode. After all, the Chinese ideograph for "crisis" combines symbols for "danger" and "opportunity."

Having a well-known and successful turnaround or restructuring on one's resume—or even having gone through a Chapter 11—is likely no longer a stigma and could possibly even be a "red badge of courage." Future employers will know that the candidate has learned firsthand that turnaround management is a process, not an event, and that corporate renewal involves realistic alternatives and is not merely a struggle—possibly in vain—to return to past glory days. Bankruptcy reorganization experience provides the valuable opportunity to learn all about the U.S. trustee, who is a Justice Department official and not to be confused with the bankruptcy trustee; and about plans of reorganization, cramdowns, and preferences. While a valuable manager such a candidate is, having crossed the River Styx and—eluding Cerberus, the three-headed dog who guards the gates of Hades—returned to tell about it!

What constitutes corporate renewal? The definition has clearly broadened. Once it meant only righting the ship, getting back on the original course, resuming the former trajectory. No longer: it's the rare turnaround today that achieves a real bounce from the experience and roars back stronger than before. Today, many turned-around companies emerge from the process slimmed down, transformed, and reoriented. Others get acquired by strategic buyers that are able to realize—and therefore pay for—more value from the operations and assets than a financial buyer can, and so the corporate existence of those businesses may change completely.

Turnaround management implicitly involves optimization—the achievement of the best result under the circumstances. And the "circumstances" involve competing stakeholders whose interests are often at serious odds in terms of what turnaround strategy is pursued. For example, in the turnaround of a retail chain, it is frequently necessary to consider closing unprofitable stores. However, if the enterprise gets smaller in order to create short-term profitability and protect creditors, it may leave the equity "out of the money," whereas keeping the store network more intact, but less immediately profitable, may be riskier but may also preserve a greater upside potential for shareholders.

A central consideration of turnaround management is risk: the identification of risks, how risks will be addressed, and how performance in the context of risks will be appropriately measured and monitored. Essentially on what does the turnaround effort depend? Upon what and whom are we depending, and how will success be measured?

Large vendors and customers deal differently with companies in turnaround mode; they take steps to avoid getting stuck in an executory contract that they will not be able to break if their trading partner files bankruptcy, even though performance is in danger of suffering. Employees start to migrate elsewhere self-selectively, with the most employable staff members leaving first. Intellectual capital and key relationships walk out the door. A feeding frenzy can begin as competitors smell blood in the water.

What skills are necessary to participate in a turnaround—or even lead one? Can these skills be taught at any business school, or is turnaround management a practicum, best learned on the job? Here are some basics, but like many other life-changing experiences, until you've been through it, it's hard to describe.

Turnaround management is often compared to the practice of medicine or, more accurately, battlefield surgery—no anesthetics, no lab tests. It's probably no coincidence that at an earlier point in my career I was an air force medical triage officer. While no two patients are exactly alike, certain principles nonetheless apply.

It is dangerous to be too doctrinaire about turnarounds or to think that there is a cookbook approach. The Turnaround Management Association (TMA), through its affiliate the Association of Certified Turnaround Professionals, has utilized a "turnaround matrix" in its review courses for the certification exam, which lists five phases that can be identified in many turnarounds: Management Change, Situation Analysis, Emergency Action, Business Restructuring, and Return to Normalcy. While these phases will likely telescope or overlap one another, the activities that each represents do regularly occur in turnarounds.

The first phase involves a change of leadership, permanent or temporary. The reasons are several: most managers are not trained for, or experienced in, turnarounds. Just as ship captains turn over the wheel to the harbor pilot when they enter the difficult tides and currents near the port, a different skill set (and, perhaps, temperament) is required for a turnaround. Difficult decisions may have to be made, affecting the lives of many people and the survivors among them who will still have to work together. A turnaround professional can serve as a lightning rod for the emotional upheaval that can accompany rationalization of facilities and downsizing, if those occur, and then hand back the helm to the permanent management once the crisis is over. Perhaps most important, lenders and creditors may have lost confidence in the previous management and may require a change at the top as a condition of their financial support.

The turnaround leader will want to do two things immediately: (1) determine short-term cash flow and (2) identify a turnaround team. Cash is not just "king," it is oxygen, it is the lifeblood of the company. The turnaround leader has to determine whether the company is approaching a wall and, if so, how far away it is. Second, the John Wayne image of turnaround leaders notwithstanding, I haven't seen many turnaround leaders that can analyze the situation, formulate alternatives, and implement action plans all by themselves. A turnaround team is needed, utilizing resources within the company to augment and leverage the turnaround leader. If the turnaround leader is from a professional turnaround firm, there will likely be other team members from the firm.

Without belaboring a point that has itself been the subject of conferences, defining the turnaround leader's role is crucial. Scope of work and goals are the starting points. Responsibility and authority must be congruent. Compensation structure must create alignment of interests. Legal niceties—especially those created if bankruptcy is a possibility—must be observed. For example, if the turnaround leader is labeled or is de facto an officer, and the company subsequently files bankruptcy, that officer and his or her turnaround firm may be disqualified from continuing to provide services. This situation is preventable with the proper planning and foresight.

In analyzing the situation, viability of the business must be confirmed. Is there a "pony under the pile"? Is a turnaround possible? Are there sufficient financial and human resources available to implement the turnaround? Is there enough time? What protective measures for assets have to be taken immediately?

Early-stage action plans will typically focus on cash. Profit-and-loss considerations, effect on earnings before interest, taxes, depreciation, and amortization (EBITDA), and other accounting concepts will typically be shoved aside while the company's survival is assured. Precious cash resources may be rationed to support critical operations and vendors. Turnaround team members may fan out to reassure employees, customers, and suppliers.

And a turnaround strategy has to be formulated. What alternatives are available? Will we kick or play? Selecting among turnaround alternatives has a lot to do with identifying and managing risk. What are the risks of each alternative? Who is being asked to bear those risks? How can these risks—and the management of the risks—be monitored and reported?

Assuming a turnaround strategy has been identified and selected, the long-term changes of the business can begin. This usually involves restructuring, both operationally and financially. A common mistake is to try to "fix the balance sheet" first, before fixing the company.

Long-term financial restructuring has to follow, not precede, the operational turnaround. What got the company into trouble? Besides the immediate symptoms, what were the root causes? Why should we reasonably expect that the future will be any different from the past? How will we measure and report progress?

If the turnaround has "taken," there will then be an effort to return things to a more normal basis. Presumably, permanent changes will have been put in place to prevent recurrences of the old problems as well as the emergence of new ones, and new yardsticks and reporting systems will have been installed to satisfy all stakeholders that there will be no relapses. If crisis or interim management has been installed, then metaphorically speaking, the helm will be handed back to the ship's captain, who may be a new face if the previous manager was part of the problem or has been too weakened by the experience.

These days there is far less patience on the part of lenders for an extended turnaround effort, especially where the lender has to take any further risk. Even where the lender is seriously "under water" in terms of how it would fare in a sale or liquidation of the business, many lenders seem to prefer an earlier out, taking whatever pain is necessary right away rather than wait. So there is a trend among lenders to require an investment banker's assessment of the salability of the business at the outset, even while the turnaround leader assesses the situation. Also, lenders are increasingly selling off loans, either individually or as a portfolio, again taking an immediate write-off rather than trying to recoup their losses. The successor to the lender's interest may have a very different viewpoint; for example, a buyer of the debt at a discount may be even more determined to capture its hoped-for profit early and might be even less inclined (or completely unable) to lend additional funds. The successor will not have had the historical relationship with the borrower, for whatever that's worth.

A word on ethics: distressed businesses often bring out the worst in otherwise good people. Just as in the Japanese proverb that states that when the water level of the pond decreases, the rocks appear, so do examples of fraud and abuse seem to escalate when things get rough. The turnaround leader has to be constantly on the alert for the signs of wrongdoing and must be especially careful not to get advertently or inadvertently caught up in such activities.

Turnaround management is usually played out with the specter of bankruptcy at least in the wings, if not as the backdrop. Stakeholders are continually measuring whether they would be better off in "a proceeding." And as many corporate officers and directors learn too late, when the business enters the zone of insolvency, their fiduciary duty is owed to creditors and not just to shareholders. It may be best to adopt what the British MI5 used to call "Moscow rules": assume the dogs are on you twenty-four hours a day, that everything you say is being recorded, and that everything you write is being shared on the Internet. Become conversant with Title 18, United States Code, Chapter 9, §§151–157 *et seq.,* the bankruptcy criminal code, since its tripwires are subtle to understand and often hidden from view.

The turnaround management community is a broad, vibrant, and varied group. The Turnaround Management Association has nearly six thousand members, of whom only about a third are turnaround professionals, with the balance dispersed among lenders; attorneys; and other service providers such as appraisers, auctioneers, liquidators, and so on. There is a TMA chapter in every major city and several foreign countries, with chapter meetings nearly every month and several regional and national programs annually. Attendance at those meetings is a good way to break into the turnaround community and learn more about turnaround management in a particular area, including employment opportunities. The Turnaround Management Association, through its affiliate the Association of Certified Turnaround Professionals, sponsors a certification program that seeks to establish a minimum credential level that distinguishes those for whom turnaround management is a professional career versus those who are just between permanent jobs and seeking turnaround consulting as the flavor of the month. The certified turnaround professional (CTP) designation requires five years experience as a turnaround professional; passage of a rigorous exam based upon a body of knowledge in law, management, accounting, and finance; references and a background check; and continuing education.

It is really heartening to see turnaround management increasingly being taught and studied in our country's business schools. I hope that this will become a regular fixture of the curriculum and not subject to the vicissitudes of the national economy and the job market. In particular, I hope that within every discipline taught in business schools there will be a "what if it don't?" component. That is, how do accounting, finance, operations, human resource management, strategic planning, business policy, international business, and on and on— how do all of these address *what to do in a turnaround?*

Note

1. *Troubled Company Reporter,* March 4, 2003.

Ethical and Legal Issues

Ethical Considerations in the Bankruptcy Decision
2. Harry Lewis: Ethical Manager

Harry Lewis, the new CEO of Fletcher Steel Inc. (FSI), was hired in December 2003 to replace Franklin Edgars, who had been CEO for the prior eighteen years. During Franklin's tenure FSI had gone from being a steady profit earner to a cash flow negative enterprise. FSI is a large unionized continuous-casting steel company established in 1916. Its mills are located in the midwestern United States, with the bulk of its products serving large industrial concerns in the automobile, appliance, and road building industries.

Franklin was a "good old boy" who had spent his lifetime in the steel industry. He accepted as facts beyond his control high industrywide union wage settlements, the encroachment of minimills, and the threat of foreign steel imports. His nearly $1 million salary and a healthy benefits and bonus package assuaged any reservations that he may have had about these issues. Unfortunately, the creditors, of whom there were many, did not feel as sanguine about FSI's future. Starting at the end of the third quarter 2003, tremendous pressures were exerted on FSI that resulted in Franklin Edgars being sacked. Creditors began their anti-Franklin campaign in January 2003 after nearly three years of negative cash flow. They were justifiably worried about the eventual repayment of their loans. As the third quarter drew to a close, FSI was in violation of several of the covenants restricting its various loans. This put FSI into technical default, greatly increasing the leverage of its lenders. Lenders insisted that Mr. Edgars be replaced and that a hard-nosed turnaround manager be brought in as the chief restructuring officer. The

---

This case was prepared by Harlan D. Platt and Thomas Allison.

board resisted and compromised by hiring Harry Lewis to replace Franklin Edgars.

Harry was not a novice to the steel industry, having spent the past six years as chief operating officer of a small minimill steel operation. However, his background with a company using a fundamentally different technology and located in the nonunion South made him a peculiar choice for the position. What impressed the board of directors of FSI about Harry was his reputation for having high ethical standards. Not only had Harry been seen on the cover of a major business newsmagazine in regard to his ethics, but he also had served on a presidential business-ethics panel. The lone dissenting voice on the board of directors asked whether a little less ethics and a little more business acumen might not be preferred. Other directors who felt that ethics were the most important attribute of a CEO following revelations about Enron and WorldCom carried the day in this debate.

FSI's immediate problem as the first quarter of 2004 was drawing to a close was making its payroll. Prior years' losses and a $141 million bad investment in a coal mine in Kentucky had nearly depleted the company's coffers. A $20 million pollution control and slag runoff fine had been imposed on the coal company shortly after the purchase was made. FSI had not expected those charges. Conversations between Harry and the CFO suggested that checks due during the next two weeks would not be a problem but that following that there would probably not be sufficient funds to pay workers, suppliers, and assorted real-estate taxes due. Harry made the rounds to FSI's lenders, private equity investors, and Wall Street seeking more funds, but he got nowhere. The recent bankruptcies of Bethlehem and National Steel had put those sources in the wrong mood. Each of them uttered the phrase "insolvent in a bankruptcy sense" repeatedly to him. While Harry had been unsure about what the phrase meant when he started his meetings, he was an expert on it by the end.

He then turned his rescue efforts to the union. Harry assembled various union bigwigs at corporate headquarters and in his most ethical manner laid out the facts about the company. His presentation concluded with the statement that he could not guarantee that workers would get paid in February. The room was silent when he finished. Then one person raised a hand and asked, "But what about the health and pension plan payments? Surely you intend to make those." Harry looked around the room. He saw that no one there, including himself, was less than fifty years of age. Moreover, over 75 percent of FSI's workforce was older than forty-eight years. He realized immediately that he would never be able to wring any wage concessions out of his workers' union. All they cared about was the value of their homes, their health insurance, and their fast approaching retirement.

As he drove home from the meeting, Harry thought about throwing in the towel and filing for bankruptcy. He felt that bankruptcy was not only the wrong thing for FSI but that it would harm his own career. The next morning Harry got some better news. One of the private investors he had visited with made an unsolicited offer of $68 million to buy the Kentucky coalfield. The offer was contingent on Harry accepting it by the end of the day and his not seeking any competing offers. Harry was torn and unsure what to do. On the one hand, the money would solve FSI's payroll and other payment issues for at least two quarters. But on the other hand, the offer was for less than half of what FSI had paid for the company just a year before, and during the interim period the price of bituminous coal had actually risen by 12 percent. Harry countered by asking for $141 million from the prospective buyer. After the laughter subsided he was told, "Look, you're out of choices. Either you take $68 million from us today, or you can file for bankruptcy tomorrow."

The news wires reported the sale of the coal company that evening at six o'clock.

Ethical Issues

3. Shrink, Inc.

A small, privately held company of 120 workers (Shrink, Inc.) has been struggling financially for the past year. The reasons for its struggle are both internal and external.

Approximately three years ago, Shrink's growth was astronomical, with orders practically doubling each quarter. Anticipating future demand to continue to grow at similar levels, the company recruited new technical employees to introduce efficiency and purchased a significant amount of equipment to increase capacity. Both recession in the economy and a slowing of demand due to competition have been responsible for much of the reduced profitability of Shrink. In addition, the outlays for capital equipment and highly priced personnel did not generate revenue as anticipated, and those expenses have kept costs of production high as competitive stress on pricing has eroded profit margins.

Although the company has sustained at least a nominal profit through its struggles, it has had serious cash flow problems, and the banks have become wary of extending Shrink, Inc., credit. The value of the company has diminished by more than 50 percent over the year. For two pay periods during the past year, owners had to lend the company money to meet payroll. Owners and management decided that the only way to keep the company financially viable was to lay off twenty-two workers who were now expendable as a result of excess capacity.

The owners generally chose which workers to terminate based on management's assessment of worker productivity and worker

This case was prepared by Suzanne Cummins.

salary. If two workers were doing the same job with the same perceived level of productivity, the one with the higher salary was generally let go. Salaries of the most senior workers were the highest,
and therefore the most senior workers were the ones laid off when
there were no other differentiating factors between employees
doing the same type of work. One of the long-term workers chosen
for layoff has a husband who is getting treatment for cancer. Hers is
the only family income, and she is frightened that she will not be
able to pay the health insurance costs that had historically been covered by Shrink.

One exception in choosing which workers to terminate involved
workers with strong technical skills, even if they weren't using those
skills at the time of the layoffs. These highly skilled workers were favored over more senior workers because of their capability to introduce more efficiency and lower production costs over time. The company views these workers (who were recruited during the "growth
spurt" three years ago) as investment in the future, and so it retained
several who were, at the time of the layoff, performing similar work
to more senior employees but at higher wages.

Three of the older, long-term employees have initiated claims
based on age discrimination. The lawyer for the company indicates
that the company's conduct is legally defensible, and although there
is some risk, she believes the company will prevail in any lawsuit that
gets filed. Management sees its decisions as crucial for corporate survival, and since Shrink is "fighting for its life," they see no choice but
to make decisions that are best for long-term economic results. The
bank and other lenders look upon Shrink's decisions favorably. The
employees, however, see management's conduct as unethical. Management made the mistake to expand when it should not have, they
hired in employees they couldn't really afford or justify at the time,
and now they (long-term loyal employees) are paying the price.

Several employees are forced to sell their homes, some under very
stressed conditions, causing them to lose most of their equity. Severance packages allowed for up to eight weeks of pay, but jobs are scarce
in the area where Shrink is located, and most of the laid-off workers
do not believe they will find other employment in eight weeks. Workers note that even though Shrink was losing shareholder value, it was
still marginally profitable. They feel their jobs were sacrificed for the
greed of shareholders. Even if no law prohibits Shrink's conduct, the
employees believe management acted without a conscience.

4. Corbesco

A builder of airplane hangars (John Corey) won a bid for building five large hangars at two airports in the San Francisco Bay area. These airport hangars were to be flat roofed, with a height of sixty feet (approximately six stories) to the roofline. The bidding was extremely competitive, but John came in at the best price. He had an established reputation as a high quality contractor.

Since John was extremely safety conscious, he asked OSHA (Occupational Safety and Health Administration) inspectors to observe the hangar sites to determine if he was meeting all regulatory requirements. On two occasions, one during framing, and one during roofing, OSHA inspectors came to the sites at John's invitation and proclaimed the working environment to meet regulatory standards.

Fred was an employee of John's who worked on roofing. Fred worked on top of the hangar roof without any safety nets or scaffolding, which was standard in the industry when working on flat-roofed hangars. In fact, OSHA regulations, in certain places, indicated a flat roof could be considered to act as a "floor" and be treated as such. One part of Fred's job involved installing insulation. To do this, he would push a long sheet of corrugated metal away from the completed portion of the roof, leaving beams exposed. Kneeling or standing on the edge of the roof, he would then shake out the insulation and place it onto the exposed beams, just as one might shake out a bedspread over a bed. Since Fred had to maintain his balance while leaning over the edge of the roof, high winds could be dangerous, and therefore John regularly sought weather forecasts from the National Weather Service.

This case was prepared by Suzanne Cummins.

18

One day, Fred was on his knees shaking out insulation when a gust of wind caught the sheet he was holding and pulled him forward. Fred lost his balance, fell sixty feet through the open beams from which he had pulled the corrugated metal away, and was killed. OSHA assessed a $1,000 penalty against John for failing to install a safety net under the roof.

After the penalty was assessed, John did install a safety net at the hangar at which Fred had worked, but he contested the OSHA penalty. At a hearing, John demonstrated that industry custom did not include the use of safety nets while working on flat roofs. He also pointed out that OSHA officers had inspected and approved the work site and that he would have had no way to know he was violating any rules.

The commissioner admitted that the industry standard and custom did not involve the use of safety nets in the relevant situation. He further noted that John would have readily been granted a variance from the safety net requirement if the cost of compliance arguably outweighed the benefits of enhanced safety need. It was noted that all the other bidders had bid the job without the use of safety nets and that "falling from the edge of a flat roof is not a common hazard in the roofing industry." It was still possible for John to get such a variance for the remaining projects. However, the commissioner found that a specific regulation had been applied to buildings such as the hangar in question and that there was consequently adequate "notice" of the requirement, notwithstanding the other factors mentioned. Although the fine was reduced, the commissioner found that the fine against John was constitutional.

John believes the government has overstepped and abused its power. He formally obtained variances for the remaining hangars, and no other injuries occurred. He has spent a great deal of time thinking about what he should have done differently. Had he bid the job with safety nets, it would have gone to his competitors who followed industry standards and bid their jobs without. Had he gotten a formal variance, Fred would still be dead—John just wouldn't be faced with any OSHA fine. John doesn't understand why, if the absence of having a safety net has gotten him into trouble, all bidders aren't required to include safety netting in their bids. He thinks that is the only fair way for things to go, but OSHA is not imposing that requirement because it allows for variances in all similar cases.

Despite the objection he has to the OSHA fine, John is very

upset about Fred's death. He has invested a great deal of time and some money to try to figure out a cost effective way to prevent that type of accident from ever occurring again, but so far, he has not been able to come up with anything. He has spoken with his other roofers to get their feedback, but all of them want to continue with things as they are. They recognize the risk and they feel really sorry for Fred's family, but they think if Fred had been more careful, the accident might not have happened. Many have been roofing for decades and have never seen that type of accident before.

John has not bid for any more hangar jobs. He is very conflicted about the entire process. His competitors, who are significantly less concerned than he is about safety, have gotten the jobs that John has ignored. Several roofers will soon face layoff since John doesn't have enough other work to keep the same crew levels that he had while building the hangars. John understands that Fred's own negligence played in part in his death but hasn't been able to reconcile that with his own feelings about the accident.

Note

This roofer case is based *very* loosely on an actual legal case, the citation for which is *Corbesco v. Dole,* 926 F.2d 422.

Developing a Plan of Reorganization

5. Toys and More, Inc.

Lester Vorkman and his wife, Julie, had founded Toys and More, Inc. (TAMI), in 1987. Their concept of high-quality educational toys quickly found a receptive audience among the burgeoning number of dual-income families with too little time to spend with their children. From 1 store in 1987 they expanded to 3 in 1989 and 7 in 1991. A public offering in 1992 raised nearly $120 million, which Lester and Julie soon leveraged with $200 million in a junk bond paying 12 percent interest. By 1999 the chain had 114 company stores, an Internet web site, and a toy-software research division. That year Lester and Julie turned the management of the enterprise over to a professional team because they had decided it was time to spend more time with their grandchildren.

Kathy Berkstone, the new CEO, had merchandising experience with a consumer products company and finance experience with an investment bank, and she was the mother of three children. Neither Kathy nor, for that matter, anyone else was prepared for the dramatic downturn in TAMI's business starting in 2000 (see tables 1 and 2). The initial pressure came from Wal-Mart stores, which that year began a big push for toy sales. That was followed in 2001 by devastating terrorist acts that sent the economy into a tailspin. Finally, the bursting of the Internet bubble in 2001 and 2002 both diminished TAMI's sales on the Web (see table 3) and also reduced the value of the Internet business. Making things still worse, the computer software division, which had not had a successful new product in eighteen months, was

---

This case was prepared by Harlan D. Platt.

experiencing an internal revolt among its developers and was in disarray.

TAMI filed for bankruptcy protection in January 2004. A team of turnaround consultants came in immediately. Janie Goodney, one of the consultants, replaced Kathy Berkstone as CEO. She immediately

TABLE 1.   Toys and More, Inc., Income Statements 2000–2003 ($ millions)

	2003	2002	2001	2000
Revenue	750.00	810.00	834.30	942.76
Cost of goods sold	525.75	566.27	579.00	650.50
Gross profit	224.25	243.73	255.30	292.26
Selling, general, and administrative expenses	215.00	230.00	236.00	254.26
R&D	1.00	1.30	1.60	2.00
Nonrecurring expense	33.0			
Operating income	−24.75	12.43	17.70	35.99
Interest	24.60	25.88	26.20	26.32
Taxes	−19.74	−5.38	−3.40	3.87
Net income	−29.61	−8.07	−5.10	5.80

TABLE 2.   Toys and More, Inc., Balance Sheet ($ millions)

	2003	2002	2001	2000
Assets				
Cash	101.30	78.57	77.90	90.98
Receivables	34.25	59.79	52.09	19.80
Inventory	172.50	198.00	190.22	216.83
Total current	308.05	336.36	320.21	327.61
Net property, plant and equipment	348.75	389.00	421.00	438.38
Goodwill	24.00	25.50	27.00	28.50
Total assets	680.80	750.86	768.21	794.49
Liabilities and owners' equity				
Payables	160.66	162.65	167.53	189.31
Bank debt	15.00	47.00	55.00	58.00
Total current	175.66	209.65	222.53	247.31
Long term debt	200.00	200.00	200.00	200.00
Total liabilities	375.66	409.65	422.53	447.31
Owners' equity	305.14	341.21	345.68	347.18
Total liabilities + owners' equity	680.80	750.86	768.21	794.49

performed a four-wall analysis on the 114 stores to find out which ones were profitable on an independent store basis (i.e., ignoring overhead charges). Following this, the bankruptcy court approved her request to shut 16 stores. Leases on these stores were rejected. TAMI assumed the leases on the remaining stores, though before doing so Janie's team successfully renegotiated their terms and conditions. For the stores that remained, lease related costs declined by 13 percent. The turnaround team also systematically analyzed the firm's operations, focusing mainly on the distribution, ordering, and back-office functions. A variety of functions were outsourced while others were made more efficient.

Janie's assessment of the Internet site was pessimistic. Her research uncovered the fact that parents buying expensive educational toys wanted to pick up and feel the items, making them unlikely web consumers. Lester and Julie, who remained on the company's board of directors and who held nineteen percent of its common stock, disputed her findings. They argued that the site had been profitable and should be profitable in the future if only the company stocked it with unique and worthy toys. Opposing comments came from the banks whose loans were secured by TAMI's inventories, accounts receivables, goodwill, and intellectual property. The bank insisted that the Internet division be shut. Certain creditors, on the other hand, were pushing Janie to liquidate the entire firm. Reluctantly, Janie sided with the creditors and closed down the web site one Friday near closing time. While this action did not improve Janie's standing with remaining employees it seems to assure support among creditors for the plan of reorganization that Janie was in the process of crafting. Finally, she agreed to sell the software division to employees for $1 plus warrants convertible into 25 percent of its stock. Any future products would be shown to TAMI for a right of first refusal.

Janie viewed the plan of reorganization as her principal assignment. The steps she followed in preparing the plan were as follows.

TABLE 3. Toys and More, Inc., Segment Sales Record

	Segment Percentage Sales			
	2003	2002	2001	2000
Stores	98.6	96.0	96.3	94.5
Web site	1.2	2.3	2.4	3.4
Software	0.2	1.7	1.3	2.1

1. Develop a pro forma estimate of profitability in a future normal year. "Normal" means after the bankruptcy and its ramifications have died down, perhaps two or three years in the future. The pro forma at this stage assumes a zero level of debt. Moreover, it reflects changes made to the firm's cost structure as a result of lease rejection and other changes.
2. Determine the present discounted value (PV) of the firm based on the pro forma estimate. To determine PV, Janie used the capitalization method, which divided the estimated net income for the single pro forma normal year by the firm's cost of capital.
3. Determine a liquidation value (LV).
4. Compare the LV to the PV. IF LV is greater than PV, liquidate; otherwise reorganize.
5. Calculate excess corporate cash by comparing working capital to historic and estimated working capital needs because companies in bankruptcy hoard cash and its equivalents.
6. Determine which liabilities can be continued as opposed to being funded in the plan. Notably this includes items such as accrued wages, which would be paid at normal monthly or biweekly times as opposed to at the end of the bankruptcy.
7. Determine the optimal capital structure for the new firm about to emerge from bankruptcy. This depends on its earning power as estimated in the pro forma but also on earning variability, lender availability, and interest rates. A comparison with historic or benchmark equivalents provides some guidance.
8. Determine the hierarchy of claims against the debtor.
9. Create a repayment plan that adheres to the absolute priority rule, as far as possible and as far as necessary.

Student Assignment

Prepare a plan of reorganization for class.

6. Clark Automotive Parts, Inc.

Clark Automotive Parts, Inc. (the "company"), operates in the passenger car and light truck segment of the automotive aftermarket distribution industry. The economic cycles and industry trends within the automotive parts manufacturing industry are highly correlated with the cycles and trends of the automotive aftermarket manufacturing industry. To assist you in your analysis of the company a summary of the automotive parts manufacturing industry is included with the analysis of the aftermarket distribution industry.

Automotive Parts Manufacturing and Distribution

The auto parts manufacturing market is highly fragmented, with companies ranging in size from mom-and-pop shops to large multinational corporations. There are four basic lines of business within auto parts manufacturing: original equipment manufacturing (OEM), replacement parts manufacturing, distribution, and rubber fabrication.[1] This analysis focuses solely on replacement parts manufacturing and distribution.

Replacement Parts Manufacturer Market

This market involves the manufacture of parts that replace or supplement parts that were originally included in the vehicle. Companics that serve this market can be independent or subsidiaries of automobile manufacturers. In addition, some participate in the original equipment market as well as the replacement market.

This case was prepared by Grant Newton, James F. Hart, and Paul N. Shields.

Do-It-Yourself (DIY) Market

The Automotive Aftermarket Industry Association reported that from 1994 to 2000 the percentage of total U.S. households performing light, medium, or heavy-duty maintenance had not changed. However, the percentage of DIY households with female DIYers had increased from 27 percent to 34 percent of the total. Nearly half of all U.S. households contained at least one automotive DIYer despite a sharp decline between 1994 and 2000 in the 25- to 44-year-old "prime" DIY age group. Two-thirds of the DIYers or DIFMers (do-it-for-me) choose aftermarket service facilities over new car dealership service because of trust, convenience, guarantee, and cost.

The sale of automotive parts accessories and maintenance items is highly competitive in many aspects, including name recognition, product availability, customer service, store location, and price, and there are many competitors. Many companies compete for both DIY and commercial customers. Suppliers include national and regional auto parts chains, independently owned parts stores, wholesalers and jobbers, car washes, and auto dealers, in addition to discount and mass merchandise stores, department stores, hardware stores, supermarkets, drugstores, and home stores that sell aftermarket vehicle parts and supplies, chemicals, accessories, tools, and maintenance parts. Many companies compete on the basis of customer service, including the knowledge of and expertise in merchandise selection and availability, price, product, warranty, store layouts, and location.

Replacement Parts Manufacturer Market Trends

The largest automakers have established a trend of spinning off their in-house parts manufacturing units. These moves will only strengthen the already cutthroat competitive environment. Additionally, the long-term trend is for the number of older model cars to increase. This trend favors parts suppliers, but at the same time, the quality of original equipment has increased steadily, which limits the growth of this segment (3 percent is projected growth rate next year, while gross margins should continue to average around 20 percent).

Replacement Parts Distribution

These market players simply distribute the parts and accessories that are used to replace or supplement original automotive parts. This market is highly fragmented, but there are some large industry players, including public companies. Distribution usually involves getting the part to the end user, either through middlemen or jobbers or by direct delivery to the end user.

Wholesalers have traditionally employed a three-step or full-service distribution process. This process involves the part manufacturer delivering to warehouse distributors who, in turn, deliver the parts to local jobbers who sell the parts to end users for installation. This type of distribution allows jobbers to provide parts to local area professionals (such as service stations and garages) and major accounts in a timely and efficient manner.

Recently, the three-step distribution process has begun to be replaced with a two-step, or direct, distribution process, which allows direct distributors to eliminate a level of distribution. Accordingly, a large jobber may purchase directly from manufacturers and sell directly to professional installers, or a warehouse distributor may skip the jobber level and sell parts directly to installers. The two-step process has evolved as a way to decrease capital needs and to halt the problems of shrinking margins. This process has proved successful in major metropolitan areas, where there are higher concentrations of professional installers.

Replacement Parts Distribution Trends
One of the largest challenges for distributors is to be able to deliver the right part to the right place in a timely and cost effective manner. This problem is only increasing as the car market expands into every area of the globe. In addition, the quality of original equipment has steadily increased, which limits sales and distribution of replacement parts. The wild card in terms of growth is how the Clean Air requirements from the U.S. Environmental Protection Agency will affect the market. Some parts manufacturers have not yet been supplied with enough information to build and service the newly required parts. This could negatively affect sales and distribution trends in the future.

Company Overview

Clark Automotive Parts, Inc., was founded in 1970 by John L. Clark. Currently, the company's executive offices are located in Atlanta, Georgia. Clark Automotive is primarily engaged in the distribution of automotive aftermarket products to jobbers and professional installers located in the Southeast and Midwest regions of the United States. The company operates in the passenger car and light truck segment of the automotive aftermarket distribution industry. The company conducts its business through ten full-service distribution centers and eight direct distribution centers. The company also owns fifty jobbing stores located in the Southeast region.

Until the mid-1990s, the company operated solely in the Southeast and had achieved operating results at par with industry norms. In 1997 (coinciding with the appointment of John Clark's son, Spencer Clark, as Clark Automotive's CEO), the company implemented a strategy to significantly expand its operations. By 2001, the company had expanded its operations to include one large jobber and three distribution centers in the Midwest. In addition, the company completed the acquisition of Jones Automotive Warehouse, Inc. ("Jones Automotive") in 2000 (the "Jones acquisition"). Jones Automotive operated three full-service distribution centers and two direct distribution centers. In addition, Jones Automotive operated forty-nine jobbing stores through its wholly owned subsidiary, Advanced Automotive, Inc. ("Advanced Automotive"). All of the Jones Automotive distribution centers and jobbing stores operated in the Southeast region. For financial reporting purposes, Jones distribution centers have been integrated with the other distribution centers.

For a number of reasons that will be discussed subsequently, Clark Automative according to management began to experience financial troubles in 2001. Over the next two years, the company's operations and financial condition continued to deteriorate. On January 15, 2003, the company filed a petition for relief under Chapter 11 of the Bankruptcy Code in the United States Bankruptcy Court for the Northern District of Georgia.

A number of factors led to the filing of the bankruptcy petition. The first factor was a significant increase in financial leverage. The company's expansion (both the addition of new distribution centers in the Midwest and the Jones acquisition) was financed predominantly with long-term and subordinated debt. Prior to this expansion, the company maintained a capital structure in line with industry norms. On average, companies within the automotive aftermarket distribution industry maintain a capital structure of 70 percent equity and 30 percent debt based on market values. At the peak of the expansion program, the company's liabilities approached or exceeded the value of its assets.

The second factor was the company's unsuccessful efforts to expand into the Midwest market. While the automotive aftermarket distribution industry is highly competitive, competition is particularly keen in the Midwest region, and the three distribution centers and one jobber established in this region never generated sufficient earnings to cover the related debt service.

The third factor was that the company overpaid for its acquisition of Jones Automotive. The company got caught up in a bidding war with a key competitor and adopted a "win at all costs" attitude toward the Jones acquisition. Furthermore, many of the company's executives had unrealistic expectations regarding the level of synergy that could be realized through the integration of Jones Automotive into the existing business.

The fourth factor was that the company created some discord with existing jobbers when they acquired Jones Automotive. As noted previously Jones Automotive owned forty-nine jobbers in the Southeast region. Some of the jobbers supplied by Clark Automotive resented the fact that, as a result of the Jones acquisition, their supplier was now competing against them. As a result, Clark Automotive lost some of its key accounts.

The fifth factor was that the company implemented an ERP (enterprise resource planning) system during its expansion phase. The company was still experiencing significant computer "downtime" and processing errors at the time the bankruptcy petition was filed. The primary processing errors were lost orders and orders that contained erroneous product codes. Not withstanding the existing problems, the company's systems consultants had made considerable progress in resolving many of the system's problems and were of the opinion that, by the summer of 2004, the company's ERP system would be fully operational.

Finally, the sixth factor leading to the Chapter 11 proceeding was that the company was behind the curve in making the transition from a full-service distribution process (or three-step process) to the direct distribution process (or two-step process).

The historical financial statements for the company are contained in exhibits 1–3.

Clark Automotive achieved operating performance in line with industry standards in 1998 and 1999 (not shown in the comparative financial statements). Subsequent to 1999, the company's operating performance began to deteriorate, with significant erosion of profitability occurring in 2001 and 2002 (see the company's financial statements reproduced in exhibits 1–3).

Operating in Chapter 11

In 2003, subsequent to the filing of the bankruptcy petition, the company began to reverse some negative trends by stabilizing gross profit margins and reducing selling, general, and administrative expenses on a percentage of sales basis. Stabilization of gross profit margins was primarily achieved through the elimination of some unprofitable customer segments, product lines, and distribution locations. Further enhancement of the company's gross profit margins should resume in the year 2005 as a result of the company's continued efforts to increase penetration into more profitable customer segments, product lines, and locations.

Another factor contributing to the stabilization of the company's gross margins was the implementation of a new computer system. While the company experienced significant cost overruns and processing problems in the early stages of its ERP implementation,[2] by mid-2002 many of the "bugs" had been worked out of the system. On a go-forward basis, the company views its state-of-the-art information system as one of its competitive advantages. Among other things, the new system employs an Internet interface that links directly to the company's inventory and purchasing systems. Accordingly, when a customer logs on to the company's web site, the system retrieves a detailed product listing, which includes the customer's pricing structure. Once the product is ordered, the order information is transmitted to the warehouse for order fulfillment and is posted to the company's inventory system. Purchasing is notified when inventory of a particular product reaches a certain level so the company can place an order for additional product with its vendors. The new ERP system is linked directly with the information systems of the company's primary vendors so that purchases can be filed more expeditiously.

Improvements in selling, general, and administrative expenses were implemented through reduction of workforce and various other cost cutting measures. Further decreases in these expenses are needed.

Company management has indicated that not only will the trend of declining sales reverse in the year 2004 but the company's top line growth will also exceed overall industry growth rates for at least the next five years. Justification for the company's sales estimates is as follows.

1. The elimination of unprofitable operations.
2. The company's expansion efforts will be directed to higher growth markets.

3. The automotive aftermarket distribution industry has begun to experience some shakeout. The shakeout will alleviate a limited amount of competitive pressure in certain locations. Furthermore, it is anticipated the company will be able to expand operations through the procurement of distribution facilities that have become available due to the insolvency of the smallest distributors.

4. The enhanced information system will enable the company to increase customer satisfaction by increasing fill rates, reducing delivery times, and providing sales and customer service representatives with more information regarding product availability and order status. The company believes increased customer satisfaction will, in time, equate to increased sales. In addition to the benefits discussed previously, the company believes that its enhanced computer system will enable it to better identify and target customer segments, product lines, and distribution locations with the highest growth potential.

The income tax rate has been calculated under the assumption that the company will be taxed at a federal income tax rate of 34.0 percent and a state income tax rate of 5.0 percent. The effective rate is 37. 3 percent due to the fact that state income taxes are deductible for federal income tax purposes.

Working capital requirements are assumed to be 8.0 percent of the increase in sales. In other words, for every $1.00 increase in sales, the company will invest $0.08 of working capital. Working capital requirements have been estimated based on the historical changes in sales relative to the historical changes in inventory, trade receivables, and trade payables for the company, as well as for publicly traded companies operating in the same industry.

The cash flow projections prepared by management for 2004–8 are included in exhibit 4 along with the estimated depreciation and capital expenditures.

Student Assignment

1. Determine the cost of capital.
2. Determine the value of Clark Automotive using the following methods.
   a. Discounted cash flow method
   b. Earnings before interest, taxes, depreciation, and amortization (EBITDA) method

3. Divide the debt into the following classes.
   a. Secured
   b. Bank debt
   c. Unsecured (balance)
4. Develop the term sheet for a plan showing the following headings.

Class	Claim Amount	Consideration			Percent Recovery
		Cash	New Debt	Equity	

EXHIBIT 1.   Clark Automotive Parts, Inc., Consolidated Schedule of Assets

	2001 ($)	2002 ($)	2003 ($)
Current assets			
Cash	1,610,000	1,007,000	1,014,000
Accounts receivable, less allowances			
(2003 – $125,000; 2004 – $150,000)			
for doubtful accounts	13,842,000	11,160,000	10,775,000
Refundable income taxes	427,000	–	–
Inventories – lower of cost (first-in			
first-out method) or market	36,695,000	28,587,000	27,384,000
Receivable due on sale of subsidiary			
assets	–	1,932,000	1,559,000
Prepaid expenses	890,000	670,000	571,000
Total current assets	53,464,000	43,356,000	41,303,000
Other assets			
Excess of purchase price over net			
assets acquired	2,260,000	2,200,000	1,689,000
Other assets	587,000	170,000	159,000
Total other assets	2,847,000	2,370,000	1,848,000
Property and equipment			
Land and buildings	733,000	659,000	626,000
Buildings under capitalized leases	3,680,000	3,222,000	3,060,000
Leasehold improvements	1,922,000	1,640,000	1,558,000
Computer equipment	2,111,000	1,810,000	1,719,000
Furniture and fixtures	3,592,000	3,143,000	2,986,000
Vehicles	2,525,000	2,183,000	2,074,000
Total property and equipment	14,563,000	12,657,000	12,023,000
Less allowances for depreciation and			
amortization	8,282,000	6,961,000	7,214,000
Net property and equipment	6,281,000	5,696,000	4,809,000
Total assets	$62,592,000	$51,422,000	$47,960,000

EXHIBIT 2. Clark Automotive Parts, Inc., Consolidated Schedule of Liabilities and Stockholders' Equity

	2001 ($)	2002 ($)	2003 ($)
Current liabilities			
Trade accounts payable and accrued expenses	15,355,000	16,086,000	1,536,000
Accrued professional fees			500,000
Dividends payable	14,000	71,000	—
Salaries, wages, and commissions	828,000	755,000	639,000
Taxes, other than income	1,017,000	534,000	391,000
Income taxes — current	—	—	—
Current portion of long-term debt and capital lease obligations	1,240,000	9,654,000	—
Obligations under credit facility[a]	21,451,000	21,241,000	—
Obligations under debtor in possession financing agreement	—	—	20,713,000
Subordinated debt (Jones acquisition)	—	3,295,000	—
Total current liabilities	39,905,000	51,636,000	23,779,000
Liabilities subject to compromise[b]	—	—	35,566,000
Long-term liabilities			
Long-term debt, less current portion[c]	6,445,000	—	—
Capital lease obligations	3,522,000	—	—
Pension	5,000,000	5,000,000	
Subordinated debt (Jones acquistion)	3,170,000	—	—
Total long-term liabilities	18,137,000	5,000,000	—
Stockholders' equity			
Preferred stock (serial), par value $1,000 — authorized 50,000 shares; issued and outstanding — 3,631 shares (callable and liquidation value: $363,100)	11,000	11,000	11,000
Common stock, par value 10 cents — authorized 3,000,000 shares; issued and outstanding — 1,222,388 shares	381,000	381,000	381,000
Additional paid-in capital	3,317,000	3,317,000	3,317,000
Retained earnings (deficit)	841,000	(8,923,000)	(15,094,000)
Total stockholders' equity	4,550,000	(5,214,000)	(11,385,000)
Total liabilities and stockholders' equity	62,592,000	51,422,000	47,960,000

[a]The line of credit is secured with a first lien in inventories and receivables.

[b]Liabilities subject to compromise consist of long-term secured debt — $3,370,000, obligations under credit facility — $1,983,000, trade payables and other unsecured claims — $14,250,000, long-term unsecured debt — $6,540,000, preferred dividends payable — $128,000, unfunded pension obligations — $6,000,000, subordinated debt — $3,295,000.

[c]Long-term debt consists of several notes with the Jim Financing Corp. at an interest rate of 11% secured by the land and building with an estimated value of $2.5 million, furniture, and fixtures; a second lien in inventory and receivables; and other assets except intangible assets.

EXHIBIT 3. Clark Automotive Parts, Inc., Consolidated Statement of Operations

	2000 ($)	2001 ($)	2002 ($)	2003 ($)
Net sales	123,239,000	113,275,000	102,906,000	97,967,000
Cost of goods sold	70,651,000	67,884,000	63,537,000	59,172,000
Gross profit	52,588,000	45,391,000	39,369,000	38,795,000
Selling, general, and administrative expenses (SGA)	47,334,000	46,638,000	43,924,000	41,111,000
Operating profit	5,254,000	(1,247,000)	(4,555,000)	(2,316,000)
Other income/(expense)				
Interest expense	(3,192,000)	(3,309,000)	(3,282,000)	(2,063,000)
Other income/(expense)	747,000	463,000	383,000	588,000
Provision for loss on disposal of subsidiary assets	—	—	(2,484,000)	(987,000)
Gain on sale of net assets of certain subsidiaries	—	—	174,000	483,000
Bankruptcy administrative expense				(1,876,000)
Total other income/(expense)	(2,445,000)	(2,846,000)	(5,209,000)	(3,855,000)
Profit before taxes	2,809,000	(4,093,000)	(9,764,000)	(6,171,000)
Income tax expense/(benefit)	1,043,000	(1,068,000)	—	—
Net income/(loss)	$1,766,000	($3,025,000)	($9,764,000)	($6,171,000)
Sales growth and percentage of sales analysis				
Annual sales growth (%)		−8.1	−9.2	−4.8
Cost of goods sold (% of sales)	57.3	59.9	61.7	60.4
SGA (% of sales)	38.4	41.2	42.7	42.0
Other expense/(income) (% of sales)	0.6	0.4	0.4	0.6
Income tax rate	37.1	−26.1	0.0	0.0

EXHIBIT 4. Clark Automotive Parts, Inc., Estimated Cash Flow

	2004 (4)	2005 ($)	2006 ($)	2007 ($)	2008 ($)
Net sales	107,764,000	122,851,000	143,736,000	158,110,000	166,016,000
Cost of goods sold	63,581,000	71,254,000	82,648,000	90,123,000	93,799,000
Gross profit	44,183,000	51,597,000	61,088,000	67,987,000	72,217,000
Selling, general, and administrative expenses	40,950,000	45,455,000	51,745,000	56,129,000	58,106,000
Operating profit	3,233,000	6,142,000	9,343,000	11,858,000	14,111,000
Other income/(expense)					
Interest expense					
Other income/(expense)	754,000	737,000	1,150,000	1,265,000	1,328,000

EXHIBIT 4—*Continued*

	2004 (4)	2005 ($)	2006 ($)	2007 ($)	2008 ($)
Bankruptcy administrative expense	(300,000)	—	—	—	—
Total other income/ (expense)	454,000	744,000	1,190,000	1,309,000	1,374,000
Profit before taxes	3,687,000	6,886,000	10,533,000	13,167,000	15,485,000
Assumptions					
Annual sales growth (%)	10.0	14.0	17.0	10.0	5.0
Cost of goods sold (% of sales)	59.0	58.0	57.5	57.0	56.5
SGA (% of sales)	38.0	37.0	36.0	35.5	35.0
Other expense/(income) (% of sales)	0.7	0.6	0.8	0.8	0.8
Income tax rate	37.3	37.3	37.3	37.3	37.3
Working capital requirements (% of the change in sales)	8.0	8.0	8.0	8.0	8.0
Capital expenditures	(650,000)	(670,000)	(715,000)	(725,000)	(595,000)
Estimated depreciation included in cost of goods sold and sales and administrative expense	400,000	420,000	440,000	450,000	420,000
Net operating loss carryforward (NOL) available each year (no NOL available after 2008)	2,000,000	2,000,000	2,000,000	2,000,000	2,000,000

Notes

1. Standard & Poor's Industry Surveys: Autos & Auto Parts, Public company 10-K file, and the Automotive Aftermarket Industry Association web site (http://www.aftermarket.org).

2. Problems associated with the implementation of the ERP system represented one of the factors that contributed to the company's bankruptcy.

7. The Creation of First City Financial Corporation: A Clinical Study of the Bankruptcy Process

I. Overview

1.1. General. A fundamental concept underlying the theory of the financially distressed firm is that if the firm is "worth more dead than alive" it should be liquidated under Chapter 7 of the Bankruptcy Code; if the post-reorganization firm value exceeds its current value, it should be rehabilitated under Chapter 11. This economic logic is straightforward, but its implementation is often not simple. A necessary step in a Chapter 11 bankruptcy proceeding is that the reorganization plan must be confirmed or approved by the court. Each plan must be accepted by formal voting.[1] In addition, the "best interests test" (¶1129 (a)(7), Bankruptcy Code) must be satisfied: each class of claims or equity interests must have accepted the plan or will receive or retain under the plan property of a value that is at least equal to what that holder would receive or retain if the firm were liquidated. The confirmation process thus relies critically on the economic values of the claims issued in the reorganization.

The post-reorganization claims are not traded at the time of the legal proceedings, and the absence of external market valuations makes the process complex and less precise. The outcome of the voting is impacted by the ongoing recontracting and negotiation during bankruptcy, which redefine the payoffs, risks, and hence values of the

---

This case was prepared by Ramesh K. S. Rao and Susan White.

claims.[2] Incentive misalignments and informational asymmetries in financially distressed firms complicate the negotiation and valuation process.[3] Equity holders have incentives to continue the firm as long as possible. On the other hand, senior creditors have an incentive to block the reorganization. Even private parties, working with managers, have incentives to influence the estimates; the cash flow estimates are endogenous ("hardwired," Kaplan and Ruback 1995).

Absent market valuations and with the informational asymmetries, competing interests, and other legal/procedural requirements, the bankruptcy proceeding becomes an administrative process wherein valuations are arrived at through negotiations and "judicial weighting of competing economic interests" (Gilson, Hotchkiss, and Ruback 2000).

1.2. Scope of Study. This paper examines the bankruptcy of First City Bancorporation of Texas and its eventual reorganization through a merger with J-Hawk, a firm specializing in distressed assets, as First City Financial Corporation (FCFC).[4] The Creditors Committee and Judge Harold Abramson approved the reorganization plan in April 1995. The court confirmed the merger in May, and FCFC emerged from bankruptcy on July 3, 1995. This complex case had numerous heterogeneous claimants.[5] To resolve the myriad contentious problems the various constituencies agreed to, and the court appointed, a court's expert (an author of this paper) to hear the concerns of the parties proposing alternate plans and to conduct an independent economic evaluation. This case draws on the vast amount of information gathered under this arrangement. This clinical study illustrates the administrative process of bankruptcy, highlights how the court conducted its judicial weighting in ensuring that the best interests test was satisfied, and explains why the merger partner was critical for the success of the confirmed plan.

1.3. Paper Organization. Section II reviews the events leading up to First City's bankruptcy. Section III discusses the competing bankruptcy plans proposed by First City management and third parties, including First City's creditors, a reorganization process that involved over five hundred lawyers representing creditors, equity holders, the FDIC, plaintiffs from shareholder lawsuits, and affirmative action claimants, among others.[6] To reduce informational asymmetries and to facilitate evaluation of the different plans, First City Bancorporation produced an Omnibus Disclosure Statement.[7] The purpose of the Omnibus Statement was to ensure that when read with each plan proponents' disclosure statements, it could provide "adequate information" as the term is defined in section 1125 of the Bankruptcy Code. It was intended to enable creditors and shareholders "to make an informed decision regarding whether to accept or reject each of the proposed competing plans for the reorganization of First City" (Omnibus Statement, p. 1). Section IV discusses informational asymmetries and incentive misalignments that were exacerbated not only because the Omnibus did not provide objective and reliable information but also because the reorganization was contingent on the FDIC settlement agreement. This section highlights some sources of contention and discusses the steps taken by the court to reduce contention and informational asymmetries. Section V shows why a merger was a superior resolution to First City Bancorporation's financial distress, and Section VI discusses FCFC's successful emergence from bankruptcy. Section VII concludes the paper.

II. First City Bancorporation of Texas

2.1. Background. First City originally owned fifty-nine state and national banks and other nonbanking subsidiaries primarily in large Texas cities. Although the original corporation had assets of $10.6 billion, its solvency was threatened in 1987 by an ailing Texas economy. With the assistance of the FDIC and an infusion of capital from a group of investors headed by A. Robert Abboud, the bank was reorganized in 1988.[8] Appendix 1 provides a time line of significant events.

Only two years after the 1988 reorganization, First City's financial condition deteriorated again. The company had high operating costs, and the credit quality of its loan portfolio was weak. The decline was triggered by a downturn in Texas real estate values, which was in turn attributed to the FDIC and Resolution Trust Corporation (RTC) selling off their large Texas real estate portfolios.

In March 1991, C. Ivan Wilson replaced Abboud as chairman of the board. The new management began a recovery plan that included increasing liquidity at its banks; cutting expenses; closing international operations; using resources of the healthier banks to shore up the weaker ones; improving asset quality; reducing the size of the management team; and raising capital, possibly through the sale of banks. The plan was at least partially successful.[9] Liquidity increased from $80 million in March 1991 to $1.5 billion in October 1992. Each bank became able to stand alone financially. Expenses were cut by

$50 million a year, and 40 percent of the highest-ranking executives left the organization. Asset quality improved through the sale of non-performing loans, and First City had reached agreements settling all of its major outstanding lawsuits.

2.2. The Bankruptcy Filing. The FDIC performed a valuation review of First City and concluded that the system would lose $1.35 billion if all the banks were liquidated, with an FDIC loss of about $698.2 million. On October 30, 1992, the FDIC declared First City's banks insolvent, seized their assets, and placed them in a receivership account. The FDIC first claimed that it would incur losses of $476.9 million because of the insolvency of First City Houston and Dallas. It assessed each of the eighteen remaining First City banks a proportionate share of the anticipated loss and demanded immediate payment. The assessment was greater than each of the remaining bank's capital, allowing the FDIC to also declare those banks insolvent.[10] The next day, some of First City's unsecured creditors filed an involuntary Chapter 11 bankruptcy petition against First City. First City's balance sheet at the time of bankruptcy filing is presented in table 1.

2.3. Lawsuit and Countersuit. First City challenged the FDIC valuation assessment by later instituting a $3 billion lawsuit against the FDIC. First City charged that the FDIC wrongfully closed the banks, it was denied due process, the banks were wrongly assessed, the regulators were negligent, and First City's property was fraudulently transferred. First City's suit demanded $1 billion in compensation

TABLE 1.   **First City Bancorporation of Texas Balance Sheet**

First City Bancorporation of Texas, Inc., Estimated
Statement of Assets and Liabilities as of 11/30/94

Assets (in $ millions)	
Cash and noncash assets in possession of debtor	36
Total assets	36
Liabilities	
Obligations to creditors and claimants	70
Proposed Krim settlement[a]	10
Total liabilities	80
Estimated equity in estate	(44)

[a]The Krim settlement refers to a $10 million settlement of a lawsuit against First City. Jerry Krim had filed a $225 million lawsuit against First City, alleging mismanagement.

plus treble damages. The FDIC countersued, seeking $364.7 million for misdeeds of the previous management.[11] The FDIC suit claimed that First City siphoned off dividends from its subsidiary banks.

2.4. *The FDIC Settlement Agreement.* First City's lawsuit against the FDIC eventually resulted in a cash settlement offer, in June 1994, under which First City could receive cash and other bank assets from the FDIC. Under the proposed settlement agreement First City would receive a dividend of about $200 million ($135 million in cash and about $65 million in noncash assets with a book value of $48 million).[12] First City would receive additional settlements of about $70 million through the closure of loss-sharing agreements with the twenty former First City banks, the FDIC, and the new owners of the First City banks.[13] Another $40–$45 million could be returned to First City after all litigation claims were settled.[14] The settlement however, was contingent on the confirmation of a reorganization plan.

2.5. *Incentives to Settle.* Without a settlement of the FDIC lawsuit, First City had a negative equity position of $44 million (table 1), but if a reorganization plan could be confirmed, the cash inflow from the FDIC would raise the net equity of First City to around $130 million. First City's postsettlement balance sheet (assuming confirmation) is presented in table 2. This potential for an asset inflow to First City arising from the FDIC settlement agreement formed the basis for the subsequent reorganization of First City. The next challenge was to ensure that the court would confirm a reorganization plan.

While legal proceedings continued, the FDIC put the twenty banks up for sale, receiving bids totaling $434.5 million more than the banks' deposits, an amount that would mean the FDIC would incur no losses as a result of its repossession of First City Bancorporation (also referred to as "old First City"). In fact, the sale of the banks plus the sale of old First City's other assets would leave the FDIC with a surplus.[15] The sale price was considerably higher than expected and 50 percent more than the price old First City expected when it was planning to sell thirteen of its banks under its pre-FDIC closure plan.[16] The FDIC attributed the higher than expected bidding to "a better market for banking franchises and improved perceptions of the economy."[17] Texas banking in particular was considered to be on the rebound. First City—minus its twenty banks—was left with its nonbank assets, its claims on the surplus generated by the FDIC sale of the banks, and net operating loss carryforwards (NOLs) available to a reorganized First City.

III. The Competing Bankruptcy Plans

3.1. Some Early Plans. Several groups initially competed to bring First City out of bankruptcy. In November 1994, three groups filed plans in Dallas bankruptcy courts to revive the bank: First City management, 21 International Holdings of New York, and a joint venture of J-Hawk and Cargill Financial Services. The group 21 International, owner of the 21 Club in New York, planned to incorporate First City into its auto finance business. In December 1994 Advanta Corp. expressed an interest in bidding for First City but withdrew its interest later that month. In January, 21 International withdrew its bid for First City.

3.2. The Joint Plan. Subsequently, First City filed a unique plan of reorganization (the "joint plan") that contained three alternatives: the

TABLE 2.   First City Balance Sheet, under the Settlement Agreement

First City Bancorporation of Texas, Inc., Pro Forma Statement of Assets and Liabilities after Payment of Initial Dividend as of 11/30/94

Assets (in $ millions)		
Initial dividend distribution from FDIC receiverships[a]		200
Adjustments to fair market value for GCR assets[b]		
GCR value	64	
Fair market value (First City estimate)	49	
		(15)
Less amounts previously distributed		−11
Cash and noncash assets in possession of debtor		36
Total assets		210
Liabilities		
Estimated payment to creditors and claimants		70
Proposed securities litigation claims settlement[c]		10
Total liabilities		80
Estimated equity after initial dividend and payment of liabilities		130

[a]As part of its settlement with the FDIC, First City received a dividend of $200 million from the $434.5 surplus generated by the sale of the old First City banks. First City would receive additional settlements of about $70 million through the closure of loss-sharing agreements with twenty former First City banks, the FDIC, and the new owners of the First City banks. Another $40–45 million could be returned to First City after all litigation claims were settled, which was the expected surplus in a fund held to satisfy such claims. This statement was contingent on court confirmation of the bankruptcy plan. If the plan were not confirmed by a specified date, there would be no settlement.

[b]GCR (gross cash recovery assets) are noncash assets within the First City bank receiverships that are valued by the FDIC at amounts higher than their market value.

[c]This amount is part of the settlement of many claims against First City, agreed to before the reorganization plan could be accepted.

primary merger alternative (PMA), the secondary standalone alternative (SSA), and a liquidation alternative. Under the PMA (management's preferred plan), postbankruptcy First City (i.e., First City minus its twenty banks) would merge with J-Hawk Corporation to form a new company specializing in valuing distressed assets.[18] If the PMA were not implemented, the plan would adopt the SSA, which was simply the joint plan but without a merger with J-Hawk. This alternative was included because it was deemed a viable plan in and of itself and because its implementation as an alternative would avoid a repetition of the expensive plan confirmation process. The SSA would provide substantially less revenue and net income than the PMA, with revenues of $31.7 million in 1996, declining to $8.8 million by 1998 and zero thereafter, with revenues obtained from the collection of loans and sale of assets received in the FDIC lawsuit. This contrasts with revenues of $25.2 million under the PMA, with revenues increasing every year to $34.7 million by 2000.

Appendix 2 discusses details of the SSA. Suffice it to say here that the primary source of value in the PMA was the merger possibility. Section V elaborates on the sources of value in the PMA.

3.2.1. The Basic Structure of the PMA. First City Financial Corporation (FCFC) would be created by merging First City with "new J-Hawk," a spun-off segment of J-Hawk Corporation (fig. 1). New J-Hawk would contribute all of its assets (book value $20 million) to the merger. First City would contribute $20 million equity from the FDIC settlement, assets not used to settle claims, and around $650 million in net operating loss (NOL) carryforwards. J-Hawk would bring in Cargill Financial Services Corporation (CFSC) as an equity partner.[19] CFSC would provide up to $100 million in subordinate debt or equity to partnerships to be organized by new First City.

FCFC would make cash payments and issue new securities to the claimants either directly or indirectly through a liquidating trust. Virtually all of FCFC's assets would be assigned to the liquidating trust, which, in turn, would issue Class A certificates to FCFC. FCFC would in turn take the Class A certificates and issue common stock and warrants to First City's creditors and shareholders. FCFC would begin with 5 million outstanding shares (estimated book value $40 million). J-Hawk would own 2,460,511 of these shares (about 49.9 percent of the stock), with First City equity holders owning about 43 percent of the company. The new company reserved 230,000 shares (about 5 percent) of common stock in a stock option plan. CFSC would receive about 100,000 shares (2 percent of FCFC shares).

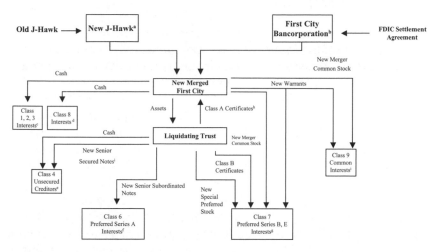

[a] J-Hawk contributed about half of the equity in FCFC from its existing assets, book value of $20 million.

[b] First City Bancorporation of Texas contributed about half of the equity ($20 million) in FCFC, primarily from its settlement agreement with the FDIC and with its assets that were not seized by the FDIC.

[c] Class 1 (priority claims), class 2 (secured claims), and class 3 (settled claims of various claimants) were unimpaired classes in the bankruptcy settlement. Class 1 and 2 claims were paid in full. Class 3 claimants were paid according to the agreed upon settlements. Class 3 claims included the EDS claim of $10.5 million, the BONY claim on $5.5 million, a group of fifty-five additional claimants, and the FDIC.

[d] Part of the settlement to class 8 (subordinated claims) included $7 million cash plus interest, and minus fees and expenses, plus First City's stock interest in Citizens State Bank in Sealy, Texas.

[e] Class 4 interests (unsecured claims) were paid $49.1 million in cash. They also received $16.9 million in new senior secured notes, maturing in six months and paying 7% interest. The settlement also included $65 to $70 million owed to unsecured creditors. Of their claim, 90% was paid in cash and 10% with new senior secured notes.

[f] Class 6 (Series A preferred stock, 635,650 shares) claims were valued at $103,968,504. These claimants received new senior subordinated notes in payment of their claim. Class 6 interests received $105.6 million in new senior subordinated notes, paying 8% interest and due two years after the first interest payment was made.

[g] Class 7 (Series B preferred stock, 2,347,396 shares valued at $172,240,224, and Series E preferred stock of 102,404 shares valued at $8,315,776). These claimants received new special preferred stock, Class B certificates, new merger common stock, and new warrants. Class 7 received $30.8 million in new preferred stock with a 15% dividend, par value of $.01/share, and nominal stated value of $14.22/share, to be redeemed three years after the first interest payment was made. Class 7 also received $33 million in Class B certificates, paying $62.8 million three years after the first payment was made. They received 1,722,638 common shares of FCFC, 35.1% of the total shares outstanding; 250,000 warrants, 50% of the warrants issued by FCFC, with a $30 exercise price, representing 5% of outstanding shares; and any residual from FCFC's asset pool.

[h] Almost all of First City's assets were assigned to the liquidating trust. The liquidating trust would, in turn, issue Class A certificates, which represented the remainder after its preferred stock and bond securities to First City claimants, to FCFC. FCFC in turn issued stock and warrants to class 7 and 9 interests.

[i] Class 9 (common interests). The residual equity holders of old First City (holders of 18,942,219 common shares) would receive new merger common stock and new warrants. These interests received 738,273 common shares of FCFC (15% of the total) and 250,000 warrants, 50% of the warrants issued by FCFC with a $30 exercise price (5% of outstanding shares). Common shareholders also would receive any residual from FCFC's asset pool. Class 10 (common equivalents) claimants, holders of old First City options and warrants, received no distribution, and their claims were canceled.

Fig. 1. The primary merger alternative (PMA)

3.2.2. Treatment of Allowed Claims under the PMA. A bankruptcy plan requires a firm to be separated into claimant classes roughly based on the priority of their claim on the bankrupt firm's assets. Figure 1 shows the type of each claim against First City and the settlement proposed under the PMA. The liquidating trust was fully responsible for settling old First City's claims and immunized the new company from claims from these creditors beyond what they received from the liquidating trust. Any assets left over after creditors were paid would become assets of FCFC. First City common shareholders would receive equity and warrants in new First City.

3.3. The Creditors' Plan. The creditors' reorganization plan contained two options: option A—continued litigation with the FDIC; and option B—the consummation of a modified FDIC settlement and the liquidation of First City's assets under the exclusive control of the creditors until such time as they were paid in full. Option A was aimed at providing First City with a quick exit from Chapter 11 because it did not depend on a settlement with the FDIC. Under option B, if the FDIC settlement was not approved by the court or consummated by the effective date, the creditors would be paid back with the assets First City had on hand and expected to recover either through a revised settlement or litigation against the FDIC.

IV. Resolving Dissension and Information Asymmetries

4.1. Disagreements about the Plans. The Creditors Committee claimed that its proposal was superior because it: (a) forced the FDIC to settle immediately or else litigation would resume; (b) continued First City as a corporation; (c) was not dependent on J-Hawk's participation, which, in the opinion of the Creditors Committee, was uncertain; (d) paid the creditors in full without the need to wait until 1997 to see if the FDIC would honor the settlement agreement; (e) allowed for the distribution of equity securities but no cash dividends or other cash payments until the creditors had been paid in full. Creditors and some shareholders objected to the joint plan primarily because they believed First City was settling its $1 billion lawsuit with the FDIC for too little. Creditors were also concerned about what they considered excessive salaries and bonuses to be paid to new management, post-merger, under the PMA.

The creditors criticized the joint plan, arguing, "the FDIC Agreement not only has an outside closing date of three years but also enjoins the Debtor from taking any action for three years in the event the agreement does not immediately close. . . . the Debtor's thought process (i.e. to do nothing) is self evident."

The joint plan proponents had their own criticisms of the creditors' plan. They noted that since the creditors' option B required significant concessions from the FDIC, which the FDIC had continually refused to make, the Creditors Committee's plan was really contained in option A, the "litigation option," in which the reorganized debtor under the control of the creditors would go back to litigating with the FDIC. The joint plan proponents noted that "There would be nothing available for distribution to Equity Security Holders unless and until there was a favorable outcome to the litigation."

4.2. The Courts' Judicial Weighting. These and other serious disagreements presented a major challenge not only to the debtors, creditors, and other claimants but also to the bankruptcy judge, Harold Abramson. How would the court handle (in the context of confirmation) the problems arising from the complexity and informational asymmetries among the debtor, creditors, and the government? How would the extreme contention among the various constituencies be resolved?[20] How would the court evaluate the veracity of the information in the competing plans? How would the court determine, before confirming a plan, whether the best interest test was, in fact, satisfied? These matters were important for at least four reasons. First, the FDIC surplus was being depleted by FDIC bankruptcy costs ($2.5 million per month). Second, resolving differences among the disparate groups with independent investment banker teams would cost the estate an additional $3 million.[21] Third, how would the judge ensure that the best interests test was met? Finally, unless the contention was resolved, the potential for an appeal of the court's eventual ruling was significant.

4.3. Reducing Contention and Informational Asymmetries. To reduce complexities from incomplete information and bargaining problems, Judge Abramson, relying on the Federal Rules of Evidence 706, appointed a court's expert to act as a common party for the various constituencies and to conduct an economic analysis of the various alternatives. This would obviate the need for expensive testimony from experts for each constituency. His motivation was that a "pooling" of all relevant information with a "disinterested person" (Bankruptcy Code section 101 (14)) can provide a more objective valuation analysis. The expert was given free access to all parties and allowed to request privileged and confidential written and oral information available from any party—the DIP (debtor in possession), equity holders, creditors, securities litigation claimants, tax consultants, the FDIC, and the Creditors Committee. He was also given permission to seek outside accounting help. The expert was asked to evaluate the economic structure of competing plans after obtaining information from the various parties, conduct independent investigations and analyses, and make a recommendation to the judge with a valuation of claims under the recommended plan. The court empowered the expert to initiate, at his sole discretion, contact with any attorney; to seek any and all information from the parties; and to resolve differences through either meetings in person or telephone conferences. The expert was authorized to examine Texas Commerce Bank's records (loss-sharing agreements). Further, the court directed the FDIC to share its confidential information with the expert, as necessary, information that neither the equity holders nor the creditors had. If the expert and the attorneys could not resolve any issue it was to be brought to the court for a resolution.[22]

The objectives of the court at the confirmation hearing were to determine whether: (a) holders of claims and equity interests would receive greater distributions under the management's plan versus Chapter 7 liquidation; and (b) the confirmed plan was fair and equitable with respect to, and did not discriminate unfairly against, any impaired class of claims.

4.4. Comparing the Competing Reorganization Plans. The subsequent discussion explains how the court's expert compared the joint plan with the creditors' plan. Let V_{PMA}, V_{SSA}, V_{OpA}, and V_{OpB} represent the economic value of the PMA, the SSA, creditors' option A, and creditors' option B, respectively. Let P_{PMA}, P_{SSA}, P_{OpA}, and P_{OpB} represent the probability that the respective plan would be implemented.

Since the joint plan contains two alternatives (to liquidation), its economic value is

$$E\ (V_J) = P_{PMA} \times V_{PMA} + P_{SSA} \times V_{SSA}.$$

Similarly, the economic value of the two alternatives in the creditors' plan is

$$E(V_C) = P_{OpA} \times V_{OpA} + P_{OpB} \times V_{OpB}.$$

It was assumed (with concurrence by the attorneys) that both the SSA and the option B alternatives were equally likely to be implemented under their respective plans ($P_{SSA} = P_{OpB}$), thus implying that $P_{PMA}/P_{OpA} = 1$. It was further agreed, in discussions with the Creditors Committee, that $V_{SSA} = V_{OpB}$. It follows that $E(V_J) > E(V_C)$ if (V_{OpA}/V_{PMA}) is less than unity. Thus, the problem was reduced to the following: if $V_{PMA} > V_{OpA}$, the joint plan is economically superior. If $V_{PMA} < V_{OpA}$, the creditors' plan has more economic value.[23]

4.5. The Best Interests Test. By cumulating the value of all claims, the market value of the PMA as submitted to the court was estimated to be $359,000,000. To evaluate whether the confirmed plan satisfies the court-required "best interests test" a summary of values received under three restructuring alternatives is contained in table 3. The estimates in table 3 clearly demonstrate that the old First City/J-Hawk merger plan provides the most overall value and is in the best interest of old First City creditors. That is, the PMA satisfies the requirements of the best interests test. As shown in table 3, the liquidation option only provides a partial payment of $40,300,000 to class 4 creditors and no payments to the remaining creditors. The SSA provides full payment to class 4 creditors and partial payment to remaining creditors, a total of $243,424,329. The PMA provides full payment to all debt holders, a total of $299,985,851, and additionally provides $58,904,633 in equity to the new corporation.

The benefit to equity holders from J-Hawk's involvement is the difference between the class 9 equity values in the merger plan versus the standalone plan, $20,366,756 minus $1,100,000, or $19,266,756.

V. Factors Favoring the PMA

The court expert eventually concluded and recommended to the court that (a) the joint plan economically dominated the creditors' plan because the PMA was superior to the creditors option A and (b) the PMA created about $20 million more value than the SSA.[24] Some of the (not mutually exclusive) factors that formed the basis for this recommendation are discussed subsequently.

Veracity of Cash Flow Estimates. The cash flow projections in the joint plan were made jointly by J-Hawk and First City's management. In its earlier business, J-Hawk first valued its potential acquisitions by estimating projected cash flows, appraising the properties, physically

TABLE 3. Valuation of Claims

Claim	Value under PMA ($)	Value under SSA ($)[a]	Value in Liquidation ($)[b]
J-Hawk (2,460,511 shares of new merger common stock −2,460,511 × $23.95)[c]	58,904,633		
Class 4 interests (old First City creditors)[d]	66,090,287	66,090,000	40,300,000
Class 6 interests (old Class A preferred stockholders)[e]	105,623,929	88,582,895	
Class 7 interests (old Class B preferred stock)[f]		87,651,434	
New special preferred stock	30,791,698		
Class B certificates	33,180,727		
New merger common stock	41,239,954		
New warrants	2,692,500		
Class 9 interests (common stockholders)[g]	20,366,756	1,100,000	
Total value	358,890,484	243,424,329	40,300,000

[a]The secondary standalone alternative is valued in appendix 2 of this paper.

[b]Note that these are the valuation amounts for impaired creditors. Administrative claims and class 3 claims were paid in full, a total amount of $5,600,000, discounted at 7.5%. The liquidation alternative valuation was provided by First City Bancorporation and is discussed in appendix 2.

[c]J-Hawk contributed half the equity of FCFC from its existing assets. The shares of FCFC were valued at $23.94 a share by the court's expert. This valuation of the stock and warrants is explained in appendix 3.

[d]Class 4 interests were paid $49.1 million in cash and $16.9 million in senior secured notes, maturing in six months and paying 7% interest. Cash flows would be $49,100,000 immediately and $17,491,500 in six months. Discounted at 5.9%, the twenty-six-week Treasury bill rate, as of March 1, 1995, the discounted value of the cash flows is $60,090,287.

[e]Class 6 interests received $105.6 million in new senior subordinated notes, paying 8% interest and due two years after the first interest payment was made. The cash flows are $2,079,370 in quarterly interest payments, with principal amount of $51,984,250 paid after one year, followed by quarterly interest payments of $1,039,685 for the second year and repayment of the remaining $51,984,254 in principal at the end of the second year. Using a discount rate of 7% (slightly higher than the risk-free rate of 5.9%), the present value of the cash flows is $105,623,929.

[f]Class 7 interests received $30.8 million in new preferred stock with a 15% dividend, par value of $.01 a share, nominal stated value of $14.22 a share, to be redeemed three years after the first dividend payment was made. They also received $33 million in Class B certificates, paying $62.8 million three years after the first interest payment was made; along with 1,722,638 common shares of FCFC, 35.1% of the total shares outstanding; 250,000 warrants, 50% of the warrants issued by FCFC, with a $30 exercise price, representing 5% of outstanding shares; and any residual from FCFC's asset pool. Cash flows for the preferred stock would be $1,312,500 every quarter for 3¼ years. The last payment would be interest plus $35 million repayment, a total of $36,312,500. With a discount rate of 20.13% (calculated in appendix 3), the present value of these cash flows is $30,761,698. Class B certificate holders would receive a payment of $62,800,000 in 3¼ years after the formation of FCFC, with a present value of $33,180,727, using a discount rate of 20.13%. New common stock and warrants are valued in appendix 3.

[g]Class 9 interests received 738,273 common shares of FCFC, about 15% of the total. They also received 250,000 warrants, 50% of the warrants issued by FCFC, with a $30 exercise price, representing 5% of outstanding shares; and any residual from FCFC's asset pool.

inspecting the sites, and using this information to determine a purchase price for each asset. Since its inception, J-Hawk had acquired over $1 billion in principal amount assets at a cost of $471.5 million. It had provided its investors with a 51 percent return on equity in 1993 and 28.6 percent in the first nine months of 1994. This track record, attributed to a great extent to its skills at forecasting flows from distressed assets, provided credibility to the plan forecasts.

Management Team. First City owned a large portfolio of distressed assets and intended to use J-Hawk's expertise to manage those assets. J-Hawk and First City's management had a comparative advantage in the distressed assets business. The management of First City, especially its president, Robert Brown, had an intimate knowledge of the assets held by First City, and it was believed that this would be an invaluable asset in the handling of the liquidating trust. This specialized information coupled with J-Hawk's experience in distressed assets was viewed as a key advantage for FCFC.

Synergies of Scope. The First City–J-Hawk merger was seen to provide several competitive advantages for the new firm. FCFC would offer a wide range of services, including portfolio valuation, management services, and disposition of assets. Many of its competitors were involved in only one or two of these areas. In addition, it would conduct operations in all parts of the country, giving it an advantage over competitors who were limited to either a specific type of distressed asset or a certain geographical area.

Involvement by J-Hawk's Prior Business Partner. J-Hawk had previously participated in joint ventures in distressed asset purchases and sales with Cargill Financial Services Corporation, which, as mentioned in note 19, is a wholly owned subsidiary of Cargill, Inc., one of the world's largest privately held companies. Under the PMA, CFSC had the right to participate as an equity investor in potential asset purchases. CFSC's involvement was considered a major plus in the merger plan.[25]

Regulatory Environment. The consolidation of financial institutions provided J-Hawk with continuing sources of distressed assets.[26] The FDIC and RTC had fewer distressed assets for sale now, and their role as the primary sellers of distressed assets had been largely replaced by commercial banks and insurance companies. Continuing consolidation in the banking industry and increasing regulatory pressure to dispose of nonperforming and underperforming assets were seen as providing continuing business for new First City. It was estimated that FCFC would acquire $70 million in distressed assets per quarter, with growth of 2 percent per quarter, which was consistent with J-Hawk's current level of business activity. The projected gross margin was 25 percent. FCFC would finance future acquisitions following its existing capital structure, with FCFC contributing 2 percent equity, CFSC 2 percent equity, senior lenders 70 percent debt, and CFSC 26 percent subordinated debt.

Access to Capital. Merging with First City gave J-Hawk better access to the public debt and equity markets, allowing it to raise new capital to expand its growing businesses. The new company would continue to need senior debt financing in order to continue growth in the distressed assets business. FCFC's partnership with CFSC was designed to ensure a continuing source of new funds. FCFC was expected to benefit from its association with CFSC through its access to that company's large financial resources.

VI. Emerging from Bankruptcy

In perfect financial markets with symmetric information, the process of evaluating whether a company should be liquidated or reorganized is, in principle, an exercise in the valuation of future cash flows. The situation, however, is dramatically complicated in a world with informational asymmetries, heterogeneous claimants, contracting rigidities, and government entities. The difficulties stem from the absence of common information, outcomes that are to be adjudicated and determined dynamically during the bankruptcy process, and contract payoffs determined not by the original contract provisions but through negotiation among the lawyers. Moreover, many contracts' payoffs are endogenous (moral hazard, political risk, nonmarketability of claims, etc.), and, in the language of Grossman (1995), they suffer from "incomplete equitization" and lack objective market valuations. The question then becomes one of exactly how the reorganization plans are to be evaluated by the court.

This paper discusses First City's bankruptcy from beginning to the end, illustrating the administrative process under which the court conducted its judicial weighting in an extremely contentious environment with severe information asymmetries and competing interests. The creation of FCFC has been described as a "very rare case" as "most banks in First City's position were liquidated and went away."[27]

Recognizing the complexities arising from the lack of common information, Franks, Nyborg, and Torous (1996) suggest that the role of the Bankruptcy Code must be to promote low-cost information production. In this regard, section 101 (14) of the Bankruptcy Code, which provides for the use of a court's expert to aid the judge in judicial weighting, may be justified on the basis of efficiency arguments in a world of informational asymmetries, unclear legal outcomes, and voluntary departures from originally contracted provisions.

With very high administrative costs and extreme complexity in First City's economic and legal environment, virtually no party had reasonable confidence in its own projections, and each party lacked the knowledge to mount any serious attack on the projections of other parties. Consider the fact that the goal of the Omnibus Disclosure Statement was to reduce informational asymmetries. First City had prepared the Omnibus Disclosure Statement. There was, in general, no independent audit of the financial information contained in the Omnibus Statement, and the numbers were derived from "numerous sources including, but not limited to, the Debtors' Books and Records, the Debtors' Schedules and Statement of Affairs, Proofs of Claim and other documents filed with the bankruptcy court, and certain documents obtained through discovery from the Federal Deposit Insurance Corporation in both its corporate capacity and as a receiver of the former First City Banks and Collecting bank" (Omnibus Statement, p. 3). Neither First City, the plan proponents, nor counsel for First City or its plan proponents would warrant or represent that the information provided was without inaccuracy. Further, both the Bankruptcy Court and the SEC explicitly stated that they would not take a position on the accuracy and adequacy of statements in the Omnibus Disclosure Statement. How, then, could the court evaluate the reasonableness of competing claims and proposals? This is a nontrivial matter because the court's confirmation decision would have both efficiency and equity (fairness) implications. Moreover, the court's decision would further be subject to postconfirmation appeals.

The judge's use of a court's expert to evaluate the available information, generate new information, and conduct independent evaluations of competing positions served as a mechanism for negotiating some agreement among seemingly intransigent factions (see Sect. 4.4). The judge's judicial weighting was based on recommendations derived from better information; independent analyses; specific agreements among the lawyers; and most important, the outcome of a process that all parties had agreed to ex ante. It was presumably used in making an informed judgment about the merits of alternative plans. Absent agreement among the various parties to abide by the judge's decision to employ a court expert, the litigation would have been prolonged. The economic costs associated with continuing litigation were enormous, and an inefficient resolution of the matter could have potentially destroyed the entire economic value that currently existed.[28] Moreover, the timing of the FDIC offer was critical for the success of the reorganization. The FDIC offer was triggered by the fact that the real estate markets were assessing the assets at far more than either First City or the FDIC had expected (Sect. 2.5). The court expert mechanism was critical for estimating the cash flows from the liquidating trust (Sect. 5). This not only speeded up the process and reduced bankruptcy costs but also lowered the possibility of postconfirmation appeals.

It is well known that mergers can be important in bankruptcy reorganizations, and this case illustrates some reasons why—the merger partner's prior track record, its expertise, and its business alliances offered the reorganized company management expertise, access to additional funds, and other competitive advantages (Sect. 4.5). The merger partner and incumbent management had a clear advantage over creditors and other groups in justifying projected cash flow estimates that were critical for plan confirmation. Issuing securities through a liquidating trust (rather than directly from FCFC; see fig. 1) was designed to immunize J-Hawk and CFSC from claims arising from First City's bankruptcy. Surprisingly, in light of the enormous uncertainty about the feasibility of using $650 million in NOLs, it was agreed to value the reorganized firm as if these tax benefits would not materialize (see note 29).

The result is an example of the use of Chapter 11 bankruptcy proceedings as the law originally intended. Bankruptcy gave First City Bancorporation a "second chance." Chapter 11 allowed the firm to divest its banking assets; retain the nonbank assets, including a portfolio of distressed real estate; and become a well-functioning company. The bankruptcy process resulted in greater value to all the participants than would have occurred in a liquidation, which might have been the result of FDIC closure of the First City banks.

The joint plan proved to be a success. FCFC officially began business on July 3, 1995, with former J-Hawk executive James R. Hawkins as chairman and C. Ivan Wilson, former First City chairman, as vice chairman of the new company. Former J-Hawk executive James T. Sartain was president, and Robert Brown, former First City president, was president of the unit overseeing the liquidating trust. After its emergence from bankruptcy, FCFC received an initial installment of $170 million ($130 million in cash and $40 million in assets) from the FDIC in July 1995, of which $66 million was immediately used to replay old First City creditors. The remainder of the settlement from the FDIC would be paid out over the next five years. On July 12, FCFC repurchased about $200 million in loans and real estate from Texas Commerce Bancshares and Cull-Frost Bankers. This purchase ended the loss-sharing agreements the FDIC had with the banks and allowed the FDIC to turn over an additional $90 million in assets to FCFC.

VII. Conclusion

The First City reorganization points to the importance of recognizing that standard valuation procedures that apply to a viable company with traded claims may not, by themselves, be adequate for evaluating the value of reorganized claims. Absent commonly accessible information and legal contingencies, the contracting and negotiation during the administrative process of bankruptcy were far more important in evaluating the economics of the competing plans. The economic analysis was based on modifications of cash flow forecasts included in the disclosure statements, with new information and additional terms and conditions "agreed upon" as "reasonable" among the lawyers and the bankruptcy court. It would be useful to study other large bankruptcies to identify common elements of the reorganization process that can provide useful information for firms, academics, legal analysts, and policymakers.

Appendix 1. First City Time Line

April 1988—First City Bankcorporation is organized as a multibank holding company headed by A. Robert Abboud, chairman of the board.

1990—First City becomes financially distressed.

March 1991—C. Ivan Wilson replaces Abboud as chairman of the board.

Summer 1992—First City proposes "Plan C," its reorganization plan that does not require FDIC participation.

October 30, 1992—First City banks in Houston and Dallas declared insolvent by FDIC.

October 31, 1992—Remaining First City banks are declared insolvent. Unsecured creditors file involuntary Chapter 11 bankruptcy petition against First City.

November 24, 1992—Creditors Committee appointed by the bankruptcy court.

November 29, 1992—First City files suits against the FDIC in Dallas civil court.

December 2, 1992—First City files adversary petition against FDIC to obtain records and certain assets.

January 27, 1993—FDIC announces sale of the twenty First City bridge banks.

February and March 1993—FDIC closes the bridge banks and places them into receivership. Assets and liabilities of the banks are transferred to the buyers.

March 8, 1993—Equity Committee appointed.

June 11, 1993—First City files additional administrative claims against the FDIC.

September 24, 1993—First City files a lawsuit against the FDIC, charging that the FDIC wrongfully seized the banks' assets.

October 8, 1993—First City and the FDIC agree to suspend the lawsuit in order to begin settlement talks.

December 17, 1993—Tentative settlement of the suit between First City and the FCIC announced.

June 1994—Proposed agreement reached between First City and the FDIC.

November 1, 1994—Three groups file plans in Dallas bankruptcy court: First City management, 21 International, and J-Hawk/Cargill Financial Services.

December 5, 1994—J-Hawk and First City file a joint bankruptcy plan.

December 23, 1994—Equity Committee announces its support for the joint merger plan.

February 24, 1995—Deadline for voting on the First City/J-Hawk plan.

March 16, 1995—Announcement of the approval of the First City/J-Hawk plan.

April 17, 1995—Creditors Committee agrees to the joint plan.

May 1995—Bankruptcy court agrees to the joint plan.

July 3, 1995—First City merges with J-Hawk, becoming First City Financial Corp.

August 11, 1995—First City Financial Corp. buys Diversified Financial Systems and Diversified Performing Assets.

Appendix 2. The Secondary Standalone Alternative (SSA) and the Liquidation Alternative

New standalone First City would also be a company specializing in managing distressed assets. After settling its bankruptcy obligations, it would seek out new ventures or liquidate. The standalone plan is illustrated in figure A2.1. As with the merger plan, administrative and unsecured creditors would be paid as detailed in the primary plan. Class A preferred stock would be converted into new senior preferred stock. Classes B and E preferred stock would be converted into new junior preferred stock equal to $55 per share.

This plan has many of the same uncertainties as the merger plan, for example, in the valuation of assets and amounts to be received from the FDIC. Management of new standalone First City would be uncertain. Under the merged plan

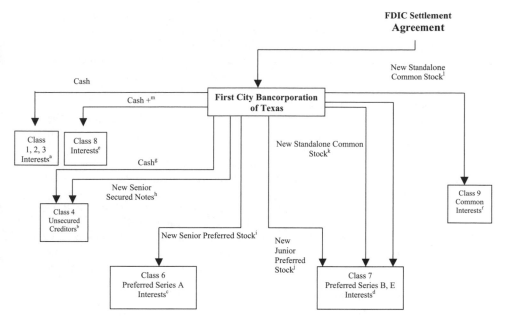

[a] Class 1, 2, 3 claimants were to be treated the same as under the primary merger alternative (PMA).

[b] Class 4 (unsecured creditors) claimants were to be treated the same as under the PMA.

[c] Class 6 (Series A preferred stock) to receive new senior preferred stock. Estimated recovery: 100%.

[d] Class 7 (Series B and E preferred stock) to receive new junior preferred stock and new standalone common stock.

[e] Class 8 (securities litigation claims) were to be treated the same as under the PMA.

[f] Class 9 (common interests) were to receive new standalone common stock. Class 10 holders of options and warrants would receive no distribution, the same as under the PMA.

[g] Class 4 claimants would receive $49.1 million in cash.

[h] Class 4 claimants would receive $16.9 million in new senior secured notes, maturing in six months and paying 7% interest.

[i] Class 6 claimants would receive $88.6 million, or 635,650 shares, of new senior preferred stock, with a stated value of $163.56/share, paying an 8% dividend.

[j] Series B holders would receive $82.6 million in new junior preferred stock, 2,336,971 shares, with a nominal value of $55/share and a 10% dividend, redeemable in ten years. Series E holders would receive $4 million in new junior preferred stock, 112,829 shares.

[k] Series B holders would receive 4,769,718 shares of common stock in the standalone company, valued at $1,049,338. Series E holders would receive 230,282 shares of new standalone common stock, valued at $50,662.

[l] Class 9 interests would receive 5,000,000 shares of new standalone common stock, valued at $1,100,000.

[m] Part of the settlement to class 8 litigation interests included $7 million cash plus interest and minus fees and expenses, plus First City's stock interest in Citizens State Bank in Sealy, Texas.

Fig. A2.1. The secondary standalone alternative (SSA)

J-Hawk's management would take over new First City operations. Other uncertainties include final settlement amounts of the various pending lawsuits, loss-sharing agreement settlement (or no settlement) amounts, availability of tax loss carryforwards, interest rates, rates on investments in marketable securities, and a possibly delayed effective date for the settlement.

Asset contributors to new standalone First City would be First City Bank Corporation of Texas[29] and the FDIC.[30]

Balance sheet and income statement data for the standalone plan show that this plan would provide substantially less revenue and net income than the primary merger plan, with revenues of $31.7 million in 1996, declining to $8.8 million by 1998, with revenues obtained from the collection of loans and the sale of assets received in the FDIC lawsuit settlement. Total assets would decline as the company's debts were paid.

The liquidation alternative provides less to creditors than either the PMA or the standalone alternative. Under Chapter 7 liquidation, classes 1, 2, and 3 would receive 100 percent of their claims, as under the PMA and SSA. Class 4 creditors would receive $50.1 million (undiscounted) of their $66 million claim. The remaining classes would not receive any distributions from the bankruptcy.

Appendix 3. Impaired Claims Valuation

Many of the cash flow projects and valuation assumptions were subject to negotiations and agreement with the various constituencies. Balance sheet and income statement projections for FCFC are contained in table A3.1. FCFC was slated to begin with $40 million in equity, with about half contributed by old First City and half by J-Hawk. Old J-Hawk and First City shareholders and old First City preferred shareholders were the shareholders in FCFC. This equity was predicted to grow at 29 percent to 48 percent annually, following the growth of net income at rates from 7 percent to 43 percent annually. The new company anticipated revenues from distressed asset servicing fees and from its acquisition partnerships to increase from $25.2 million in 1995 to $34.7 million in 2000. Book value per share was expected to climb from $8 at the inception of the new company to $33.20 by 2000. Similarly, earnings per share were expected to grow from $3.29 in the first full year of operation, 1996, to $7.60 by 2000, representing a growth rate of 7 percent increasing to 37 percent per year by 2000. This represents a return on equity averaging 27.6 percent per year and a return on investments averaging 40.4 percent per year. Table A3.1 also contains information on the projected cash flows for the reorganized First City.

Classes 4, 6, and 7 receive securities issued by the liquidating trust rather than from FCFC. This provision was designed to immunize FCFC, J-Hawk, and CFSC from claims arising from First City's bankruptcy. The liquidating trust issued all securities to satisfy First City claims, with FCFC receiving any residual after all claims were paid. Thus, to value the new senior secured notes, new senior subordinated notes, new special preferred stock, and Class B certificates, the information in Table A3.1 is insufficient; one must estimate the expected cash flows from the liquidating trust. Since the joint plan made no attempt to sepa-rately identify the cash flows from the liquidating trust, these were developed by the court expert based on responses to specific questions sent out to the various parties. The cash flows for the liquidating trust are presented in table A3.2, which shows sources of cash from the FDIC settlement, interest earned on cash bal-ances, and proceeds from the sale and collection of loans received in the FDIC settlement.

FCFC expected to receive cash and assets from the FDIC over a three-year period of time from 1995 to 1998. The line "Cash allocated to A certificates" is the money allocated to unsecured creditors and old Series A preferred shareholders, the money left over after higher priority claimants were paid. The unsecured cred-itors were paid $66.5 million in 1995 at the inception of FCFC, with $57.2 million available to remaining creditors, now also equity holders in FCFC. The unsecured creditors and Series A preferred shareholders creditors were to receive repay-ment in full of their new debt in 1996 and 1997. Debt repayment included pay-ment of a $25 million note to the FDIC, part of the lawsuit settlement in 1996. Special preferred stock of $35 million, issued to old Series B and E preferred shareholders, was scheduled to be redeemed in 1999. This plan called for sizable balances remaining to holders of the B certificates issued to old Series B and E preferred shareholders, as noted in the line "Cash allocated to B certificates."

An equity discount rate is needed to value new common stock and warrants. The capital asset pricing model (CAPM) was used to estimate the discount rate on equity. Beta was estimated using the pure play method.[31] There are few di-rectly comparable firms in the distressed asset disposal business that are publicly traded. This analysis evaluated firms recommended by J-Hawk and others based on the standard industrial classification (SIC) system. Comparable firms first were classified as nondepository credit institutions, insurance agents, brokers and ser-vice, real estate, holding and other investment companies, and business services. Table A3.3 lists firms selected as comparable to new First City.

In this sample, the average beta of the comparable firms is 1.39, the highest beta is 2.49, the average price/earnings (P/E) ratio is 15, and the lowest P/E is 8.

The historic average risk-free rate is 3.7 percent, and the historic average market return is 10.3 percent.[32] From the CAPM: $E(R_i) = R_F + \beta_i[E(R_m) - R_F]$ = 0.037 + 2.49[0.103 − 0.037 = 20.13 percent. The annual rate of 20.13 percent, or quarterly rate of 5.0325 percent was used in the equity calculations.

Dividend Growth Model

The analysis also assumes that no dividends are paid until the end of the fourth year, the last period for which financial statements are provided. Half of the pro-jected net income of $41,800,000[33] at the end of the fourth year is assumed to be paid out as dividends. This is a fairly high dividend payout ratio and will lead to more conservative estimates of value. The amount of the dividend, $20,900,000, is assumed to be paid out quarterly, giving a quarterly dividend of $5,225,000. It is also assumed that the warrants are exercised in year 4, adding 500,000 shares

TABLE A3.1. New Merged First City Projected Schedule of Cash Flow for Ongoing Operations

		As of April 1, 1995, and the Five Years Ending March 31, 2000 (in $ millions)				
	1-Apr 1995 (inception)	Year Ending 31-Mar 1996	Year Ending 31-Mar 1997	Year Ending 31-Mar 1998	Year Ending 31-Mar 1999	Year Ending 31-Mar 2000
Balance sheet data						
1. Cash	21.3	27.2	34.5	46.4	85.6	123.3
2. Equity in investments of acquisition partnerships	17.7	28.2	38.5	47.9	54.3	58.3
3. Other assets	1.0	1.0	1.0	1.0	1.0	1.0
4. Total assets and new common equity	40.0	56.4	74.0	95.3	140.9	182.6
Income statement data						
5. Trust assets service fees		6.0	3.3	1.1	0.0	0.0
6. Other servicing fees		6.4	9.2	11.3	13.0	14.7
7. Equity in earnings of acquisition partnerships		12.8	13.7	15.2	17.2	20.0
8. Total revenue		25.2	26.2	27.6	30.2	34.7
9. Administrative expenses		9.8	11.1	11.9	12.2	12.9
10. Income taxes expense[a]		0.4	0.4	0.5	0.7	0.9
11. Interest on cash balances		1.5	2.8	6.1	13.2	20.9
12. Net income		16.5	17.5	21.3	30.5	41.8
Cash flow data						
13. Net income		16.5	17.5	21.3	30.5	41.7
14. Less partnership income		(12.8)	(13.7)	(15.2)	(17.2)	(20.0)
15. Adjusted net income		3.7	3.8	6.1	13.3	21.7
Acquisition partnerships						
16. Distributions		8.2	9.9	12.7	18.4	24.1
17. Investments		-5.9	-6.4	-6.9	-7.5	-8.1
18. Proceeds from warrants					15.0	
19. Net cash flow		6.0	7.3	11.9	39.2	37.7
Beginning cash		21.3	27.2	34.5	46.4	85.6
Ending cash		27.3	34.5	46.4	85.6	123.3
20. Average cash		24.3	30.9	40.5	66.0	104.5
Per share information ($)						
21. Earnings per share[b]	8.00	3.29	3.50	4.26	5.55	7.60
22. Book value per share[c]		11.28	14.80	19.06	25.62	33.20
23. Shares outstanding (mil)	5	5	5	5	5.5	5.5

Financial statistics

26. Return on equity[d]	34	27	25	26	26
27. Tax provision rate[a]	2.12	2.12	2.12	2.12	2.12
28. Interest rate on cash	6	9	15	20	20
29. Return on investments[e]	56	41	35	34	36
Growth (%) of					
30. Cash[f]	28	27	34	84	44
31. Investments[g]	59	37	24	13	7
32. Equity	41	31	29	48	30
33. Other servicing fees[h]	−10	44	23	15	13
34. Equity in earnings of acqusition partnerships[i]	198	7	11	13	16
35. Administrative expenses[j]	−4	13	7	3	6
36. Net income[k]	239	6	22	43	37
37. Adjusted net income[l]		3	61	118	63
Acquisition partnerships					
38. Distributions[m]		21	28	45	31
39. Investments[n]		8	8	9	8
40. Earnings per share[o]		7	22	30	37
41. Book value per share[p]		31	29	34	30

Note: Information is taken from the Joint Plan of Reorganization Disclosure Statement, unless otherwise noted.

[a] Rate from Omnibus, p. 70. See references. Taxes are low because of the use of net operating losses. FCFC would only have to pay the alternative minimum tax, estimated at 2% of income before taxes.

[b] Line 12/line 23.

[c] Line 4/line 23.

[d] Line 12/(prior year line 4 + line 4)/2.

[e] Line 7/((prior year line 2 + line 2)/2)].

[f] [(Line 1 − prior year line 1)/prior year line 1].

[g] [(Line 2 − prior year line 2)/prior year line 2].

[h] [(Line 6 − prior year line 6)/prior year line 6].

[i] [(Line 7 − prior year line 7)/prior year line 7].

[j] [(Line 9 − prior year line 9)/prior year line 9].

[k] [(Line 12 − prior year line 12)/prior year line 12].

[l] [(Line 13 − prior year line 13)/prior year line 13].

[m] [(Line 14 − prior year line 14)/prior year line 14].

[n] [(Line 15 − prior year line 15)/prior year line 15].

[o] [(Line 21 − prior year line 21)/prior year line 21].

[p] [(Line 22 − prior year line 22)/prior year line 22].

TABLE A3.2. New Merged First City Liquidating Trust Cash Flows

	New Merged First City (in $ millions)				
	1-Apr 1995 (Inception)	Year Ending 31-Mar 1996	Year Ending 31-Mar 1997	Year Ending 31-Mar 1998	Year Ending 31-Mar 1999
Sources of cash					
From debtor[a]	19.2				
From FDIC settlement[a]	124.5	20	20		
Interest on cash balances[b]		1.5	1.5	4.6	1.5
Proceeds from sale of					
Collection of loans		11.3	11.3	5.7	
FDIC and debtor assets		12.1	19.5	8.8	
Loss-sharing-pool assets		60	60	30	
Loan loss recovery			20		
Total sources of cash	143.7	104.9	132.3	49.1	1.5
Uses of cash					
Interest on senior note[c]		0.6			
Interest on subordinated note[d]		8.3	4.2		
Dividends on special preferred		5.3	5.3	5.3	1.3
Servicing expenses		6.0	3.2	1.1	
Direct trust expenses		2.5	2.3	2.0	
Investment in new company	20.0				
TCB loss-sharing agreement[a]		52.0			
Interest on FDIC note[c]		2.0			
Total uses of cash	20.0	76.7	15.0	8.4	1.3
Net cash flow	123.7	28.2	117.3	40.7	0.2
Beginning cash balance	0.0	57.2	(8.5)	56.9	97.7
Cash before allocations	123.7	85.4	108.8	97.6	97.9
Cash allocated to A certificates	66.5	93.9	52.0	0.0	35.0
Cash allocated to B certificates	57.2	(8.5)	56.8	97.6	62.9
Reconciliation of Class A certificates					
Proceeds from trust	66.5	93.9	52.0	0.0	35.0
Payments to bankruptcy creditors at inception					
Administrative claims	3.0				
Tax and gap claims	0.4				
Class 3 creditors[c]	14.0				
Class 4 creditors[c]	49.1				
Class 5 creditors	0.0				
Total payments to creditors	66.5				
Principal payments of					
Senior secured notes[c]		16.9			
Subordinated notes		52.0	52.0		

TABLE A3.2—*Continued*

		New Merged First City (in $ millions)			
	1-Apr 1995 (Inception)	Year Ending 31-Mar 1996	Year Ending 31-Mar 1997	Year Ending 31-Mar 1998	Year Ending 31-Mar 1999
Redemption of special preferred FDIC note[a]		25.0	0.0	0.0	35.0
Total principal payments	0.0	93.9	52.0	0.0	35.0
Total cash used by Class A	66.5	93.9	52.0	0.0	35.0

Note: Numbers taken from the joint plan of reorganization and from information provided by the court's expert.

[a]From Omnibus Disclosure Statement.

[b]Average at 6%.

[c]Numbers taken from information from the court's expert after the joint plan of reorganization was prepared.

[d]Balance at 8%.

to the existing 5,000,000 shares outstanding. This means dividends per share will be $0.95.[34]

The dividend growth rate (g) is estimated to be equal to the retention ratio times the return on equity. The retention ratio is 50 percent. The return on equity (ROE), as calculated from the financial statements in table A3.1, is 34 percent in year 1, 27 percent in year 2, 25 percent in year 3, and 26 percent in year 4. The average ROE is 27.6 percent. To be conservative, the lowest ROE of 25 percent is

TABLE A3.3.   Firms Comparable to First City Financial Corporation

Firm	Market	Symbol	Beta	P/E
Advanta Corp.	NASDAQ	ADVNB	1.65	12
Alleghany Corp.	NYSE	Y	0.50	8
American General Corporation	NYSE	AGC	1.50	24
Amresco Inc.	NYSE	BCN	0.70	
Beneficial Corporation	NYSE	BNL	1.20	12
Countrywide Credit Industries Inc.	NYSE	CCR	2.20	13
Countrywide Mortgage Investments	NYSE	CWM	0.80	
First American Financial Corp.	NYSE	FAF	0.70	12
Green Tree Financial Corporation	NYSE	GNT	2.49	14
Household International, Inc.	NYSE	HI	2.30	13
Mercury Finance Company	NYSE	MFN	1.49	22
Stewart Information Services Corp.	NYSE	STC	1.40	11
Sumamerica Inc.	NYSE	SAI	2.30	11
United Asset Management Corp.	NYSE	UAM	1.60	18
World Acceptance Corp.	NASDAQ	WRLD	0.03	25

used in the analysis. These numbers produce a dividend growth rate of 12.5 percent a year, or a quarterly dividend growth rate of 3.125 percent: $g = (0.50)(.25) = .1250$.

The value of the stock at the end of the fifteenth quarter discounted to the present using the equity rate of return is $50.00(0.4788)$, or $23.94.[35]

The value of a share of FCFC common stock is $23.94. The total value of new common stock to class 9 interest is 738,273 shares times $23.94, or $17,674,256. The value of the remaining 250,000 warrants issued to common shareholders is 250,000($10.77), or $2,692,500. The total value to new First City shareholders is the sum of these, or $20,366,756.

Value of New First City Warrants

It was agreed that the warrant would be valued at its minimum value (stock price minus the exercise price). Compounding the value of the stock at a rate of one-fourth of the equity return of 20.13 percent, the value at the end of the sixteenth period (four years) is $52.50. The value for a warrant at the end of four years is $52.50 − $30, or $22.50, and its present value using the equity rate of return of 20.13 percent is $10.77.

FCFC common stock can also be valued using price/earnings (P/E) ratios. The P/E ratio is a widely used common stock analysis statistic. P/E ratio is equal to price per share divided by earnings per share. It can be used to value stock using the following relationship:

P/E ratio × earnings per share = price per share.

The earnings per share (EPS) for each year projected by the PMA are

Year 1: $3.29
Year 2: $3.51
Year 3: $4.26
Year 4: $5.54
Year 5: $7.60

Using a conservative (average) P/E ratio from the comparative firms in this appendix, and using the lowest EPS given previously, the price per share is estimated as

Price per share = (15)($3.29) = $49.33.

The present value of this amount at the effective date of the merger is

$49.35/\text{PVFO}_{.0503, 16} = $49.35(0.4560) = $22.50.$

Notes

1. At least one class of claim holders must accept a plan for it to be confirmed. Acceptance for a single class is defined as acceptance by a two-thirds majority of creditors in that class. A majority of the total claim holders must favor a plan in order for it to be accepted. Impaired creditors are those who would either receive alternative securities or would have part or all of their claim dismissed. Even if all impaired classes do not accept the plan, it may still be confirmed as long as at least one impaired class of claims has accepted a plan. Under the "cramdown procedure" [§ 1129 (b) of the Code] an impaired class may be required to accept a plan as long as that class and all the classes below it in priority are treated according to the absolute priority rule, which requires that investors be paid according to their seniority, with senior debt and secured creditors first, then junior debt holders, then preferred shareholders, and finally equity holders.

2. An early discussion of the incentives of the various parties to renegotiate during the confirmation process is contained in Miller 1997.

3. See, for example, Franks and Torous 1989, Bernardo and Talley 1996, Rao, Sokolow, and White 1996, and Weiss and Wruck 1998. The Bankruptcy Code allows managers to remain in place during the bankruptcy (the debtor in possession [DIP]), and management has the right to propose a reorganization plan. This creates incentives for incumbent managers to propose reorganization rather than a liquidation using optimistic cash flow projections. Indeed, Hotchkiss (1995) finds evidence consistent with this forecasting bias. In analyzing pre-reorganization cash flow projections and comparing them to post-reorganization performance, Hotchkiss finds that these firms consistently underperformed.

4. First City Bancorporation of Texas, Inc., Debtor; Case 392-39474-HCA-11; in the United States Bankruptcy Court for the Northern District of Texas, Dallas Division.

5. There were several lawsuits pending. There were affirmative action claims; Director and Officer Liability Claims; claims filed by the FDIC, by EDS Corporation, the Bank of New York; Employment Discrimination Claims; Employee Benefit Claims; a class action suit alleging misrepresentation and omissions in First City's proxy statements; 90 claims filed by individual bondholders; 293 claims filed by equity holders; 10 claims by depositors involving banks; 953 former employee claims for severance pay; trade claims for $680,000; various indemnification claims, and so on.

6. Information about the number of lawyers from First City president, Mr. Robert Brown, in private communication.

7. "Omnibus Disclosure Statement for each of the Competing Plans of Reorganization for First city Bancorporation of Texas, Inc. under Chapter 11 of the Bankruptcy Code," December 23, 1994.

8. After serving as chairman of First Chicago Corp. and president of Occidental Petroleum, Abboud, with a group of investors, bought First City

Bancorporation. Abboud put up $5 million of his own money along with $970 million from the FDIC. See "The Nine Lives of Bob Abboud: Number Three," *Business Week,* Feburary 15, 1988.

9. In the summer of 1992 First City developed its own non-FDIC-assisted recapitalization plan, called Plan C. Plan C included debt deferral by the bank's bondholders, sale of thirteen banks that represented about a third of First City's assets, renegotiation of bank building lease agreements, and raising $120 million from outside sources. Unlike the reorganization that occurred several years earlier, which included over $1 billion in FDIC assistance, First City's Plan C did not require FDIC aid. First City successfully implemented parts of the plan. It negotiated debt deferral with its bondholders; found buyers for the thirteen banks for $50 million; renegotiated leases, which settled $266 million in future liabilities and would have meant an $83 million reduction in lease reserves for its remaining banks, which would have been added to the banks' capital. The bank also had letters of intent for $90 million of new capital and was working on the remaining $30 million required.

10. This FDIC policy has been since legally challenged. In a July 28, 1994, ruling, a Washington, D.C., federal judge ruled that the FDIC cannot seize solvent banks in the process of shutting down insolvent ones. This action, known as cross-guaranteeing between sister banks, was part of the 1989 Financial Institutions Recovery, Reform and Enforcement Act (FIRREA). The court, however, ruled that such an action would require government compensation if the subsidiary bank was operated as a separate entity and had no reasonable expectation of becoming involved in the parent bank's business.

11. Three former First City executives were jailed for defrauding the bank: Frank Cihak, former vice chairman, was sentenced to thirteen years in prison for siphoning off $9 million in bank funds along with his coconspirators, Lloyd Swift, who was sentenced to eight years, and William Allen, who was sentenced to seventy months.

12. The noncash assets consisted of $27.2 million in loans and $20.8 million in other than real estate (ORE). The ORE had a market value of $32 million. The loans consisted of $11 million in performing loans and $16.2 million in nonperforming loans.

13. Loss-sharing agreements were agreements between the FDIC and banks that purchased the former First City banks. The FDIC guaranteed recovery by the acquiring institutions of about $2 billion in loans made by First City before the closing of the banks.

14. This consisted of $50 million in a claims reserve fund, First City's estimate of $10 million paid out of this fund to settle claims, and interest of up to $5 million on the remainder.

15. Texas Commerce Bank (TCB), a unit of New York's Chemical Banking Corp., bought 73 percent of old First City's assets, including its Houston and Dallas banks, for $347 million. TCB laid off about eighteen hundred old First City employees and closed down the Houston headquarters when it consolidated old First City's assets into its own. Frost National Bank of San Antonio bought 6 percent

of First City's assets for $38 million, and Mercantile Bank of Brownsville bought 5 percent of the assets for $14 million. Other purchasers included Victoria Bank and Trust; First National Bank of Lubbock, Texas; Alice Bank of Texas; FBOP Corp. of Oak Park, Illinois; First National of Olney, Texas; and Corpus Christi National Bank. About forty groups bid for all or parts of First City's assets.

16. This sale was terminated when the FDIC closed the old First City banks.

17. "FDIC Sells First City Bancorp of Texas to 12 Banks," Bloomberg News Service, January 27, 1993.

18. J-Hawk was founded in 1986, and by 1994 it had become one of the largest independent providers of distressed asset services. In 1994 J-Hawk had about a hundred employees in its five offices in Texas, South Carolina, Connecticut, Pennsylvania, and Virginia. Other than its Texas headquarters, all the offices were temporary—opened as convenient locations to service its portfolios and closed once the portfolios were sold.

19. CFSC was a wholly owned subsidiary of Cargill, Inc., one of the world's largest privately held companies. CFSC would pay certain of J-Hawk's fixed expenses and half of all approved valuation expenses incurred in J-Hawk's search for prospective portfolio puchases.

20. A columnist dubbed First City "Fist City" because of the contentious nature of the stakeholders in the company. ("First City Bancorp. Common Seen Worth $3 a Share in Liquidation," Bloomberg News Service, October 6, 1994.)

21. This estimate and discussion of the potential for an appeal are from a 1/10/95 letter to Judge Abramson from the law firm of Harvey Greenfield, counsel for the class action litigants ("the Krim litigation").

22. The practice of appointing a court's expert although not routine, is not uncommon. Generally, this procedure leads to a court's confirmation decision because the judge's choice of expert is approved by the relevant competing parties.

23. Under this procedure for comparing the plans, the question of how to value the creditors' option B became moot. The court expert had maintained that the creditors' option B numbers were not consistent with the discussion in their disclosure statement.

24. The net present value (NPV) of J-Hawk's investment under the PMA was estimated to be almost $37 million.

25. CFSC's primary business is investing in funds, trading financial instruments and assets, securitizations, leasing, and investing in emerging markets. CFSC, founded in 1984, manages about $6 billion in assets through its seventeen worldwide offices.

26. Financial institutions like commercial banks and insurance companies must allocate more regulatory capital to underperforming and nonperforming assets, making it more cost effective for the institutions to sell such assets.

27. See "Nothing Succeeds Like Distress," *Business Week*, December 23, 1996.

28. The competing plans were filed in December 1994, and the confirmation of the reorganization was in May 1995. However, there were prior reorganizations, and it is difficult to meaningfully compare the time First City spent in

bankruptcy with that of other similar companies in bankruptcy. Hard data is difficult to come by. Anecdotal evidence suggests that the average time for a large bankruptcy resolution is about four years.

29. Existing assets plus $650,000,000 in NOLs.

30. $200,000,000 in initial receivership distribution ($124,500,000 in cash; $10,500,000 paid by the FDIC receiver on behalf of First City; $65,000,000 in assets, including real estate of $20,777,000 and loans of $27,223,000) plus additional future distributions based on the liquidation of FDIC receiverships ($110,000,000 with loss-sharing agreements or $125,000,000 without loss-sharing agreements).

31. Project risk was estimated conservatively. The betas listed are equity betas, which means effects of leverage are included in beta; in other words, beta reflects both asset risk and financing risk. Normally, pure play analysis would reduce betas by removing the leverage effects. To be conservative, this was not done. Second, rather than take the average beta for the sample, the highest beta is used, further raising the required rate of return.

32. These estimates are from *Stock, Bonds, Bills, and Inflation 1993 Yearbook* (Ibbotson Associates, Chicago, Ill.). These numbers are the average for the period 1926–92. This figure is the average on all common stocks and provides a more conservative return estimate than if the return on small stocks is used. The return on small stocks during this period was 12.2 percent.

33. This number is from table A3.1, net income for the year 2000.

34.
$$Div_{16} = \frac{\dfrac{\$41,800,000(0.5)}{4}}{5,500,000} = \$0.95/\text{share.}$$

35. The value of the new common stock is

$$S_{15} = \frac{Div_{16}}{k_S - g} = \frac{\$0.95}{0.0503 - 0.0313} = \$50.00.$$

Here, S_{15} is the stock price at the beginning of the first dividend payment period, Div_{16} is the first dividend paid, k_S is the equity rate of return, and g is the dividend growth rate.

References

Bernardo, Antonio E., and Eric L. Talley. "Investment Policy and Exit-Exchange Offers within Financially Distressed Firms." *Journal of Finance* 51 (1996): 871–88.

Betker, Brian L. "An Empirical Examination of Prepackaged Bankruptcy." *Financial Management* 24 (spring 1995): 3–18.

"Committee of Unsecured Creditors' Disclosure Statement with Respect to Its First Amended Plan of Reorganization for First City Bancorporation of Texas, Inc., under Chapter 11 of the United States Bankruptcy Code, as

Modified." United States Bankruptcy Court, Northern District of Texas, Dallas Division. December 23, 1994.

Franks, Julian R., K. G. Nyborg, and Walter N. Torous. "A Comparison of US, UK, and German Insolvency Codes." *Financial Management* 25 (autumn 1996): 86–101.

Franks, Julian R., and Walter N. Torous. "An Empirical Investigation of U.S. Firms in Reorganization." *Journal of Finance* 44 (1989): 747–69.

Gilson, Stuart C., E. H. Hotchkiss, and R. S. Ruback. "Valuation in Bankrupt Firms." *Review of Financial Studies* 13 (2000): 43–74.

Grossman, Sanford. "Dynamic Asset Allocation and the Information Efficiency of Markets." Presidential address. *Journal of Finance* 50 (1995): 773–87.

Hotchkiss, Edith Shwab. "Postbankruptcy Performance and Management Turnover." *Journal of Finance* 50 (1995): 3–21.

"The Joint Plan of Reorganization by First City Bancorporation of Texas, Inc., the Official Committee of Equity Security Holders of First City, and J-Hawk Corporation." United States Bankruptcy Court, Northern District of Texas, Dallas Division. December 24, 1994.

Kaplan, Steven N., and Richard Ruback. "The Valuation of Cash Flow Forecasts." *Journal of Finance* 50 (1995): 1059–94.

Miller, Merton H. "Tax Obstacles to Voluntary Corporate Restructuring." *Journal of Applied Corporate Finance* 4, no. 3 (1991): 20–23.

———. "The Wealth Transfers of Bankruptcy: Some Illustrative Examples." *Law and Contemporary Problems* 41 (1977): 38–46.

"Omnibus Disclosure Statement for Each of the Competing Plans of Reorganization for First City Bancorporation of Texas, Inc., under Chapter 11 of the Bankruptcy Code. United States Bankruptcy Court, Northern District of Texas, Dallas Division. December 23, 1994.

Rao, Ramesh K. S., with D. S. Sokolow and D. White. "Fiduciary Duty à la Lyonnais: An Economic Perspective on Corporate Governance in a Financially Distressed Firm." *Journal of Corporation Law* 22 (fall 1996): 53–78.

Weiss, Lawrence A., and Karen H. Wruck. "Information Problems, Conflicts of Interest, and Asset Stripping: Chapter 11's Failure in the Case of Eastern Airlines." *Journal of Financial Economics* 48 (1998): 55–98.

Wruck, Karen H. "Financial Distress, Reorganization, and Organizational Efficiency." *Journal of Financial Economics* 27 (1990): 419–44.

Investigation Phase

Predicting Distress

8. Enron Red Flags Case

Jon Goodwin is the head of investment banking services for Barra Partners, a small investment banking firm with headquarters in San Francisco. In May 2002, Jon was meeting with Seamus Hatch, the newly hired managing director of research.

JON: Our firm is excited about a new business opportunity that all these financial accounting and investment banking scandals have created. With the Securities and Exchange Commission (SEC) pushing for the separation of investment banking and research functions, we should be able to develop our independent research services. I want you to expand our basic industry and company research capabilities.

SEAMUS: Thanks. This opportunity was the major reason I wanted to work for your firm. Hopefully, we will not have the appearance of a conflict of interest between investment banking and research activities, like the big investment banking firms. For example, one big firm actually fired an analyst for changing his rating to a "sell" recommendation on Enron at $38 per share, and another firm told its analysts to maintain a "buy" recommendation for Enron no matter what!

JON: Barra usually executes transactions within a valuation range of $15 million to $50 million. The big New York investment banking firms usually won't touch any transactions under $50 million. With the big firms' research credibility as

This case was prepared by Hugh Grove, Tom Cook, and Jon Goodwin.

"sell-side" analysts being questioned, we should have an opportunity to expand our research capabilities to sell both
basic industry and company research to the mutual funds, insurance companies, and other "buy-side" analysts and investors. We will first focus on the investment prospects of a
select group of growth industry sectors and then recommend companies within such industries that have the ability
to develop a sustainable competitive advantage. A major
issue, of course, is how to profit from providing such comprehensive research. In the past, many investors had not valued such painstaking research, but they should now, due to
the credibility problems of the big firms constantly "touting"
individual companies in order to be awarded large investment banking fees.

SEAMUS: All the negative publicity from the New York attorney
general fining Merrill Lynch $100 million for such question-
able business practices should help smaller firms like us who
are interested in expanding their research services.

JON: One way we may be able to create a market for our research
services is to develop a set of red flag procedures that help
identify companies using earnings management and other
deceptive financial reporting strategies. I have always been
surprised about how little knowledge of financial accounting
and financial reporting bankers and financial analysts have.
That is why I went back to school to get a Master of Accountancy degree. Your first task will be to develop a set of
red flags. Then, I'd like you to back test them against companies such as Enron, WorldCom, Qwest, Global Crossing,
etc. Start your red flag analysis with Enron. If the red flags
don't work for Enron, they probably won't work on any
firm. Contrary to what all the "sell-side" analysts said in
congressional testimony, I can't believe that no red flags existed in Enron's reported financial numbers!

SEAMUS: I am excited about your proposal to create a set of red
flags. Such a capability should enhance our research contract
proposals to the "buy-side" analysts and investors. Starting
with Enron should be very interesting since it was such a
high profile case.

JON: Independent, unbiased, basic industry research and related
company research are fundamental to both our merchant

banking investments and our major investment banking activities of strategic advice, financial advisory services, corporate finance, and mergers/acquisitions. This project is very important to us as a small investment banking firm, especially as we need to maintain the trust of our existing investors and expand our networks of investor relationships. I look forward to seeing your report. Let's meet at the end of next week to discuss it.

Barra Partners Company Background

Barra partners is a private research, investment, and merchant banking partnership serving the needs of emerging growth companies. Its capabilities include providing timely strategic research and advice; raising private debt and equity financing; arranging mergers, acquisitions, and divestitures; advising on financial restructurings; and valuing businesses and corporate securities. It has engaged in transactions with a valuation range between $15 million and $500 million. Its industry sector expertise has included biotechnology, medical devices, wireless communications, energy, power generation, transportation, recreational products, and financial services. Headquartered in San Francisco, Barra has maintained small offices in Denver; New York; Chicago; Dallas; Kuala Lumpur; Malaysia; and Chenni, India. Barra currently has three managing directors, nine other full-time employees, and twelve independent contractors.

Barra was founded in 1997 by Mike Bock, managing director of the merchant banking group at Barra. Prior to joining Barra, Mike operated his own investment banking firm for twenty-four years, specializing in private equity investments in public companies, project finance, and project development in the international power industry. Prior to that, Mike was the director of corporate finance at Boettcher and Company. Mike was a graduate of the U.S. Air Force Academy and also earned an MBA from Harvard.

Jon Goodwin joined Barra in May 2001 as managing director of strategic advisory services. Prior to joining Barra, Jon was a vice president in the telecommunications investment banking group of Gerard Klauer Mattison & Company in New York City. Before that, he spent six years with International Capital Strategies (ICS), a New York–based boutique investment banking firm providing private equity and merger/acquisition advisory services. Prior to ICS, Jon earned a Master of Accountancy degree in 1992 from the University of Denver. Jon had begun his financial services career in 1984 (after earning an undergraduate business degree from the University of Denver) with Capital Services Group, a Denver asset-based finance firm and sponsor of tax-advantaged limited partnerships. Before he returned to school in 1991, he had become vice president of syndications.

Seamus Hatch joined Barra in May 2002 with a sixteen-year background in technology firms that did digital asset management, web site management, data modeling, and business modeling. Prior to that, Seamus was a director in the investment research department of Hoare Govett, a UK-based investment bank. He started his career at Andersen Consulting, specializing in the design of securities trading systems in both London and New York. His undergraduate degree in computer science and accounting was from the University of Manchester, England.

Barra's principals have extensive investment banking experience. Collectively, they have completed over 150 transactions with an aggregate market value in excess of $3.5 billion. As a result, they have developed close relationships with numerous strategic and financial investors. More information on Barra partners may be obtained from their web site: http://www.barrapartners.com.

Financial Red Flags: Starting Point

As a starting point for creating financial red flags, Seamus decided to use the five "irrational" ratios from prior earnings manipulation research. These five ratios were the most significant ones in detecting 1990s earnings manipulations, based upon a comparison of nonmanipulators' mean indexes to manipulators' mean indexes. Seamus also decided to use eleven key "investor" ratios that were provided for each company tracked by Yahoo Finance, the most heavily used financial web site. These ratios were grouped by Yahoo Finance into four major categories: valuation, income statement profitability, management effectiveness, and financial strength.

Also, from various financial press articles, Seamus had compiled ten nontraditional or "emerging" ratios that various short sellers, mutual fund managers, and other investors had used to flag financial reporting problems at Enron, Qwest, WorldCom, and other recent financial accounting scandals. For example, several analysts had advocated a comparison of generally accepted accounting principles (GAAP) and cash effective tax rates to help indicate financial reporting problems. Concerning Enron, a citizens' taxpayer group had alleged that Enron had not paid any U.S. income taxes in the last three years. For this effective tax rate comparison, Seamus made the following excerpts from Enron's 2000 10-K footnotes. For 2000, 1999, and 1998, Enron's GAAP income tax expenses were $434 million, $104 million, and $175 million, respectively, but its income taxes actually paid in cash were $62 million, $51 million, and $73 million, respectively.

Seamus classified these emerging ratios into four categories: operating cash flow, long-term debt solvency, effective tax rate, and economic value added. Seamus realized that it was just as important to understand why certain ratios did not work as red flags as it was to identify the ones that did work. (See tables 1–3.)

From previous company research and investment banking experiences, both Jon and Seamus believed that about 80 percent of a company's success was having a good management team. They thought the other 20 percent was having the technology and marketing to exploit business ideas and opportunities. Thus, they decided that more Enron company background was needed before Seamus started his red flag analysis.

TABLE 1. Irrational Ratios for Earnings Manipulation Detection

| | | Benchmarks | |
| | | Nonmanipulators' | Manipulators' |
	Ratio Formula	Mean Index	Mean Index
Days' sales in receivables	$(Accounts\ Receivable_t/Sales_t)/$ $(Accounts\ Receivable_{t-1}/$ $Sales_{t-1})$	1.031	1.465
Gross margin	$(Sales_{t-1} - Cost\ of\ Sales_{t-1}/$ $Sales_{t-1})/(Sales_t - Cost\ of$ $Sales_t/Sales_t)$	1.014	1.193
Asset quality	$(1 - Current\ Assets_t + Net$ $Fixed\ Assets_t/Total$ $Assets_t)/(1 - Current\ As$-$sets_{t-1} + Net\ Fixed$ $Assets_{t-1}/Total\ Assets_{t-1})$	1.039	1.254
Sales growth	$Sales_t/Sales_{t-1}$	1.134	1.607
Total accruals to total assets	Changes: (Working Capital − Cash − Current taxes payable) − D&A/Total Assets	0.018	0.031

Source: Joseph Wells, "Irrational Ratios," *Journal of Accountancy* August (2001): 80–83.
Note: D&A = depreciation and amortization.

TABLE 2. Key Ratios for Investing

	Ratio Formula	Benchmarks S&P 500 (year 2000)	Benchmarks Industry Average
Valuation ratios			
Price/Book	Common Share Price/ Book Value per Share	4.10	2 to 3
Book value per share	Total Stockholders' Equity/Basic Common Shares Outstanding	4.10	2 to 3
Price/Earnings	Common Share Price/ Diluted Earnings per Share	35.70	20 to 25[a]
Diluted earnings per share	Net Income/[Common Shares Outstanding + Stock Options + Convertible Common Shares]	35.70	20 to 25[a]
Price/Sales	Common Share Price/Sales per Basic Common Share	1.90	
Price/Cash flow	Common Share Price/ Operating Cash Flows per Basic Common Share	15.10	
Income statement probability			
Profit margin	Net Income/Sales		4%–8%
Top-line growth	Sales Change (Prior Year to Current Year)/Prior Year Sales		5%–20%
Bottom-line growth	Net Income Change (Prior Year to Current Year)/ Prior Year Net Income		5%–15%
Management effectiveness			
Return on assets	Net Income/Total Assets		8%–12%
Return on equity	Net Income/Total Stock- holders' Equity		9%–16%
Financial strength			
Current ratio	Current Assets/Current Liabilities		≥2
Debt/Equity ratio	Total Debt (Short-Term + Long-Term)/Total Stockholders' Equity		≥0.50

Source: Yahoo Finance, the most heavily used financial web site.
[a]Benchmark: Industry average (1990s).

Enron Company Background

In 1985, Houston Natural Gas merged with InterNorth, a natural gas company based in Omaha, Nebraska, to form Enron, an energy company with a thirty-seven thousand mile interstate and intrastate gas pipeline. In 1986 Kenneth Lay was appointed chairman and CEO of Enron. He had a vision for Enron that went far beyond that of a traditional energy company. He understood that deregulation of the energy business would offer new opportunities and hired Jeffrey Skilling, an industry consultant, in 1991 to help take advantage of them. Enron was a pioneer in trading natural gas and electricity and by 1997 had become one of the largest natural gas and electricity trading companies. Revenues increased from $9.2 billion in 1995 to $100.8 billion in 2000, and its stock returned 500 percent over that period.

TABLE 3. Emerging Red Flag Ratios

	Ratio Formula	Benchmark
Operating cash flow (OCF) ratios		
Quality of earnings	OCF/Net Income	≥ 1.5
Quality of earnings before interest, taxes, depreciation, and amortization (EBITDA)	OCF/EBITDA	≥ 1.0
Cash flow liquidity	OCF/Current Liabilities	≥ 2.0
Cash flow solvency	OCF/Short- and Long-Term Debt	≥ 0.5
Long-term debt solvency		
Sales comparison	Long-Term Debt/Sales	
Equity comparison	Long-Term Debt/Stockholders' Equity at Year End Market Value	
Effective tax rate		
Generally accepted accounting principles (GAAP) effective tax rate	(GAAP Current + Deferred Income Tax Expense)/Net Income before Taxes	
Cash effective tax rate	Cash Income Taxes Paid/Net Income before Taxes	
Economic value added		
Return on invested capital	Net Income/Long-Term Debt + Stockholders' Equity at Year End Market Value	
Weighted average cost of capital	(calculated by Chanos for Enron as 9%–12%)	

In January 1997, Skilling was named president and chief operating officer of Enron. His strategy was to create an "asset light" company by applying Enron's trading and risk-management skills to power plants and other facilities owned by outsiders. Enron would become more like an investment bank than an industrial company weighed down by tangible assets.

Skilling's strategy focused on expanding Enron's energy trading expertise into a vast array of new commodities to sustain earnings growth. He operated on the belief that Enron could commoditize and monetize anything from electronics to pollution-emission tax credits to advertising space. In August 1997, Enron expanded beyond energy trading by introducing commodity trading of weather derivatives (based on actual temperature deviations from 65 degrees for risk management by energy companies). In July 1998, Enron paid $2.4 billion for a British water company for its new global water business. It also had purchased a $3 billion power plant in India in the early 1990s and a $1.3 billion power distributor in Brazil in July 1998.

Skilling developed the belief that older, stodgier competitors had no chance. At an industry conference, Skilling told these competitors that he was "going to eat their lunch." A banner in Enron's lobby said: "The World's Leading Company." Skilling was credited with creating a system of forced rankings for all employees, in which those rated in the bottom 20 percent would be fired. Employees attempted to crush not only outsiders but each other. They believed that they could handle increasingly exotic risks without danger and often traded just for the sake of trading, as opposed to using trading as a part of a corporate strategy.

To maintain a high credit rating and raise capital for business expansion, Skilling hired Andrew Fastow, who subsequently became the CFO of Enron. In a 1999 interview, Fastow explained that the key to Enron's trading business was the fact that "the counterparties who enter into these contracts with Enron have to be able to take Enron counterparty risk and, thus, Enron needed to have strong investment-grade credit." Fastow chose to maintain such a credit rating for Enron not by the traditional methods of issuing equity (which would cause dilution) or selling assets outright (since cash doesn't earn much). Instead, Fastow shifted debt off the balance sheet through special purpose entities (SPEs) and other unconsolidated affiliates. He said: "We had to be very creative but we're very conservative in our accounting approach."

Prior to Fastow, Enron had used a publicly traded subsidiary to raise off-balance-sheet debt. However, Fastow preferred private SPE partnerships for this purpose because he said: "they were much more cost-effective and flexible." For such creativity, Fastow was given the 1999 CFO Excellence in Capital Structure Management Award, cosponsored by the *CFO* magazine and Arthur Andersen. The award guidelines were "to applaud strong and creative individuals who have taken bold steps to add value for shareholders, employees, partners, and/or customers."

By 1999, Enron had moved many of its assets and debt off the balance sheet into hundreds of SPEs and had approximately thirty-five hundred subsidiaries and affiliates. In 1999, Enron created three new private investment limited partnerships (SPEs), Cayman, Raptor, and Condor, to be operated by Fastow. To help capitalize these SPEs, Enron issued its own common stock in exchange for SPE note receivables. Subsequently, Enron increased these SPE note receivables and its own earnings from a series of transactions with these SPEs.

For example, Enron had made a $10 million pre-IPO (pre–initial public offering) or insider investment in Rhythms NetConnections, a Colorado corporation that went public in early 1999. As Enron's investment increased in value by $290 million, Enron recognized this holding gain as other revenue, using the mark-to-market investment accounting method. However, pursuant to the typical pre-IPO security lockup regulations, Enron could not sell this Rhythms stock for two years, until early 2000. To hedge against the Rhythms stock price going down after the IPO, Enron wanted to sell a put option, but no investor would buy such an option. Thus, Enron forced the Cayman SPE to grant a put option to Enron to lock in the Rhythms holding gain. However, the Cayman SPE, capitalized primarily with appreciated Enron common stock, did not have enough cash to cover the put option unless Enron's stock continued to increase in value.

Fastow earned more than $30 million from managing these partnerships while still CFO of Enron. Enron's financial statements disclosed Fastow's SPE management arrangement as "a senior officer of Enron" and did not disclose that such SPE partnership deals had credit "triggers." Such "triggers" would make Enron responsible for the partnership debt if its stock price fell below a certain price or if its credit rating dropped below investment grade.

Enron's management had developed a "culture of arrogance," according to outsiders who had dealt with the company. These managers

would scoff at the notion that Enron's business and financial statements were complicated. This attitude, expressed with barely con-
cealed disdain, especially by senior executives in dealing with Wall
Street, was that anyone who couldn't understand its business just didn't
"get it." They dismissed criticism by financial analysts as ignorance or
sour grapes for failing to win Enron's investment banking business.

However, in mid-1999, Veba, a German utility company, pieced
together a view of Enron's finances so disturbing that it called off a
proposed merger with Enron. Veba had become very concerned with
the debt levels and aggressive accounting practices of Enron. Veba
determined that Enron had swept millions of dollars of debt off its
books through complex accounting and deal making to make its balance sheet appear stronger than it really was. Veba adjusted Enron's
debt-to-equity ratio from 54 percent to 72 percent. One of Veba's
merger consultants said: "We were wondering why this wasn't common knowledge, or why it wasn't discovered by those people whose
business it was to discover these things."

In November 1999, Skilling launched EnronOnline, a Net-based
commodity trading platform, and introduced trading of broadband
capacity. Enron invested $1.2 billion in fiber-optic broadband net-
works to facilitate such trading, but the broadband market later became overbuilt with excess capacity. Enron started online trading of
metals in July 2000 and wood products in September 2000. At the end
of 2000, Skilling was promoted to CEO effective February 2001.

In her March 2001 *Fortune* article, "Is Enron Overpriced?"
Bethany McLean became the first reporter to question Enron's value
in the financial press. She noted that Enron's Price Risk Management
division had 1,217 different trading books for pricing strategies of
various commodities. When questioned, Fastow claimed that any details on how Enron made money on trading were proprietary and
said: "We don't want anymore to know what's on those books. We
don't want to tell anyone where we're making money." McLean also
noted that another large Enron division, Assets and Investments, was
just as "mysterious." It involved building, operating, and selling
power plants around the world with very little disclosure. Analysts
were concerned that Enron was liquidating its asset base while booking such asset sales as recurring revenue. McLean concluded: "The
problem, as we know from innumerable failed dot-coms, is that the
potential new market doesn't always materialize on schedule. Enron
isn't leaving itself a lot of room for the normal wobbles and glitches

that happen in any developing business. In the end, it boils down to a question of faith."

In August 2001, after six months as CEO, Skilling quit for "personal reasons" and forfeited approximately a $20 million severance package. He then had to repay a $2 million loan that Enron would have forgiven if he had stayed until the end of 2001, but he had made $78 million from selling Enron stock since 2000. Over the past decade, Enron executives had sold over $1 billion in stock from their stock option grants. Seventeen of the eighteen "sell-side" financial analysts who followed Enron at that time still had buy recommendations the day after Skilling quit.

Ken Lay returned to the CEO position. He tried to reassure nervous investors in a conference call on October 23, 2001. It was generally viewed as a disaster. One analyst said: "Enron wiggled, squirmed, and gave a bunch of non-answers." After the call, Prudential's sell-side analyst, Carol Coale, downgraded Enron to a sell and said: "not because of things that we know, but because of things that we potentially don't know." Fastow was forced out the next day on October 24, 2001.

On November 8, 2001, Enron filed with the SEC a Form 8-K that restated its prior financial statements in order to consolidate its major SPEs. Its auditor, Arthur Andersen, contended that Enron had not made available a side agreement concerning these SPEs that would have required them to be consolidated. Such consolidation eliminated $591 million (about 20 percent) of Enron's earnings over the last four years. For Enron's 2000 financial statements, debt was increased by $628 million, and the following items were reduced: assets by $728 million, total shareholders' equity by $1.164 billion, and net income by $132 million. For 1999, debt was increased by $685 million, and the following items were reduced: assets by $182 million, total shareholders' equity by $834 million, and net income by $250 million.

On November 28, 2001, the proposed merger with Dynegy collapsed when Dynegy's bankers discovered that debt coming due in the fourth quarter had increased from under $1 billion to $2.8 billion per a final draft of Enron's fourth quarter 10-Q (primarily due to Moody's downgrade of Enron's debt on October 29, 2001). Also, cash on hand, to which Dynegy had recently contributed $1.5 billion, had shrunk from $3 billion to $1.2 billion, and Enron's new CFO had no explanation for the missing cash.

On November 28, 2001, Standard & Poors downgraded Enron's

debt below investment grade to "junk" bond status, triggering the immediate acceleration of almost $4 billion in off-balance-sheet (OBS) debt and forcing Enron to seek bankruptcy. (Previously, in February 2001, Skilling had said Enron's OBS debt was nonrecourse to Enron. However, he failed to mention that a downgrade of Enron's on-balance-sheet debt below investment grade would force Enron to repay the OBS debt that had thus become recourse debt.) In summary, Enron had taken four years to build its market capitalization from $10 billion in 1997 to $67 billion in 2000 but only ten months in 2001 to destroy it all. The Enron employee 401(k) retirement accounts that held primarily Enron stock lost more than $1 billion.

Enron generated huge fees for Arthur Andersen. In 2001, a total of $52 million was paid: $25 million for audit fees and $27 million for consulting fees. $5.7 million of those fees came from providing advice to Enron on the accounting treatment of the SPE partnerships. Back in 1993, Andersen took over Enron's internal-audit function. Enron's financial management team was dominated by former Andersen partners. Enron also generated huge fees for its investment bankers, primarily JP Morgan/Chase, Citigroup, and UBS Paine Webber, who maintained buy recommendations for Enron.

On January 12, 2002, an internal memo was released to the public. It was written on August 15, 2001, to Ken Lay by an Enron employee at that time, Sherron Watkins, who questioned Enron's financial accounting. (Lay never took any action on this memo. In fact, two months later when Lay announced third quarter financial results, he said: "The continued excellent prospects in Enron's businesses and Enron's leading market position make us very confident in our strong earnings outlook.") Key statements from this memo were noted as follows:

> Has Enron become a risky place to work? For those of us who didn't get rich over the last few years, can we afford to stay? Skilling's abrupt departure will raise suspicions of accounting improprieties and valuation issues. Enron has been very aggressive in its accounting—most notably the Raptor SPE transactions. The spotlight will be on us, the market just can't accept that Skilling is leaving his dream job.
>
> I think that the smaller SPE receivable write-offs can be combined with the new required goodwill impairment in 2002 but how do we fix the huge Raptor deals? We have recognized over

$550 million of fair value gains on IPO stocks via our Raptor swaps or hedges; much of that stock has declined significantly: Avici by 98% (from $178 million to $5 million) and New Power Co by 70% (from $20/share to $6/share). The value in those swaps won't be there for Raptor, so once again Enron will issue stock to offset these losses. It sure looks to the layman on the street that we are hiding losses in a related company and will compensate that company with Enron stock in the future. In 2000, Enron has lost $500 million in value from several IPO investments. These losses were offset by booking gains from our price risk management (hedging) transactions with Raptor, recording a corresponding accounts receivable from Raptor. That's a $500 million related party transaction—it's 51% of NI [net income] pre tax and 33% of NI after tax in 2000.

I am incredibly nervous that we will implode in a wave of accounting scandals. My 8 years of Enron work history will be worth nothing on my resume; the business world will consider the past successes as nothing but an elaborate accounting hoax. Skilling is resigning now for "personal reasons" but I think he wasn't having fun, looked down the road and knew this stuff was unfixable and would rather abandon ship now than resign in shame in 2 years.

In March 2002, the Senate Governmental Affairs Committee released data showing that ten of fifteen analysts who followed Enron still were rating the stock as a "buy" or "strong buy" as late as November 8, 2001. On that date, Enron's stock price had fallen to under $10 from over $80 at the beginning of 2001. A group of these "sell-side" financial analysts testified before this committee, and all blamed Enron and its auditors for providing misleading financial statements. However, the committee chairperson, Senator Joseph Lieberman, said: "Analysts should have alerted investors to the fiscal fissures in Enron's foundation. No matter what the market does, analysts just seem to keep saying buy." He suggested one reason is that the analysts' employers, the investment banking firms, earned millions of dollars arranging mergers or stock offerings for the companies being analyzed. He said: "These influences compromise analysts' objectivity and mean that the average investor should take their bottom-line recommendations with at least a grain of salt, if not a whole bucket."

Final Thoughts

To analyze the financial ratios as potential red flags for earnings manipulation and financial reporting problems, Seamus made excerpts from Enron's 10-K report for the fiscal year ended December 31, 2000. These reported financial numbers were available by the March 31, 2001, due date at the SEC, well before Enron blew up. In accordance with Jon's instructions, he wanted to see if these reported numbers yielded any red flags, as opposed to the congressional testimony of all the "sell-side" analysts who said no red flags existed.

In developing red flag procedures, Seamus wanted to see if changes in a company's stock price could be linked to financial red flags as well as nonfinancial red flags, concerning major company-related events. Thus, he obtained historical information on Enron's stock price performance. Enron's stock had traded in the $10 to $20 price range from 1995 to 1997. By the end of 1998, it was up to $30, and by the end of 1999, it had steadily risen to $50. It peaked at $90.75 in August 2000 as Enron's revenues had grown from $31 billion in 1998 to over $100 billion, making it the seventh largest company on the Fortune 500. Enron's stock price stayed around $80 until February 2001 when it began to fall steadily (although there were several upward ticks) to $35 by October 10, 2001. It then fell steadily to below $1 on November 28, 2001 when Enron set a record for the heaviest single-day trading volume for a NYSE- or NASDAQ-listed stock. Enron had lost over $67 billion in total market capitalization in just one year. Meanwhile, the level of short-selling positions not yet closed out had risen from 2 million in August 2000 to 8 million at year-end 2000 to 33 million by October 31, 2001, and increased to 88 million by November 30, 2001. He decided to use October 10, 2001, as the cutoff date for identifying leading red flags since that date was the last time Enron's stock price ever went up (to $35 per share) before its continuous decline to below $1 by November 28, 2001.

Before Seamus went off to apply his red flag procedures to Enron for his report to Jon, he summarized a financial press interview with James Chanos, a widely known short seller. Chanos was among the first to short Enron and had made his reputation as a short seller in the 1970s by shorting the Baldwin Piano Company, primarily based upon his own cash flow analysis techniques. At that time, most analysts had disagreed with and strongly criticized Chanos until Baldwin went bankrupt a year later. Seamus also made notes from an inter-

view about Enron's financial reporting practices with Doug Carmichael, the former chief accountant of the American Institute of
Certified Public Accountants (AICPA) and current accounting professor at Baruch College in New York. Seamus concluded that the
use of SPEs and the "mark-to-market" accounting method for deriv-
ative contracts did not violate generally accepted accounting principles, but he thought that Enron's limited and complex disclosures
about these items did violate GAAP.

Appendix A

Enron Corp. and Subsidiaries Consolidated Income Statement ($ millions, except per share amounts)

	Year Ended December 31		
	2000	1999	1998
Revenues			
Natural gas and other products	50,500	19,536	13,276
Electricity	33,823	15,238	13,939
Metals	9,234	—	—
Other	7,232	5,338	4,045
Total revenues	100,789	40,112	31,260
Cost and expenses			
Cost of gas, electricity, metals, and other products	94,517	34,761	26,381
Operating expenses	3,184	3,045	2,473
Depreciation, depletion, and amortization	855	870	827
Taxes, other than income taxes	280	193	201
Impairment of long-lived assets		441	
Total costs and expenses	98,836	39,310	29,882
Operating income	1,953	802	1,378
Other income and deductions			
Equity in earnings of unconsolidated equity affiliates	87	309	97
Gains on sales of nonmerchant assets	146	541	56
Gain on issuance of stock by TNPC, Inc.	121	—	—
Interest income	212	162	88
Other income (net)	(37)	181	(37)
Income before interest, minority			
Interests and income taxes	2,482	1,995	1,582
Interests and related charges, net	838	656	550
Dividends on company-obligated preferred securities			
of subsidiaries	77	76	77
Minority interests	154	135	77
Income taxes expenses	434	104	175
Net income before cumulative effect of accounting changes	979	1,024	703
Cumulative effect of accounting changes, net of tax	—	(131)	—

(continued)

	Year Ended December 31		
	2000	1999	1998
Net income	979	893	703
Preferred stock dividends	83	66	17
Earnings per share of common stock	896	827	686
Basic			
Before cumulative effect of accounting changes	1.22	1.36	1.07
Cumulative effect of accounting changes	—	(0.19)	—
Basic earnings per share	1.22	1.17	1.07
Diluted			
Before cumulative effect of accounting changes	1.12	1.27	1.01
Cumulative effect of accounting changes	—	(0.17)	—
Diluted earnings per share	1.12	1.10	1.01
Average number of common shares used in computation			
Basic	736	705	642
Diluted	814	769	695

Enron Corp. and Subsidiaries Consolidated Statement of Comprehensive Income ($ millions)

	Year Ended December 31		
	2000	1999	1998
Net income	979	893	703
Other comprehensive income			
Foreign currency translation adjustment and other	(307)	(579)	(14)
Total comprehensive income	672	314	689

Enron Corp. and Subsidiaries Consolidated Balance Sheet: Assets ($ millions)

	Year Ended December 31	
	2000	1999
Current assets		
Cash and cash equivalents	1,374	288
Trade receivables (net of allowance for doubtful accounts of $133 and $40, respectively)	10,396	3,030
Other receivables	1,874	518
Assets from price risk management activities	12,018	2,205
Inventories	953	598
Deposits	2,433	81
Other	1,333	535
Total current assets	30,381	7,255

	Year Ended December 31	
	2000	1999
Investments and other assets		
Investments in and advances to unconsolidated equity affiliates	5,294	5,036
Assets from price risk management activities	8,988	2,929
Goodwill	3,638	2,799
Other	5,459	4,681
Total investments and other assets	23,379	15,445
Property, plant and equipment, at cost		
Natural gas transmission	6,916	6,948
Electric generation and distribution	4,766	3,552
Fiber optic network and equipment	839	379
Construction in progress	682	1,120
Other	2,256	1,913
Total property, plant, and equipment	15,459	13,912
Less accumulated depreciation, depletion, and amortization	3,716	3,231
Property, plant and equipment, net	11,743	10,681
Total assets	65,503	33,381

Enron Corp. and Subsidiaries Consolidated Balance Sheet: Liabilities and Shareholders' Equity ($ millions, except shares)

	Year Ended December 31	
	2000	1999
Current liabilities		
Accounts payable	9,777	2,154
Liabilities from price risk management activities	10,495	1,836
Short-term debt	1,679	1,001
Customers' deposits	4,277	44
Other	2,178	1,724
Total current liabilities	28,406	6,759
Long-term debt	8,550	7,151
Deferred credits and other liabilities		
Deferred income taxes	1,644	1,894
Liabilities from price risk management activities	9,423	2,990
Other	2,692	1,587
Total deferred credits and other liabilities	13,759	6,471

(continued)

	Year Ended December 31	
	2000	1999
Commitments and contingencies		
Minority interests	2,414	2,430
Company-obligated preferred securities of subsidiaries	904	1,000
Shareholders' equity		
Second preferred stock, cumulative, no par value, 1,370,000 shares authorized, 1,240,933 shares and 1,296,184 shares issued, respectively	124	130
Mandatorily convertible junior preferred stock, Series B, no par value, 250,000 shares issued	1,000	1,000
Common stock, no par value, 1,200,000,000 shares authorized, 752,205,112 shares and 716,865,081 shares issued, respectively	8,348	6,637
Retained earnings	3,226	2,698
Accumulated other comprehensive income	(1,048)	741
Common stock held in treasury, 577,066 shares and 1,337,714 shares, respectively	(32)	(49)
Restricted stock and other	(148)	(105)
Total shareholders' equity	11,470	9,570
Total liabilities and shareholders' equity	65,503	33,381

Enron Corp. and Subsidiaries Consolidated Statement of Cash Flows ($ millions)

	Year Ended December 31		
	2000	1999	1998
Cash flow from operating activities: reconciliation of net income to net cash provided by operating activities			
Net income	979	893	703
Cumulative effect of accounting changes	—	131	—
Depreciation, depletion, and amortization	855	870	827
Impairment of long-lived assets (including equity investments)	326	441	—
Deferred income taxes	207	21	87
Gains on sales of nonmerchant assets	(146)	(541)	(82)
Changes in components of working capital	1,769	(1,000)	(233)
Net assets from price risk management activities	(763)	(395)	350
Merchant assets and investments:			
Realized gains on sales	(104)	(756)	(628)
Proceeds from sales	1,838	2,217	1,434
Additions and unrealized gains	(1,295)	(827)	(721)
Other operating activities	1,113	174	(97)
Net cash provided by operating activities	4,779	1,228	1,640
Cash flow from investing activities			
Capital expenditures	(2,381)	(2,363)	(1,905)
Equity investments	(933)	(722)	(1,659)
Proceeds from sales of nonmerchant assets	494	294	239

| | Year Ended December 31 | | |
	2000	1999	1998
Acquisition of subsidiary stock	(485)	—	(180)
Business acquisitions, net of cash acquired	(777)	(311)	(104)
Other investing activities	(182)	(405)	(356)
Net cash used in investing activities	(4,264)	(3,507)	(3,965)
Cash flows from financing activities			
Issuance of long-term debt	3,994	1,776	1,903
Repayment of long-term debt	(2,337)	(1,837)	(870)
Net increase (decrease) in short-term borrowings	(1,595)	1,565	(158)
Net issuance (redemption) of company-obligated preferred securities of subsidiaries	(96)	—	8
Issuance of common stock	307	852	867
Issuance of subsidiary equity	500	568	828
Dividends paid	(523)	(467)	(414)
Net disposition of treasury stock	327	139	13
Other financing activities	(6)	(140)	89
Net cash provided by financing activities	571	2,456	2,266
Increase (decrease) in cash and cash equivalents	1,086	177	(59)
Cash and cash equivalents, beginning of year	288	111	170
Cash and cash equivalents, end of year	1,374	288	111
Changes in components of working capital			
Receivables	(8,203)	(662)	(1,055)
Inventories	1,336	(133)	(372)
Payables	7,167	(246)	433
Other	1,469	41	761
Total	1,769	(1,000)	(233)

Enron Corp. and Subsidiaries Consolidated Statement of Changes in Shareholders' Equity ($ millions, except per share amounts; shares in thousands)

| | 2000 | | 1999 | |
	Shares	Amount	Shares	Amount
Cumulative second preferred convertible stock				
Balance, beginning of year	1,296	130	1,320	132
Exchange of convertible preferred stock for common stock	(55)	(6)	(24)	(2)
Balance, end of year	1,241	124	1,296	130
Mandatorily convertible junior preferred stock, Series B				
Balance, beginning of year	250	1,000	—	—
Issuance	—	—	250	1,000
Balance, end of year	250	1,000	250	1,000

(continued)

	2000		1999	
	Shares	Amount	Shares	Amount
Common stock				
Balance, beginning of year	716,865	6,637	671,094	5,117
Exchange of convertible preferred stock for common stock	1,509	6	465	(1)
Issuance related to benefit and dividend reinvestment plans	28,100	966	10,054	258
Sales of common stock	—	—	27,600	839
Issuances of common stock in business acquisitions	5,731	409	7,652	250
Other	—	330	—	174
Balance, end of year	752,205	8,348	716,865	6,637
Retained earnings				
Balance, beginning of year		2,698		2,226
Net income		979		893
Cash dividends				
Common stock ($0.5000, $0.5000 and $0.48 per share in 2000, 1999 and 1998, respectively)		(368)		(355)
Cumulative second preferred convertible stock ($13.652, $13.652 and $13.1402 per share in 2000, 1999 and 1998, respectively)		(17)		(17)
Series A and B preferred stock		(66)		(49)
Balance, end of year		3,226		2,698
Accumulated other comprehensive income				
Balance, beginning of year		(741)		(162)
Translation adjustments and other		(307)		(579)
Balance, end of year		(1,048)		(741)
Treasury stock				
Balance, beginning of year				
Shares acquired	(1,338)	(49)	(9,334)	(195)
Exchange of convertible preferred stock for common stock	(3,114)	(234)	(1,845)	(71)
Issuances related to benefit and dividend reinvestment plans	—	—	181	4
Issuances of treasury stock in business acquisitions	3,875	251	9,660	213
Balance, end of year	(577)	(32)	(1,338)	(49)
Restricted stock and other				
Balance, beginning of year		(105)		(70)
Issuances related to benefit and dividend reinvestment plans		(43)		(35)
Balance, end of year		(148)		(105)
Total shareholders' equity		11,470		9,570

**Appendix B. Financial Press Excerpts from Enron Short
Seller and Accounting Expert Interviews**

The following notes were from a November 5, 2001, *Wall Street Journal* interview
with James Chanos, an Enron short seller:

- In October 2000, short seller James Chanos struggled through Enron's
  annual report and began questioning Enron's financial reporting, especially its related party transactions with a senior officer of Enron being
  the managing member of three related parties that were private investment companies. (This senior officer turned out to be Andrew Fastow,
  Enron's chief financial officer (CFO).)
- Mr. Chanos said: "We read the disclosure over and over and over again,
  and we just didn't understand it—and we read footnotes for a living. Not
  only was it impossible to understand what it meant, but it also raised a
  conflict-of-interest issue."
- He accumulated an eighteen-inch stack of regulatory filings and other
  Enron material that raised multiple red flags, such as the following:
- Enron had plenty of tangible assets such as pipelines and utilities. However, it appeared to be a hedge fund in disguise since much of its growth
  came from taking positions in the trading of energy contracts. However,
  Enron refused to detail the return on capital that the trading business
  generated, instead pointing to reported earnings. By the late 1990s,
  Enron's tangible asset portfolio had been mostly added to its trading operations for reporting purposes. Chanos noted that Enron was selling
  those assets and recognizing such sales as recurring earnings. Enron also
  took equity stakes in many companies and included results from those
  investments as recurring earnings.
- The chief operating officer of Chanos's investment company called
  Enron "a giant hedge fund sitting on top of a pipeline." In September
  2001, another short seller and investment manager, David Tice, called
  Enron "a hedge fund in drag." Even though Enron was not as profitable
  as an average hedge fund, Wall Street loved it because it had consistently
  met or beaten earnings targets for the last twenty consecutive quarters.
- Chanos said: "What struck us was, despite their market-leadership position, just how poorly they were doing in terms of returns." He estimated
  that Enron's return on invested capital (ROIC) was 7 percent for the
  rolling four quarters through September 30, 2000, versus his estimate of
  Enron's cost of capital (COC) between 9 percent and 12 percent. He
  thought that the ROIC should exceed the COC by 3 percent to 5 percent
  to justify an investment.
- Enron's shares were trading at about six times book value in late 2000.
  He compared that result to Wall Street brokerage firms, typically priced
  at two to three times book value, and hedge funds, typically priced right
  at book value.

- In February 2001, Enron's stock was trading at $72, which was forty times the analysts' consensus earnings per share estimate for 2001. He said: "The market is priced for perfection here whereas it looks like things may be anything but."
- Insider stock sales occurred through the second half of 2000 while the Wall Street, sell-side analysts still had buy recommendations for Enron. The analysts told investors just to trust management, given the difficulty of analyzing how earnings were derived.
- Mr. Chanos said: "You look for patterns in my business. The fact that this was a 'trust me' story while management was voting with its feet was another check. While we didn't have a smoking gun, we certainly saw a reason to perhaps not trust management at its word that these earnings were what they said they were."
- In an April 2001 conference call, Enron's CEO, Jeffrey Skilling, responded to another short seller's criticism that Enron hadn't provided a balance sheet by calling him a donkey-related name. Mr. Chanos said: "For the first time, I got a sense that the company was now getting tough questions and was not happy about it."

The following notes were from an Enron-related interview in a November 5, 2001, *Wall Street Journal* article with Douglas Carmichael, an accounting expert:

- The nation's accounting-standard setters have never offered any clear guidance on whether a company's financial disclosures should be understandable only to sophisticated people with specialized training or to a broader audience.
- How murky were Enron's related party disclosures concerning its private investment company partnerships? A summary of the 2000 10-K footnote followed: The company disclosed that it transferred assets valued at $1.2 billion, including $150 million in notes payable; 3.7 million restricted Enron shares, and the right to receive as many as 18 million Enron common shares in March 2003, subject to certain conditions. It also transferred to the partnerships other assets valued at $309 million, including a $50 million note payable and an investment in an entity that indirectly holds warrants convertible into common stock of an Enron equity method investee. In return, Enron said it received economic interests in the entities, $309 million in notes receivable, and an additional $1.2 billion in notes receivable as part of a special distribution.
- Doug Carmichael said: "The raw numbers may all be there but any objective person would be hard pressed to understand the effects of these disclosures on the financial statements. The quality of the disclosure is low, which creates uncertainty about the quality of their accounting."
- Enron didn't even pretend to be cooperative in responding to questions about related party transactions. The CFO Fastow said that such details were confidential since Enron didn't want the information to get into the

market. He said that the partnerships were used for unbundling and re-assembling various contract components. He said: "We strip out price risk, we strip out interest rate risk, we strip out all the risks. What's left may not be something that we want." The partnerships were sold "what was left," and such transactions were backed by Enron stock.

- Carmichael said: "Enron's explanation of why it entered into the transactions seems to defy imagination." In the year-end financial statements, Enron said that the purpose was to hedge certain merchant investments and other assets, including energy assets whose values are prone to widespread fluctuations. However, the related party footnote disclosure shows that Enron chose to use its own shares and options of its own stock as its chief hedging instrument even though their price movements wouldn't appear to be directly related to the value of the investments Enron was trying to hedge.
- Professor Carmichael said: "I don't see how that possibly hedges any of Enron's risks or assets." These disclosures have generated widespread speculation that Enron's actual purpose was to use its off-balance-sheet transactions to shift losses off its books and hide debt to preserve its credit rating.

Note

9. AOL LATIN AMERICA (B)

On February 8, 2002, Charles Herington, chief executive officer (CEO) of AOL Latin America; Javier Aguirre, chief financial officer (CFO); and Carlos Trostli, president of AOL Brazil, arrived at AOL Time Warner's (AOLTW) headquarters, in Washington, D.C., to discuss the company's need for additional operating funds (see exhibits 1–4).

Prior to the meeting, AOLTW CFO Wayne Pace reviewed AOL Latin America's "Altman Z-Score," a rough, but usually accurate, measure of a company's financial health (see app. A). By inputting a few items from the company's income statement and balance sheet, such as retained earnings, revenues, and market value of equity, into the model it generated the following numbers.[1]

David Wesley prepared this case under the supervision of Professor Harlan Platt solely to provide material for class discussion. The authors do not intend to illustrate either effective or ineffective handling of a managerial situation. The authors may have disguised certain names and other identifying information to protect confidentiality.

Fiscal Year Ending	Z-Score[2]
June 30, 1999	5.36
June 30, 2000	−7.44
December 31, 2000	−3.87
December 31, 2001	−20.15

As everyone gathered around the boardroom table, Herington took his place at the front of the room. Pace and AOL CEO Gerald Levin[3] listened attentively as Herington opened the discussion:

> When you look at an industry as young as the Internet is in Latin America, we believe that the best way to evaluate the performance of America Online and other companies is actual membership growth. And we have the revenue growth, as well, coming along with it. We are creating an industry. It's a young industry, and it's off to a great start.
>
> But the losses are actually a reflection of the investment we're making in order to create awareness of the Internet in Latin America and awareness of the benefits of AOL in Latin America. And the growth in subscriber revenues is actually what tells you the growth in paying members. If you look at that track, quarter after quarter you'll see that not only is it growing very healthy, but it's growing faster than any other Internet service provider in Latin America.[4]

In the process of funding that "growth," AOL Latin America had seen its working capital decline to less than $1 million.[5] Herington explained bluntly that without an additional $160 million to fund operations through to the end of 2002, the company would soon be insolvent:

> We anticipate that the cash on hand and the cash to be raised through the issuance of the senior convertible notes to AOLTW will be sufficient to fund operations through the end of the 2002 calendar year, based upon our current operating budget. A portion of this cash may be used for the acquisition and subsequent funding of technologies, products or businesses complementary to our business.
>
> The projected spending is comprised primarily of discretionary items that could be adjusted, when, or if, necessary. Subsequent financing will be required before we expect to become

cash self-sufficient. In order to fund our post-2002 cash needs, we will seek to sell additional equity or debt securities or to enter into credit facilities, although we cannot be sure that funding will be obtained on favorable terms.[6]

Herington finished by noting that it had taken AOL nine years to reach the one million subscribers mark, while AOL Latin America had reached that mark in only 21 months[7] (see app. B).

Despite these words of confidence, AOL Time Warner's management team was concerned. One expressed worry that Internet services in Latin America were a fad and that high growth rates were not sustainable. Another suggested that Herington would be back in another year to ask for more money. After all, it had been less than two years since Herington promised that his company would be profitable by the end of 2001. Now, some wondered if it would ever show a profit (see exhibit 5).[8]

Herington countered:

The big fundamentals are still there. It's not a fad, it's a trend. Even now, growth in the industry is in the double-digits, so I think the space to compete is there. I continue to be very impressed that in a region that has undergone the trouble it did last year that, adjusted for local currency, we were able to grow revenue 25 percent in 2002. That is the real metric of progress of the business. We feel we are on the right track. If it hasn't been noticed, it eventually will.

AOL Time Warner has been very clear in stating that you won't fund plans that do not have a clear business plan, and we are absolutely in agreement with that. While we are not profitable yet, we feel we are on the path to get there and it is definitely a key priority.[9]

AOLTW was already reeling from more than 700 million dollars in noncash writedowns from its investments in GM Hughes, AOL Latin America, and Time Warner Telecom. Advertising revenues, in particular, were hard hit by a U.S. recession that followed terrorist attacks on New York and Washington on September 11, 2001 (see exhibit 6). While management loathed the thought of further losses, they wondered how they could justify withdrawing from one of the fastest growing regions in the world for Internet services.

Company Background

Brazil represented the largest potential marker for AOL Latin America's online services, accounting for more than half of Internet users in the region. AOL Brazil's first president, Francisco Loureiro, served from May 1999 to December 1999, when he resigned to take a more lucrative position with an AOL competitor (see below). Loureiro was the first and only senior manager in Brazil to have Internet and telecommunications industry experience. He was replaced by Manoel Amorim, a former marketing manager for Procter and Gamble. Under Amorim, AOL Brazil focused on creating brand awareness through extravagant advertising events, such as a rock concert that cost the company $20 million to sponsor.

In November 2000, Amorim also resigned to take a position with the Brazilian subsidiary of Spain's Telefónica, a leading provider of fixed-line telephony in Brazil and an AOL competitor (see Terra-Lycos below). AOL Latin America CEO Charles Herington managed the Brazilian operations until May 2001, when the company hired Carlos Dan Trostli, its third Brazilian president in less than two years. Trostli had previously served as president of the Brazilian branch of Quaker Oats and had also worked as a marketing and sales manager for Procter and Gamble.

At the end of 2001, AOL Brazil service was available in 227 cities. The company also offered service in 58 cities in Mexico and 22 cities in Argentina. In addition, AOL Time Warner transferred its existing customer base in Puerto Rico to AOL Latin America, where bilingual English/Spanish language service was available (see exhibit 7).

Competition

StarMedia

The first president of AOL Brazil, Francisco Loureiro, became chief operating officer (COO) of StarMedia in December 1999. On June 1, 2001, he resigned. In the difficult period that followed the dot-com decline, Loureiro could not accept StarMedia's policy of gaining market share at the expense of profitability, as had been common during the dot-com bubble of 1999 and early 2000. Loureiro's departure followed a financing deal with BellSouth that infused $31.2 million into StarMedia. Loureiro announced:

This kind of money evaporates very quickly. For BellSouth, this is an interesting and appropriate deal. But it doesn't seem to me that this value of money for the company guarantees long-term sustainability. . . . I never believed that a company could sustain itself with external financing. Rather it has to generate results internally.[10]

Loureiro echoed the sentiments of other former employees of StarMedia, who questioned the company's free-spending policy. Shortly before Loureiro's departure, one former employee stated:

They were like a bunch of kids playing at running a company. People would travel to Argentina for a two-hour meeting, fly business class, and no one would ever ask how the meeting went. There were no controls or accountability.[11]

In Brazil, StarMedia's most important market, the company had slid to tenth place among portals, prompting one Brazilian executive to comment:

StarMedia is amazing. They are the biggest hype in the history of the Internet on Wall Street. But they're a non-player in Brazil, and if they don't make it here, they're bust.[12]

By early 2001, StarMedia shares had dropped to just under $2 per share from a high of more than $60 per share in 1999, and the company dismissed 15 percent of its workforce. Then in February 2002, the company was delisted from the NASDAQ stock exchange when shares fell to $0.38 and the company failed to submit quarterly statements. (See exhibit 8.)

Universo Online

With 1.1 million subscribers, Universo Online (UOL) was the largest Internet service provider (ISP) in Brazil. The company admitted that it started as a clone of AOL, but as a Brazilian-based company, it was able to provide regional enhancements that allowed it to attract a larger market share than its foreign competitor (see exhibit 9). Even so, UOL was a loss-making entity that had originally hoped to fund its expansion through a NASDAQ initial public offering (IPO). As U.S. capital markets collapsed in 2001, UOL had to find private venture capital, raising $200 million from Portugal Telecom in exchange for an equity stake of approximately 18 percent. It also sold Access-net, a telecommunications technology that managed Internet traffic, for another $100 million.[13] These two transactions effectively provided the working capital needed to continue operations. In 2001, UOL reported a loss of approximately $108 million on revenues of $158 million, double the loss reported in 2000.[14]

Terra Lycos

At the end of 2000, Telefónica Interactive of Spain acquired U.S.-based Lycos, a leading Internet portal founded by Northeastern University alumnus Robert Davis in 1995. The acquisition resulted in the creation of Terra-Lycos. With $2.9 billion in cash, Terra-Lycos had one of the strongest cash positions of any Internet company in the world.[15] According to Executive Chairman Joaquim Agut, the new company's goal would be to become one of "the world's largest Internet companies."[16]

In Latin America alone, Terra-Lycos employed more than twelve hundred people and held leading market positions in numerous countries throughout the region, including Argentina, Brazil, Chile, Colombia, Costa Rica, Dominican Republic, El Salvador, Guatemala, Honduras, Mexico, Nicaragua, Panama, Peru, Uruguay, and Venezuela. While the company boasted that it had 4.3 million subscribers to its Internet service, only 1.3 million of those were paying customers. The remainder accessed free services, which were funded primarily through advertising (see exhibit 10). As this model became more questionable, Terra-Lycos attempted to convert more of its subscribers to paying customers by offering improved services, such as broadband (high-speed), or by discontinuing free services in specific markets. Accordingly, the company invested heavily in new hardware, such as high-speed access lines. In 2001, the company lost $586.3 million on revenues of $693.5 million compared to a year 2000 loss of $555.2 million on $307.5 million in revenues.

Other Competitors

AOL Latin America competed against numerous small- and medium-sized Internet service providers in each of its markets. The company also faced large regional competitors that were backed by state telecommunications firms or foreign multinationals. These included the state telephone company, Telmex in Mexico (which forged an alliance with Microsoft to offer service under the Prodigy brand), and Arnet in Argentina, also owned by that country's state telecom provider.

In Brazil, where telephone companies charged for local phone calls, free Internet access proved very popular. Although several service providers, such as UOL and Terra-Lycos, terminated their free service, others continued to flourish. One such company was Internet Gratis (translated Free Internet), which was owned by a Rio de Janeiro–based telephone company.

The company did not solely rely on advertising revenues, but instead offered value-added revenue generating services such as wireless content, online pizza delivery service, an electronic boutique, and high-speed connection services (see exhibit 11). Internet Gratis was also one of the few Latin American Internet companies to post a profit in 2001.[17]

EXHIBIT 1. AOL Latin America Revenues and Losses by Segment ($000s)

Revenues	Year Ended 31-Dec-01	Year Ended 31-Dec-00	Year Ended 30-June-00	Period from 15-Dec-98 to 30-June-99
Brazil				
Subscription revenues	17,853	6,950	2,154	
Advertising and commerce	8,870	5,470	3,292	
Total Brazil	26,723	12,420	5,446	
Mexico				
Subscription revenues	19,579	2,379		
Advertising and commerce	5,557	996		
Total Mexico	25,136	3,375		
Argentina				
Subscription revenues	7,388	420		
Advertising and commerce	1,766	665		
Total Argentina	9,154	1,085		
Corporate and other				
Subscription revenues	5,098	2,042	3,694	1,644
Advertising and commerce	332	106	60	
Total corporate and other	5,430	2,148	3,754	1,644
Total revenues	66,443	19,028	9,200	1,644
Loss from operations				
Brazil	(147,731)	(161,070)	(82,477)	
Mexico	(71,550)	(50,221)		
Argentina	(39,663)	(34,565)		
Corporate and other	(36,124)	(25,444)	(17,447)	(1,750)
Total consolidated loss	(295,068)	(271,300)	(99,924)	(1,750)

Source: AOL Latin America, SEC 10-K405, FY 2001.

EXHIBIT 2. Consolidated Balance Sheet for Years Ending December 31 ($000s)

Assets	2001	2000
Current assets		
Cash and cash equivalents	46,676	63,509
Short-term investments		69,357
Total cash and short-term investments	46,676	132,866
Trade accounts receivable, less allowances of $1,979 in 2001 and $501 in 2000	6,144	3,724
Other receivables	4,713	12,269
Prepaid expenses and other current assets	5,410	15,200
Total current assets	62,943	164,059
Property and equipment, net	11,958	11,307
Investments, including securities available for sale	1,361	754
Product development and other intangible assets, net	988	1,876
Other assets	7,134	1,035
Total assets	84,384	179,031
Liabilities and stockholders' equity		
Current liabilities		
Trade accounts payable	18,114	25,024
Payables to affiliates	15,198	10,976
Other accrued expenses and liabilities	14,570	9,236
Deferred revenue	3,656	3,187
Accrued personnel costs	9,004	3,450
Other taxes payable	1,595	943
Total current liabilities	62,137	52,816
Deferred revenue	692	1,957
Other noncurrent liabilities	432	437
Total liabilities	63,261	55,210
Commitments and contingencies		
Stockholders' equity		
Preferred stock, $.01 par value; 500,000,000 shares	2,274	1,997
Common stock, $.01 par value; 1,750,000,000 shares	671	629
Additional paid-in capital	800,714	651,491
Unearned services	(189,191)	(230,671)
Accumulated other comprehensive (loss) income	(3,334)	71
Accumulated deficit	(590,011)	(299,696)
Total stockholders' equity	21,123	123,821
Total liabilities and stockholders' equity	84,384	179,031

Source: AOL Latin America, SEC 10-K405, FY 2001.

EXHIBIT 3. Consolidated Statement of Operations ($000s, except share and per share amounts)

	Year Ended December 31		Six Months Ended December 31	
	2001	2000	2000	1999
Revenues				
Subscriptions	49,918	11,791	8,050	2,106
Advertising and commerce	16,525	7,237	4,423	537
Total revenues	66,443	19,028	12,473	2,643
Cost and expenses				
Cost of revenues	120,772	53,808	38,270	4,828
Sales and marketing	191,024	201,977	150,951	19,521
Product development	8,124	5,718	4,120	927
General and administrative	41,591	28,825	19,247	6,108
Total costs and expenses	361,511	290,328	212,588	31,384
Loss from operations	(295,068)	(271,300)	(200,115)	(28,741)
Other income, net	4,753	1,623	204	592
Loss before income taxes				
Provision for income taxes	(290,315)	(269,677)	(199,911)	(28,149)
Net loss	(290,315)	(269,677)	(199,911)	(28,149)
Less: Dividends on Series B and C preferred shares	17,005	5,711	5,711	
Net loss applicable to common stockholders loss per common share	(307,320)	(275,388)	(205,622)	(28,149)
Basic and diluted	(5)	(11)	(4)	
Weighted average number of common shares outstanding	66,017,796	24,447,518	48,496,436	

Source: AOL Latin America, SEC 10-K405, FY 2001.

EXHIBIT 4. Consolidated Cash Flows ($000s)

	Year Ending December 31		Six Months Ended December 31	
	2001	2000	2000	1999
Operating activities				
Net loss	(290,315)	(269,677)	(199,911)	(28,149)
Adjustments to reconcile net loss to net cash used in operating activities				
Provision for uncollectible accounts	2,210	358	284	361
Depreciation and amortization	4,920	2,304	1,545	91
(Gain) loss from investment securities	(385)	3,705	3,705	
Noncash marketing expense	41,845	21,094	21,094	
Noncash stock-based compensation expense	324	252	252	
Noncash asset impairment charges and lease reserves	1,473			
Changes in operating assets and liabilities				
Trade accounts receivable	(9,741)	(1,313)	(2,805)	(1,757)
Other operating assets	7,322	(28,278)	(23,279)	(728)
Operating liabilities	6,658	30,678	20,737	8,062

EXHIBIT 4—*Continued*

	Year Ending December 31		Six Months Ended December 31	
	2001	2000	2000	1999
Deferred revenues	(376)	223	854	1,003
Payables to affiliates	8,173	8,051	5,000	2,758
Net cash used in operating activities	(227,892)	(232,603)	(172,524)	(18,359)
Investing activities				
Capital spending	(5,998)	(10,893)	(4,454)	(2,690)
Product development costs	(194)	(1,622)	(225)	(770)
Purchase of short-term investments		(128,519)	(128,519)	
Sale of short-term investments	69,357	59,162	59,162	
Net cash provided by (used) in investing activities	63,165	(81,872)	(74,036)	(3,460)
Financing activities				
Net proceeds from affiliate capital contributions	148,853	77,000	70,000	23,000
Payments of subscription receivable from affiliate		77,979		
Dividend for CompuServe subscribers		879		
Proceeds from IPO, net of offering costs		203,132	206,124	(46)
Net cash provided by financing activities	148,853	358,990	276,124	22,954
Cash and cash equivalents				
Effect of exchange rate changes on cash and cash equivalents	(959)	(1,219)	624	1,362
Net (decrease) increase in cash and cash equivalents	(16,833)	43,296	30,188	2,497
Cash and cash equivalents at beginning of period	63,509	20,213	33,321	17,716
Cash and cash equivalents at end of period	46,676	63,509	63,509	20,213

Source: AOL Latin America, SEC 10-K405, FY 2001.

EXHIBIT 5. AOL Latin America Pro Forma Income Statement (for years ended December 31)

	2002	2003
Revenues		
Subscriptions	60,000	80,000
Advertising and commerce	32,000	38,000
Total revenues	92,000	118,000
Cost and expenses		
Cost of revenues	138,000	165,200
Sales and marketing	180,000	160,000
Product development	10,000	12,000
General and administrative	50,000	55,000
Total costs and expenses	378,000	392,200
Loss from operations	(286,000)	(274,200)

Source: Case writer estimate based on Bear, Stearns; Epsilon S.A.; Lehman Brothers; Salomon Smith Barney consensus data provided by Yahoo! Finance.

EXHIBIT 6. AOL Time Warner Consolidated Statement of Operations ($ millions)

	2001	2000
Revenues		
Subscriptions	16,543	14,733
Advertising and commerce	8,487	8,744
Content and other	13,204	12,736
Total revenues	38,234	36,213
Cost of revenues	(20,704)	(19,887)
Selling, general and administrative	(9,596)	(9,550)
Amortization of goodwill and other intangible assets	(7,231)	(7,032)
Gain on sale or exchange of cable television systems	—	28
Merger-related costs	(250)	(155)
Operating income (loss)	453	(383)
Interest income (expense), net	(1,379)	(1,373)
Other income (expense), net	(3,539)	(1,356)
Minority interest expense	(310)	(264)
Income (loss) before income taxes and cumulative effect of accounting change	(4,775)	(3,376)
Income tax provision	(146)	(551)
Income (loss) before cumulative effect of accounting change	(4,921)	(3,927)
Cumulative effect of accounting change, net of $295 million income tax benefit	—	(443)
Net income (loss)	(4,921)	(4,370)
Preferred dividend requirements	—	(14)
Net income (loss) applicable to common shares	(4,921)	(4,384)
Basic income (loss) per common share before cumulative effect of accounting change	(1)	(1)
Cumulative effect of accounting change	—	—
Basic net income (loss) per common share	(1)	(1)
Average basic common shares	4,429	4,301
Diluted income (loss) per common share before cumulative effect of accounting change	(1)	(1)
Cumulative effect of accounting change	—	—
Diluted net income (loss) per common share	(1)	(1)
Average diluted common shares	4,429	4,301

Source: AOL Time Warner, SEC 10-K405, FY 2001.

EXHIBIT 7. AOL Latin America portal

Source: www.aola.com (March 10, 2003).

STARMEDIA

EMAIL CHAT JUEGOS POSTALES AMOR

Tu gente.Tu idioma

Lunes 10.3.2003 | El tiempo

Busca en la web   **BUSCA** Búsqueda avanzada

SERVICIOS
Email
Chat
Amor
Postales
Páginas personales
Foros
Clasificados

CANALES
Noticias
Entretenimiento
Deportes
Humor
Juegos
Música
Horóscopo
Software
Tecnología
Finanzas
Salud
Mujer
Estudiantes
Familia
Formación
Gay
Trivia

ACTUALIDAD

Chile busca una resolución alternativa ante propuesta sobre Irak
La canciller Alvear reiteró que Chile reafirma la necesidad de que Irak alcance un desarme inmediato, íntegro y efectivo, pero en un contexto de paz y al amparo de las Naciones Unidas.
Cine latinoamericano >> Ocupa lugar de privilegio en festival suizo
Mundial >> Beckenbauer ve viable la ampliación a 36 equipos

HOY TE RECOMENDAMOS

Los beneficiados de Irak
Según un estudio, Venezuela, México o Argentina saldrían beneficiados de una guerra en Irak

Tu media naranja
No existe la perfección...¿Seguro? Cupido puede buscarte tu pareja ideal. ¿Por qué no lo intentas?

CLASIFICACIONES

COPA LIBERTADORES
Chile: Cobreloa 13 ptos.
Perú: Cienciano 6 pts.
Parag.: Libertad 12 pts.
Ecuador: Nacional 6 pts.

Cámara indiscreta
No son especialistas... pero los golpes que se dan son de película. ¡Mira estos videos!

Lo vendemos todo >> Entra y verás
Juegos >> Ponte al día con las novedades
Formación >> Profesiones con futuro
Estudiantes >> Apuntes y trabajos a tu alcance

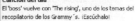
StarMedia DEPORTES

A UN CLICK

Canción del día
El 'boss' vuelve con 'The rising', uno de los temas del recopilatorio de los Grammy´s. ¡Escúchalo!

¿Estás en las nubes?
¡Despierta! Deja que los internautas interpreten tus sueños

EN NUESTROS CANALES

Del tabú, al 'tatoo'
Marcarse la piel con un tatuaje se ha convertido en un fenómeno social. Sin embargo, la moda 'tatoo' data de miles de años. ¡Conoce los orígenes!
Mónica Naranjo >> Su video en inglés
Recetas >> Paso a paso con estos vídeos
Por los pelos >> Rituales mágicos con cabello

ENCUESTA
¿Qué obtendrá Chile si apoya a USA en una posible guerra contra Irak?
○ Beneficios en el TLC
○ Dinero del FMI

Descarga del día

¿Es la voz de Kylie Minogue lo que más te gusta?

EXHIBIT 8. StarMedia Web portal
Source: www.starmedia.com (March 10, 2003).

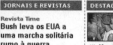

EXHIBIT 9. UOL Brazil portal
Source: www.uol.com.br (March 10, 2003).

EXHIBIT 10. Terra-Lycos Brazil portal
Source: www.terra.com.br (March 12, 2003).

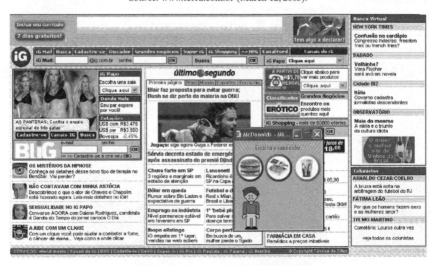

EXHIBIT 11. Internet Gratis Web portal
Source: www.ig.com.br (March 12, 2003).

Appendix A. The Altman Model

Edward Altman studied 33 bankrupt and 33 nonbankrupt firms over the period 1946 to 1965. With them he built a model that correctly predicted 97 percent of the surviving firms and 94 percent of those that failed. The Z-score is derived using a statistical technique known as multiple discriminate analysis or MDA. MDA is similar to regression analysis except that, unlike regression analysis, which seeks to minimize the squared errors of a fitted line from the original values, MDA seeks to develop a function that minimizes the squared error within each group (bankrupt or nonbankrupt) while maximizing differences between groups. Altman's Z-score model takes the form

$$Z = (1.2X_1) + (1.4X_2) + (3.3X_3) + (.66X_4) + (1.0X_5)$$

where

$$X_1 = \frac{Working\ capital}{Total\ assets}$$

$$X_2 = \frac{Retained\ earnings}{Total\ assets}$$

$$X_3 = \frac{EBIT}{Total\ assets}$$

$$X_4 = \frac{Market\ value\ of\ equity}{Book\ value\ of\ debt}$$

$$X_5 = \frac{Sales}{Total\ assets}$$

The numerical values are estimated coefficients, and the Xs are the five financial ratios selected as best by Altman. Z is the value of the function. Note that estimated coefficient values do not convey by their size the importance of particular variables; coefficient size depends, as well, on the typical size of each variable.

Interpreting Z is tricky. Altman hit upon a straightforward approach. He evaluated the Zs for the sixty-six companies in his sample. Companies whose Zs exceeded 2.99 never failed, while those with Zs below 1.81 always failed. He described these two values as his "cut-off" points. The area between 2.99 and 1.81 he called a zone of ignorance.[18]

Companies with Z-scores in the zone of ignorance have an uncertain future; if their Z-score value is falling (rising) from one year to the next, then bankruptcy (survival) is more likely. Using these critical points, 95 percent of the companies in Altman's sixty-six-company sample are properly categorized as bankrupt or nonbankrupt in a follow-up evaluation exercise.

Nonpublic companies, whose common equity is not traded in a market, are incapable of using Altman's original model specification since they lack information for one of the variables, X_4. To surmount this obstacle, Altman reestimated the model and derived a Z that included only variables that are accessible to nonpublic companies.

Appendix B

To Our Stockholders

For AOL Latin America, 2001 was a year of substantial growth and progress, as we brought the AOL interactive experience to an even larger audience in Latin America. We have been successful in building one of the largest and most vibrant online communities in the region. At the same time, we were able to record substantial revenue increases from 2000 levels—with increased revenue from our existing service in Brazil, as well as the addition of revenues from the services in Mexico, Puerto Rico and Argentina—while we narrowed our net loss each quarter. Importantly, we have continued to focus on the member experience, to expand our dial-up network, to roll out our newest software, and to provide members with the very best features and content.

These accomplishments are particularly noteworthy given the difficult environment in which we operated last year, including the economic crisis in Argentina and the weakening of the global advertising marketplace. AOL Latin America's ability to continue growing against this backdrop underscores the tremendous commitment to our employees, the strong support of our partners America Online, the Cisneros Group of Companies and Banco Itaú, and the attractiveness of the AOL experience.

During the year, AOL Latin America:

- Surpassed 1 million members, just 21 months after the launch of our first service, AOL Brazil. This membership milestone represented the fastest growth of any major interactive services provider in the region.
- Expanded our local dial-up network to 263 cities at the end of the year.
- Established relationships with key marketing distribution partners such as Hewlett-Packard, Samsung, Microtec, SBT and Wal-Mart.
- Began rolling out our newest software, AOL 7.0, in the markets we serve. The launches began in Puerto Rico in October 2001, and since year-end have been completed in Mexico, Brazil and Argentina.
- Launched a new Latino content area on AOL's 26 million member U.S. service. Known as AOL Latino (AOL Keyword: Latino), this area provides AOL members in the U.S. with a unique array of Spanish-language offerings.
- Unveiled redesigned Web portals for Brazil, Mexico and Argentina that provide added convenience in allowing members to access their AOL e-mail and other AOL member features when they are traveling.

- Added exciting content providers to further strengthen our rich offerings. Some of these new content partners added to the roster in 2001 include: Dow Jones, EFE, Hispanic Business, Agencia Estado and LanceNet.
- Provided advertisers with unique opportunities to reach their audiences. Advertisers included: Coca-Cola, Kraft, IBM, Philips, Volvo, McDonald's, Pfizer, MasterCard, Ford, Nike, Sony, Shell, Nestlé, Siemens and Nextel.
- Sponsored Rock in Rio: For a Better World, the 7-day music festival in Brazil attended by 1.2 million concert-goers.
- Through our presence, we succeeded in making the word "fácil" (easy) synonymous with AOL Brazil.

Going forward into 2002, we will continue to focus on improving the member experience and honoring our commitment to provide the very best interactive services in Latin America. We will work to both introduce consumers to the AOL experience and to better target higher value members. As our business continues to evolve, we will evolve with it. And, as the interactive medium becomes an increasingly important part of everyday life in Latin America, we intend to be there, offering prospective new members the advantages of AOL's hallmark ease-of-use and convenience.

We are excited about the future of both the interactive medium and this Company in the months and years to come.

Warm regards,
Charles M. Herington, President and Chief Executive Officer

Notes

1. An online Altman Z-score calculator is available at http://www.jaxworks .com/calc2.htm (accessed March 26, 2003).

2. A Z-score greater than 2.99 indicates financial health, with a bankruptcy during the next year being unlikely. A score below 1.81 suggests a likely bankruptcy within the next 12 months. The model is uncertain between the two scores.

3. Levin had already announced plans to step down as CEO in May 2002.

4. From a conversation with Neil Cavuto, Fox News Network, September 5, 2001.

5. All currency references are in U.S. dollars unless otherwise stated.

6. America Online Latin America, Inc., SEC Form: 10-K405, April 1, 2002.

7. More than half of those one million represented free trial memberships. And despite having some of the lowest rates in the world (unlimited service for less than $10 per month), nearly 10 percent of subscribers defaulted on their payments. Meanwhile, market leader Universo Online (UOL) boasted 1.1 million subscribers in Brazil alone.

8. Independent analysts predicted continued losses. A pro forma income statement based on analyst predictions is provided in Exhibit 5.

9. Adapted from: "'AOL Latam Has No Plans to Go Private,' CEO Says," *Reuters,* February 11, 2003.

10. "Loureiro Bows out of StarMedia with Bite," *Reuters,* June 4, 2001.

11. "StarMedia fixes Its Gaze on Latin America," *Upside,* March 28, 2001.

12. Ibid.

13. "UOL Makes Capital out of Steve Jobs' Business Model," *Financial Times,* August 31, 2001.

14. "Losses Double for UOL in 2001," *Online Journalism Review,* April 8, 2002.

15. The company's cash position declined to $2.2 billion at the end of 2001.

16. Terra-Lycos 2001 Annual Report.

17. "In Brazil an ISP Still Roams Free," *Wired News,* August 9, 2001.

18. Three zones of recognition are what most textbooks report for Altman's model; however, Altman concluded that 2.675 is the value to use when a single cut-off score is required.

Deciding What to Do

10. Periwinkle Software, Inc.

Jake Periwinkle graduated with a B.A. in computer science in 1990 from a prestigious university. After receiving an M.B.A. degree two years later from another school, he immediately incorporated Periwinkle Software, Inc., to sell a scheduling program that he had written in his spare time during business school. The timing was perfect, as many companies were buying their first computer systems about this time and few already had scheduling programs. Jason quickly developed the company using $100,000 of equity financing from friends and family, a small loan from Tri-city Bancorp Inc., and reinvested profits from early adopters to find this growth plan. Tables 1 and 2 show financial results for Periwinkle.

In 1994 Jake hired Sheila McGriff as head of sales. Sheila had worked in the sales department of a large Minneapolis-based mainframe computer company that had let her go when it scaled back its workforce. Jake's board of directors (his parents and uncle) argued against the hire solely because Sheila was out of work. Jake ignored them and brought Sheila on board. Her impact was felt immediately. Sales jumped by nearly 300 percent in 1995 as Sheila brought in seventy-three new customers. She also added a service department so that revenues in 1995 were comprised of 94 percent sales and 6 percent service. The margin on service revenue was smaller than on new sales, but Sheila argued that it would stabilize the company by creating a steady base of sales. The service share continued to grow, reaching 12 percent in 1996.

Midyear 1995, Sheila returned from a sales trip and told Jake

This case was prepared by Thomas Hays and Harlan D. Platt.

about how customers were literally begging to be sold a new type of software that could integrate across several corporate departments. Jake was reluctant to enter a new market because his background was in scheduling and he wasn't sure that he could handle the technical issues involved. Moreover, he wasn't sure that Periwinkle was ready to be a "big company." Sheila was persuasive and convinced Jake to hire two additional programmers who would take over the bulk of the programming area, thereby allowing Jake to devote himself to management.

To fund this decision, Jake approached Tri-city Bancorp Inc. with a plan to borrow $3,000,000. The bank was reluctant, but Jake was impassioned. He reminded the bank how Perinwikle had repaid its earlier loans on time, and he proudly showed the bank the 1995 income

TABLE 1.   Periwinkle Software, Inc., Historical Income Statements ($000)

	1992 (partial)	1993	1994	1995	1996
Sales	4.3	174.2	893.0	2,344.5	6,982.1
Cost of goods sold	5.7	166.9	459.8	1,109.4	2,359.4
Gross margin	(1.4)	7.3	433.2	1,235.1	4,622.7
Sales, general, and administrative expenses	12.5	87.9	245.6	823.9	1,110.5
Operating profit	(13.9)	(80.6)	187.6	411.2	3,512.2
Interest expense	0.0	23.0	26.5	0.0	270.0
Taxes	—[a]	—[b]	18.9	164.5	1,296.9
Net income	(13.9)	(57.6)	142.2	246.7	1,945.3

[a]Carryforward of (4.0).
[b]Carryforward of (41.5).

TABLE 2.   Periwinkle Software, Inc., Historical Balance Sheet (December 31) ($000)

	1992 (partial)	1993	1994	1995	1996
Current assets	88.9	253.8	608.5	538.8	5,452.7
Fixed assets	1.7	47.9	97.9	111.8	649.6
Total assets	90.6	301.7	706.4	650.6	6,102.3
Notes payable	0	255.6	350.0	0	3,000
Total current liabilities	4.5	277.7	540.3	237.8	3,744.2
Owners' equity	86.1	24.0	166.1	412.8	2,358.1
Total liabilities + owners' equity	90.6	301.7	706.4	650.6	6,102.3

statement that included over $100,000 in profits. Jake did not reveal to the bank how sales were beginning to move from sales to service; his view was "if they don't ask then don't tell them." The bank was not convinced. It finally agreed to the loan provided that Periwinkle secured the loan with all of its assets including patents and that Jake and his parents, then the sole members of the board following the resignation of his uncle, put up their homes as collateral. Jake's attorney told him that banks never enforced those clauses anyway so that he had little to worry about.

The new software was a hit, reaching sales of $4,300,000 in 1996. Jake's concerns about the scheduling product were rebuffed by Sheila, who said that the entire sales team had focused on the new product so that the low growth rate of the old product "was not a real concern." As 1996 drew to a close, Sheila reported that her old employer had asked her to return. Jake was frantic. He knew that she was largely responsible for the huge profit to be earned in 1996. Again his board advised against Sheila and told Jake to let her go back if she wished. Jake again ignored the board and agreed to double Sheila's pay (to more than his own), made her an officer of the corporation, gave her 10 percent of the stock and an option to buy 40 percent more, and put her on the board of directors. His parents were so furious with him that they quit the board, leaving Sheila and Jake as its sole members.

The year 1997 proved to be less sanguine for Periwinkle. The economy was less rosy in 1996, with the software market being especially hard hit; several large new competitors entered the corporate integration software market; and corporate costs exploded as the manufacturing and programming departments encountered troubles trying to maintain two separate product lines. Perhaps worst of all, the competitors were offering a marginally superior product to Periwinkle's but at a substantially lower cost. When Jake asked Sheila about marketing plans that might help hold onto their market shares she could only describe new selling ideas. Jake was aghast when she explained that she had been paying purchasing agents under the table to get them to consummate transactions with Periwinkle. Combined sales of the two products in 1997 fell to just $4,309,000, with operating profits being negative at $4,000. Periwinkle was overdue on bank interest and seemingly unable to repay the loan. Worse still, bickering between the two board members was intense, and nothing good came from their frequent meetings. As one senior employee put it, "The company was at a standstill in a pool of quicksand."

Further complicating the situation was a letter received in December 1987 from the Environmental Protection Administration asking Periwinkle, Inc., to comment about a leakage from its warehouse that was currently contaminating local drinking water wells. Sheila had opened the letter and had stormed into Jake's office demanding an explanation. He mumbled something about "Dad took care of that years ago" before he started to leave the room. When he got to the door, he turned around and said that a large account working with the FBI had called that morning about an alleged bribe that Sheila had made to complete a sale. "I don't know which problem is worse," he said.

Tri-city Bancorp asked your firm to meet with Sheila and Jake. Initially the goal was mediation, but after the first meeting you reported to the bank that perhaps something more hands on was needed. A meeting with the programming staff convinced you that the two products were technically good though not breakout fantastic. The future market for the software was also tantalizing but unsure.

Operating and Leadership Issues

11. Manchester Wholesale Distributors (A)

When Thomas E. Fillingim joined the executive MBA (EMBA) program at Northeastern University in January 1995, he hoped it would help prepare him to own and manage his own company. A successful senior executive and former president of the Wholesale Marketers Association, Fillingim resigned from his $150,000-a-year position as executive vice president of a major New England wholesaler to apply himself full-time to his academic endeavors.

One evening, Fillingim received a call from Henry Vachon, vice president of the Wholesale Marketers Association and owner of

David Wesley prepared this case under the supervision of Professors Paul Croke and Henry W. Lane solely to provide material for class discussion. The authors do not intend to illustrate either effective or ineffective handling of a managerial situation. The authors may have disguised certain names and other identifying information to protect confidentiality.

Manchester Wholesale Distributors (MWD). Vachon's company had a long successful history as a tobacco and sundries distributor for southern New Hampshire. A year earlier, Fillingim had heard of MWD's acquisition of a distributor in northern New Hampshire and assumed the company was doing well to be able to expand so aggressively. Therefore, he was more than surprised to discover that MWD was failing and that the bank had presented Vachon with a sixty-day foreclosure notice. Vachon was grave: "I just don't know what to do." Having only completed three months of the EMBA program, Fillingim did not relish the idea of sidetracking his education to plunge himself headlong into an effort to rescue a wholesaler not unlike the company he had just left. Not surprisingly then, Filingim's first response was, "But I am in school now. I want to apply my efforts to the program."

After some persistence, Fillingim agreed to visit MWD to assess the situation and decide then, and only then, what, if anything, he could do. Some weeks later, Fillingim found himself inside the old converted textile mill that served as MWD's warehouse. Before making any commitment to help, he wanted to review the company's financial statement. It was at that point Fillingim realized that the situation was more than serious. Indeed, it was desperate.

Company Background[1]

In 1939, Robert Vachon founded the Vachon Tobacco Company after his job with a distributor of tobacco, candy, and beer was eliminated through bankruptcy. These early beginnings were difficult because he had to work out of his apartment and use his personal sedan as the company delivery vehicle. The business grew quickly, however, and within a few months he had to seek larger quarters. In 1956, after acquiring new warehousing facilities in downtown Manchester, New Hampshire, the company was renamed Manchester Tobacco Company.

In his youth, Robert's son, Henry, helped his father with the family business and, after graduation from college, took a full-time role in the company operations. Henry evaluated and added product lines to gain a greater share of the ever changing distribution market. He added paper products, sundries, snack lines, and grocery and beverage lines to the company mix of product. The business continued to grow during the 1960s and 1970s as the company added more product and additional staff and increased the number of delivery routes. In 1975, when his father retired, Henry assumed full leadership of the family business. In order to reflect the greater diversity of products, in 1987 the business was renamed Manchester Wholesale Distributors.

Beyond basic health coverage, MWD did not offer many employee benefits. Nevertheless, it was a good company to work for, and the company's staff was committed to the long-term success of the business. Many had served MWD for more than ten years. Henry had been personally generous with his staff, offering them personal loans and other assistance when needed. That concern for his workers translated into unwavering loyalty to the company among its long-term employees.

MWD also enjoyed a favorable reputation with customers, offering services not available with other wholesalers, such as shelf stocking, store setup, and equipment repair. The company served convenience stores, theaters, restaurants, hotels and resorts, school cafeterias and small supermarkets.

Key competitors were other midsized wholesalers, such as Pine State Trading Company and New Hampshire Tobacco, as well as big box stores such as Berkley and Jenson Co. (BJs) and Costco. Large food service companies, such as Sysco, were not direct competitors because they required minimum purchase of $5,000 and did not allow case lots to be broken up. MWD, on the other hand, required only a $250 minimum order and would sell single items from a case. Weekly orders ranged from $250 to $15,000 per customer. Industry-wide, net income averaged approximately 1.2 percent of sales.

On March 31, 1994, the company acquired Chenard Wholesale in northern New Hampshire, further diversifying the product mix with the addition of produce and food service items. A second warehouse (the Chenard facility) was added under a lease arrangement as part of this acquisition to service customers from the White Mountain area to the Canadian border and into eastern Vermont.

Combined 1993 sales from Chenard and MWD amounted to approximately $33 million. Following the acquisition, MWD employed a total of forty-seven management, warehouse, and field staff.

Thomas E. Fillingim

Tom Fillingim was one of eight children born to a working class family in Boston. Although his father worked hard to provide the best for his family, he could not afford many luxuries for his children. If one of the children wanted a bicycle, for example, it would have to be earned. At the age of eleven, Fillingim began to rise at four o'clock each morning to deliver newspapers. His father encouraged him when needed, saying that he had to "get the job done." Later he paid his own way through a private high school, graduating in 1967.

At the age of eighteen, Fillingim had saved enough to purchase his first home on Cape Cod. The built-to-order house was based on plans that Fillingim had personally selected, and it served as his summer home for many years. Within eight years, he had completely paid off the mortgage. Later, he began purchasing rental properties in Florida, eventually accumulating ten properties.

Fillingim was an inquisitive youth who decided to attend the Skip Barber Racing School after attending the Indy 500, where he marveled at the ability of the drivers to turn corners at two hundred miles per hour. After studying racing and aerodynamics, Fillingim returned to Boston, where he began his career in convenience goods merchandising.

Upon returning to Boston, Fillingim began an entry-level job with a Boston-area convenience store chain. The company was expanding with new stores throughout the area south and west of Boston. One day, Fillingim was assisting the general manager responsible for acquiring new properties. Upon arriving at a prospective site, Fillingim, who knew something about real estate from managing his Florida properties, asked, "Why are you going to build a store here? There are no apartment or residential buildings close by." The manager replied, "Don't worry. I know what I am doing!" Within four months of opening, the store was closed for lack of sales. Management began to take notice of Fillingim's business acumen, and before long, he was promoted to vice president.

Reflecting on his experience, he noted, "What I learned from my early working career is that you have to have a team. I always had people working around me who could get the job done."

Rini and Sons Merchandising Corporation

In 1976, Fillingim joined Rini and Sons Merchandising Corporation (RSM), a Boston-area convenience goods wholesaler, where he worked nights as operations manager, filling customer orders. At the time, RSM was losing money on $18 million in annual revenues. Within six months of joining RSM, Fillingim was promoted to vice president, eventually rising to executive vice president. His primary goals for the company in the late 1970s and early 1980s were to retire high-interest debt that was consuming much of the company's potential earnings and to invest the savings back into the business. By the early 1990s, RSM was debt free and consistently posted strong earnings.

Fillingim personally oversaw the company's expansion into New England and upstate New York as the company grew to over $100 million in sales. Ralph Rini, the company president and owner, had essentially turned over the day-to-day responsibility for managing the company to Fillingim. Rini, recalled Fillingim, was an avid golfer, who preferred to spend much of his time at the Spring Valley Golf and Country Club.

During his tenure at RSM, Fillingim also became president of the Wholesale Marketers Association (Henry Vachon was vice president). The association's prestigious annual meeting drew owners and executives from across the country, including representatives from major manufacturers, such as Philip Morris, Hershey, and Warner-Lambert. This event, among others, afforded Fillingim with an opportunity to become well acquainted with numerous industry leaders.

Although Fillingim was responsible for much of RSM's success, he nevertheless remained an outsider in the family-owned company. Earning a respectable salary was not enough. Instead, Fillingim hoped that he would someday be offered a chance to purchase the company.

Λ Dream Shattered

Every year, State Street Bank invited top clients to an exclusive dinner at the Algonquin Club of Boston, where company executives mingled with senior bankers. Most of all, it was an opportunity for companies to brag of their successes. During the 1994 event, one of the bankers congratulated Ralph Rini on RSM's success and asked how he had managed to grow the company by as much as 15 percent a year. To Rini's embarrassment, another banker interjected to say that Fillingim, not Rini, had been responsible for the company's good fortune. "You're talking to the wrong guy," he said to the other banker. Rini turned red. An uncomfortable silence beset the rest of the evening.

The next morning, Rini approached Fillingim. "Tom, you're going to find out that this is my company, not yours," he exclaimed. At that moment, Fillingim realized that if he stayed with RSM, he would never be able to run his own company. Meanwhile, "Rini was pulling over a million dollars a year from the business and contributing very little," he noted.

Shortly after his confrontation with Rini, Fillingim decided to resign from RSM and pursue his MBA. Fillingim's success and experience made him well qualified for the EMBA program. He recalled his thoughts at the time:

> I didn't know exactly what I wanted to do, but I did not want anyone looking over my shoulder and second-guessing everything I did. I wanted to run my own show. I didn't want some guy who couldn't make [the company successful] himself telling me what I was doing wrong while I was making him rich.

The Chenard Wholesale Acquisition

In 1993, Manchester Wholesale Distributors had a net income of $163,000 on $23 million in sales. Everyone was optimistic as the company moved forward on plans to acquire Chenard Wholesale in northern New Hampshire for approximately $300,000[2] (goodwill value) plus an additional amount of $955,000 for the inventory, receivables, and other assets. Chenard would add $10 million to the company's sales and provide MWD with statewide coverage.

After the acquisition was finalized in April 1994, however, MWD began losing money. The company's $149,000 dollar profit in 1993 turned into a $380,000 loss in 1994 (see exhibits 1–4).

Responding to Vachon's request for help, Fillingim decided to drive to the company's Manchester headquarters to review the situation for himself. Immediately upon reviewing the company's yearly and interim financial statements, he noticed that sales had plummeted dramatically. In its most recent month, the company had managed to reduce overall expenses by approximately 4.5 percent from the previous year, while revenues for the same period were down by more than 15 percent (see exhibit 5). He recalled:

> The two companies' combined sales in 1995 for the year *should* have brought sales in the $33 million range. However, with the price increases that were initiated at the end of 1994, business

was leaving at a pace that would have put the company back at the $23 million level at best. The decline was clear in the interim financials through April 29 of 1995. Year-to-date sales on the interim statement are at $7.8 million. With the sales from both companies combined, the sales figures at that time should have been at the $11 million level. Over $3 million in sales had already gone away in four months!

Higher debt servicing costs associated with the acquisition further contributed to MWD's decline. To finance losses, the company borrowed on its line of credit, for a total commitment of $2.2 million at the end of April. Operations remained essentially the same as they had been prior to the acquisition of Chenard, and none of the staff from either operation had been released (see exhibit 6).

Regarding MWD's acquisition, Fillingim noted, "Chenard was already in trouble, and they overpaid for it." For one thing, Chenard had spent $100,000 on a Snapple franchise in a part of the state where few people consumed Snapple products. Under the terms of the franchise, MWD had to pay for advertising and exclusive vending machines but received little revenue in return.

Salaries were another area of concern. Initially, the company's pay rate was consistent with industry norms. Like most enterprises, MWD offered pay increases to compensate for inflation and seniority. Gradually, however, a policy of automatic annual pay raises placed the company increasingly out of line with competitors. By 1995, MWD employees received salaries that averaged 20 percent more than at other companies in the region.

Still, cutting jobs or salaries went against Vachon family policy. In late 1994, the company's accountant suggested that MWD raise the overall margin on goods sold, from 9.5 percent to 18 percent. "Income must be increased if the company ever hopes to make its interest payments, and raising prices is the fastest way to achieve higher income," he suggested.

The expected increase in earnings never materialized. Moreover, the company's position worsened, as more than two hundred customers defected to the competition.[3] The company's remaining customers refused to pay higher prices, and in order to stem the tide of customer defections, sales agents were offering discounts that essentially wiped out the price distinction. Fewer customers paid their bills on time, as some $350,000 in receivables remained unpaid for more than thirty days.

In January 1995, Vachon met with the Flint Bank loan officer to discuss the company's precarious situation. At that point, the bank decided to transfer the account to its "work out" department. The loan officer also recommended a consultant, who would work in the company to identify any opportunity, however small, to generate cash to repay the outstanding debt.

At the end of April the MWD line of credit came up for renewal. Flint Bank offered the company two thirty-day extensions as part of a "sixty-day" package, which provided the bank with several advantages. It had the ability to opt out at the thirty-day juncture; plus it charged renewal fees (amounting to $11,000) for each thirty-day period and a $3,000 preparation fee that brought the total cost of the loan extension to $25,000. Furthermore, Flint Bank increased the company's borrowing rate from 0.5 percent above prime to prime plus 2 percent, amounting to an extra $2,750 per month in interest. The bank also informed Vachon that he was to pay off the loan at the end of the sixty days. Vachon had no choice but to agree to these demands, as the MWD account was "unbankable" at other institutions and his only other option, on such short notice, was to close the business. Fillingim sat down with Vachon to discuss the situation. "Henry was distraught and did not know what to do," he observed. Vachon was a personal guarantor for the company's loans, and a bank foreclosure would financially ruin the family. Discussing the matter with the bank would be futile, as the loan officer refused to return calls. He now had less than forty days to pay the $2.2 million owed to Flint Bank or face insolvency.

As he returned home that evening, Fillingim thought to himself, "These are all nice people, and they could be on the street in three weeks." He wondered what made this company any different from the one he left a few months before joining the EMBA program. It, too, was a family-owned wholesaler that was losing money when he joined in 1976. Was there any hope for saving the company? Should he distract himself from his studies so early in the EMBA program? If the company failed, how would he get paid for his services? Moreover, an affirmative answer to the first two questions still left Fillingim wondering whether the Vachon family and other managers in the company would be willing to follow his direction and take whatever steps would be necessary to salvage Manchester Wholesale Distributors.

EXHIBIT 1. Statement of Income, Years Ended December 31, 1994 and 1993

	1994		1993	
	Amount ($)	Percentage	Amount ($)	Percentage
Sales	28,597,463.85	100.0	23,040,235.47	100.0
Cost of goods sold	(25,911,295.92)	(90.6)	(20,985,213.87)	(91.1)
Gross profit	2,686,167.93	9.4	2,055,021.60	8.9
Operating expenses				
Selling expenses	589,608.13	2.0	342,309.81	1.5
Delivery expenses	455,543.59	1.6	194,202.46	0.8
Warehouse expenses	934,921.76	3.3	587,737.46	2.6
Administrative expenses	706,529.67	2.5	563,381.42	2.4
Total operating expenses	2,686,603.15	9.4	1,687,631.15	7.3
Net operating income (loss)	(435.22)	0.0	367,390.45	1.6
Other income (expenses)				
Interest expense	(238,104.20)	(0.8)	(135,914.92)	(0.6)
Depreciation and amortization	(138,067.98)	(0.5)	(115,127.00)	(0.5)
Bad debts expense	(54,000.00)	(0.2)	0.00	0.0
Finance charge income	33,425.97	0.1	19,157.07	0.1
Rental income	16,950.00	0.1	14,442.89	0.1
Other income	10,547.50	0.0	13,080.33	0.0
Write-off of intangible assets	(11,644.30)	0.0	0.00	0.0
Provisions for income tax	1,716.00	0.0	0.00	0.0
Total other income (expense)	(379,177.01)	(1.3)	(204,361.63)	(0.9)
Net income (loss) before taxes	(379,612.23)	(1.3)	163,028.82	0.7
Provision for income tax	0.00	0.0	(14,400.00)	(0.1)
Net income (loss)	(379,612.23)	(1.3)	148,628.82	0.6

Note: In exhibits 1–4, figures for 1993 do not include amounts for Chenard Wholesale (1994 figures are for the combined entity). Revenues for Chenard Wholesale in 1993 were approximately $10 million.

EXHIBIT 2. Income Statement Schedule, Years Ended December 31, 1994 and 1993

	1994		1993	
	Amount ($)	Percentage of Gross Profit	Amount ($)	Percentage of Gross Profit
Operating expenses				
Selling expenses				
Wages — sales	439,056.41	16.3	254,809.86	12.7
Payroll taxes	36,439.05	1.4	21,448.57	1.1
Employee benefits	28,907.19	1.1	18,959.08	0.9
Salesman expenses	60,619.10	2.2	34,226.60	1.7

(continued)

EXHIBIT 2—*Continued*

	1994		1993	
	Amount ($)	Percentage of Gross Profit	Amount ($)	Percentage of Gross Profit
Credit and collection expense	15,575.13	0.6	11,232.58	0.6
Equipment lease	5,735.36	0.2	0.00	0.3
Marketing promotion expense	3,275.89	0.1	1,633.12	0.1
Total selling expenses	589,608.13	21.9	342,309.81	16.7
Delivery expenses				
Wages — delivery	185,054.77	6.9	74,262.76	3.7
Payroll taxes	16,190.97	0.6	6,614.29	0.3
Employee benefits	24,691.21	0.9	13,275.65	0.7
Insurance — fleet	27,601.38	1.0	31,933.49	1.6
Vehicle expenses	101,800.00	3.8	63,254.42	3.2
Uniforms	5,905.85	0.2	4,861.85	0.2
Truck lease expense	33,821.41	1.3	0.00	0.0
Freight expense	60,478.00	2.3	0.00	0.0
Total delivery expenses	455,543.59	17.0	194,202.46	9.7
Warehouse expenses				
Wages — warehouse	487,533.33	18.2	328,306.76	16.4
Payroll taxes	38,563.20	1.4	26,595.62	1.3
Employee benefits	64,636.05	2.4	48,820.09	2.4
Rent	137,180.00	5.1	67,459.31	3.4
Utilities	65,089.66	2.4	41,088.25	2.0
Property taxes	40,722.39	1.5	27,000.98	1.3
Insurance	30,267.11	1.1	24,360.20	1.2
Equipment expense	15,166.98	0.6	5,053.26	0.3
Building expense	4,160.64	0.2	4,739.33	0.3
Warehouse expense	28,796.90	1.1	14,313.66	0.7
Equipment lease	22,805.50	0.8	0.00	0.0
Total warehouse expenses	934,921.76	34.8	587,737.46	29.3

Note: This schedule provides a detailed breakdown of expenses for the income statement in exhibit 1.

EXHIBIT 3.   Statement of Cash Flows

	1994	1993
Cash flows from operating activities		
Net income (loss)	(379,612.23)	148,628.82
Noncash items included in net income		
Depreciation and amortization	138,067.98	115,127.00
Reserve for last-in first-outs (LIFO) valuation	28,698.00	(98,004.00)
Loss on write-off of intangible assets	11,644.30	0.00
Gain on sale of assets	(8,947.50)	0.00
(Increase) decrease in		
Due from vendors	22,945.59	(15,579.00)
Accounts receivable	(560,852.91)	111,040.94

EXHIBIT 3—*Continued*

	1994	1993
Notes receivable	58,404.04	15,521.67
Due from stockholder	(55,000.00)	6,229.10
Prepaid expenses	25,380.11	(12,414.91)
Intangible assets	(78,052.45)	(17,132.51)
Inventory	(386,884.55)	223,154.77
Refundable taxes	(2,400.00)	2,000.00
Deposits	(19,717.29)	0.00
Increase (decrease) in		
Accounts payable	187,945.52	(302,301.92)
Accrued expenses	20,520.29	8,030.92
Net cash from operating activities	(997,861.10)	184,300.88
Cash flows from investing activities		
Proceeds from sale of assets	10,788.50	0.00
Purchase of fixed assets	(180,704.25)	(105,787.19)
Net cash used by investing activities	(169,915.75)	(105,787.19)
Cash flows from financing activities		
Payments on long-term debt	614,789.29	(60,127.41)
Payment on notes payable	0.00	(3,132.17)
Net proceeds from line of credit	626,611.29	0.00
Proceeds from long-term debt	876,000.00	0.00
Proceeds for subordinated debt	300,000.00	3,505.54
Payments in subordinated debt	(15,051.00)	0.00
Net cash from financing activities	1,172,771.00	(59,754.04)
Net increase in cash	4,994.15	18,759.65
Cash at beginning of period	20,514.11	1,754.46
Cash at end of period	25,508.26	20,514.11

EXHIBIT 4. Balance Sheet

	1994		1993	
	Amount ($)	Percentage	Amount ($)	Percentage
Current assets				
Cash	25,508.26	0.6	20,514.11	0.6
Accounts receivable	1,367,210.50	31.6	807,408.15	24.4
Due from vendors	21,052.41	0.5	43,998.00	1.3
Allowance for bad debts	(28,572.37)	(0.7)	(29,622.93)	(0.9)
Inventory	1,814,591.78	42.0	1,427,707.23	43.2
LIFO reserve	(93,050.05)	(2.2)	(64,352.05)	(1.9)
Prepaid expenses	37,612.37	0.9	62,992.48	1.9
Loan receivable officer	55,000.00	1.3	0.00	0.0
Refundable taxes	2,400.00	0.1	0.00	0.0
Total current assets	3,201,752.90	74.1	2,268,644.99	68.6

(continued)

EXHIBIT 4—*Continued*

	1994		1993	
	Amount ($)	Percentage	Amount ($)	Percentage
Property and equipment				
Land, buildings, and improvements	1,326,421.95	30.7	1,243,959.23	37.6
Equipment	828,828.36	19.2	858,621.83	26.0
Total before depreciation	2,155,250.31	49.9	2,104,581.06	63.6
Accumulated depreciation	(1,159,565.04)	(26.8)	(1,165,246.04)	(35.2)
Net property and equipment	995,685.27	23.1	939,335.02	28.4
Other assets				
Notes receivable	11,805.77	0.3	70,209.81	2.1
Deposits	19,717.29	0.4	0.00	
Intangible assets, net	91,484.98	2.1	30,231.81	0.9
Total other assets	123,008.04	2.8	100,441.62	3.0
Total assets	4,320,446.21	100.0	3,308,421.63	100.0
Current liabilities				
Line of credit	1,660,425.25	38.4	1,033,813.96	31.2
Accounts payable	795,381.28	18.4	607,435.76	18.4
Accrued expenses	68,515.53	1.6	47,995.24	1.5
Current portion of long-term debt	96,599.00	2.2	61,709.00	1.9
Total current liabilities	2,620,921.06	60.6	1,750,953.96	53.0
Long-term debt				
Notes and mortgages payable	874,992.95	20.3	603,382.24	18.2
Less current portion	(68,467.00)	(1.6)	(61,709.00)	(1.9)
Total long-term debt	806,525.95	18.7	541,673.24	16.3
Other liabilities				
Subordinated debt	291,734.54	6.8	6,785.54	0.2
Less current portion	(28,132.00)	(0.7)	0.00	0.0
Total other liabilities	263,602.54	6.1	6,785.54	0.2
Total liabilities	3,691,049.55	85.4	2,299,412.74	69.5
Stockholders' equity				
Common capital stock, no par value Authorized 300 shares, issued 300 shares	60,000.00	1.4	60,000.00	1.8
Retained earnings, January 1, 1994 and 1993	949,008.89	22.0	800,380.07	24.2
Net income (loss) for the year December 31, 1994 and 1993	(379,612.23)	(8.8)	148,628.82	4.5
Total retained earnings	569,396.66	13.2	949,008.89	28.7
Total stockholders' equity	629,396.66	14.6	1,009,008.89	30.5
Total liabilities and stockholders' equity	4,320,446.21	100.0	3,308,421.63	100.0

EXHIBIT 5. Departmental Income Statement, April 1995

	Current Period				Year to Date				YTD Net Change	
	This Year $	%	Last Year	%	This Year	%	Last Year	%	Amount	Var %
Sales										
Cigarettes	1,063,750.83	57.6	1,323,757.93	60.8	4,583,199.56	58.1	4,740,391.41	64.2	(157,191.85)	(3.3)
Tobacco and cigars	50,943.71	2.8	55,051.33	2.5	209,720.26	2.7	167,187.01	2.3	42,533.25	25.4
Candy and snacks	276,958.04	15.0	330,240.31	15.2	1,192,332.26	15.1	1,218,033.07	16.5	(25,700.81)	(2.1)
Groceries and beverages	172,337.40	9.3	182,326.08	8.4	720,081.92	9.1	599,863.97	8.1	120,217.95	20.0
Food service	112,409.40	6.1	102,976.36	4.7	482,131.00	6.1	205,394.68	2.8	276,736.32	134.7
Paper and cleaning	76,181.83	4.1	73,288.30	3.4	320,043.87	4.1	158,254.00	2.1	161,789.87	102.2
Health and beauty aids	26,373.58	1.4	26,510.66	1.2	112,678.44	1.4	106,783.51	1.4	5,894.93	5.5
Sundries and seasonal	41,413.64	2.2	47,824.99	2.2	149,834.24	1.9	154,099.70	2.1	(4,265.46)	(2.8)
Produce and provisions	26,535.45	1.4	33,490.77	1.5	118,752.84	1.5	33,490.77	0.5	85,262.07	254.6
Service	643.18	0.0	–	0.0	1,878.87	0.0	–	0.0	1,878.87	100.0
Total sales	1,847,547.06	100.0	2,175,466.73	100.0	7,890,653.26	100.0	7,383,498.12	100.0	507,155.14	6.9
Cost of sales										
Cigarettes	1,014,240.91	54.9	1,257,570.03	57.8	4,388,422.13	55.6	4,522,156.52	61.2	(133,734.39)	(3.0)
Tobacco and cigars	42,109.54	2.3	47,068.89	2.2	177,983.40	2.3	142,932.92	1.9	35,050.48	24.5
Candy	235,500.05	12.7	277,712.07	12.8	991,568.36	12.6	1,032,040.64	14.0	(40,472.28)	(3.9)
Groceries and beverages	143,773.16	7.8	158,264.63	7.3	606,752.63	7.7	517,585.67	7.0	89,166.96	17.2
Food service	58,414.02	3.2	80,321.56	3.7	373,795.56	4.7	162,171.18	2.2	211,624.38	130.5
Paper products	52,656.59	2.9	54,325.47	2.5	240,083.35	3.0	117,950.24	1.6	122,133.11	103.5
Health and beauty aids	18,705.64	1.0	23,161.70	1.1	84,960.01	1.1	91,287.19	1.2	(6,327.18)	(6.9)
Sundries and seasonal	30,801.47	1.7	36,687.79	1.7	112,930.92	1.4	113,681.35	1.5	(750.43)	(0.7)
Produce and provisions	19,520.92	1.1	28,299.70	1.3	58,888.91	0.7	25,299.70	0.3	33,589.21	132.8
Service	227.97	0.0	–	0.0	(147.41)	(0.0)	–	0.0	(147.41)	100.0
Total cost of sales	1,615,950.27	87.5	1,963,411.84	90.3	7,035,237.86	89.2	6,725,105.41	91.1	310,132.45	4.6

(continued)

EXHIBIT 5—Continued

	Current Period				Year to Date				YTD Net Change	
	This Year $	%	Last Year	%	This Year	%	Last Year	%	Amount	Var %
Gross profit										
Cigarettes	49,509.92	2.7	66,187.90	3.0	194,777.43	2.5	218,234.89	3.0	(23,457.46)	(10.7)
Tobacco and cigars	8,834.17	0.5	7,982.64	0.4	31,736.86	0.4	24,254.09	0.3	7,482.77	30.9
Candy and snacks	41,457.99	2.2	52,528.24	2.4	200,763.90	2.5	185,992.63	2.5	14,771.27	7.9
Groceries and beverages	28,564.24	1.5	24,061.45	1.1	113,329.29	1.4	81,978.30	1.1	31,350.99	38.2
Food service	23,995.38	1.3	22,654.80	1.0	108,335.14	1.4	43,223.50	0.6	65,111.64	150.6
Paper products	23,825.24	1.3	18,962.83	0.9	79,960.52	1.0	40,333.76	0.5	39,626.76	98.2
Health and beauty aids	7,667.94	0.4	3,648.96	0.2	27,718.43	0.4	15,496.32	0.2	12,222.11	78.9
Sundries and seasonal	10,611.97	0.6	11,137.20	0.5	36,903.32	0.5	40,418.35	0.5	(3,515.03)	(8.7)
Produce and provisions	6,714.56	0.4	5,191.07	0.2	29,863.93	0.4	5,191.07	0.1	24,672.86	475.3
Service	415.21	0.0	–	0.0	2,026.28	0.0	–	0.0	2,026.28	100.0
Gross profit	201,596.62	10.9	212,355.09	9.8	825,415.10	10.5	655,122.91	8.9	170,292.19	26.0
Setting expenses										
Wages—sales manager	3,800.00	0.2	3,600.00	0.1	16,150.00	0.2	15,300.00	0.2	850.00	5.5
Wages—sales supervisor	5,760.00	0.3	5,760.00	0.2	24,480.00	0.3	5,760.00	–	18,720.00	325.0
Wages—outside sales	17,666.76	0.9	17,760.00	0.8	74,118.03	0.9	60,304.06	0.8	13,813.97	22.9
Wages—inside sales	4,132.44	0.2	3,777.68	0.1	11,603.91	0.2	17,641.09	0.2	(37.18)	0.2
Wages—purchasing	2,100.00	0.1	2,100.00	0.1	8,925.00	0.1	2,100.00	–	6,825.00	325.0
Wages—service	1,923.58	0.1	2,275.00	0.1	9,175.59	0.1	2,275.00	–	6,900.59	303.3
Payroll taxes	2,817.11	0.1	3,044.88	0.1	13,959.00	0.1	10,138.05	0.1	3,820.95	37.6
Group insurance	1,871.65	0.1	2,318.39	0.1	6,885.83	–	5,894.29	–	991.54	16.8
Workers' compensation	665.12	–	445.13	–	2,814.01	–	1,195.47	–	1,618.54	135.3
Salesmen expenses	5,067.53	0.2	5,472.28	0.2	20,029.17	0.2	14,242.30	0.2	5,786.87	40.6
Snapple Cooler lease	716.92	–	–	–	2,867.68	–	–	–	2,867.68	100.0

Commission expense	–	–	–	–	–	–	26.86	–	(26.86)	(100.0)
Collection fees	1,308.80	–	3,441.54	0.1	4,556.89	–	4,749.50	–	(192.61)	(4.0)
Credit insurance	651.67	–	742.48	–	2,606.68	–	2,969.92	–	(363.24)	(12.2)
Advertising and promotion	1,054.64	–	–	–	1,775.80	–	150.0	–	1,625.80	–
Total setting expenses	49,536.22	2.6	50,737.38	2.3	205,947.59	2.6	142,746.54	1.9	63,201.05	44.2
Delivery expenses										
Wages – delivery	10,797.45	0.5	14,981.11	0.6	46,927.76	0.5	36,249.02	0.4	10,678.74	29.4
Payroll taxes	1,126.79	–	1,615.49	–	4,866.60	–	3,874.76	–	991.84	25.6
Group insurance	240.13	–	332.66	–	2,234.80	–	1,257.60	–	977.20	77.7
Workers compensation	1,056.68	–	2,304.47	0.1	4,642.56	–	5,854.29	–	(1,211.73)	(20.7)
Insurance – fleet	1,500.00	–	2,834.09	0.1	6,000.00	–	11,336.36	0.1	(5,336.36)	(47.0)
Vehicle expense	7,407.24	0.4	6,594.91	0.3	31,617.64	0.4	20,003.09	0.2	11,614.55	58.0
Uniforms	558.60	–	355.60	–	2,674.55	–	1,563.65	–	1,110.90	71.0
Delivery truck lease	3,474.44	0.1	3,895.43	0.1	13,897.76	0.1	3,895.43	0.1	10,002.33	256.7
PNA trucking fees	5,812.20	0.3	6,513.00	0.3	26,131.30	0.3	6,513.00	–	19,618.30	301.2
Total delivery expenses	31,973.53	1.7	39,426.76	1.8	138,992.97	1.7	90,547.20	1.2	48,445.77	53.5
Warehouse expenses										
Wages – warehouse manager	5,512.00	0.3	5,992.00	0.2	23,426.00	0.3	16,392.00	0.2	7,034.00	42.9
Wages – warehouse	30,256.68	1.6	29,765.33	1.3	123,560.13	1.5	97,997.70	1.3	25,562.43	26.0
Payroll taxes	3,538.05	0.1	3,447.82	0.1	14,969.20	0.1	11,409.97	0.1	3,559.23	31.1
Gross insurance	1,027.99	–	1,720.06	–	4,118.79	–	4,957.46	–	(838.67)	(16.9)
Workers' compensation	2,410.94	0.1	6,119.38	0.2	10,372.61	0.1	18,971.72	0.2	(8,599.11)	(45.3)
Rent	13,565.00	0.7	13,565.00	0.6	54,260.00	0.6	30,260.00	0.4	24,000.00	79.3
Utilities	6,051.99	0.3	3,293.81	0.1	27,196.20	0.3	15,421.88	0.2	11,774.32	76.3
Property taxes	3,774.68	0.2	4,418.97	0.2	16,468.33	0.2	11,934.84	0.1	4,533.49	37.9
Insurance	2,155.41	0.1	1,449.45	–	8,721.64	0.1	6,771.80	–	1,949.84	28.7
Equipment rental	–	–	–	–	576.35	–	232.04	–	344.31	148.3
Equipment repair	2,531.71	0.1	409.94	–	6,396.55	–	2,799.45	–	3,597.10	128.4
Building repair	318.40	–	–	–	1,852.66	–	5.34	–	1,647.32	802.2
Warehouse expense	1,617.61	–	1,695.20	–	5,856.18	–	8,574.10	–	(2,717.92)	31.7
Warehouse equipment lease	2,911.34	0.1	1,645.24	0.1	11,645.36	0.1	1,645.24	–	10,000.12	607.8
Total warehouse expenses	75,671.80	4.1	73,522.20	3.3	309,420.00	3.9	227,573.54	3.0	81,846.46	35.9

(continued)

EXHIBIT 5—Continued

	Current Period				Year to Date				YTD Net Change	
	This Year $	%	Last Year	%	This Year	%	Last Year	%	Amount	Var %
Administrative expenses										
Management fees	15,000.00	0.8	18,000.00	0.8	60,000.00	0.7	72,000.00	0.9	(12,000.00)	(16.6)
Wages—electronic data processing manager	2,800.00	0.1	2,700.00	0.1	11,900.00	0.1	11,775.00	0.1	125.00	1.0
Wages—office	10,005.09	0.5	12,695.71	0.5	52,092.78	0.6	38,215.10	0.5	13,877.68	36.3
Payroll taxes	1,151.99	—	1,724.99	—	6,219.51	—	5,355.68	—	863.83	16.1
Group insurance	1,218.99	—	1,353.63	—	4,537.46	—	2,372.27	—	2,165.19	91.2
Workers' compensation	84.28	—	246.53	—	381.87	—	648.36	—	(266.49)	(41.1)
Payroll processing	568.95	—	607.83	—	3,062.70	—	2,570.93	—	491.77	19.1
Office expense	2,289.93	0.1	3,562.30	0.1	6,300.88	—	8,300.67	0.1	(1,999.79)	(24.0)
Order forms	2,751.98	0.1	3,436.62	0.1	7,280.24	—	7,182.28	0.1	97.96	1.3
Maintenance agreement	300.00	—	396.00	—	1,262.98	—	396.00	—	866.98	218.9
Bank service charges	1,142.48	—	984.86	—	4,477.06	—	3,627.98	—	849.08	23.4
Bank loan charegs	—	—	—	—	—	—	1,914.56	—	(1,914.56)	(100.0)
Travel and entertainment	1,334.36	—	564.98	—	3,308.21	—	3,366.48	—	(58.27)	(1.7)
Deferred wages	400.00	—	400.00	—	1,600.00	—	1,600.00	—	—	—
Computer expense	1,043.67	—	1,029.30	—	3,719.95	—	3,822.75	—	(102.80)	(2.6)
Telephone	3,521.59	0.1	3,018.39	0.1	14,022.88	0.1	10,061.81	0.1	3,961.07	39.3
Dues and publications	418.60	—	507.65	—	4,724.26	—	1,692.26	—	3,032.00	179.1
Professional services	4,595.00	0.2	4,736.40	0.2	12,838.32	0.1	13,822.04	0.1	(983.72)	7.1
Licenses and permits	84.00	—	1,277.80	—	697.80	—	1,502.80	—	(805.00)	(53.5)
Contributions and gifts	(70.00)	—	1,381.78	—	1,165.50	—	3,396.78	—	(2,231.28)	(65.6)
Insurance—other	—	—	—	—	1,200.00	—	1,220.00	—	—	—
Total administrative expenses	48,640.91	2.6	58,624.77	2.6	200,812.40	2.5	194,843.75	2.6	5,968.65	3.0
Total operating expenses	205,822.46	11.1	222,311.11	10.2	855,172.96	10.8	655,711.03	8.8	199,461.93	30.4
Net operating income	(4,225.84)	(0.2)	(9,956.22)	(0.4)	(29,757.86)	(0.3)	(588.12)	—	(29,169.74)	—

Other income (expenses)

Interest expense	(23,973.85)	(1.3)	(19,172.66)	(0.8)	(89,345.29)	(1.1)	(52,327.01)	(0.7)	(37,018.28)	(70.7)
Depreciation	(10,000.00)	(0.5)	(9,000.00)	(0.4)	(40,000.00)	(0.5)	(36,000.00)	(0.4)	(4,000.00)	(11.1)
Amortization	(411.11)	—	(948.85)	—	(2,719.92)	—	(2,403.85)	—	(316.07)	(13.1)
Bad debts	(2,000.00)	(0.1)	(2,000.00)	—	(8,000.00)	(0.1)	(8,000.00)	(0.1)	—	—
Finance charge income	2,656.02	0.1	2,518.80	0.1	11,419.63	0.1	7,085.45	0.1	4,334.18	61.1
Rental income	1,250.00	—	1,150.00	—	5,000.00	—	5,450.00	—	(450.00)	(8.2)
	−32,478.94	(1.70)	(27,452.7)	(1.2)	(123,645.6)	(1.5)	(86,195.4)	(1.1)	(37,450.2)	(43.4)
Net income before taxes	(36,704.78)	(1.9)	(37,408.93)	(1.7)	(153,403.44)	(1.9)	(86,783.53)	(1.1)	(66,619.91)	(76.7)
Business profits tax	(149.00)	—	—	—	(149.00)	—	—	—	(149.00)	100.0
Net income (loss)	(36,853.78)	(1.9)	(37,408.93)	(1.7)	(153,552.44)	(1.9)	(86,783.53)	(1.1)	(66,768.91)	(76.9)

Note: The YTD figures for the previous year include combined MWD and Chenard Wholesale amounts for the month of April 1994 only. YTD figures prior to the March 31, 1994, acquisition date are for MWD only. Figures for the current period reflect postacquisition combined amounts for both the current year and previous year.

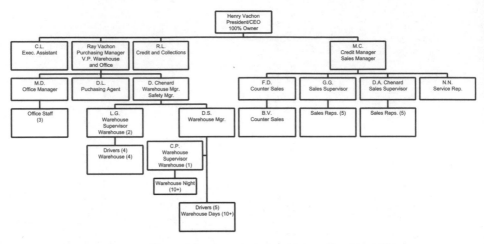

EXHIBIT 6. Organizational chart, April 1995. Initials and/or titles without accompanying names indicate individuals who are not family members.

Notes

1. The information in the "Company Background" section is adapted from company documents, with additions by the case writer.

2. The company issued a $300,000 debenture to finance the purchase.

3. Lost sales from the October to December period accounted for most of the company's decline in revenues for the year.

Industry Analysis

12. Clean Harbors

Alan McKim, president and chief executive officer (CEO) of Clean
Harbors, Inc., and a 1988 graduate of Northeastern University's executive MBA (EMBA) program, contemplated how to react to the
company's rapidly deteriorating earnings. For the first time in its history, the highly successful environmental services company had
begun posting losses, despite a two-year, $4-million reorganization of
the company that started in 1994. Toward the end of 1996, the entire

Richard Ivey School of Business
The University of Western Ontario

David Wesley and Professor Daniel McCarthy prepared this case solely to provide material for class discussion. The authors do not intend to illustrate either effective or ineffective handling of a managerial situation. The authors may have disguised certain names and
other identifying information to protect confidentiality.

industry was depressed by predatory pricing and underutilized capacity, with little relief in sight. Most recently, some analysts advised that McKim consider selling the company to a larger competitor. McKim, who had built up the company from nothing, did not relish the idea of letting go of his "baby," but he knew that ultimately he had to make the right decision for the company's employees and shareholders.[1]

Company Background

In the late 1970s, McKim was an engineering student attending night classes at Northeastern University. However, financial difficulties forced him to drop out of the program before completing his degree, and he instead went to work for a small oil spill recovery firm. When McKim's employer suffered a fatal heart attack in 1979, the twenty-four-year-old decided to strike out on his own with $15,000 savings and a mortgage on his home. He recalled the struggles of starting Clean Harbors.

> We were working out of a trailer in front of the garage of a friend's house. There were a lot of sleepless nights the first couple years; a lot of payless pay days; a lot of running to the mailbox to see if a customer had paid a bill so that we could meet payroll.

Leveraging the relationships McKim had developed with his former employer's clients, Clean Harbors was able to post $600,000 in revenues its first year. The company doubled in size every year for the next seven years, which set the stage for a well-received initial public offering in October 1987.

Through a combination of internal growth and acquisitions, Clean Harbors continued to grow rapidly throughout its history. By 1996, the company had sales and service centers in twenty-four states and operated twelve licensed waste management facilities in the northeastern and midwestern United States.

The company's fully integrated hazardous waste disposal services were offered within three broad service categories, namely treatment and disposal of industrial waste, on-site field services, and treatment and disposal of laboratory chemicals and household hazardous wastes. In addition, Clean Harbors offered training and consulting services to customers and maintained a twenty-four emergency response team to react to major oil and chemical spills. While industrial accidents such as oil spills were relatively profitable, they were also unpredictable.

Among the company's clients, chemical and allied products companies accounted for 19 percent of revenues, while gas and electric utilities accounted for another 14 percent. Additional revenues were derived from petroleum and transportation companies; universities; medical laboratories; and federal, state, and municipal governments. Approximately 80 percent of company revenues were from repeat customers with recurring needs for treatment and disposal services, including more than three hundred Fortune 500 companies.

Environmental Legislation

Federal and state environmental regulation had created a major source of revenue for the industry, as industrial firms attempted to comply with existing laws. Many producers of hazardous waste were ill equipped to undertake compliance measures on their own and instead relied on specialized service firms such as Clean Harbors.

The numerous regulations and permits required to store, transport, and dispose of hazardous waste created a barrier to entry for any new companies wishing to enter the industry. In order to avoid some of the difficulties associated with developing new sites, companies already in the industry often chose instead to acquire existing facilities from other firms in the industry. Field services, which involved the removal of waste, but not necessarily its transport and disposal, was the only component within the industry with low barriers to entry since it could be typically undertaken without special permits.

While environmental service firms generally benefited from government regulations, they also faced liability for contamination; accidents; and violations, such as improper labeling, transportation, or storage. Although most firms in the industry had to pay fines and cleanup costs, these typically amounted to no more than several hundred thousand dollars and usually did not have a material impact on the operations of these companies. However, occasional serious violations and accidents, particularly those involving bodily injury to employees or the public, could result in lawsuits of several million dollars (see "Accidents and Lawsuits"). Clean Harbors purchased insurance that covered many of these contingencies.

The most important act governing hazardous waste was the Resource Conservation and Recovery Act (RCRA),[2] which prohibited the disposal of hazardous substances in standard landfills and directed their cleanup and transportation. Companies engaged in the transportation, storage, and disposal of hazardous waste were required to obtain RCRA permits for each facility, including warehouses, depots, and incinerators. In the mid-1990s, the federal government also began requiring previously unregulated industrial incinerators to obtain RCRA permits before accepting hazardous wastes.[3]

Another important act was the Comprehensive Environmental Response, Compensation, and Liability Act of 1980, also known as the Superfund Act.[4] This law required industrial sites contaminated by hazardous waste to be restored to their natural state. Although the government initially funded the studies and cleanup necessitated by compliance with Superfund, the costs were to be ultimately recovered from those responsible for the contamination, regardless of the legal status of these wastes when the contamination occurred. Clean Harbors normally derived around 5 percent of its revenues from Superfund cleanup operations.

Under Superfund and RCRA, producers of hazardous waste retained responsibility for safe disposal, even when third parties such as Clean Harbors were hired to undertake remediation efforts on their behalf. Therefore, knowledgeable customers who did not wish to be held responsible for further cleanup resulting from improper disposal placed great importance on reliability and frequently audited contractors like Clean Harbors to ensure compliance. Clean Harbors had its own compliance team that assisted companies and government officials with these audits and provided monitoring and advice within Clean Harbors. The manager of the compliance function reported directly to McKim.

The Clean Air Act, which regulated air pollution, was another important federal law affecting Clean Harbors. To prevent the introduction of certain toxins into the air, certain wastes required pretreatment, such as that offered by Clean Harbors. Additionally, the act regulated pollutants generated by incinerators.

Environmental regulations were monitored by U.S. Environmental Protection Agency (EPA) and state equivalents. Clean Harbors was also subject to state regulations similar to RCRA, as well as local bylaws and zoning regulations.

Industry

1980s Growth

The introduction of environmental legislation in the late 1970s and early 1980s brought with it annual growth in the environmental remediation industry that approached 20 percent, as industrial companies attempted to comply with the new regulations.[5] During the latter half of the decade, Clean Harbors experienced growth on the order of 100 percent per year. However, the number of cleanup sites reported to the EPA "had declined steadily since 1985," and a significant amount of new business under federal contract was the result of the backlog created during the early 1980s.[6]

McKim hoped that Clean Harbors would eventually become a fully integrated company that could offer a complete "cradle-to-grave" service to clients. With that goal in mind, in the late 1980s, the company began to develop a state-of-the-art incinerator in Braintree, Massachusetts, a suburb of Boston. However, environmentalists and local residents protested the decision. After spending $19 million on project site planning and testing, Clean Harbors abandoned the idea. Reflecting on the event, McKim noted,

> It is very emotional for people who live in the communities. [The incinerator project] damaged our reputation in the state, and people began looking at us as part of the problem rather than the solution [to environmental problems]. People in the community don't want us there. They don't look at us positively. They do [look at us favorably] when there is an emergency, and we're the guys with the white hats who come in and clean up a chemical spill or something.
>
> We are now trying to be more proactive using technology as a way to reduce waste instead of using more archaic disposal methods. From a public standpoint, that is a good image to portray and it is something we want to build our reputation on.

1990s Decline

Large industrial waste producers, such as chemical and petroleum companies, often treated hazardous waste themselves, and only 5 percent of hazardous waste produced in the United States was handled by specialty firms. However, several accidents in the 1980s had seriously eroded public confidence in these industries. Perhaps the most notorious of these was the Union Carbide chemical leak at Bhopal, India, in 1984, which killed thousands of local residents and injured up to half a million others. By the end of the decade, public dissatisfaction with the chemical industry was at an all-time high. In an attempt to rebuild confidence, the Chemical Manufacturers Association established an environmental program, dubbed Responsible Care, and mandated compliance as a condition of membership. The program's goal was less successful than hoped, and public dissatisfaction remained high. However, member companies continued to implement hazardous waste reduction plans as part of the program. Rhone-Poulenc, for example, implemented a program to cut hazardous waste by 78 percent at its West Virginia facility, resulting in cost savings of approximately $1.8 million in 1995.[7]

Chemical companies that handled their own waste soon experienced excess capacity at their treatment and incineration facilities and began to offer environmental remediation and consulting services to third parties. Among Clean Harbors' new competitors were chemical giants Rhone-Poulenc, Monsanto, and DuPont. In 1994, Dow Chemical was added to the roster when it formed a wholly owned subsidiary known as Dow Environmental. The company planned to generate annual revenues of $1 billion by 2000 from its waste treatment and consulting services.[8]

In the 1990s, more companies sought to minimize the liabilities associated with hazardous wastes by introducing waste minimization projects. These efforts resulted in average annual waste reduction of between 10 percent and 15 percent during the first half of the decade, which translated into a 20 percent drop in demand for incinerators. Meanwhile, newer and more efficient incinerators were being constructed, which only exacerbated industry overcapacity.[9] This situation was expected to eventually correct itself as cement kilns, some of which had a difficult time meeting increasingly stringent EPA emissions guidelines, were retired from service.[10] Clean Harbors, which at the time had no incinerator of its own, had to pay third parties to incinerate waste handled by the company. Overcapacity benefited Clean Harbors as incinerators reduced prices in response to competitive pressures, which in turn reduced Clean Harbors' disposal costs.

The EPA also began transferring authority for monitoring cleanup projects to state agencies. Many state programs tolerated less thorough cleanups when companies offered to undertake remediation projects voluntarily. Real estate developers wishing to rehabilitate prime areas for other commercial uses had to pass state environmental standards before title transfers or rezoning could take place. However, less costly nonpermanent solutions were often deemed acceptable, such as constructing a parking lot over a contaminated site to seal in contaminated soil, which, under federal regulations, would have been removed and incinerated.[11]

"Some voluntary programs did not require cleanup of contaminated groundwater," while others allowed for only "partial soil cleanups" that did not "address all of the chemicals that threaten human health or the environment." A few states provided financial assistance to volunteers, and most states agreed to limit future liability for companies participating in voluntary programs. In Massachusetts alone, some five thousand sites were voluntarily addressed under the state program between 1993 and 1996. Contaminated sites with low real estate value, such as those in lower income areas, were rarely addressed under these programs.[12]

By 1994, the overall demand for waste services had dropped to five hundred thousand tons, while industry capacity remained at approximately eight hundred thousand tons.[13] The downward trend was expected to continue as the U.S. government planned to relax hazardous waste regulations, allowing some forms of untreated waste to be deposited in regular landfills. Furthermore, site cleanups would be prioritized on the basis of public risk, which meant that some sites would be dropped from the list of federal priorities.[14]

Industry Trends

Some industry players reacted to further declines in revenue by downsizing, consolidating, and liquidating assets. In 1995, one of Clean Harbors' main competitors gradually began to focus more on nonhazardous solid waste while reducing the number of RCRA licensed facilities.[15]

Other companies began to look for opportunities abroad. In the developing world, liberal environmental policies allowed many companies to continue producing products that were hazardous to the environment and to human health. For example, Ethyl Corporation, the Virginia-based company that developed leaded gasoline in the 1920s, continued to promote leaded fuels in less-developed countries long after these products had been banned in Europe and North America. As a result, nearly half the children in smog-plagued Mexico City were regularly exposed to "dangerous levels of lead."[16] With the globalization of trade, however, more governments were implementing sustainable environmental policies in response to pressures from foreign governments, trade bodies (such as the World Trade Organization), and environmentalists.

In Asia, where governments were beginning to deal with the problem of hazardous waste, the market for environmental services was expected to grow significantly, especially among higher growth economies. One U.S. company that hoped to benefit from this trend was Waste Management International, which became the first company to open a hazardous waste treatment facility in Indonesia.[17] In Europe, on the other hand, demand for such services was in sharp decline as corporations responded to governmental and public pressures to reduce hazardous waste production.

In the mid-1990s, Clean Harbors began talks with a European company to develop a joint venture in the United Kingdom. However, McKim was concerned about how to deal with the regulatory differences on a foreign venture while the company was still concerned with its U.S. expansion.

Acquisitions

The industrywide decline meant companies that had been very profitable in the 1980s quickly began posting losses. McKim, however, saw the eroding valuations of his competitors as an opportunity to expand the company's geographical reach and add additional services. In 1989, Clean Harbors began to more aggressively pursue acquisitions of smaller competitors and additional licensed facilities. By 1996, the company had made seven major acquisitions and expanded well into the midwestern states (see exhibit 1). McKim commented,

Many of the large Fortune 500 companies required us to grow geographically to meet their needs. They are trying to reduce the number of venders they do business with and to reduce their liability. . . . One hundred customers represent over half of our business. Out of those customers, they have about a thousand plants, so you can understand the impact losing one customer has on your business.

Expanding geographically allowed the company to reduce costs by shifting transportation of waste between regions, based on fluctuations in demand. Also, by increasing the number of facilities, the company could reduce the distance required to transport waste to its storage and disposal facilities. In 1993, Clean Harbors implemented a satellite tracking system for all its trucks to further enhance the efficiency of the company's transportation network.

In 1995, Clean Harbors purchased its first incinerator from Ecova, a subsidiary of Amoco, for $15 million plus royalties.[18] The never-used, state-of-the-art incinerator, which was completed in 1993, cost $66.8 million to build and had a capacity to burn forty-five thousand tons of waste per year. It was the only incinerator in the United States authorized to delist waste ash as nonhazardous, thereby all but eliminating any future cleanup liabilities. The property included fifteen buildings on 617 acres of land, as well as an on-site landfill.[19]

The incinerator was located near the community of Kimball, Nebraska, an agricultural town that grew out of an oil boom in the 1950s. In 1962, Kimball changed its title from "Oil Capital of Nebraska" to "Missile Center—U.S.A." after the U.S. government completed construction on four hundred nuclear missile silos which ringed the town.[20] The twenty-five hundred residents of Kimball overwhelmingly supported the incinerator and viewed the hundred jobs created by the project as a boon to the local economy.

Accidents and Lawsuits

Due to the nature of the industry, accidents and corresponding legal actions were not uncommon, and all environmental companies experienced such events. In 1996, two major lawsuits filed by employees and their families were pending against Clean Habors. The first resulted from the accidental discharge of chlorine gas that damaged the lungs of a company truck driver who sued for $9 million to cover personal damages and potential medical expenses.[21] Then, on October 7, 1995, a drum that had been mislabeled by a customer as nonhazardous exploded after being stored at a Clean Harbors site for an extended period. The explosion killed a company foreman and set fire to the company's warehouse. The foreman's family filed a damages suit against Clean Harbors and Lancaster Synthesis, the producer of the waste.[22]

While such incidents could paint a negative public image for a company within the industry, Clean Harbors continued to enjoy a good reputation. For example, while Clean Harbors had been cited for 73 noncompliance violations between 1990 and 1995, the company's main competitor, Safety Clean, received 599 noncompliance citations over the same period.[23]

Next Steps

As company earnings began to quickly decline in 1994, Clean Harbors began to implement a two-year plan that was expected to result in $10 million in annual savings (see exhibit 2). The company closed several administrative offices, shed noncore assets, and decreased the number of employees. At the same time, a new computer system was implemented to increase operating efficiency through more effective tracking and transportation of waste.[24] The total implementation cost was $4.2 million, a significant portion of which had been spent on fees to a leading management consulting firm. Nevertheless, in 1995, for the first time in its history, Clean Harbors posted a financial loss for the year.

Despite efforts to reduce costs and increase efficiency, in July 1996, after a 10 percent drop in revenues, the company decided to lay off an additional 3.6 percent of its workforce. Drum and bulk waste handled by the company continued to decline by 21 percent and 12 percent in volume, respectively. By the end of 1996, annual losses rose to almost $7 million from $2.6 million[25] in 1995 (see exhibit 3). Clean Harbors chief operating officer (COO) David Eckert lamented, "The industry is not growing and there is severe price competition."[26]

EXHIBIT 1. Major Acquisitions, 1980–96

	Company	Assets Acquired	Purchase Price ($)	Stock ($)	Cash ($)	Assumed Liabilities ($)
Apr-85	Clean Harbors of Braintree	transfer station	3,240,335		3,240,335	
Sep-85	Pollution Control	waste oil facility[a]	1,500,000		1,500,00	
Apr-88	Mid Atlantic Refinery	field service	1,229,000		1,229,000	
Aug-88	Alliance Technologies	analytical laboratory	1,486,928		1,486,928	
Sep-88	General Welding & Design	welding and design	1,650,000		1,650,000	
Jan-89	Murphy's Oil	waste oil facility	300,000		300,000	1,000,000
Jan-89	ChemClear, Inc.	transfer station	45,949,925	15,683,000	11,935,000	18,331,925
Feb-92	Mr. Frank	trucking broker	2,155,000	2,155,000		
Jun-92	Connecticut Treatment	transfer station	2,383,000		2,383,000	
Jun-94	Spring Grove Res. Rec.	transfer station	7,000,000	5,600,000	1,400,000	
May-95	Kimball Incinerator	incinerator	5,000,000			10,000,000
Sep-95	Chicago Facility	transfer station	0			Still pending

[a]Under Massachusetts law, waste oil was classified as hazardous.

EXHIBIT 2.   Company Reorganization: Estimated Savings

Task	Monthly Savings ($)	Total Savings, 1996 ($)
Workforce reduction: wages and benefits	515,333	6,183,996
Sale or lease of real estate properties	125,500	1,506,000
Reduction in consultants	62,000	744,000
Reduction in transportation expense	83,000	996,000
Sale of trucks	0	450,000
Refinancing truck leases	37,000	450,000
Pay truck drivers by mile instead of hour	50,000	600,000
Reduce air travel by 50%	50,000	600,000
Reduce accounts receivable by 5 days	12,000	144,000
Eliminate car phones	20,000	240,000
Reduce data communications costs	50,000	600,000
Total	1,004,833	12,513,996

EXHIBIT 3.   Selected Financial Data ($000s, except per share amounts)

	1996	1995	1994	1993	1992
Income statement data					
Revenues	200,213	209,250	207,073	200,114	176,193
Cost of revenues	154,608	156,779	146,132	134,525	116,473
Selling, general, and administrative expenses	36,326	39,574	38,910	42,296	35,923
Depreciation and amortization of intangible assets	9,827	10,081	10,250	10,319	8,884
Nonrecurring charges	—	4,247	1,035	—	—
Income (loss) from operations	(548)	(1,431)	10,746	12,974	14,913
Interest expense (net)	9,170	8,657	7,432	7,198	7,064
Income (loss) before provision for income taxes and extraordinary item	(9,718)	(10,088)	3,314	5,776	7,849
Provision for (benefit from) income taxes	(2,775)	(3,195)	1,619	2,645	2,774
Income (loss) before extraordinary item	(6,943)	(6,893)	1,695	3,131	5,075
Extraordinary loss related to early retirement of debt, net of income tax benefit of $823,000	—	—	1,220	—	—
Net income (loss)	(6,943)	(6,893)	475	3,131	5,075
Balance sheet data					
Working capital	14,245	11,053	20,814	18,320	15,487
Total assets	177,997	186,444	159,875	167,358	153,939
Long-term debt, less current portion	68,668	70,391	60,465	62,507	64,565
Stockholders' equity	53,587	60,374	67,326	67,371	58,065

EXHIBIT 3—*Continued*

Stock Price ($)	May-90	May-91	Mar-92	Mar-93	Mar-94	Mar-95	Mar-96	Sep-96
High	11.50	15.00	14.50	17.50	9.25	5.13	3.88	3.38
Low	5.75	9.25	9.00	12.50	6.63	3.38	2.38	1.50
Avg.	8.63	12.13	11.75	15.00	7.94	4.25	3.13	2.44

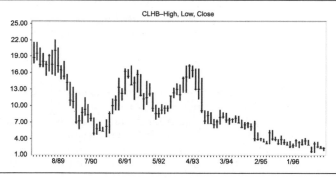

Notes

This case was made possible through the generous support of Darla and Frederick Brodsky through their endowment of the Darla and Frederick Brodsky Trustee Professorship in International Business.

1. McKim held approximately one-third of the company shares.

2. Enacted in 1976 to cover large quantity waste production and amended in 1984 to include smaller producers of hazardous waste.

3. Cement companies charged a fee to burn hazardous waste in kilns that were used to generate energy for cement production.

4. The act was called Superfund because of the large amount of funds ($16 billion) set aside by the government to finance environmental remediation projects. These funds were mainly obtained through a levy on chemical and petroleum companies.

5. "Chemical Companies Play the Environmental Market," *Chemical Week,* January 18, 1995.

6. "Superfund," United States General Accounting Office, November 29, 1994.

7. "Response Care, Chemical Makers Still Counting on It to Improve Image," *Chemical and Engineering News,* May 29, 1995.

8. "Chemical Companies Play the Environmental Market."

9. "Waste Management '94," *Chemical Marketing Reporter,* December 5, 1994.

10. "Chemical Companies Play the Environmental Market."

11. "State Voluntary Cleanup Programs," United States General Accounting Office, April 1997.

12. "State Voluntary Cleanup Programs," United States General Accounting Office, April 1997.

13. "Waste Management '94," *Chemical Marketing Reporter,* December 5, 1994.

14. "Tough Times for TSD," *Environment Today,* October 1995.

15. "Regulation," *Safety Clean 1995 Annual Report.*

16. "Back to the Future," *Institute for Local Self-Reliance,* September 9, 1997.

17. "Hazardous Waste Consolidation Continues," *Chemical Week,* January 4, 1995.

18. Clean Harbors agreed to pay royalties amounting to a percentage of total waste incinerated over a period of ten years.

19. Although the ash produced from the incinerator was considered nonhazardous, the landfill met hazardous waste landfill standards.

20. A Titan 1 missile shell was proudly erected in the town's park in 1968.

21. "$9 Million Settlement for Father Injured in Hazardous Waste Job," *Chicago Daily Law Bulletin,* February 28, 1996.

22. "Family Accuses Waste Firm," *Boston Globe,* July 3, 1996.

23. "Regulation," *Safety Clean Annual Report,* 1995.

24. Each shipment was assigned a bar code to allow for constant tracking. Waste could then be routed to the most efficient location for treatment or disposal.

25. This figure excludes a nonrecurring charge of $4.2 million incurred in 1995 to implement a reengineering plan, as discussed above.

26. "Clean Harbors' Losses Prompt Layoff of 50," *Boston Globe,* August 2, 1996.

13. NextCard

On the morning of Wednesday, July 10, 2002, Andrew Watson placed an order for two books at Barnes & Noble's web site (bn.com). Strange though it may seem, the credit card he used bore the logo of bn.com's main competitor: Amazon.com. He used this Amazon Visa card for many transactions a month. Whenever he used it, he earned "Amazon points." When he had accumulated enough of these points, Andrew could cash them in for certificates that could be spent at Amazon.com. The web site at which he cashed in the points for certificates was that of the credit card issuer, NextCard. The points program, often combined with other Amazon enticements, meant that Andrew got some great bargains at Amazon.com.

An order placed on June 21, 2002, provides an example of one of these bargains. Andrew placed an order for five books and a CD, which would normally have cost $68.22 including shipping. He had a $50 certificate, generated by using the Amazon Visa, and Amazon was at the time offering free shipping. This offer was subject to restrictions, but none of them applied to the June 21 order. The final cost was $9.28, so he paid Amazon less than $10 for the six items.

Yet on July 10 it was from Barnes & Noble, rather than Amazon, that Andrew was ordering. The reason was that Barnes & Noble was also offering free shipping but with fewer restrictions than Amazon. Barnes & Noble's offer applied to orders comprising at least two items.

Soon after placing the order, Andrew checked for the expected email from bn.com. But his email contained an unpleasant surprise: "We [bn.com] are experiencing difficulty in placing your order be-

---

This case was prepared by Andrew Watson and Alison Sauve.

cause your credit card issuer is not accepting this charge." Andrew made sure he hadn't mistyped the credit card number or expiration date. He rejected the fleeting thought that bn.com wouldn't accept a card with which its rival Amazon was affiliated. He then called the toll-free phone number on the back of the credit card.

A recorded message told him that his account had been closed due to the failure of NextBank. He was further informed that an attempt to sell the account had been unsuccessful. He'd known for a while that NextCard had been in trouble, but this was very sudden. When he got home that evening, there was a letter from the FDIC (Federal Deposit Insurance Corporation) waiting for him. The letter told him that in February NextBank (a subsidiary of NextCard) had failed and that since then it had been run by the FDIC as receiver. It added that his NextCard account was closed as of July 10, and it expressed regret for any inconvenience.

Andrew knew that NextCard was a credit card issuer specializing in e-commerce. He'd come to suspect that they were having trouble, since they had stopped accepting applications for new credit cards. This had been a disappointment to a friend of Andrew's who spent too much money on books and was interested in a card that would earn Amazon points and thus save money.

Andrew wondered what had gone wrong for NextCard. At first glance, it didn't seem as though NextCard's niche had been a bad one: e-commerce, although it had seen many firms fail, had been growing.

How Credit Cards Work

Evans and Schmalensee's book *Paying with Plastic*[1] identifies many "characters" in the credit card story. Here are some of the main ones, with an account of the part each plays in making credit cards work.

Systems, such as Visa and Mastercard, are actually joint ventures between the issuing institutions. Not all cards issued by Visa and Mastercard are credit cards. Many such cards, particularly in Europe, are debit cards, linked directly to the cardholder's bank accounts.

Issuing institutions, such as NextCard, collect money from both the cardholder and the merchant. For example, many cards charge annual fees to cardholders; all charge interest to cardholders who do not pay off their balances in full each month, unless they are running a particularly generous promotion. If you use a Citi Mastercard to buy from the university bookstore, the store (merchant) gives around 2 percent of the transaction value to Citi (issuing institution).

Many credit card issuers are banks. However, there are or have been some large nonbank issuers, such as AT&T and GM. Even among banks, there are considerable differences. MBNA, like Next-Card, specializes in issuing credit cards; indeed, the "About MBNA" page at its web site starts with the sentence "MBNA is the world's largest independent credit card issuer."[2] In contrast, credit cards are one of many financial services offered by Citi.[3]

Affiliates comprise the last set of characters we will introduce here. Amazon was affiliated with NextCard, as we can see if we look at the now-useless NextCard Visa cards, which bear the name of Amazon (affiliate), as well as the names of NextCard (issuer) and Visa (system). Cards like this are called "cobranded cards" or "affinity cards." There are two incentives for an organization to affiliate with a credit card issuer.

- Payment from the issuing institution. Amazon, at the time of its agreement with NextCard, expected to receive up to $150 million in fees over a five-year period.[4]
- Increased loyalty from the cardholder. Amazon points, earned by using the card, made cardholders more likely to shop at Amazon in the future. Of course Amazon had to buy this loyalty with points and hence with certificates.

It is quite possible, and not uncommon, for the same organization to be both merchant and affiliate for a given transaction. This was the case when Andrew used his Amazon Visa at Amazon.com but not when he used it to make purchases elsewhere.

The U.S. Credit Card Industry

Dolores Smith, the director of the Federal Reserve Board's Division of Consumer and Community Affairs, testified to a House of Representatives subcommittee that "Recent estimates suggest that in 2000, consumers used about 1.4 billion credit cards (or roughly 9 cards per holder) to purchase nearly 1.5 trillion dollars in goods and services in more than 20 billion individual transactions. It is estimated that at year-end 2000, consumers in the U.S. owed nearly $675 billion on general purpose credit cards."[5]

Most of the characteristics of the U.S. credit card industry identified in *Paying with Plastic*[6] still apply. In particular, the industry is characterized by the following.

- At the system level there is extremely high concentration, with Visa and Mastercard dominating.
- At the issuer level, on the other hand, there are a large number of competitors, with no few issuers dominating. In terms of 1997 bankcard charge volume, the largest issuer was Citibank (15.16 percent), followed by MBNA (9.36 percent). However, there is a trend toward consolidation. This is due in part to mergers and acquisitions in the banking industry, with further consolidation occurring as some issuers exit the industry by selling their card portfolios.
- Risk for issuers is high. Issuers offer to cardholders unsecured loans of indeterminate duration. Charge-offs (amounts owed by cardholders to issuers but deemed uncollectable) are the second-highest cost (32 percent of issuer costs in 1996), behind only cost of funds (40 percent). Issuer profitability declined from 1999 to 2000, with provisions for future losses accounting for much of the decline. Even after the decline, credit cards compared favorably with other commercial bank lines of business.[7] One of the sources of losses on credit card operations is fraud, to which issuers lose about a billion dollars every year (with merchants losing much more).[8]
- Competition between issuers is intense. Issuing banks spent about $10 billion marketing credit cards in 2001.[9]

One industry characteristic that has changed is growth rate, which was rapid up until the late 1990s[10] but has since slowed. The statistic that 150 million new credit cards were issued in 2001 may suggest that growth is still rapid, but two further statistics put it in perspective. First, almost 100 million existing cards were canceled by either the holder or the issuer, so that the net number of new cards in 2001 was about 50 million. Second, the gross figure of 150 million is a drop from the 200 million new cards issued in 2000.[11]

It is worth noting that not all descriptions of the industry are as uncritical as those presented in *Paying with Plastic* and in this case so far. A more critical account appears in Manning's *Credit Card Nation*.[12]

A more recent and specific criticism comes from the Consumer Federation of America (CFA).[13] In early 2001, credit card issuers were lobbying for changes to the federal bankruptcy laws. Their marketing and lending practices had been particularly aggressive in the previous year. These practices would, according to the CFA, increase the number of consumers who would get into credit trouble, just in time for them to be denied the option of bankruptcy by the legislative changes being sought by the very issuers who had encouraged their use of credit.

The CFA buttressed its criticism of the issuers by asserting that credit card profits in 2000 were at their highest level in five years. This presents a contrast to the preceding statement that profits were lower in 2000 than in 1999. The difference between the profitability statistics arises, at least in part, from the measure of profit employed. Pretax return on assets rose to 3.6 percent from 3.1 percent, while pretax earnings as a percentage of outstanding balances fell to 3.1 percent from 3.3 percent.

The Rise and Fall of NextCard

From Launch to Amazon

Jeremy and Molly Lent founded NextCard in 1996 with Jeremy as chairman and chief executive officer. He had previously been chief financial officer of Providian Financial, itself a specialist credit card issuer.[14] NextCard's mission was consistent from its foundation to its closing, by the FDIC, in mid-2002. It was an innovative, Internet-oriented issuer of credit cards.[15] Given the growth of e-commerce, shown in exhibit 1, this seemed to identify a promising niche.

Early press coverage was favorable. In 1998, Stewart Alsop told the readers of his *Fortune* magazine column how NextCard's technology enabled its execution (as reflected in the application process) to match its mission. He applied for a Visa at NextCard.com. His application was approved within two minutes. He was then shown the balances on his existing credit cards and asked which balances he would like to transfer to his minutes-old NextCard account.[16]

The following year, a *Business Week* article provided more detail on the technology and its advantages. NextCard posted banner advertisements across thousands of web sites, from which users could click to NextCard.com. Once there, they could apply for a Visa card and learn the outcome of their applications in seconds. The site approved one in every five applications; this was near the industry average. When NextCard's server approved an application, it offered a card with terms, such as the annual percentage rate (APR) of interest, set according to the customer's credit profile.

NextCard took more online applications for credit cards than did any other issuer, with about one in every four online applications being made at its site. However, some traditional card issuers were seeing the advantages of taking applications online.[17] Some of them charged a higher APR when they issued a card in response to an application made online than when they issued a card in response to an application made through other channels; they did so because they perceived a higher level of risk.[18]

NextCard's technology enabled it to track the sites at which it advertised, as well as the customers to whom it advertised and issued cards. Due to this ongoing assessment of the sites at which it advertised, NextCard was able to decrease its customer acquisition cost by 70 percent from 1998.[19]

NextCard's initial public offering (ticker NXCD, on NASDAQ) on May 14, 1999, was successful, in that the shares opened at a premium. NextCard offered six million shares at $20 each; trading opened at $36 (and closed that day at $33.50).[20] Some of this success may have been due to the boom in dot-com stocks.

NextCard won recognition and awards from several quarters. It was named the number one Internet credit card by *Gómez,* ranked as a leader in the Internet-driven economy by *Internet 500,* and listed as one of the 100 most important and influential Internet companies in the Internet economy by *The Industry Standard.*[21]

NextCard also received the approval of Amazon.com. Amazon was the largest online retailer. Exhibit 2 charts its sales and net income and thus illustrates Amazon's determination to "get big fast."[22] In November 1999, NextCard announced that it would offer the Amazon credit card. The deal was exclusive for five years, over the course of which Amazon expected to receive about $150 million in fees from NextCard.[23]

The advantages for NextCard were many. Amazon brought to the deal its thirteen million customers, a warrant to take an equity stake of just under 10 percent in NextCard, and its brand name. NextCard's stock price went up by over 50 percent on the morning of the deal's announcement. A columnist at the *Motley Fool* investment web site hailed NextCard for the Amazon deal and for its low charge-off rates.[24]

From Clouds to the Wreck

The same columnist identified a cloud on the horizon, in the form of what economists (and fools, apparently) term *adverse selection*. A year and a half later, the low charge-off rates persisted, but so did the cloud. In the NextCard context, adverse selection is "the process by which too many people with bad credit histories take advantage of the ease of the internet to apply for credit cards."[25]

NextCard's annual report for 2000, posted of course at its web site,[26] showed awareness of potential problems but took a confident tone. Jeffrey Lent, now chairman and chief strategy officer, noted in his letter to shareholders that NextCard had exceeded expectations, despite the turbulence of the markets in which it operated. He asserted that "the proof is in the numbers." Exhibit 3 shows some of the numbers provided in the annual report. The report did not provide full financial statements. John Hashman, president and chief executive officer, was consistent with Lent, emphasizing that the firm was ready for any weakening of the economy in the year ahead, having increased its reserves.

It appeared that the "new economy" was already weakening. NextCard's share price reached almost $37 in January 2000 but dropped below $5 by the end of the year. While its stock suffered along with much of the rest of the NASDAQ, fluctuating interest rates made life more difficult for NextCard as a credit issuer. The weaker economy also resulted in reduced demand for consumer credit. Given the competitive nature of the consumer credit business, such drops in demand tempt credit issuers to consider lending to customers of marginal creditworthiness.[27]

The turning point for NextCard came at the end of October 2001. As late as October 23, a press release about online holiday shopping showed optimism. But the last day of the month saw another press release, announcing that NextCard was under "new regulatory limitations."

The Company announced that it is taking several steps to increase reserves and limit certain lending activities of its wholly owned banking subsidiary, NextBank, N.A. (the "Bank"). These steps are being taken as a result of discussions with the Bank's regulators, the Office of the Comptroller of the Currency (the "OCC") and the Federal Deposit Insurance Corporation (the "FDIC," collectively with the OCC, the "Regulators"), as well as in consideration of the worsening economic situation.

As an additional result of discussions with the Regulators, the Company has further tightened its underwriting criteria to limit new account originations.

These steps were necessary in part due to a regulator-required re-classification of losses. Credit losses impose greater capital requirements on lending institutions than do fraud losses: "The Bank has determined that, effective in the third quarter of 2001, it will classify as credit losses certain loan losses which were previously recognized as fraud losses and reflected as other expenses in the Company's financial statements. The Company believes that a substantial portion of these losses are related to fraudulent account origination activity specific to the Internet channel."

As a result of this increase in capital requirements, NextCard was considered "significantly undercapitalized." It simply did not have enough capital relative to the volume of its credit losses. Next-Card retained the investment bank of Goldman Sachs to explore the sale of the firm to a "larger and better-capitalized entity." No such buyer was found.

The bad news does not end there. Less than a month after NextCard issued their press release, a press release from the law firm of Kaplan Fox announced the filing of a class action lawsuit against NextCard and "certain of the Company's officers and directors" on behalf of stockholders. The stockholders had certainly suffered losses; the October 31 press release led to a one-day decline of 84 percent, to $.87, in the stock price.

> The complaint alleges that during the Class Period, defendants knew but failed to disclose that the Company's financial statements were materially false and misleading and violated GAAP [generally accepted accounting principles] because, among other reasons, defendants: 1) improperly failed to adequately record provisions for NextCard's loan loss reserves; 2) overstated the gains recorded on the securitization of NextCard's credit card re-

ceivables; and 3) improperly classified certain losses on loans as "fraud losses" rather than as "credit losses." Because of this improper accounting, NextCard's reported earnings for fiscal 1999, 2000, and the first two quarters of fiscal 2001 were materially misstated.[28]

What's the Next Card after NextCard?

Andrew, as a cardholder rather than a stockholder, was not affected by this and other suits brought against NextCard. However, he had been affected by the termination of his card. Having a card refused can be inconvenient or embarrassing. He needed another credit card. But what should he check in order to avoid a similar incident with whatever credit card he got next?

In July 2002, Amazon did not offer new credit cards from Next-Card or from any other issuer. They did offer what they called a credit account, but it could only be used at Amazon.com, and did not earn Amazon points. Thus the Amazon credit account compared unfavorably in almost every respect with the Amazon credit card, which could be used anywhere that accepted Visa and did earn points. However, the card suffered from the overwhelming disadvantage that it no longer existed. Assuming that the world's leading online retailer would issue another credit card, what should Amazon check to avoid history repeating itself in the form of more Amazon cards being canceled?

Underlying both the question for Andrew and the question for Amazon is the more basic question: why did NextCard fail?

EXHIBIT 1. Growth in E-Commerce

	E-commerce ($ millions)	Percentage Increase from Previous Year	E-commerce as Percentage of Retail
1998	5,005		0.2
1999	15,004	200.0	0.5
2000	28,152	87.6	0.9
2001	34,382	22.1	1.1

Source: United States Census Bureau, "E-Stats: Measuring the Electronic Economy," http://www.census.gov/eos/www/ebusiness614.htm (accessed April 16, 2003).

Note: Figures for 2000 are the revised figures in the report for 2001 (rather than those originally published in the report for 2000). Figures for 1999 are the revised figures in the report for 2000. The percentages are computed from the revised figures.

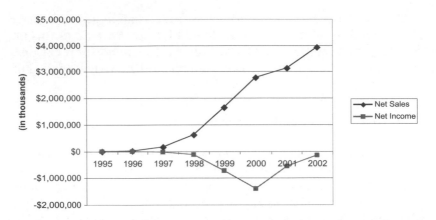

EXHIBIT 2. Amazon's sales and profits

EXHIBIT 3.   NextCard Numbers

	2000	1999	Comment
Assets under management ($ millions)	1,312	416	up from 66 in 1998
Accounts	708,000	220,000	up from 40,000 in 1998
Employees	820	287	up from 105 in 1998
Earnings (losses) per share ($)	(1.56)	(2.54)	This looks like a trend toward profit, especially given the 1998 figure of (5.07).
Charge-offs (%)	3.1		percentage of managed loans, up from 1999 but "well below industry average" (per Hashman, CEO)
New account acquisition cost ($)	65		record low for NextCard and lower than cost for the traditional direct mail acquisition channel

Source: 2000 Annual Report.

Notes

1   David S. Evans and Richard Schmalensee, *Paying with Plastic* (Cambridge, MA: MIT Press, 1999).

2. "Success Is about Getting the Right Customers . . . and Keeping Them," http://www.mbna.com/about_index.html (accessed April 11, 2003).

3. "How Citigroup Is Organized," http://www.citi.com/citigroup/about/index.htm (accessed April 11, 2003).

4. Brian Graney, "NextCard Links up with Amazon," *Motley Fool,* November 10, 1999, http://www.fool.com/news/1999/nxcd991110.htm (accessed April 11, 2003).

5. Dolores S. Smith, testimony, http://www.federalreserve.gov/boarddocs/testimony/2001/20011101/default.htm (accessed April 11, 2003).

6. Evans and Schmalensee, *Paying with Plastic.*

7. Board of Governors of the Federal Reserve System, "The Profitability of Credit Card Operations of Depository Institutions," June 2001, http://www.federal reserve.gov/boarddocs/rptcongress/creditcard/2001/ccprofit.pdf (accessed April 11, 2003).

8. Cardweb.com, "Card FAQs: Statistics," http://www.cardweb.com/cardlearn/stat.html (accessed April 11, 2003).

9. Cardweb.com, "Card FAQs."

10. Evans and Schmalensee, *Paying with Plastic.*

11. Cardweb.com, "Card FAQs."

12. Robert D. Manning, *Credit Card Nation* (New York: Basic, 2000).

13. Consumer Federation of America, "Credit Card Issuers Aggressively Expand Marketing and Lines of Credit on Eve of New Bankruptcy Restrictions," http://www.consumerfed.org/travpr.pdf (accessed April 21, 2003).

14. Heather Green, "How NextCard Hooks 'Em in the Clickstreams of Cyberspace," *Business Week e.biz,* August 3, 1999, http://www.businessweek.com/ebiz/9908/ec0803.htm (accessed April 11, 2003).

15. "About Us," formerly at NextCard.com (accessed October 18, 2002).

16. Stewart Alsop, "The First Powerhouse Bank of the Virtual World," *Fortune,* September 7, 1998, 159.

17. Green, "How NextCard Hooks 'Em."

18. Edgar, Dunn & Company, "The US Consumer Credit Market," March 28, 2002, http://www.dti.gov.uk/ccp/topics1/pdf1/ccusreport.pdf (accessed April 11, 2003).

19. Green, "How NextCard Hooks 'Em."

20. "NextCard, Inc.," *Hoovers Online,* http://www.hoovers.com/co/arc_ipo/3/0,2657,59443,00.html (accessed April 11, 2003).

21. "Awards," at NextCard.com (accessed October 18, 2002).

22. Robert Spector, *Amazon.com: Get Big Fast* (New York: HarperCollins, 2002).

23. Graney, "NextCard Links up with Amazon."

24. Graney, "NextCard Links up with Amazon."

25. Jeff Makos, "E-Payments; Thriving when it should have failed," *Credit Card Management,* May 2001, http://www.cardforum.com/html/ccmissue/may01epy.htm (accessed April 11, 2003).

26. NextCard, "2000 Annual Report," at NextCard.com (accessed October 18, 2002).

27. Constance Lozios, "NextCard Charges Ahead," *Business 2.0,* April 2001, http://www.business2.com/articles/mag/0,1640,14633,FF.html (accessed April 11, 2003).

28. "Kaplan Fox Seeks to Recover Losses for Investors Who Purchased Nextcard, Inc. Common Stock," November 16, 2001, http://www.kaplanfox.com/press/index.php?id=47 (accessed April 11, 2003).

Strategic Issues

Affecting Strategy:
What Does It Take?

14. A Hard Turnaround for Software

While executing a turnaround in any industry can be a difficult task, digging a software business out of trouble is a Herculean one. Certain product, financial, and labor market forces unique to the sector reinforce one another when a software company is performing well—and also when things start to go wrong. With the right formula, companies can ride a wave to fantastic success. When the environment changes, they must battle mightily to avoid being sucked into the abyss.

The odds against turning a software company around are thus extremely high. A McKinsey study showed that out of 492 companies defined as struggling, only 13 percent were subsequently able to revive themselves (see "About the Research" below)—an unusually low proportion. Yet turnarounds *are* possible, and the rewards make the effort worthwhile.

Why Is It So Difficult?

Software turnarounds are tough because, at the first signs of trouble, forces specific to the industry can combine to create a deadly downward spiral.

Take product market forces. Software is a winner-takes-all business in which three factors—the need for compatible technology in networked environments, high switching costs, and increasing returns to scale—unite to ensure that only a small number of players in most market segments survive in the long run. SAP, the German provider of enterprise-resource-planning (ERP) software, illustrates

---

This article was prepared by Mark Blumling, Kevin A. Frick, and William F. Meehan III.

the phenomenon: by the mid-1990s, it was such a clear leader in its market segment that it was able to claim, "We spend more on R&D than our competitors have revenues." This winner-takes-all phenomenon favors companies as they race toward market leadership but exacerbates the difficulties of companies that fall on hard times. Switching costs, for example, are high because software is expensive to integrate into corporate information technology (IT) systems; this hurts the losers because once a network has been configured around new software and employees have been trained to use it, the company isn't likely to switch to a vendor that might not be around to provide upgrades and service in years to come.

Forces in financial markets are another consideration. The volatility of share prices in the software sector reflects the cyclical nature of demand for information technology and, more important, the intangible nature of assets such as employees, customer relationships, and technology. The importance of these intangible assets—the essential drivers of economic value for software companies—is magnified by their scalable character and the winner-takes-all dynamic of the business. But it is notoriously difficult to price them, so investors must rely on revenue and earnings streams as proxies for their value. Software companies benefit when their performance is rising, as their return on invested capital can exceed 50 percent and grows extremely quickly. During a downturn, however, they are hit twice—once for their actual financial performance and again for what it implies about the value of their assets. If insolvency looms, investors flee because there are few residual assets to divide.

Finally, labor market forces contribute to the spiral. In most software companies, stock options form a large part of the employees' compensation. Once a company starts to fail, it can suffer a massive attrition of its workforce as options lose their appeal. The most valuable employees tend to leave first, diluting the company's intangible-asset base at the time of greatest need. If the company tries to hang on to this talent by increasing pay, net income suffers, thus further reinforcing the vicious cycle.

How to Turn around a Software Company

To escape from this spiral, a company must address huge challenges: revitalizing its core business, investing in new category killers, and ruthlessly cutting everywhere else. It must also regain the trust of financial markets by achieving liquidity, profitability, and growth. Finally, to attract and retain talent and to create a commitment-based culture and organization, the company must staff a core turnaround team and enable it to act quickly. This is a tall order, but companies such as PeopleSoft and Intuit have shown that it can be done.

Revitalize the Core Business

During boom times, the "land grab" mentality of most software companies drives them headlong into new geographies, products, channels, and customer segments. Given the overriding importance of scale within the industry, this approach is not only sensible but frequently imperative. When changing market conditions, strategic mistakes, new technologies, or shifts in customer demand abruptly end the boom, though, companies that have grown unselectively or neglected their core business find themselves saddled with bloated costs and with poorly defined products and services.

The first requirement for such a company is to peel back the layers it added during the land grab phase and to locate the distinctive part of its business—the part that once made it a market leader. This is usually the core software product, along with the customer and network relationships and the customer channels connected with it. More often than not, it suffered from neglect and underinvestment as the company expanded into other areas.

A practical starting point is the use of a handful of key customers—preferably leaders in the industry—to guide the company's redirection of its business. The loyalty of this group will also provide a base of customers who can serve as references for new business. Such endorsements are very important in software, since it is an "experience-based" product. PeopleSoft, which suffered from overexpansion and a downturn in the ERP market in 1998, revived its core ERP business by responding to the demand of its leading customers that it replace the client-server architecture of its previous products with a new World Wide Web–enabled product, PeopleSoft 8.

Ariba too is working with leading customers in an effort to restore itself to health. The company saw its market capitalization dive to $1 billion, from $40 billion, between October 2000 and October 2001 as the bottom fell out of the market for e-marketplaces, in which it had invested heavily. Ariba had neglected its core franchise: the provision of enterprise procurement software to help business manage their spending on office supplies. The company has now turned to its customers to discover what really drives procurement savings—limitations on purchases from nonapproved suppliers, for example—so that it can prioritize its R&D investments and so refine its principal offering.

Software companies targeting the broader consumer market should also examine ways to develop their core franchise. Intuit fell on hard times in the mid-1990s, when the market for consumer financial software began to mature and the company's Quicken software for personal financial management was challenged by a powerful new competitor: Microsoft Money. After Intuit found that its customers increasingly used the Internet for financial services, it responded by investing heavily in the development of server-based financial-services software through the web. The resulting Quicken.com software was one of the first successful online offerings in the consumer and small-office segment. Because the package was quick to access and easy to integrate with online financial services, it became a great success.

Invest in New Category Killers

Revitalizing the core business is just the first step. Software companies also need to come up with new category killers: products that will claim a market share of at least 30 percent. As with efforts to revitalize the core franchise, senior managers should draw on the views of leading customers, analysts, and partners.

Choosing investment opportunities is important, of course, but in all likelihood the most difficult challenge for senior managers will be actually turning these investments into concrete and distinctive successes. To have even a chance of winning against specialized competitors in this highly competitive industry, a company must have tremendous financial and human resources as well as a keen focus. Most unsuccessful companies handicap themselves by diluting their efforts across a variety of growth options.

Growth initiatives can be generated internally. Lotus, for example, suffered in the late 1980s, when Microsoft Excel challenged its core franchise: the Lotus 1-2-3 spreadsheet. The company responded by investing heavily in programmer Ray Ozzie's vision of a software platform that would foster collaboration in large networked organizations. The result, Lotus Notes, became one of the most widely used enterprise software applications in the industry's history.

Some companies have difficulty creating growth options in-house. In these cases, mergers and acquisitions, though fraught with risk, can offer a quick way to establish a position in a new market. When PeopleSoft looked for a product to complement its ERP package, it decided that its weak position in the fast-growing area of customer relationship management warranted the strategic acquisition of Vantive, then the second-largest firm in that sphere. PeopleSoft paid $426 million—quite a sizable amount relative to its market capitalization. But the resulting marriage of front-office (customer relations) and back-office (ERP) applications created a comprehensive e-business suite that no rival could match. Coupled with the introduction of PeopleSoft 8, the acquisition helped the company's share price to rebound from $16 in June 1999 to $43 two years later.

An acquisition also helped revive Manugistics, a developer of supply-chain-optimization software. The company hit a low point in 1998, when its stock price plunged by 72 percent, to $12.50. In 2000 it acquired Talus Solutions with the aim of expanding into the nascent field of pricing- and revenue-optimization products and services. Manugistics built its complete e-business supply-and-demand network by integrating its original product with Talus's profitability-optimization solutions, which fine-tune the scheduling and pricing of processing time. That same year, the stock price of Manugistics soared to $241.

Cut Ruthlessly Everywhere Else

Heavy investment in winning products must be paid for with cuts elsewhere. PeopleSoft, for instance, halted three of its large product-development projects, laid off 15 percent of its workforce, and redirected its remaining fifteen hundred engineers to develop PeopleSoft 8. The same relentless focus is necessary when a company develops new category killers. Any project that lacks the potential to achieve hundreds of millions of dollars in revenue must be scrutinized and, probably, eliminated. A company that fails to make these hard decisions has a poor shot at restoring its business to health.

Win Back the Trust of Financial Markets

A software company can reestablish its credibility with investors by setting clear expectations and consistently delivering on them. The most pressing need is often to establish liquidity through a one-off infusion of cash—because where tangible assets are few, equity investors can become skittish if a lack of cash becomes an issue.

Improving the use of working capital is the usual way of generating a one-off infusion of capital internally. A company can shorten its collections process for receivables and extend the process for payables, to give an example, while making sale and leaseback arrangements for its few fixed assets. Externally, short-term loans can sometimes be secured against the value of receivables. Given the lack of tangible assets, long-term debt options tend to be limited. But issuing new equity or equity-linked instruments is a possibility—albeit not a cheap one, since investors tend to buy at a discount when companies are in trouble.

As a second step, a company must increase its profitability. Profits are a measure of the health of intangible assets; without profits, investors will question whether the company really has a successful franchise in a market where leadership is crucial. Profitability and liquidity are also essential to make the financial community believe in businesses that compete in an industry in which 90 percent of a growing company's share value may reflect cash flows that will be generated more than ten years in the future. Moreover, a higher share price is vital if cash-strapped companies are to improve their strategic growth possibilities, such as mergers and acquisitions, because it provides a currency they can use to execute deals.

There are several ways to improve profitability in short order. A company can change the scope of its operations by eliminating products, customer segments, distribution channels, and geographies that are not linked tightly to its core franchise or growth options. It can increase its efficiency by improving the deployment and processes of its staff. And it can control outlays on IT equipment, office supplies, travel, and outside services—areas that might account for 30 to 40 percent of overall spending but that are often overlooked in the search for cost cuts. On such items, our experience demonstrates, savings of from 10 to 20 percent can be achieved, thereby enhancing a company's operating income by 3 to 8 percent. With a view to reducing total expenditures by 15 to 20 percent, PeopleSoft, for instance, reduced perks such as catered lunches and took a hard look at spending on telecommunications, travel, and information technology.

Appoint a Turnaround Team

Regaining the confidence of the market is one thing, but companies must look to their own organizations as well. When a company is sliding, senior executives tend to lose credibility, attrition within the ranks becomes rampant, and organizational discipline grows slack owing to poor management during the land grab years, when growth at all costs was rewarded.

To put all this right, a company must give a turnaround team the power to act fast. First, the board of directors should decide whether the current CEO—who often has an entrepreneurial mind-set and might have forfeited the respect of customers, investors, and employees by making too many unfulfilled promises—has the skills to execute the transition from growth to cost cutting and organizational discipline. The worse the situation, the more probable it is that the CEO will be forced out and an outsider brought in to manage the turnaround.[1]

A CEO hired from outside is likely to turn over the management of the company in order to change its skill sets and improve its credibility. He or she must first select five to ten senior lieutenants, who, whether old or new to the company, must receive professional and financial incentives to stay for at least two years (usually the time interval needed to reestablish stability) as well as the latitude to act quickly.[2] When the time came to arrest the declining fortunes of PeopleSoft, for example, founder and CEO Dave Duffield recognized that his dislike of bureaucracy and budgets did not make him the best-qualified person to provide day-to-day operational discipline. He brought in as CEO Craig Conway, an experienced software chief executive with strong operating skills who promptly replaced two-thirds of the company's senior managers with more seasoned executives.

As soon as the turnaround team is in place, the company should identify and secure the loyalty of its top twenty-five to fifty leaders in product development, sales and marketing, and services, for they can represent a substantial part of its intangible capital. The presence of these people, whose skills, charisma, and leadership qualities set an example for other staff members, usually helps stem the tide of defections. To retain and attract crucial talent, the company must offer career opportunities, financial incentives, and a compelling vision of its future. PeopleSoft, for instance, gave vitally important employees a special retention bonus of share options and cut the vesting time[3] in half.

Impose Organizational Discipline

With this top talent secured, the company has to introduce a disciplined organizational framework. The product-development unit, for example, must ensure that it meets its release deadlines no matter what external pressures emerge in the market, while the sales unit must implement rigorous account-management processes. At PeopleSoft, Conway quickly imposed strict accounting controls that prevented any investment greater than $100,000 from being made without his approval.

Tightening the reins is essential to turnarounds in any industry. The difference in software is that companies often need to put essential skills and controls in place *before* starting to tighten discipline. One provider of enterprise application software, with revenues of almost $1 billion, had to institute a budgeting process before it could rein in spending.

Only one software turnaround in eight succeeds. While the principles we have outlined provide a blueprint for recovery, management's commitment is just as important. Checking boxes isn't enough; success depends upon making the truly hard decisions.

About the Research

To determine the probability that a software company could achieve a successful turnaround, we studied the ups and downs of all U.S. publicly traded software companies in business for two or more years from 1990 to 2001, a time frame that covers varying economic climates, several product generations, the popularization of the Internet, and the dot-com boom and bust. Of 814 companies, the total returns to shareholders of 492 declined by 50 percent over a two-year period relative to the S&P Computer Software & Services Index. Using the 50 percent figure as the baseline, we then analyzed the performance of these 492 troubled software companies over the subsequent two years.

Only 13 percent (64) had a successful turnaround, defined as a 30 percent or more increase in total returns to shareholders relative to the index. Included were companies (such as BEA Systems, Oracle, and PeopleSoft) that have since claimed a place among the world's 25 most valuable software companies. Another 13 percent halted further declines in value, while 15 percent were acquired. The value of 59 percent continued to erode (exhibit 1).

Performance of 492 troubled software companies, 1990–2001, number of companies[a]

			Examples	Price per share	
				Start	Finish
Successful turnarounds[b]		64	• PeopleSoft • BEA Systems	• $16 (June 1999) • $5 (Oct 1998)	• $43 (June 2001) • $72 (Oct 2000)
Plateau[b]		63	• BMC Software • Advent Software	• $8 (Jan 1992) • $10 (Aug 1996)	• $8 (Jan 1994) • $10 (Aug 1998)
Further decline[b]		292	• J. D. Edwards	• $48 (Sept 1998)	• $26 (Sept 2000)
Acquired[b]		73	• Lotus Software • Tivoli Systems		

Source: Compustat; Thomson Financial; McKinsey analysis.

[a]From April 1990 to April 2001, the U.S. Department of Labor listed 814 businesses as prepackaged software companies under Standard Industrial Classification (SIC) code 7372. Of these companies, we selected 492 whose total returns to shareholders (TRS) declined by 50% relative to the S&P Computer Software and Services index over any 24-month period during those years.

[b]For the purposes of this article, successful turnarounds involved companies that outperformed the S&P Computer Software and Services index by 30% over the 24 months from the point when they first qualified as troubled (as defined in note a); companies that hit a plateau tracked the S&P Computer Software and Services index within a range of +30 to −30 during the 24 months after they first qualified as troubled; companies that experienced a further decline underperformed the S&P Computer Software and Services index by 30% over the 24 months after they first qualified as troubled; acquired companies were purchased within 24 months after they first qualified as troubled.

EXHIBIT 1. Turnarounds are tough.

Notes

1. A McKinsey study of the performance of more than 200 companies from 1986 to 1996 showed that those whose CEOs had been forced out performed three times as badly (as measured by share price performance relative to the index) in the run-up to their departure as companies whose CEOs left voluntarily. The odds of bringing in an outsider as CEO were five times greater when a departure was forced, indicating that boards are truly looking for a new approach.

2. George C. Mueller and Vincent L. Barker, in "Upper Echelons and Board Characteristics of Turnaround and Nonturnaround Declining Firms," *Journal of Business Research* 39, no. 2 (1997): 119–34, note that companies in turnarounds are more likely to have CEOs who also hold the title of chairman, indicating that they have greater authority.

3. The time period after which the employee gains the right to the options.

15. Symantec's Strategy-Based Transformation

One of the sacrosanct rules of sustaining shareholder value is to underpromise and overdeliver. Never is this rule truer, nor are the consequences of delivering less than what's promised worse, than in a corporate turnaround situation. So when the Symantec Corporation, a global software technology company based in Cupertino, California, put together a business plan committing to annual revenue growth of 20 percent and delivered something closer to a flat line, Wall Street's punishment was swift and severe: 38 percent of the company's value vanished in a day. That was in June 2001, five quarters after John Thompson, a twenty-eight-year IBM veteran, had been recruited to "fix" the Silicon Valley software company. One quarter after becoming Symantec's chairman, president, and chief executive officer in April 1999, Mr. Thompson announced a transformational strategy to take the company "upmarket," from its roots in consumer software, to sell so-called enterprise systems, the software installations used by big corporations. He also promised to nearly double revenues and break the $1 billion ceiling that separates minor software players from majors.

Conceptually, the strategy was a simple one. Symantec dominated the consumer market for personal computer antivirus software, programs that users install to help block bits of rogue code from invading their machines. Many companies already used Symantec's antivirus product, but as large enterprises embraced the Inter-

---

This article was prepared by Lawrence M. Fisher.

net, they would need more robust and more varied software solutions to keep their data safe and secure. Symantec's strategy was to become the complete provider of security products.

But the real world has a way of intruding on the best-laid strategies of even the most capable leaders. As Symantec's leadership team turned its attention to acquiring and building capabilities and products for the enterprise customer, the company's consumer business was blindsided by a series of market disruptions that slashed year-over-year sales by 21 percent in the quarter ended June 30, 2001. "It was the darkest hour of my career because I knew the team had worked really hard," Mr. Thompson reflected in a November 2002 interview at Symantec's Cupertino headquarters. The setback "caused us to pause to think about how we were, in fact, going to manage ourselves in a very, very challenging time—a time when we had become confident in our strategy, but we weren't really sure that the market was going to allow us to execute the strategy given where we were," he says. "What's even more relevant is, How do you recover? And how do you rebuild your credibility?"

How Symantec recovered and ultimately did deliver on Mr. Thompson's billion-dollar promise is a lesson in the realities of corporate transformations. A strategy-based transformation is an opportunity to make a significant change and lasting improvement in the economic value of a company by taking it in a new direction using any number of different approaches—mergers, restructurings, new business models, new markets, or a combination thereof. Symantec's transformation involved acquiring technology and management capabilities, learning new sales and marketing approaches, and skillfully positioning business leaders to drive change and execute strategy. "John came in and gave the company a greater sense of purpose by doing a small number of moves that seemed obvious after he did them. Some of it's like Management 101, but his execution has been brilliant," says Roger McNamee, cofounder and general partner of Integral Capital Partners, which counts Symantec among its ten largest stockholdings.

But as the consequences of Symantec's bad quarter show, a company in such a transition must be as resilient as it is flexible to recover from stumbles along the way. And recover Symantec did, taking its market capitalization from about $600 million to more than $6 billion within three years, even as the stock values of most software companies were plummeting.

Listen, Learn, Plan

Founded in 1982, Symantec was one of the earliest PC software companies and a long-term survivor, even as once-brighter lights like the Lotus Development Corporation, Borland International, and Word-Perfect dimmed or disappeared through acquisitions. Symantec produced a broad range of mostly acquired products, ranging from software development tools for programmers to ACT, the most popular contact management program. The 1990 acquisition of Peter Norton Computing Inc., maker of the leading antivirus product, Norton Utilities, cemented Symantec's hold on the market for PC utilities, which are programs that help diagnose and fix disk-drive errors and perform other bits of computational housekeeping.

But by the end of the 1990s, Symantec's sales and earnings were erratic; aggressive competition had eroded profit margins, and, after five workforce reductions in five years, morale was low. The company had largely missed the Internet boom. In the fiscal year ended March 31, 1999, Symantec shares were trading at about one times revenues, which then stood at $644 million. Other software companies were commanding five times revenues or more. That Symantec's valuation was so low when Mr. Thompson joined the company was testimony to a company that had lost its way. "The situation was untenable," says George Reyes, a Symantec board member and former vice president and treasurer of Sun Microsystems Inc. "It was either fix the company or continue to unravel and go into a death spiral."

At that time, Symantec, with just more than two thousand employees, had three business units: Remote Productivity Solutions, Security and Assistance, and Internet Tools. Remote Productivity encompassed fax software; the ACT contact manager software; and PC Anywhere, a software that allows users to connect multiple PCs. Security and Assistance products included Norton AntiVirus as well as programs for encrypting e-mails and keeping hard drives healthy. Internet Tools offered a set of software that developers could use to create interactive Internet sites and applications using the Java programming language.

Each of these business units had some market-leading products. However, the products had little in common besides a distribution channel, and even some of the popular programs were consistently unprofitable because of high development and support costs. Plus, customers did not closely identify the best-selling product, Norton

AntiVirus, with the Symantec brand. In fact, the product still carried a prominent picture of Peter Norton, founder of the acquired company, on its box.

"Part of the problem was [Symantec] did too many things, and many of them not too well," recalls Mr. McNamee. Mr. Thompson, who saw this problem immediately, pushed the company to focus on what it already did well, rapidly jettisoning weaker products, and even some strong ones, that fell outside his new strategy.

"The idea I had was I would just listen for ninety days, and within a hundred days we would have a plan," Mr. Thompson says. "But a couple of things became clear right away. The Internet Tool business had no linkage to anything else—we didn't even use the product ourselves—and it was losing money. The company had no strategy for an Internet-based economy; there was no web distribution, and there were no web-based products."

At an offsite meeting about seventy-five days into his tenure, Mr. Thompson brought together senior managers to determine the company's new direction. The first decision was to concentrate on security, which was clearly the company's strong suit. Another early decision was to restructure Symantec according to customer sets, rather than by products or geographies.

At the same time, a core leadership team, consisting of two Symantec veterans and two new recruits, was formed to drive change. Stephen Cullen, a senior marketing executive who had joined the company in 1996, was to lead the consumer business, and Gail Hamilton, recruited from the Compaq Computer Corporation, was put in charge of the new enterprise initiative. Rounding out the team were Symantec's chief financial officer, Greg Myers, and a longtime IBM colleague of Mr. Thompson's, Donald Frischmann, who was recruited to head communications and brand management.

The biggest challenge facing a change agent can be the task of gaining support from subordinates. As John P. Kotter of Harvard Business School notes in his recent book, *The Heart of Change: Real-Life Stories of How People Change Their Organizations,* "today, a single individual cannot effectively handle large-scale, fast-paced change alone. It is important to get the right people in place who are fully committed to the change initiative, well-respected within the organization, and have power and influence to drive the change effort at their levels."

In driving the transformation of Symantec, the core leaders created four teams, composed of their respective direct reports, to look at markets, evaluate opportunities, and identify those with substantial potential revenues and long-term viability. The teams considered a diverse range of customers and markets, such as Internet service providers, the managed-services market, IT systems management, and remote PC connectivity. And through a collaborative process, they determined that the company would move aggressively into the corporate computer security market. "John set expectations, and he got key leaders involved in determining where we would go," Mr. Cullen says. "It was easy for these leaders, because they were already working on these projects, to see our direction when we laid out all of the strategic alternatives. Then we made decisions and said how we thought they were going to impact the company."

As Professor Kotter suggests, the team structure helped gain acceptance of these decisions throughout Symantec, even in pockets of the company where some of the least successful products still had intense support. Some decisions were easy, like spinning off the money-losing Internet Tools business, and some were harder, like selling the popular ACT program. But although ACT had defined the category of contact management for a generation of PC users, it had no connection to security, so Mr. Thompson felt it had to go. "It's important when a company goes through a change like this to create some sense of focus," Mr. Thompson says. "ACT, while profitable, did not grow very fast. It was a development and support distraction. Selling ACT helped people realize I was serious."

Still, to be taken seriously in the enterprise security market, the company had to build or buy capabilities it lacked. "It went from top to bottom, there were so many things that needed to be addressed to make this transition," says Ms. Hamilton, who had led enterprise units at both Compaq and Hewlett-Packard Company. "Immediately, we needed new development processes, with a level of performance testing and scale to ensure we were developing products that could serve hundreds of thousands of users," she says. "Second, we had to establish a much closer relationship with customers. We needed to share our plans with them, we needed to understand their businesses and the problems they faced going forward rather than just immediate issues."

Symantec's needs were all the more urgent because as a company that published (i.e., packaged and marketed) software rather than developing its own, the company had no technological base, aside from the antivirus expertise acquired in the Peter Norton deal and some smaller technology acquisitions from IBM and the Intel Corporation. As a publisher, Symantec was hard pressed to attract programmers, who at the time were being courted with big equity stakes in Internet startups.

Indeed, the software-publisher business, an intermediary model that had flourished in the early days of PC software, had largely disappeared with the consolidation of the industry and the spread of the World Wide Web, which let any enterprising programmer distribute his or her software directly to consumers. Companies such as Broderbund Inc., which resold independent developers' programs, were gone. The might of the industry now lay with larger software developers that could leverage an essential technological base, as the Microsoft Corporation did with the Windows operating system and the Oracle Corporation did with its relational databases.

A Serial Acquirer

Symantec had no time to build a technological base, so it had to buy one. The acquisitions had to follow the evolution of security needs. In the early days of the personal computer, hacker attacks were primarily associated with viruses, little programs that, like their biological counterparts, used their hosts to replicate—sometimes benignly, sometimes not. Security software used to be synonymous with antivirus software, and blocking these intruders was a simple matter of scanning for known code patterns. But because hackers have become more sophisticated, and attacks have mutated to include industrial espionage and potential terrorist actions, enterprises now face a broad range of so-called blended threats.

Combating these more varied threats requires a more varied, and more proactive, approach to security software. Vulnerability assessment programs help enterprises determine their risk exposure; intrusion detection identifies unauthorized uses of the network before they cause damage; virtual private networks and authentication services allow remote privileged users to get past the firewalls designed to keep intruders out. Security management keeps track of all these systems, chronicles security "events," and distinguishes genuine threats from false alarms.

The only piece of this extensive puzzle that Symantec already owned was antivirus, so the company had to become a serial acquirer. Its historic strategy had been to buy disparate products to pump through its distribution channel; now each acquisition was intended to add a piece to the business portfolio and broaden its base in enterprise security technology. Each deal strengthened Symantec's position in the security market; each added to the company's technology base and, perhaps even more important, to its talent pool.

"At that point in time, it was almost impossible for Symantec to hire anybody," Mr. Thompson says. "We were not hip; we were a publisher, not a developer; we were not a dot-com; and we had a history of layoffs. My strategy was to acquire little companies and pay about $1 million a head. I felt that would get us the talent we needed and hopefully some technology, too."

In February 2000, it acquired L3 Network Security, which offered products and consulting services designed to help enterprises assess their vulnerability to hacker attacks and rapidly detect systems intrusions when they did occur. Some of the world's largest companies were already using L3's Retriever and Expert products to design, implement, and manage network security.

Symantec followed that deal with an $18 million investment in Brightmail Inc., which makes products that enable service providers to manage and protect their e-mail systems. Symantec had previously partnered with Brightmail, whose technology filters messages to block spam and e-mail-borne viruses and could be extended to provide other forms of content control.

To enter the enterprise market, not only did Symantec need new engineering talent, it needed sales talent. The logistics of selling $100,000 products to corporations are vastly different from those of selling $100 products to consumers. Add one of the critical differences between consumer software and the enterprise business is the sales channel. Symantec sold products such as Norton Utilities and ACT through big distributors, who in turn sold them to retailers who stacked the yellow boxes on shelves for consumers. Some of the products were also sold preinstalled on personal computers from such companies as the Dell Computer Corporation and Compaq. A limited number were sold by subscription, with upgrades delivered online.

In contrast, corporate customers are used to buying software directly from the manufacturer. Entry in this marketplace pitted Symantec against the well-trained sales forces of companies like IBM and Cisco Systems Inc., both of which are significant players in the enterprise security business. These companies also field armies of consultants and engineers, who generate additional revenues by aiding in the implementation of the programs they sell.

Symantec gained some of those capabilities, 750 people, and vital products and technology in the December 2000 acquisition of Axent Technologies Inc. for $990 million in stock. Axent's Enterprise Security Manager and Prowler series were the industry's leading vulnerability-assessment and intrusion-detection products, used by 45 of the Fortune 50. Axent also had the global reach of a network of qualified value-added resellers (VARs), as well as its own enterprise sales force.

For Symantec management, the deal was part of a logical transition. Initially, the company had focused on buying technology assets and engineering talent. With Axent, it was adding to its technology base yet again, and it was also moving into a new phase by acquiring marketing and sales capabilities aimed directly at enterprise customers. "Early on we bought technical talent, not sales talent. In the second phase, the last two-and-a-half years, we've started to bring into the company people with strong direct-relationship sales capabilities," says Symantec CFO Greg Myers.

But, following the series of smaller acquisitions, the Axent deal took Wall Street by surprise. Symantec's market cap dropped by 28 percent the day after the announcement. "They didn't expect me to do one that big," Mr. Thompson says. "Also, there was a strong belief that Axent was damaged goods. They had a tough 1999 and appeared to be struggling against the competition. The reality was that Axent had some terrific technology and people who knew what we needed to get done. It was in my mind a transformational transaction, and it really did catapult our company's enterprise strategy more profoundly than anything we had done."

Nevertheless, Symantec could never acquire its way to sales or support parity with established enterprise software players. Instead, the company adopted a new distribution channel, which included creating a network of some fourteen thousand partners and introducing its first partner certification program. These partners, from large accounting firms and IBM itself to VARs, supplement Symantec's small sales force and add their own implementation services.

The Axent acquisition was also the catalyst for changing Symantec processes to support an enterprise business. Axent had systems in place for serving major corporate customers, and just as important, its senior executives had an understanding of the service and support needs of that market. As the former Axent executives assumed leadership roles at Symantec, they helped guide the company's investment in and deployment of new systems to undergird the new enterprise thrust.

As a global enterprise, for example, Symantec needed to become euro compliant. It needed better overall enterprise resource planning (ERP) to make sure management was in control of critical processes. Because Symantec's customer relationships had historically been with the distribution channel, not the end user, it now needed end-user-centered systems to track problems and make sure they got solved, and to track relationships on a global basis.

Team Transformation

Not every executive bought into Symantec's rapid change scenario, and those who did not were politely but rapidly moved out of the company. The leadership team welcomed it. Mr. Thompson says that increased turnover is actually desirable in a company undergoing a transformation. "Of the nine people who are on the senior management team, only two are left from the day when I arrived," he says. "Today, we are just shy of four thousand people; we had a little over two thousand when I arrived. Of those four thousand people, more than half have less than two years of service in our company. So, as we have retooled our strategy, we have completely retooled the team as well to work that strategy, because those two things in my mind truly go hand-in-glove."

Some members of the new team came from acquired companies; others had been Mr. Thompson's colleagues at IBM. But in many cases, Symantec's key executives were senior people, like Ms. Hamilton, the former Compaq executive, who were recruited from market leaders. "John went out and got high-priced talented leadership and positioned them throughout the company," says Greg Myers, one of the two remaining members of the old team.

Mr. Thompson also changed the compensation system. As a typical young aggressive technology company, Axent had based a large percentage of its compensation on stock options, which were allocated according to rank and performance. Because Symantec's shares had long underperformed those of other Silicon Valley companies, it had compensated employees with higher-than-typical salaries, and perks, like BMWs. One of the ways the company aligned internal processes with the new strategy was to shift to a more incentive-based compensation structure.

"As a method for attracting and retaining talent, the prior leadership had used salary and cash compensation a little above the norm," Mr. Thompson says. "As such, they had more assured compensation rather than risk-based compensation, higher than I expected for a team in a high-tech arena. Option grants were not related to the performance of an individual; it was more socialistic where everybody gets the same. So we lowered the base rate, but accelerated the growth rate." Now employees get far fewer options to start but gain many more, and more rapidly, if they exceed performance expectations. Option grants are also more heavily weighted to senior management than was previously the case at Symantec.

Mr. Thompson, no fan of distributed management, was quick to address organizational issues. At a time when many companies are implementing a "centerless" corporation organizational model, which is based on minimizing overhead and hierarchy while pushing critical decision rights to the periphery, Symantec has pulled those responsibilities back to corporate headquarters. Mr. Thompson blames the old structure, in which regions and business units each determined their own policies, for much of the old company's lack of focus.

Centralized decision making means Symantec now has fewer meetings, with fewer people attending. "We used to have this monthly meeting with all the executive staff; everybody would show up in Cupertino from all over the world," Mr. Thompson says. "We'd talk about issues, and then people would go away and do whatever they wanted to do."

"Strategic decisions are corporate decisions, not regional," Mr. Thompson says. "It was time for some of our regional leaders to accept that they were part of a team rather than feudal lords."

Mr. Thompson is also a bit of a contrarian when it comes to product strategy. Although individual PC users (and corporations buying PCs for employees) have largely given up buying a word-processor program from WordPerfect, a spreadsheet from Lotus, and a database from Ashton-Tate in favor of Microsoft's all-in-one Office suite, enterprise customers select business-process software mostly by clinging to a best-of-breed approach. That is, corporations often buy what they perceive is the best application in each category and let their internal information technology staffs integrate them. For example, they continue to buy human resource management software from PeopleSoft Inc., or customer relationship management (CRM) software from Siebel Systems Inc. and ERP products from SAP AG, rather than buying Oracle's E-Business Suite. Symantec itself buys business applications in this way.

Security software has been purchased the same way. According to the International Data Corporation (IDC), security software includes security management, access control, authentication, virus protection, encryption, intrusion detection, vulnerability assessment, and perimeter defense. Symantec provides virus protection, firewall and virtual private network, vulnerability management, intrusion detection, Internet content and e-mail filtering, remote management technologies, and managed security services.

But Mr. Thompson believes companies will choose to buy an integrated security system rather than purchase antivirus from one vendor, firewall technology from another, and so forth. "Our strategy is different from every other security software company's in the industry; we are not following a best-of-breed, point-product strategy," he says.

The idea is that, although one vendor may offer a security component that outperforms a Symantec product, the cost and complexity of integrating multiple products outweigh any benefit to a corporation. This argument is similar to Oracle's pitch for its E-Business Suite, which has yet to take significant market share away from the established players. It is not clear whether the enterprise security market will be any different.

"We buy best of breed when it comes to product," says one customer, Jeff Moore, president of EcommSecurity Inc. in Atlanta. "We don't recommend 100 percent of the Symantec product line."

Ms. Hamilton counters, however, that most buyers of corporate security products are trying to reduce the number of vendors they deal with but continue to buy from multiple sources. Although she believes Symantec's offerings are competitive across the spectrum, she also stresses their ability to operate with other companies' products. "Our strategy is not, 'here's a bundled suite that all works together, and take it, it's all or nothing,'" she says. "It's modular, and customers can take different pieces over time, blending our product with others."

In any case, its product strategy appears to be working, allowing Symantec to claim the No. 1 spot in the $6 billion worldwide security market in 2002, with a 12 percent share, according to IDC. Using slightly different criteria, a November 2002 Gartner Dataquest report also shows Symantec as the world's leading security software provider on the basis of new license revenue and market share in 2001. That report showed that Symantec's market share of the worldwide security industry increased from 14.7 percent in 2000 to 21 percent in 2001, leading the list of the world's top twenty-one security software vendors.

The Comeback

What happened in that wretched quarter back in 2001, and how did Symantec recover from it? Part of the problem was that while the company's management was focused intently on its transformation goal to become a leader in serving the enterprise customer, the mainstay consumer business suffered. Some products were not upgraded rapidly enough to match competitors' products, and the consumer unit's marketing efforts remained diffuse.

More critically, a confluence of external events struck the company in that quarter. Worldwide sales for all consumer software went into recession; the dollar strengthened against the euro and the yen, negatively affecting the 45 percent of Symantec's sales that came from overseas; and the company's Macintosh-related business unexpectedly dropped 50 percent, possibly because of the perception that Apple Computer Inc.'s new operating system was less vulnerable to viruses.

"Most companies can suffer or endure one body shock in a quarter, but it's unlikely a company can endure three," Mr. Thompson says. "That made it very challenging for us to recover. We had to take some actions to shore up the business." Some of those actions were obvious, like refreshing the consumer product line. Others seem counterintuitive, like raising prices on the basis of what turned out to be the correct hunch that the company's primary competitor, Network Associates Inc., would follow suit to improve its own profit margins. At the same time, Symantec consolidated its marketing activities in a few key markets, rather than spreading them all over the globe.

Finally, Symantec got a boost from an unexpected quarter: hackers. Highly publicized viruses, like Code Red and Nimda, coupled with heightened security awareness of all kinds after the attacks of September 11, 2001, led many customers to consider Symantec's products for the first time.

"We did get the benefit of what I've called the most insidious, malicious code environment in the history of the security industry over the last two years," Mr. Thompson says. "No one could have ever forecast the level of activity by hackers and virus writers that we've seen. And we've just been reasonably well positioned to be able to take advantage of that when it did occur."

Sales growth in the September 2002 quarter was 7 percent, jumping to 20 percent in the December 2002 quarter. For fiscal year 2002, which ended on March 31, Symantec's sales grew 14 percent, to $1.071 billion, with earnings of $65.1 million, or 41 cents a share.

This strong performance has continued. For the fiscal second quarter 2003, ended September 30, 2002, Symantec posted revenues of $325 million, a 34 percent increase over the year-earlier quarter. Pro forma net income before one-time charges and the amortization of acquisition-related intangible assets was $60 million, or 38 cents a share, compared with $42 million, or 28 cents a share, for the same quarter a year earlier.

A Suite of Challenges

Still, challenges remain. Old competitors, like Network Associates, Trend Micro Inc., and McAfee, are rapidly following Symantec's move to the enterprise market. Established enterprise players, such as Computer Associates, Checkpoint Systems Inc., and Cisco, are ceding little ground. Firewalls are a natural product for a network systems vendor such as Cisco, which can build them into its servers at very little additional cost, and Computer Associates can easily add security processes to its systems management software, in much the same way Microsoft has slipped features from Norton Utilities into Windows over the years.

Symantec has continued to buy companies, rolling the acquired technologies into its security portfolio. This strategy presents two challenges. The first is the cultural challenge created by any acquisition; the second the technical difficulty of integrating products created by disparate development teams.

On cultural matters, Symantec treads a middle line between the laissez-faire approach historically used by Novell Inc., which allowed acquired companies to retain much of their own cultures and many of their own processes, and the strict discipline of Cisco, which erases the old company's identity and plants the Cisco flag the day the deal closes. Symantec's flexible approach is visible in small ways, like the shorts and flip-flops favored by employees at the former Santa Monica home to Peter Norton, which contrast with the khaki culture of the Silicon Valley headquarters.

"We have a pretty aggressive integration process, but we're not at the point where we say you have to think the Symantec way," says Robert Clyde, Symantec's vice president and chief technology officer, who joined with the Axent acquisition. "We show up the next day with the benefit packages, with as many answers as we can, because it's uncertainty that causes the most pain."

With respect to the other challenge, integrating products created by disparate development teams, Mr. Clyde says the technical integration of the acquired products has been simplified by something called the Symantec Enterprise Security Architecture. "Rather than every product integrating with every other, with each acquisition, we move products onto that common architecture," he says. "It's phased, so there's some easy integration that happens right away, and the more difficult stuff takes longer. This way we can integrate acquired products quickly."

The pace of migration away from the Norton brand is another issue for Symantec. The company's leadership would like the entire product line branded with the Symantec name, and the enterprise offerings all are, as in Symantec Enterprise Firewall 7.0, Symantec Enterprise Security Manager 5.5, and so on. But the consumer products all still carry the Norton name; their yellow color, which Peter Norton adopted so his boxes would stand out on store shelves, is now Symantec's official hue. The Symantec name is gradually getting bigger on the boxes, and Mr. Norton's face is gone, but even many enterprise customers still know the company primarily as the publisher of Norton products.

"There were suggestions that we change the name of the company to Norton, but Norton is very heavily associated with $29.95 products," says Mr. Frischmann, Symantec's senior vice president of communications and brand management, a 30-year IBM employee who was Mr. Thompson's first executive hire. "We've accomplished a lot by associating Symantec with the enterprise. We've made a few steps toward moving Symantec into the consumer market, but we're moving slowly. I believe we can have one brand, but it could take five years or more," he says.

Five years in the software industry is a very long time. Although the Norton products don't command the six- and seven-figure price tags of the enterprise offerings, or the healthy profit margins, they do generate a tremendous amount of cash flow, and Symantec is not going to make the branding change until they know their position in the consumer space is secure. Despite the focus on the enterprise, the consumer business is still growing at a faster rate. In the quarter ended September 30, 2002, Symantec's worldwide enterprise security business grew 30 percent from the same quarter the previous year and was 44 percent of total revenue, while the consumer business grew by 68 percent during the same period and was 38 percent of total revenue.

Analysts differ on whether the continued importance of the consumer business is a problem for Symantec. Whereas some view it as a weight slowing the enterprise initiative, others see it as fueling the whole company's growth.

"While the enterprise opportunity is the bigger one over the long term, the consumer market is still underpenetrated, and nobody can compete with Symantec, given the company's 70 percent share of the market today and their strong brand with Norton," says Jonathan Ruykhaver, an analyst with Raymond James. "The strength of the consumer business has allowed Symantec to be acquisitive, to buy some strong emerging technologies. It gives them the opportunity to educate the enterprise market and capture that opportunity over time."

Others say Symantec should move away from consumer products, which sell at very low prices but still require a high level of technical support. "All they have in that space are products that are painfully hard to support at the prices they're getting through retail," says Jeff Tarter, editor and publisher of *Softletter,* an industry newsletter based in Watertown, Massachusetts. "They get that $15, but they have to be constantly finding viruses, fixing them, making the product better than McAfee. If they had any sense, they'd get out of the consumer business, but they can't."

Mr. Thompson says this view is simply wrong. "There's no question the consumer business is growing faster at this moment, but at a time when the enterprise software business around the world is contracting, ours has grown 30 percent," he says.

Of course, 34 percent revenue growth and 43 percent earnings growth are problems most software companies would love to have right now. Mr. Thompson says he is not concerned about the pace of change or the big players Symantec will increasingly face as his strategy proceeds.

"Companies that win in this industry are willing to make big bets, and they're able to get their team rallied behind what they're trying to do," Mr. Thompson says. "The fact that somebody bigger than you has an idea doesn't mean you should run away from it. I can outrun. I can outthink. I can outexecute. If you can do these things, size doesn't matter."

References

Kotter, John P. *The Heart of Change: Real-Life Stories of How People Change Their Organizations.* Cambridge: Harvard Business School Press, 2002.

Lane, Ray. "The Future of Enterprise Software." *s+b enews*, July 16, 2001.

Marshall, Jay, and Daryl R. Conner. "Another Reason Why Companies Resist Change." *s+b* (first quarter 1996).

Pasternack, Bruce A., and James O'Toole. "Yellow-Light Leadership: How the World's Best Companies Manage Uncertainty." *s+b* (second quarter 2002).

Shapiro, Benson P., Adrian J. Slywotzky, and Richard S. Tedlow. "How to Stop Bad Things from Happening to Good Companies." *s+b* (first quarter 1997).

Note

Reprinted with permission from *strategy+business*, no. 30 (spring 2003), the award-winning quarterly management magazine published by Booz Allen Hamilton. http://www.strategy-business.com.

Scope/Orientation/Scale

16. Global Foods Inc.: A Corporate Renewal Engagement

Global Foods Inc. (Global) is a midsize manufacturer that specializes in the production of imitation (i.e., store brand or in house brand) food items sold to large supermarket chains. Global specializes in look alike products that stores put next to national brands. Store brand items sell at an average 20 percent discount from national brands but return a 25 percent gross margin, nearly double what grocers earn on national brand sales.

Otis Young, a twenty-four-year-old graduate of Northeastern University, founded Global in 1974. During five years of cooperative education work assignments arranged by the university, Young worked for Market Shoppers Inc., the largest local supermarket chain, where he eventually rose to become an assistant store manager. Upon graduation the firm offered him a full-time job as the manager of its original store. Store-brand items accounted for approximately 3 percent of sales, and generic goods represented another 2 percent of sales. Generic brands, sold in plain white packages with crudely stenciled labels and inferior-quality products inside, were a short-lived idea that came into vogue during the economy's adjustment to higher energy prices following the oil embargo crisis in 1974. As a store manager, Young knew well that his store's bottom line and his own personal bonus improved with sales of off-brand items. Consumer brand loyalty, reinforced by coupons and advertising, limited sales of off-brand items.

This case was prepared by Harlan D. Platt.

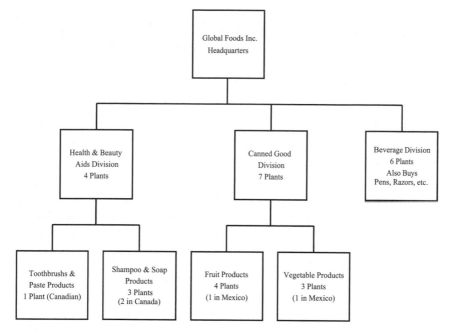

Fig. 1. Global Foods divisional chart

Three years of working full time (sixty-plus hours per week) for someone else fired Young's entrepreneurial spirit. Working at night, he developed a business plan for Global and with the help of his parents and two college roommates raised $250,000 of startup capital. Before quitting his job, Young arranged to sell his first knockoff product, mouthwash, to Market Shoppers. Young's plan was simple. He imported the English strategy, developed by Sainsbury Inc., of matching or even surpassing the quality of national brands with his knockoffs. He kept his costs and prices low and easily attracted new customers. The company expanded in two ways: new accounts and new products.

Profitability began in year one. Sales grew astronomically: 104 percent annually from 1974 to 1988 and 36 percent annually from 1980 to 1990. Soon Global became a national player in the imitation-brand business (see fig. 1). Table 1 summarizes Global's income statement. Global expanded from one product in 1974 to four hundred stock keeping units (SKUs) in 1996.[1] Global manufactures most of the products itself at seventeen manufacturing sites in the United

TABLE 1. Global Foods' Income Statements ($ millions)

	1974	1975	1976	1977	1978	1979	1980	1981	1982	1983	1984	1985	1986	1987
Sales	0.41	1.01	2.23	3.14	8.20	15.82	29.58	47.74	71.43	104.15	141.83	152.14	180.14	234.12
Cost of goods	0.20	0.47	1.03	1.48	3.77	6.96	13.67	22.44	32.86	44.78	62.41	64.07	81.06	110.04
Gross margin	0.21	0.54	1.20	1.66	4.43	8.86	15.91	25.30	38.57	59.37	79.42	88.07	99.08	124.08
Total general and administrative expense (G&A)	0.10	0.21	0.53	0.63	2.39	4.08	7.40	12.82	18.54	30.18	39.74	42.89	48.65	60.90
Depreciation	0.04	0.06	0.10	0.12	0.30	0.60	1.10	1.80	2.70	4.25	6.00	6.50	8.10	10.28
Earnings before interest and taxes (EBIT)	0.07	0.27	0.58	0.91	1.74	4.18	7.42	10.69	17.33	24.93	33.68	38.68	42.32	52.91
Interest	0.05	0.08	0.12	0.15	0.40	0.85	1.55	2.40	3.65	6.05	8.55	8.90	10.40	13.40
Taxes	0.01	0.10	0.23	0.38	0.67	1.67	2.93	4.14	6.84	9.44	12.57	14.89	15.96	19.75
Net income	0.01	0.10	0.23	0.38	0.67	1.67	2.93	4.14	6.84	9.44	12.57	14.89	15.96	19.75
Dividends	–	–	–	–	–	–	–	–	1.71	1.71	3.14	3.14	3.99	3.99

	1988	1989	1990	1991	1992	1993	1994	1995				1996			
								Total	Health	Foods	Bev.	Total	Health	Foods	Bev.
Sales	397.14	523.62	639.25	672.80	731.64	727.57	709.36	702.62	333.55	185.42	183.65	694.39	396.79	188.48	109.12
Worker salaries								207.87	102.19	35.35	70.33	255.69	153.94	67.94	33.80
Plant manager salaries								10.78	4.65	2.98	3.15	13.07	5.80	3.81	3.46
Fixed plant and warehouse costs								71.36	20.54	19.99	30.83	93.45	30.67	25.36	37.42
Raw materials and packaging								64.81	39.62	18.76	6.43	97.20	62.21	27.25	7.73
Cost of goods	198.57	261.81	326.02	349.86	391.43	381.97	365.32	354.82	167.00	77.08	110.74	459.40	252.62	124.37	82.42
Gross margin	198.57	261.81	313.23	322.94	340.21	345.60	344.04	347.80	166.55	108.34	72.91	234.99	144.18	64.11	26.70
Gross margin percentage	50	50	49	48	47	48	49	50				34			

Distribution															
Employee salaries								29.18	10.98	8.34	9.86	25.79	11.26	8.81	5.72
Shipping								71.17	33.97	13.49	23.71	67.90	37.24	14.69	15.98
Maintenance, rent, and other fixed costs								24.77	5.31	9.34	10.12	26.38	6.44	9.73	10.22
Total distribution								125.12	50.26	31.17	43.69	120.07	54.93	33.22	31.92
Corporate															
Corporate staff								25.67	12.30	7.12	6.25	24.27	12.39	7.55	4.33
Corporate management								46.09	25.07	9.63	11.39	46.40	25.78	9.88	10.75
Total corporate								71.76	37.37	16.75	17.64	70.67	38.16	17.43	15.08
Total G&A	95.30	115.24	140.28	154.70	175.60	196.51	191.48	196.88	87.63	47.92	61.33	190.75	93.09	50.65	47.00
Total G&A percentage	24	22	23	24	27	27	28					27			
Depreciation	13.33	15.88	19.77	22.48	25.88	28.73	31.29	37.91	8.67	13.89	15.35	42.58	10.43	16.52	15.64
EBIT	89.95	130.70	153.19	145.76	138.73	120.36	121.27	113.01	70.25	46.53	(3.77)	1.66	40.65	(3.06)	(35.93)
Interest	17.90	19.40	23.25	26.25	27.75	27.75	27.75	34.00	8.43	14.69	10.88	47.00	11.66	20.30	15.04
Taxes	36.02	55.65	64.97	59.76	55.49	46.30	46.76	39.51	—	—	—	—	—	—	—
Net income	36.02	55.65	64.97	59.76	55.49	46.30	46.76	39.51	61.82	31.84	(14.65)	(45.34)	28.99	(23.36)	(50.97)
Dividends	9.01	13.91	39.41	39.41	39.41	39.41	39.41	39.41				39.41			

States, Canada, and Mexico.[2] Next to most manufacturing sites is a companion distribution center. Global remained headquartered in Chelsea, Massachusetts.

Worker loyalty at Global is steadfast, based partly on an affinity for Young but also on a perception that Global's compensation plan is fair. In fact, wage levels lag the industry by approximately 5–7 percent. Almost 25 percent of employees are part-timers earning 20 percent less than full-time workers and ineligible for most benefits. Full-time employees receive 80 percent medical coverage at their choice of HMO; a $500 annual dental allowance; ten vacation days after the first year, rising to twenty after ten years of employment; seven holidays off; and a defined contribution pension plan that matches the employee's contribution up to 5 percent. The pension plan's principal investment has been Global stock; it now owns approximately 21 percent of the company.

Global's balance sheet and sources and uses of funds are presented in tables 2 and 3 in slightly abbreviated form. Global's crisis began at the end of 1995. Trade creditors demanded that Global reduce its days payable. Young exhorted them to relent and bought some time by reminding them of prior business dealings and future business possibilities. Table 4 shows Global's largest creditors. Only the first creditor is secured, by inventory and receivables. Dividends to shareholders were ended as of the fourth quarter of 1996.

Global's relationships with its bank and long-term creditors also are in peril. A sinking fund obligation of $32.5 million per year for ten years on the pre-1996 debt load commences in 1997. The $50 million bank credit line is converted into a one-year-term loan if, among other things, notes payable hit the $50 million limit or stockholders' equity falls below $100 million. At the end of 1996, the bank syndicate delivered two cautionary letters to Global documenting indenture-agreement violations by its inventory turnover and debt-equity ratios. The letters stated that Global needed to submit a plan to ameliorate the violations.

Young and his two college roommates owned 76 percent of Global's equity and served as its president and CEO, COO, and CFO, respectively. In 1990, investment bankers proposed an initial public offering indicating a value in excess of $1.5 billion. The three friends rejected the proposal, preferring to retain control and maintain their investment in Global. However, much of this value had evaporated along with Global's net income. Cash flow in 1996 was negative; there were $45.34 million in losses, dividends of $39.41 million, and depreciation of $42.6 million.

Global's difficulties started in 1990 with two unanticipated events.

1. Sainsbury and other non-U.S. grocery behemoths began to buy up U.S. grocery chains and demand price concessions from suppliers like Global or else substituted some of their own goods for U.S. supplies.
2. Branded-goods producers whose sales had felt the impact of imitations responded by sharply cutting prices. The two leaders in this movement were Kellogg's in the cereal arena and Philip Morris in the tobacco and cookie business.

Global responded by cutting its margins and introducing still more products. The latter strategy derived from Young's belief that Global could always profit by introducing new look-alike products until the name-brand manufacturer felt the competition and cut its price. The race to introduce new products and maintain profits began in 1991, when Global had 135 products, mainly canned goods, health and beauty aids, and beverages.

Finally one night in November 1996 at the pre–board meeting dinner, Young's mother, a board member, asked, "How come we're making more products and less money?" No one answered her. Young knew the company needed to be restructured.

Young had always been a hands-on manager, doing almost everything himself, from choosing new plant locations to setting prices to testing new products in development. Not being familiar with corporate renewal, he read a number of books. He learned that entrepreneurs have difficulty dismantling what they have assembled, so the corporate renewal task should be assigned to an outsider.

Global's accountants knew Young intended to restructure and suggested he talk with the corporate recovery team in the consulting arm of the firm. Following a meeting in which the consultants cataloged their accomplishments, the board agreed to hire the team to prepare a restructuring plan. The management team would remain in charge of daily operations and business decisions. Information gathered by the team is presented in tables 5–9 and figures 2 and 3.

TABLE 2. Global Foods' Balance Sheet ($ millions)

	1974	1975	1976	1977	1978	1979	1980	1981	1982	1983	1984	1985	1986
Assets													
Current assets													
Inventory	0.01	0.03	0.07	0.10	0.26	0.53	1.06	1.50	2.00	2.87	4.21	4.41	5.82
Accounts receivable	0.05	0.12	0.28	0.38	1.03	2.08	3.87	6.07	9.32	14.04	19.58	20.92	26.75
Cash and other assets	0.23	0.41	0.44	0.73	0.94	1.84	3.05	4.20	7.28	12.16	17.05	28.58	29.92
Total current assets	0.29	0.56	0.79	1.21	2.23	4.45	7.98	11.77	18.60	29.07	40.84	53.91	62.49
Fixed assets	0.80	1.10	1.90	2.40	5.90	11.90	21.90	35.90	54.00	85.00	120.00	130.00	162.00
Accumulated depreciation	0.04	0.10	0.19	0.31	0.61	1.20	2.30	4.09	6.79	11.04	17.04	23.54	31.64
Net fixed assets	0.76	1.01	1.71	2.09	5.30	10.70	19.61	31.81	47.21	73.96	102.96	106.45	130.36
Total assets	1.05	1.56	2.50	3.30	7.53	15.15	27.58	43.58	65.81	103.03	143.80	160.37	192.85
Liabilities and owners' equity													
Notes payable	0.20	0.25	0.50	0.75	1.50	3.00	5.50	5.50	5.50	5.50	5.50	4.03	4.03
Accounts payable	0.08	0.21	0.46	0.63	1.64	3.09	5.59	8.95	13.54	19.03	25.37	26.68	32.18
Current liabilities	0.28	0.46	0.96	1.38	3.14	6.09	11.09	14.45	19.04	24.53	30.87	30.71	36.21
Long-term debt	0.25	0.50	0.70	0.70	2.50	5.50	10.00	18.50	31.00	55.00	80.00	85.00	100.00
Stockholder equity	0.52	0.62	0.84	1.22	1.89	3.56	6.49	10.63	15.76	23.49	32.93	44.67	56.65
Total	1.05	1.56	2.50	3.30	7.53	15.15	27.58	43.58	65.81	103.03	143.80	160.37	192.85
Sale/Net fixed assets	0.54	1.00	1.30	1.50	1.55	1.48	1.51	1.50	1.51	1.41	1.38	1.43	1.38
Debt/Equity	1.13	1.86	2.56	2.28	4.38	4.91	5.02	5.03	5.58	6.38	6.98	5.48	5.45

	1987	1988	1989	1990	1991	1992	1993	1994	1995	1996 Health	Foods	Beverages	Total
Assets													
Current assets													
Inventory	8.32	15.02	20.73	25.63	28.56	33.03	32.65	31.53	32.18	19.25	12.44	12.36	44.05
Accounts receivable	35.86	62.89	83.35	102.10	106.54	116.66	116.41	114.86	113.96	47.39	47.12	19.64	114.15
Cash and other assets	38.57	53.37	71.08	72.13	87.52	75.26	56.22	44.95	14.43	2.25	1.07	0.62	3.94
Total current assets	82.74	131.27	175.16	199.87	222.62	224.95	205.29	191.34	160.57	68.89	60.63	32.62	162.14
Fixed assets	205.50	266.50	317.50	395.30	449.60	517.60	574.60	626.60	759.20	210.50	330.30	312.70	853.50
Accumulated depreciation	41.92	55.24	71.12	90.88	113.36	139.24	167.97	199.26	237.17	68.15	82.46	129.14	279.75
Net fixed assets	163.59	211.26	246.39	304.42	336.24	378.36	406.63	427.34	522.04	142.35	247.85	183.56	573.76
Total assets	246.33	342.53	421.54	504.29	558.86	603.31	611.92	618.68	682.60	211.24	308.47	216.18	735.90
Liabilities and owners' equity													
Notes payable	4.03	4.03	4.03	12.50	12.50	12.50	12.50	12.50	15.00				45.00
Accounts payable	39.90	64.09	86.36	105.08	109.31	122.67	124.38	123.80	125.12				133.17
Current liabilities	43.93	68.12	90.39	117.58	121.81	135.17	136.88	136.30	140.12				178.17
Long-term debt	130.00	175.00	190.00	220.00	250.00	265.00	265.00	265.00	325.00				425.00
Stockholder equity	72.41	99.41	141.15	166.71	187.05	203.14	210.04	217.39	217.47				132.73
Total	246.33	342.53	421.54	504.29	558.86	611.92	611.92	618.68	682.60				735.90
Sale/Net fixed assets	1.43	1.88	2.13	2.10	2.00	1.93	1.79	1.66	1.35	2.79	0.76	0.59	1.21
Debts/Equity	5.71	5.50	4.00	4.45	5.05	6.26	9.55	22.15	(23.62)				(4.10)

TABLE 3. Global Foods' Sources and Uses of Funds ($ millions)

	1974	1975	1976	1977	1978	1979	1980	1981	1982	1983	1984	1985
Cash	0.50	0.23	0.41	0.44	0.73	0.94	1.84	3.05	4.20	7.28	12.16	17.05
EBIT	0.07	0.27	0.58	0.91	1.74	4.18	7.42	10.69	17.33	24.93	33.68	38.68
Interest	(0.05)	(0.08)	(0.12)	(0.15)	(0.40)	(0.85)	(1.55)	(2.40)	(3.65)	(6.05)	(8.55)	(8.90)
Taxes	(0.01)	(0.10)	(0.23)	(0.38)	(0.67)	(1.67)	(2.93)	(4.14)	(6.84)	(9.44)	(12.57)	(14.89)
Dividends	–	–	–	–	–	–	–	–	(1.71)	(1.71)	(3.14)	(3.14)
Depreciation	0.04	0.06	0.10	0.12	0.30	0.60	1.10	1.80	2.70	4.25	6.00	6.50
Change in notes payable (NP) and long-term debt	0.45	0.30	0.45	0.25	2.55	4.50	7.00	8.50	12.50	24.00	25.00	3.53
Change in accounts payable (AP)	0.08	0.12	0.25	0.17	1.01	1.45	2.50	3.35	4.60	5.49	6.34	1.30
Change in inventory	(0.01)	(0.02)	(0.04)	(0.03)	(0.17)	(0.26)	(0.53)	(0.44)	(0.50)	(0.87)	(1.33)	(0.20)
Change in accounts receivable (AR)	(0.05)	(0.07)	(0.16)	(0.10)	(0.64)	(1.06)	(1.79)	(2.20)	(3.25)	(4.72)	(5.55)	(1.34)
Capital expenditures	(0.80)	(0.30)	(0.80)	(0.50)	(3.50)	(6.00)	(10.00)	(14.00)	(18.10)	(31.00)	(35.00)	(10.00)
Ending cash balance	0.23	0.41	0.44	0.73	0.94	1.84	3.05	4.20	7.28	12.16	17.05	28.58
Days payable	74.8	74.2	75.3	73.1	72.8	71.3	69	68.4	69.2	66.7	65.3	64
Receivable days	45.1	44.2	46.1	44.7	45.7	48.1	47.8	46.4	47.6	49.2	50.4	50.2
Inventory days	20.1	22	23.4	24.5	25.6	27.6	28.2	24.4	22.2	23.4	24.6	25.1
Outstanding loans	0.45	0.75	1.20	1.45	4.00	8.50	15.50	24.00	36.50	60.50	85.50	89.03
Interest rate (%)	10	10	10	10	10	10	10	10	10	10	10	10
Interest paid	0.05	0.08	0.12	0.15	0.40	0.85	1.55	2.40	3.65	6.05	8.55	8.90
Tax rate (%)	50	50	50	50	50	50	50	50	50	50	50	50

	1986	1987	1988	1989	1990	1991	1992	1993	1994	1995	1996
Cash	28.58	29.92	38.57	53.37	71.08	72.13	87.52	75.26	56.22	44.95	14.43
EBIT	42.32	52.91	89.95	130.70	153.19	145.76	138.73	120.36	121.27	113.01	1.66
Interest	(10.40)	(13.40)	(17.90)	(19.40)	(23.25)	(26.25)	(27.75)	(27.75)	(27.75)	(34.00)	(47.00)
Taxes	(15.96)	(19.75)	(36.02)	(55.65)	(64.97)	(59.76)	(55.49)	(46.30)	(46.76)	(39.51)	—
Dividends	(3.99)	(3.99)	(9.01)	(13.91)	(39.41)	(39.41)	(39.41)	(39.41)	(39.41)	(39.41)	(39.41)
Depreciation	8.10	10.28	13.33	15.88	19.77	22.48	25.88	28.73	31.29	37.91	42.58
Change in NP and long-term debt	15.00	30.00	45.00	15.00	38.47	30.00	15.00	—	—	62.50	130.00
Change in AP	5.50	7.72	24.19	22.28	18.72	4.22	13.37	1.71	(0.59)	1.33	8.05
Change in inventory	(1.41)	(2.50)	(6.69)	(5.71)	(4.91)	(2.93)	(4.47)	0.38	1.12	(0.65)	(11.88)
Change in AR	(5.83)	(9.11)	(27.03)	(20.46)	(18.76)	(4.44)	(10.12)	0.25	1.55	0.90	(0.19)
Capital expenditures	(32.00)	(43.50)	(61.00)	(51.00)	(77.80)	(54.30)	(68.00)	(57.00)	(52.00)	(132.60)	(94.30)
Ending cash balance	29.92	38.57	53.37	71.08	72.13	87.52	75.26	56.22	44.95	14.43	3.94
Days payable	65.2	62.2	58.9	60.2	60	59.3	61.2	62.4	63.7	65	70
Receivable days	54.2	55.9	57.8	58.1	58.3	57.8	58.2	58.4	59.1	59.2	60
Inventory days	26.2	27.6	27.6	28.9	28.7	29.8	30.8	31.2	31.5	33.1	35
Outstanding loans	104.03	134.03	179.03	194.03	232.50	262.50	277.50	277.50	277.50	340.00	470.00
Interest rate (%)	10	10	10	10	10	10	10	10	10	10	10
Interest paid	10.40	13.40	17.90	19.40	23.25	26.25	27.75	27.75	27.75	34.00	47.00
Tax rate (%)	50	50	50	50	50	50	50	50	50	50	50

TABLE 4. List of Major Creditors (excluding long term debt)

Creditor	Amount Owed ($)
Bank of Shawmut	45,000,000
Consolidated Dairies Inc.	15,528,000
Orange Growers Coop Inc.	11,793,000
Stairs Container Corp.	9,135,000
Interstate Truckers Ltd.	9,068,000
Guaranteed Trucking Inc.	8,195,000
Quail Pharmaceuticals Co.	7,899,000
Health and Beauty Inc.	7,453,000
Ready Glow Products Co.	7,854,000
Verity Meats Poultry and Dairy Inc.	6,368,000

TABLE 5. Global Foods' Plant Information ($ millions)

	Location	Year Built	Fixed Costs[a]	Plant Capacity[b]	Utilization in 1996 (%)	Total Employed[c]	Book Value	Original Value
				Health and Beauty				
1	Mass.	1974	10.2	0.91	90	1,292	2.18	29.99
10	Texas	1987	5.0	0.86	49	346	39.35	27.80
11	Canada	1987	9.4	1.34	83	1,092	33.00	51.83
16	Mexico	1995	11.9	2.95	99	1,658	53.65	97.47
	Total		36.5	6.06		4,389	128.18	207.09
				Food Division				
5	California	1983	5.5	0.70	85	562	9.37	25.10
6	Georgia	1984	2.0	0.34	0	—	9.50	9.58
7	Georgia	1986	3.6	0.64	73	316	14.50	19.01
9	Alabama	1987	2.1	0.39	0	—	31.05	11.64
14	Texas	1989	3.4	0.62	82	336	30.78	21.90
15	Florida	1990	5.4	0.93	58	377	41.60	33.01
17	Mexico	1995	7.2	1.78	24	208	48.10	58.97
	Total		29.2	5.40		1,799	184.90	179.20
				Beverage Division				
2	Mass.	1978	7.1	0.75	76	215	4.35	25.37
3	California	1981	6.2	0.73	93	228	9.75	26.73
4	Mass.	1982	4.7	0.58	81	153	7.80	19.58
8	Alabama	1986	6.6	1.20	87	229	37.80	34.98
12	Florida	1988	8.9	1.44	54	191	42.00	51.66
13	Florida	1989	7.4	1.24	98	288	45.00	45.20
	Total		40.9	5.94		1,303	146.70	203.51
	Company total		106.5			7,492	459.77	

[a]Fixed costs includes maintenance, rent, and fixed overhead.
[b]Plant capacity combines fixed investment dollars with plant/age, giving relative capacity across all plants.
[c]Includes plant workers and managers.

TABLE 6. Global Foods' Distribution Centers ($ millions)

Location	Year Built	Fixed Costs[a]	Plant Capacity[b]	Utilization in 1996 (%)	Workers Employed[c]	Book Value	Original Costs
			Health and Beauty				
Mass.	1974	2.4	1.11	92	112	2.4	2.38
Texas	1987	2.0	1.50	95	97	6.3	1.99
Canada	1987	2.1	1.30	91	96	5.5	2.06
Total		6.4	3.92		305	14.2	6.44
			Food Division				
California	1983	2.7	1.57	92	77	4.6	2.70
Mass.	1983	2.4	1.29	62	46	4.2	2.40
Missouri	1984	1.9	0.95	65	38	7.2	1.90
Georgia	1986	0.9	0.39	94	26	6.1	0.90
Texas	1989	0.8	0.70	87	22	15.4	0.80
Canada	1992	1.0	0.50	36	11	25.6	1.03
Total		9.7	5.40		222	63.0	9.73
			Beverage Division				
Mass.	1978	2.7	1.42	86	71	1.4	2.70
California	1981	2.1	1.15	72	46	5.1	2.10
Missouri	1984	1.9	0.95	83	48	6.4	1.90
Alabama	1986	1.5	1.21	31	14	7.4	1.50
Florida	1988	1.1	0.82	24	8	8.0	1.10
Canada	1989	0.9	0.68	47	13	8.5	0.92
Total		10.2	6.23		200	36.9	10.22
Company total		26.4			727	114.0	

[a]Fixed costs includes maintenance, rent, and fixed overhead.

[b]Plant capacity combines fixed investment dollars with plant/age, giving relative capacity across all plants.

[c]Includes plant workers and managers.

TABLE 7. Global Foods' Product Summary

	Year Introduced	Plants Producing	Market Share (%)[a]	Retail Price ($)	Wholesale Price ($)	Margin 1995	Margin 1996	Units (millions) Sold 1996	Sales Revenue 1996	Gross Margin 1996
			Health and Beauty							
Bleach	1975	1, 10, 11, 16	38	1.15	0.86	34	28	60.56	52.23	14.62
Dental floss	1981	1, 10, 11, 16	24	1.35	1.01	63	33	25.24	25.60	8.45
Deodorant	1991	1, 10, 11, 16	5.0	1.60	1.20	54	40	15.94	19.12	7.65
Ear cleaners	1985	1, 10, 11, 16	13	1.20	0.90	39	32	8.29	7.46	2.39
Fabric softener	1995	1, 10, 11, 16	2.0	3.99	2.99	28	24	9.56	28.61	6.87
Hair conditioner	1988	1, 10, 11, 16	1.0	1.35	1.01	60	48	3.19	3.23	1.55
Hair spray	1995	1, 10, 11, 16	2.0	2.69	2.02	30	30	9.56	19.29	5.79
Laundry detergent	1987	1, 10, 11, 16	17	2.69	2.02	49	40	81.28	163.98	65.59
Mouthwash	1974	1, 10, 11, 16	13	2.69	2.02	49	48	10.36	20.90	10.03
Nail polish remover	1989	1, 10, 11, 16	7.0	0.99	0.74	43	41	22.31	16.57	6.79
Shampoo	1981	1, 10, 11, 16	4.0	1.11	0.83	48	43	12.75	10.63	4.57
Shaving cream	1984	1, 10, 11, 16	2.0	1.11	0.83	42	36	9.56	7.97	2.87
Soap	1993	1, 10, 11, 16	1.0	0.99	0.74	25	21	9.56	7.10	1.49
Spray starch	1984	1, 10, 11, 16	0.5	2.79	2.09	24	18	0.80	1.67	0.30
Tampons	1995	1, 10, 11, 16	0.5	2.80	2.10	62	45	1.59	3.35	1.51
Toothbrushes	1977	1, 10, 11, 16	3.0	2.20	1.65	47	44	4.78	7.89	3.47
Other (average)	various	1, 10, 11, 16	3.5	1.43	1.07	26	20	1.12	1.20	0.24
Total									396.79	144.18

Food

Applesauce	1985	5, 7, 15, 17	18	0.99	0.74	41	31	21.21	15.75	4.88
Frosted cereal	1990	5, 7, 15, 16, 17	11	2.09	1.57	50	33	17.28	27.09	8.94
Frozen broccoli	1982	5, 7, 15, 16, 17	5	0.69	0.52	27	23	7.86	4.07	0.93
Frozen corn	1982	5, 7, 15, 17	17	0.59	0.44	27	23	40.06	17.73	4.08
Frozen peas	1982	5, 7, 15, 17	16	0.59	0.44	27	23	31.42	13.90	3.20
Oatmeal	1988	5, 7, 15, 16, 17	28	1.69	1.27	49	45	11.00	13.94	6.27
Popcorn	1982	5, 7, 15, 17	23	1.09	0.82	44	33	18.07	14.77	4.87
Pretzels	1980	5, 7, 15, 17	38	1.09	0.82	39	39	44.78	36.60	14.28
Salt	1979	5, 14	68	0.79	0.59	39	34	8.90	5.27	1.79
Sugar	1978	5, 14	35	1.99	1.49	48	43	13.75	20.52	8.82
Whole wheat	1985	5, 7, 15, 16, 17	9	1.09	0.82	36	36	17.67	14.45	5.20
Other (average)	various	5, 7, 15, 17	5	1.49	1.12	29	19	3.93	4.39	0.83
Total									188.48	64.11

Beverage

Beer	1992	2, 12	1	3.00	2.25	37	26	0.80	1.79	0.47
Cola	1983	2, 3	18	0.79	0.59	35	19	14.31	8.48	1.61
Ginger ale	1984	2, 3	38	0.79	0.59	35	22	15.11	8.95	1.97
Milk[b]	1981	3, 4, 8	49	1.39	1.04	32	24	48.71	50.78	12.19
Orange juice	1982	3, 4, 8, 13	28	1.49	1.12	31	27	27.83	31.10	8.40
Root beer	1983	2, 3	38	0.79	0.59	35	25	7.56	4.48	1.12
Seltzer water	1984	2, 3	58	0.59	0.44	35	26	5.77	2.55	0.66
Tomato juice	1988	2, 3, 8	3	0.99	0.74	38	38	0.30	0.22	0.08
Wine	1993	2, 12	0.5	3.00	2.25	48	40	0.20	0.45	0.18
Other (average)	various	2, 3, 12	5	0.84	0.63	16	8	0.50	0.31	0.03
Total									109.12	26.70

[a]In stores where products are sold.
[b]Some markets.

TABLE 8. Global Foods' Age, Salary, Managerial Compensation, and Worker Salaries

Age Distribution by Division

	Age Distribution (%)			Number of People			People Years		
	Health	Food	Beverage	Health	Food	Beverage	Health	Food	Beverage
60+	4	23	6	210	529	106	13,238	33,298	6,691
50–59	10	36	9	525	827	159	28,892	45,500	8,762
40–49	35	28	33	1,839	643	584	82,735	28,955	26,285
30–39	31	10	35	1,628	230	620	56,995	8,043	21,683
20–29	20	3	17	1,051	69	301	26,265	1,724	7,523
Total	100	100	100	5,253	2,298	1,770	208,124	117,520	70,942
Average age by division							39.6	51.1	40.1

Salary Distribution by Division (without benefits)

	Breakdown (%)			Number of People			Salaries		
	Health	Food	Beverage	Health	Food	Beverage	Health	Food	Beverage
$100K+	1.0	1.0	1.0	53	23	18	6,566	2,873	2,213
80–99	1.5	2.0	1.5	79	46	27	7,092	4,136	2,390
60–79	2.5	2.0	5.5	131	46	97	9,193	3,217	6,815
40–59	14	19	5	735	437	89	36,771	21,831	4,425
20–39	24	31	13	1,261	712	230	37,822	21,371	6,903
<20	57	45	74	2,994	1,034	1,310	50,902	17,580	22,267
Total	100	100	100	5,253	2,298	1,770	148,345	71,008	45,011
Average salary by division							28,240	30,900	25,430

Average Managerial Compensation (1996) (without benefits)

	Distribution (%)			Number of Managers			Total Salaries ($000)		
	Health	Food	Beverage	Health	Food	Beverage	Health	Food	Beverage
125K	1.0	1.0	1.0	53	23	18	6,566	2,873	2,213
90	1.5	2.0	1.5	79	46	27	7,092	4,136	2,390
70	2.5	2.0	5.5	131	46	97	9,193	3,217	6,815
50	0	0	0	—	—	—	—	—	—
30	0	0	0	—	—	—	—	—	—
17	0	0	0	—	—	—	—	—	—
Total	5	5	8	262.65[a]	114.9[b]	141.6[c]	22,851	10,226	11,417
Average salary for a manager per division							87,000	89,000	80,625

Average Worker Salaries (without benefits)

	Distribution (%)			Number of Workers			Total Salaries ($000)		
	Health	Food	Beverage	Health	Food	Beverage	Health	Food	Beverage
125K	0	0	0	—	—	—	—	—	—
90	0	0	0	—	—	—	—	—	—
70	0	0	0	—	—	—	—	—	—
50	14	19	5	735	437	89	36,771	21,831	4,425
30	24	31	13	1,261	712	230	37,822	21,371	6,903
17	57	45	74	2,994	1,034	1,310	50,902	17,580	22,267
Total	95	95	92	4,990	2,183	1,628	125,494	60,782	33,595
Average salary for a worker per division							25,147	27,842	20,630

[a]210 work at corporate headquarters, 48 in plants, and 5 at distribution centers.
[b]80 work at corporate headquarters, 33 in plants, and 3 at distribution centers.
[c]103 work at corporate headquarters, 35 in plants, and 5 at distribution centers.

TABLE 9. Global Foods' Employee Distribution

	Health and Beauty	Food	Beverage	Total
Worker breakdown				
Corporate	349	196	163	708
Plants	4,342	1,768	1,270	7,380
Distribution	299	218	195	712
Management breakdown				
Corporate	210	80	103	393
Plants	47	31	33	116
Distribution	5	3	5	13

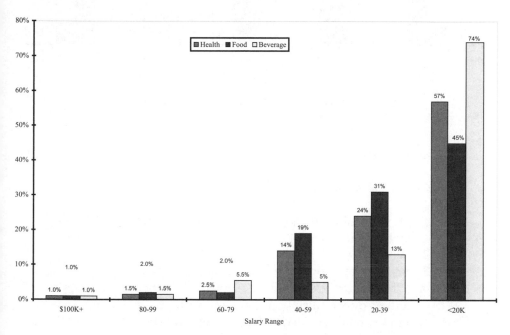

Fig. 2. Nonmanagerial salary breakdown (5,253, 2,298, and 1,770 employees per division, respectively)

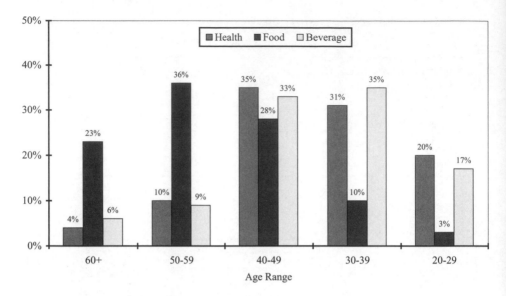

Fig. 3. Age distribution (5,253, 2,298, and 1,770 employees per division, respectively)

Student Assignment

Answer the following questions.

1. How should targets be set in a restructuring: people, financial, products, etc.?
2. Who should be laid off?
3. Should any products be discontinued? Which ones?
4. What incentives should be given to induce employees to leave? Be specific about blue and white collar employees.
5. How can Global insure that the best workers remain and the least qualified leave?
6. Does Global have an age discrimination problem to contend with? Sex discrimination?
7. Which plants should Global shut?
8. Which processes should Global change?
9. How and when should Global inform its customers of these changes? When should the changes occur?
10. Do ethical concerns arise in restructurings? What about at Global?

11. Are there good alternatives to a restructuring?
12. What information do you need to prepare a reengineering report?
13. What other guidance would you give the board?
14. What other questions need to be asked?

Notes

1. A typical grocery store stocks approximately 2,500 items. Super stores may stock 4,000 or 5,000 items.

2. Mexican labor costs in 1996 were 25 percent of U.S. wages up from 23 percent in 1995. Canadian labor costs equaled 90 percent of U.S. levels in both years.

Strategic Turnaround Analysis

17. American Motors Corporation (B)

This case was prepared in the 1960s and of necessity refers to the events of that time as breaking news. It was included in this volume because of its robust representation of the decline of a large corporation.

With profits falling, its share of the U.S. auto market down to little more than half what it was five years ago, and its Rambler being outsold in America even by Volkswagen, American Motors Corp. yesterday (August 2, 1965) took its most drastic step yet to loosen a growing financial squeeze: it cut its quarterly dividend in half. On September 20, it will pay 12½ cents a share to common stockholders of record August 20; previously it had paid 25 cents quarterly.

The move was hardly unexpected. For the last two years AMC has been raising eyebrows in Detroit and on Wall Street by reporting slipping sales while the bigger three U.S. automakers were pushing sales to undreamed-of-heights. Its latest profit report, released yesterday with news of the dividend cut, makes it plain the trend is continuing.

But if the dividend cut startled few, it is bound to stir debate over AMC's future role. Fresh in the minds of many, of course, is the decision by Studebaker Corp. eighteen months ago to close its U.S. auto plants after nearly five decades and move all output to Canada.[1]

This was not the only side of the story, however. In a speech to the Automobile Analysts of New York in June 1965, Mr. Abernethy pointed out that

> American Motors is like no independent automobile manufacturer that ever existed before. We have the kind of volume base

---

This case was prepared by Chuck Hofer.

that no other independent has ever reached before . . . and we have done and are continuing to do right things to move ahead.

Our position in automotive history is unique.

We've come through more than half a century of competitive battles in an arena that has seen more than a thousand companies come and go.

Sales of a billion dollars a year is the new plateau on which we are building. Our sales this year (1965) should be again in that area. (These figures are gross.)

We have a far better foundation than ever before. At the end of our fiscal year, last September 30, assets totaled $421 million. Five years ago the figure was $288 million.

Going into the current fiscal year, our investment in property, plant and equipment was more than $126 million. Five years ago, it was $59 million.

Over the past five years, the company invested $90 million in capital improvements . . . $127 million in new model tooling[2] and $26 million in subsidiaries. In addition, we paid off some staggering debts. Meanwhile, we have paid stockholders $115 million in dividends, more than half of this in the past three years. Since we resumed dividend payments in 1959, we have paid our stockholders $17 million more than Chrysler has.

All our expansion to date has been paid for completely out of earnings retained in the business. Working capital as a result was down somewhat going into our current fiscal year. But the total figure of 94.6 million is far above the $46 million we showed in 1957, when so many people were writing American Motors off.

This case describes the automotive strategy of American Motors during the period 1962–65. It focuses on the changes which have occurred in the automotive market since 1962, on the modifications which have occurred in the strategies of the automobile companies as a result of the changes in the market, and on AMC's competitive position at the end of the 1965 model year. Some consideration is given to AMC's position in foreign markets during this interval and to forecasts about the nature of the domestic market in the years ahead.

The Changing Car Market: 1962–65

The three trends—market growth, proliferation of models, and an emphasis on luxury—which were developing in the domestic car market in late 1962 continued and matured during the 1963, 1964, and 1965 model years.

The car market recovered from the 1960–61 recession and entered a period of rapid growth. From 5,516,000 units in 1961, sales increased each year to an estimated 8,840,000 units in 1965, the first 8,000,000 car year in history. This growth was attributed to such factors as the general rise in the economic prosperity, the emergence of an affluent youth market, and the increase in two and three car families. According to *Fortune*, this growth was expected to continue for the remainder of the decade, with a 10,000,000 car year forecast by 1970.

The second major change which occurred in the automobile market between 1962 and 1965 was the proliferation of models, sizes, and styles offered by the automobile manufacturers. This increased variety allowed the buyer to select that particular model, size, and style which met both his or her driving and his or her personal needs.

Largely as a result of this proliferation of models, the segment of the market captured by compact cars expanded from the 4 percent Rambler held in 1958 to 40 percent in 1962 and remained at that figure through 1965. However, during the 1962–65 period, the definition of a compact car changed somewhat. Originally, the compact car had a wheelbase of 105 inches or less, while the standard cars were about 115 inches or greater. Between 1962 and 1965 a third car size, the intermediate car, between 105 and 115 inches, was developed, while the standard cars increased in size to about 119 or more inches. The first intermediate car was the Fairlane, which Ford introduced in 1961. GM then introduced the Chevelle in 1962 and increased the wheelbase on its B-O-P compacts by 4 inches in 1964 to put them in the intermediate size class. Both Chrysler and American Motors introduced models in this intermediate segment in 1965. Chrysler brought out the Dodge Coronet and the Plymouth Belvedere as intermediate cars, while AMC increased the size of its Ambassador by 5 inches to put it at the upper end of its segment at 116 inches. The intermediate cars were still grouped with the compacts by the industry in determining share of market for the compact segment, however.

Another manifestation of the proliferation of the market was the development of the "sporty" car and the resurgence of an emphasis on the performance. The "sporty" car trend started with the introduction of the Corvair Monza in 1961 and the Pontiac GTO in 1963. It really caught fire with the introduction of the Ford Mustang and the Plymouth Barracuda in 1964. To complete the representation, AMC brought out the Marlin in 1965.

The final major change in the car market was the trend toward luxury and the development of the "personalized" motor car. This trend apparently did not hurt the compact or intermediate market segments per se but rather reduced the market share of stripped down, "economy" models in all size ranges.

Business Week, in discussing this trend, noted that

Last model year (1962), 76% of Chevy Corvair buyers ordered the sporty, more expensive Monza; this model year (1963), 79% are specifying the Monza. Chevy's standard sized Impala and intermediate sized Chevy II introduced super sport models last fall, with high performance and bucket seats. Since October, 32% of all Impala sales and 35% of Chevy II Nova sales have been for these models.

It is much the same at Ford. The premium-priced Galaxie 500 and 500 XL a year ago accounted for 54% of the Ford Division's sales of standard sized cars; this year they account for 64%. . . . Ford Division's economy-orientated Falcon compact declined 28% last year and is still falling behind larger and plusher compacts. Ford notes, though, that 37% of Falcon buyers are paying extra for deluxe vinyl interior trim this year, compared to 15% last year.

Even American Motors Corporation, champion of the compact cars, found its most compact lines withering. Midway last year, it dropped its smallest car, the Metropolitan, for lack of demand; the small American dropped 12% while AMC's over-all sales were rising 20%.

Even auto men are surprised at how well the expensive cars they term "personal transportation" are selling. By March, for example, Pontiac sold more of its 1963 Grand Prix models than it did in all of the 1962 model year.[3]

Thus the trend toward luxury was not a trend from a Chevrolet to a Cadillac but rather a trend toward higher priced models for the same car, that is, a trend from a Chevrolet Biscayne to a Chevrolet Impala Super Sport. As a result the more costly body styles such as two-door hardtops and convertibles increased in demand at the expense of the two-door and four-door sedans. In 1964, for example, two-door hardtops captured 33 percent of the $2,500–$3,000 market segment to surpass four-door sedans for the first time in history in that price segment.

Another aspect of the trend toward luxury was the development of options and accessories as a major market. The period from 1962 to 1965 saw the auto manufacturers offer more optional equipment than ever before, particularly on the lower priced models. For example, 17.9 percent of the 1964 cars had air conditioning installed at the factory, while 14.1 percent were installed in 1963 and only 8 percent as recently as 1961. The rate of V-8 engine installation was increased to 73.2 percent (through June 30) in 1965 compared to 52.9 percent in 1961. Similar increases were noted for such items as four-speed manual transmissions, bucket seats, vinyl tops, AM-FM radios, limited slip differentials, and movable steering wheels. This wide range of options and accessories permitted the buyer to "personalize" his new car by selecting just those options and accessories which fit his individual needs.

Just as the Rambler had been the embodiment of the "economy" car market, the Mustang could be viewed as the fulfillment of the "personal" car market. It combined a compact body style, a "sporty" flair, a wide range of accessories, and unique styling in a package whose price brought the personal motor car concept within the reach of the mass market. The appeal of such a package was immediately demonstrated in the marketplace. From the time of its introduction in April 1964, the Mustang sold 303,000 units during the 1964 model year, which placed it sixth among all domestic cars in market share at 3.92 percent. During its first full year on the market, the Mustang sold over 450,000 units—the most ever for a new car. And for the first six months of the 1965 model year the Mustang sold 311,000 units to capture 6 percent of the market. This represented third place, behind the big Chevrolet and big Ford.

How the Companies Fared: 1963–65

During the period of change from 1962 to 1965, the Big Three continued the strategies they developed during "campaign counterattack." They offered the consumer a variety of sizes, styles, and horsepower ratings, giving the consumer a wide range of choice, particularly in the $2,000 to $3,000 price range. Beyond this, their strategies diverged. Ford and Chrysler emphasized compacts and lower-priced standard cars, while GM placed much more emphasis on the big car market with its B-O-P series of cars. In addition, Ford and Chrysler emphasized performance by giving factory backing to entries in the major stock car races in an attempt to appeal to the youth market. GM, on the other hand, withdrew from racing competition and deemphasized performance as a selling appeal.

American Motors continued to emphasize the compact car. However, the company broadened its concept of the Rambler compact car:

> Because Rambler became distinctively known for its trimmer length and for its unusual operating economy—and because the earliest competitive imitations of Rambler stressed these characteristics excessively—the word "compact" tended to become associated with "small, economy." ... However, the Rambler idea is the maximum consumer benefit is best achieved through a balance of all elements in car design that makes for total usefulness. ... In summary, the Rambler compact car concept is the balanced combination of the major elements of car design, packaged to meet the new problems of more intensive car use while squarely meeting American standards of interior roominess, riding comfort, performance, luxury, and pride of ownership.[4]

During these years of change, the fortunes of the Big Three rose and fell. The period started with the GM onslaught of 1963. In that year, GM's market share reached 55 percent during the spring months and averaged 53.4 percent for the year. The total unit sales of 4,078,000 was a GM record. This domination of the market was achieved primarily by GM's strength in the standard, medium, and luxury car lines, which had all been restyled for this model year. This year also saw the resurgence of Chrysler, which completely restyled all its cars and began to emphasize performance again by giving factory support to entries in drag strip and stock car racing. Chrysler's market share increased from 10.3 percent in 1962 to 13.1 percent in 1963. American Motors registered the highest unit sales volume in its history in 1963, even though its market share declined 0.3 percent. While sales of the Classic and Ambassador series, which had been redesigned for the 1963 model year, increased 25 percent over 1962, sales of the American dropped 12 percent. Ford was the primary victim of the GM onslaught in 1963, however, as its market share declined 2.2 percent to 25.7 percent. Ford was caught in a vise between the strength of GM's standard sized cars and the resurgence of Chrysler in the compact market.

The Mustang was the vanguard of the Ford counterattack in 1964 and 1965. With a newly designed Thunderbird and the success story of the year in the Mustang, Ford rebounded to capture 26.3 percent of the market in 1964. A totally new Mercury, styled in the Lincoln Continental tradition, and a Ford with a new body combined with the Mustang to continue the Ford advance in 1965. Together with the Thunderbird and the Lincoln, these cars enabled Ford to strengthen its image as a producer of luxurious, "sporty," personalized motor cars as well as compact and standard cars and helped Ford cut into GM's penetration in the standard, medium, and luxury price classes.

Chrysler continued its advance in 1964 by increasing its market share to 14.7 percent, which represented gains in all market segments. Chrysler continued its emphasis on performance, which was enhanced by the victories of Dodge and Plymouth entries in several major stock car races in 1964. Chrysler also brought out the Barracuda, a fastback "sporty" version of the Valiant, in the late spring of 1964 to offer some competition to the Mustang. In 1965, the Chrysler received a new body as did the large Dodges and Plymouths. In addition, two intermediate sized Dodges and Plymouths were introduced, the Dodge Coronet and Plymouth Belvedere. This gave Chrysler a more complete coverage of the lower priced market, which it continued to emphasize. Dodge also introduced a larger, more luxurious edition called the Monaco which was intended to compete against the Pontiac Grand Prix and Buick Wildcat. As a result, Chrysler continued to increase its market share in 1965 but at a slower rate than the preceding two years.

The Ford counterattack and continued advance by Chrysler cut into GM's market share in 1964, which dropped to 51.1 percent, down 2.3 percent from 1963. GM's total unit sales also slipped in 1964 by 100,000 units to 3,957,000. During 1964, GM lost sales to Ford and Chrysler in the standard, medium, and luxury price classes but led by its lengthened B-O-P compacts increased its penetration in the compact market segment. For 1965, all GM's noncompact cars from Chevrolet to Cadillac received new bodies. In addition, the Corvair received a new body, a new suspension system, and a new engine, which allowed it to compete more directly with the Mustang. During the beginning of the 1965 model year, GM's market share remained approximately the same as in 1964, but during the latter half of 1965 its share of the market began to creep up slightly. This slow start may have been the result of shortages of cars caused by the UAW strike against GM in the fall of 1964.

With Ford and Chrysler advancing in 1964 and 1965 and GM

holding its own, American Motors lost market position during these years. AMC entered the 1964 model year with a completely restyled American line, while the Classic and Ambassador series had received only minor face-lifts. However, Rambler did offer two-door hardtop models as well as more luxury appointment in top-of-the-line models for the first time this year. Nevertheless, both the Classic and the Ambassador experienced sharp sales declines in 1964: over 33 percent for the Classic and more than 50 percent for the Ambassador. A 50 percent sales increase in the newly designed American prevented a disastrous year for AMC. In total, Rambler sales dropped 70,000 units, which represented a 1.2 percent loss of market share. According to the *Wall Street Journal:*

> The company said sales were hurt by an "image lag." [Richard Cross, chairman, and Roy Abernethy, president, stated that]: Buyers identified the company's Rambler cars with conservative design and economy . . . this lag should be corrected by the 1965 Rambler models which represent the most sweeping changes in our history. While maintaining the basic virtues that established Rambler popularity, all three Rambler lines are now dramatically in the three divisions of the most active segment of the automobile market.[5]

The only silver lining available to AMC in 1964 was that its foreign sales were up 28 percent over 1963 to 72,000 cars.

In implementing an attack on this problem of "image lag," AMC took several steps before and during 1965. First, the Classic and Ambassador series received a complete restyling, and a clear difference was created between these lines in the 1965 models. Second, the company planned to introduce a "sporty" car, the Marlin, about the first of the year to help attract younger buyers and to modify the product image of the company. Third, AMC broadened the range of accessories which it offered on all models. Finally, the company changed advertising agencies and also its method of advertising.

Even after taking these major steps, AMC's total domestic sales lagged during the 1965 model year. The Classic and the Ambassador both experienced gains in 1965. While the Classic only had a modest gain of 5,000 units, the Ambassador's sales more than tripled to reach an estimated 62,000 units. With only minor styling changes, however, the American experienced a drastic sales decline—over 50,000 units—so that for the entire year AMC's sales were about 3,000 units less in 1964. Thus while the Big Three were all experiencing sales gains and having record years, AMC not only lost market share but also suffered a decline in total sales.

The Situation at AMC at the End of the 1965 Model Year

By the end of the 1965 model year, Rambler's market share had dropped to an estimated 3.6 percent, nearly 50 percent below the peak of 7.1 percent reached in 1960. The sales decline, coupled with much higher tooling costs, naturally damaged the company's earnings. For the fiscal quarter ending March 30, 1965, earnings were 31 percent a share, 9 cents below last year's second quarter earnings; its first half profits were only 59 percent a share, compared with 98 cents for the first half of 1964.

According to the *New York Times:*

> None of this means, of course, that American Motors is headed for sudden collapse. The company still sells about $1 billion in products a year, is debt free and has about $100 million in working capital. But the company's continued sales decline is prompting knowledgeable auto men to wonder whether even a billion dollar corporation has the resources to compete head-on with the industry's three giants—the General Motors Corporation, the Ford Motor Company, and the Chrysler Corporation.
>
> Roy Abernethy, the finger-jabbing salesman who is president of American Motors, admits that "everyone seems to be asking what's next for American Motors" and wondering if competition has "boxed us in." But he firmly asserts that the company can compete. . . .
>
> "American Motors is like no independent automobile manufacturer that ever existed before," Mr. Abernethy thunders. "We have the kind of volume base that no other independent ever reached before, and we have done and are continuing to do the right things to move ahead."
>
> Mr. Abernethy says the company's domestic auto sales are running at an annual rate of around 380,000 units. . . . This level of output, Mr. Abernethy asserts, enables American Motors to obtain the same production economies achieved by larger producers. He calculates that American Motors can compete in this regard as long as its volume holds about 360,000 units a year.[6]

Product Line

With its 1965 models, AMC spanned the compact car market with more progressively styled cars than it ever had before. For 1966, the company planned to introduce a completely redesigned American, while the larger Classics and Ambassadors were to receive only a minor face-lift. However, according to *Ward's Automotive Reports:*

> AMC is changing its policy of humping its three car lines under the name "Rambler." For 1966, AMC is calling them the American Rogue and the Classic Rebel while the Ambassador hardtop will be the Ambassador DPL, with the initials standing for "Diplomat."[7]

In maintaining these models and in developing the Marlin, AMC appeared to be competing head-on against the Big Three. To some, this seemed unwise:

> There is widespread view among auto men, however, that American Motors should return to offering a distinctively different car, such as a vehicle smaller than anything now produced in the United States. This would, of course, require the company to walk away from current market trends and gamble its future on a single concept.
>
> Mr. Abernethy dismisses the idea. The market for cars smaller than the Rambler American is 500,000 units a year and is not likely to grow, he says. He doubts the company could attain enough volume in such a market, where Volkswagen already has over half the business.[8]

Mr. Abernethy further expounded his views on this subject in a briefing to the company's new ad agency, Benton and Bowles:

> We have no plans for a significantly bigger car, or for anything in the subcompact area. Of course, there is room within our general size range to be somewhat flexible. We can add an inch or so here and there as necessary to be competitive and give real added value to our customers.
>
> Nor are we—as some people have recommended—going to confine ourselves to a specialized product. We plan to appeal to

the broad spectrum of the automobile market with cars that ad-
here to our design concepts. Within this concept, we believe we
can satisfy most automobile tastes and demands. We don't want
to be known just as an economy car builder. We build sporty cars,
high performance cars, roomy cars, luxurious cars, stylish cars,
and basic, all-around economy cars.

But, all will stay within our established design precepts of trim-
ness, maneuverability, efficiency and avoidance of excess.[9]

While still dedicated to the concept of the compact car, AMC's
primary thrust in 1965 was, therefore, to change, or at least modify, its
image in order to broaden its market appeal. The problem was aptly
stated by a Midwest Rambler dealer: "Most of my customers are
older, more conservative people. We see those 28 to 35 years old driving by in Pontiacs and Impala convertibles."[10]

Roy Abernethy further elaborated the problem and gave some
indication of AMC's response in his remarks in *1965 Product Review*
to members of the communications media:

The basic challenge, of course, is in the attitude of people. We
have a very powerful economy image . . . one we are proud of.

But there has been a swift change toward buying up in recent
months. . . . During this market transition period, we have continued to have a strong appeal for conservative owners, as in the
past. . . . We have not adequately made the public aware of the extent to which we have broadened our appeal. . . . Our challenge is
to create a new picture of Rambler in the minds of the public—a
picture that contains the best of both—the best of the established
Rambler concept and the best of the new. We will move toward
this challenge with the best tools I think we ever had for breadth
of appeal to buyers of every type.

As you have seen, we will have three distinctly different Rambler lines, each with fresh and strong curbstone identification and
each with a different appeal to a different segment of the market—all within our basic concept of sense and balance.

The big *visible* change in the Rambler line—in beauty and size
of package—gives us a positive and realistic basis for the en-
largement of our product image. The American will compete in
price, size, roominess, style and power with the Falcon, Valiant,
and Chevy II. . . . The Classic will compete with the Fairlane,

Chevelle, Dart, and Comet. Their power range with their sixes runs from 170 for the Comet to 200 for the Fairlane—while we will have 199–232.[11] . . . The Ambassador will compete with the Tempest, Special, F-85, Plymouth Belvedere, Dodge Coronet and on up. . . . In addition to an excellent power position, with the edge in most cases, we'll have a roominess advantage. . . . And we'll have the options, trim, luxury and looks to match their best.

How do we meet the challenge of 1965 from a policy and advertising approach?

As I emphasized, we must *enlarge* our identity, not trade it all in for a new one. We have roughly 2.4 million Ramblers on the road. A large share of our owners bought the established Rambler image. Essentially, what most of them bought was common sense.

They represent a great potential backlog of repeat sales. It would be a stupid business decision to desert them and millions more like them who moved toward the Rambler idea. You don't sneeze at a mass of buyers who account for close to 40 percent of the total market—and who have made their moves in a very short space of time, because of the excitement of a fresh new appealing idea.

Our objective is to keep them—and add their cousins. We're in a green pasture that we've plowed and fertilized and dropped some sweat and blood in—and we're not going to jump the fence and run to a pasture that just looks greener.

The idea is to move the fence.

In the main, our advertising decisions seem to involve two starting issues:

1. Is the word "compact" a handicap for all or part of our product approach?
2. Does our public policy on horsepower promotion limit us in getting our performance story across?

I don't believe we should continue to have our thinking clouded up by wasteful debate on when and how the word "compact" is used. This is like being hung up on a meat-hook.

Let's sell our concept.[12]

After Ford withdrew its support (in 1963) of the 1957 Automobile Manufacturer's Association resolution that sought to deemphasize the promotion of speed, horsepower, and racing and Chrysler began giving factory support to entries in major stock car races in 1963, the subject of performance received more attention than it ever had since the 1957 resolution. In *1965 Product Review,* Mr. Abernethy commented on AMC's policy in this area:

> The subject of horsepower is getting a great deal of attention—from two directions. On the one side, certain competitors in the industry are on a speed and horsepower binge. On the other side, automotive deaths and casualties are at a record level.
>
> Perhaps the view of our position has changed since we were joined by General Motors, which has now come out sled-length [*sic*] for the policy we have been fighting for alone in the industry for the past two years. Our judgment has been confirmed.
>
> There have been some suggestions that our *policy* position has hurt us in sales.
>
> I don't believe this. To the extent that horsepower may have influenced us adversely, this would be largely due to under powering.
>
> We believe that the combination of wholly adequate horsepower in our cars . . . and a public position against manufacturer participation in racing and against promotion of advertising or excessive speed and horsepower . . . will win us growing public approval.
>
> We're on the right side in this issue. But you need to help make our position clear. We're not opposed to adequate horsepower. We have plenty and we will have more. We *are* opposed to over stimulating the motorist with heavy advertising and promotion of excessive speed and horsepower.
>
> Essentially, the Rambler concept is one of balance. The challenge for you is to come up with the most effective means of getting this balance story across.
>
> In summary:
>
> 1. We want to keep our heritage and our traditions—retain what we have and expand to the broadest appeal.
> 2. We want to increase public understanding of the Rambler concept.

3. We want to use our horsepower policy position to win public approval for our stand—and at the same time get in the one-two punch on performance.
4. We want to enlarge the public idea that we are different and part of this project must be to have advertising that is plainly different.
5. We must emphasize quality and find new ways to tell both our quality and warranty stories.[13]

Marketing

The marketing program had as its main objective the goal of changing the American Motors corporate image. To continue with the *Times:*

> American Motors has been seeking to alter its image as an economy-car producer by broadening its lines and putting more emphasis on luxury and power. The company added the Marlin early this year to give its line a sporty flavor and has hired a new advertising agency to promote the new theme. Benton & Bowles, Inc. has the account.[14]

Additional facets of the image AMC was trying to project were revealed in Mr. Abernethy's briefing of Benton and Bowles:

> In developing the public's concept of us as a company, we face the interesting challenge of building confidence in our ability, and strength, while at the same time exploiting our underdog position.
>
> We seek ways to be distinguished from other automobile companies . . . to be seen as more scrappy, more independent, more creative and more concerned with the customer. We want people to feel confident they'll get extra value, better service, and better all-around satisfaction from American Motors.
>
> We have also been speaking out on other growing problems stemming from automobile use, such as abandoned cars and urban traffic problems.
>
> This is characteristic of our corporate personality. We want people to know that American Motors *cares* about these things.[15]

Dealer Organization

American Motors dealerships reached a high around thirty-one hundred in late 1963. These dealers were smaller than the industry average, since AMC had 10 percent of the industry's dealers but only 6 to 7 percent of the industry's sales. It was perhaps for this reason that AMC was the first in the industry to move into dual dealerships, i.e., to encourage their dealers to handle other lines or to try to entice other dealers to handle the AMC line. After 1963, however, AMC tried to discourage this practice. In 1964, AMC lost approximately 100 dealers, which left the dealer count at about 3,000. Mr. Abernethy described AMC's 1965 distributions system to the Automotive Analysts of New York:

> We have a strong and profitable dealer organization ... the best an independent company has ever enjoyed. While the numbers are down slightly this year—to about 2,900 from around 3,000 a year ago—dealer quality is continuing to improve. Dealer net worth has continued to move up steadily, and was $220 million going into the current fiscal year—an all time high.

> Nevertheless, there were still some problems in 1965, since according to the *New York Times:* "dealer's inventories at June 30, 1965, stood at a 123 day supply, against 90 days a year earlier and 44 days for the industry."

Finance and Control

At the end of 1965 AMC still remained as the only U.S. automobile manufacturer free of long-term debt. However, because of reduced earnings and the higher tooling costs associated with more extensive and more frequent model changes, there was, according to the *New York Times:*

> a feeling both in Detroit and on Wall Street that American Motors will have to borrow money to reshape its products and image successfully. Mr. Abernethy says there is "nothing at the moment" planned, but adds that "whether we have future financing or not remains to be seen."[16]

Should American Motors seek long-term financing to reshape its product line, it could follow the example of Chrysler Corporation. In 1954, Chrysler secured a 100 year, $250 million loan from the Prudential Insurance Company in order to help finance a major redesign of its entire product line. Some estimate of what it might cost AMC to develop totally new cars in order to widen its product line can be gained from competitors' experience. The Mustang, for example, cost Ford about $50 million, which was considered low for the industry. On the other hand, the $250 million spent to develop the ill-fated Edsel was considered high.

Production Policies and Facilities

American Motors continued its policy of lack of integration, which allowed a low breakeven point. However, with the increase in tooling costs necessary for more frequent model changes and the increase in capacity to 700,000 units, the breakeven point was raised to approximately 360,000 units.

According to *Fortune:*

> While AMC does not deny that its profit margins are smaller, the company emphatically rejects the notion that dependence on outside suppliers is a prime cause. The hotly competitive nature of the automobile-supply business, officials say, automatically keeps suppliers' costs in line. The company periodically reviews its "make-buy" policy, and if it ever saw fit to buy out a supplier or to make a part now bought outside—which it hasn't—it has the resources to do so. To make doubly sure it is getting value for its money, the company has set up a twenty-man "purchase analysis" department under John C. Secrest, the youthful vice president for purchasing analysis whom it hired away from Ford.
>
> This "dependence" on suppliers also has its benefits, A. M. men say. One is flexibility. "Take the grille as an example," says Bernard A. Chapman, the executive vice president who oversees engineering, styling and purchasing. "The grille can be die cast, it can be an extrusion, or it can be a stamping. Since we haven't got a lot of money tied up in capacity for any of these, we have complete freedom of choice. Another is that A. M. gets the benefit of suppliers' own research and development, thus multiplying the effectiveness of its own relatively small engineering staff. Most important of all,

the low degree of integration enables A. M. to operate on a relatively small investment." It was able to boost its capacity from 250,000 cars a year in 1957 to nearly 700,000 today for less than $45 million—absolute peanuts by Big Three standards. Because it has less money invested in making parts than its competitors, American Motors' return on stockholders' equity—as distinguished from its low return on sales—is quite good. It earned 13.8 percent in equity last year, less than GM's 22.4 percent, but slightly more than Ford's 13.1 percent and considerably more than some of its suppliers.

Fortune continued with a description of AMC's plant complex:

Some of American Motors' production facilities are behind the times, the critics say. The charge is leveled not at the company's Kenosha assembly line, which is certainly modern enough, but at such operations as the Milwaukee body shop. This plant is a five-story affair, so crammed with uphill and downhill conveyer lines that it looks like an amusement-park fun ride. The same could be said for the former Simmons Co. plant at Kenosha that American Motors has leased since 1959. The company insists that these facilities are as efficient as any brand-new one-story plant; if they weren't, it would replace them. But it has a long-standing policy against investing in bricks and mortar except where it is absolutely unavoidable. Just to prove the company can build when necessary, officials cite the brand-new, $34-million engine plant at Kenosha, finished last February. The new facility, as up to date as anything the Big Three have, turns out the company's completely new six-cylinder engine.

Granting that American Motors' plant is reasonably up to date, can a company this size produce the variety of cars needed in today's compact car market? Absolutely, says Roy Abernethy. "When you have production volume of 400,000 to 500,000 cars a year, as we have," he says, "you're playing in the big leagues." Romney, he notes, once estimated the most efficient automobile-production volume at between 330,000 and 440,000 cars a year. Below 330,000 efficiency suffers; above 440,000, a company has to go into multiplant operation, as the Big Three have done. With all production concentrated in the Kenosha area, American Motors men say, the company operates well above the lower figure.

Indeed, its volumes in recent years have been at least 100,000 a year greater than was ever achieved by any of the industry's other, now defunct, independents, and its single assembly plant is the biggest in the U.S., with a capacity of 2,200 cars in a two-shift day. Shipping all over the U.S. from Kenosha presents no cost problem, officials contend. Romney once declared it costs less to ship finished cars to California than to ship components there to be assembled, and his successors say the argument is even more valid with the advent of trilevel railroad rack cars. . . . Most Big Three compacts have production runs of only 150,000 to 330,000 a year, and the Classic and American have been in this range in recent years.

In sum, American Motors faces no serious economic handicaps if it can keep its production at the 400,000-a-year level.[17]

Labor Relations

In remarks at the annual meeting of the stockholders on February 3, 1965, Mr. Abernethy noted:

Our production employees are now working under a new labor contract and a revised form of progress sharing [profit sharing]. Although all the auto industry contract settlements last fall could be said to be "generous," American Motors came out with two basic improvements. To a degree, our cost picture in relation to our competitors was improved by reducing the gap between their basic relief-time allowance and ours. In addition, a ceiling was put on distribution of profits under progress sharing.

Management Techniques

At the same meeting, Mr. Abernethy continued:

We have been doing what is necessary to apply the new, more sophisticated tools of management techniques to the larger-scale level of business at which this company now operates.

Our new data processing program is an example of the kind of planning and preparation that has been done.

We have complete systems in operation now that reflect our determination to continue to improve quality . . . give us better distribution of our products . . . give us more cars and the right cars when we need them.

Within a year, we'll be able to tell immediately the status of each car in our distribution channels, by pushing a button. Within minutes we will be able to locate and identify any car, anywhere in the U.S.

We've been testing date processing by computers in parts distribution for about three months in certain zones—and the things this system can do to expedite orders are amazing. The system in our Milwaukee Parts Center is programmed to automatically dial the zones at intervals, pick up the parts orders and put them on IBM cards, transmit the order to the proper warehouse—wherever the inventory indicates, Milwaukee, regional or zone—place the order and prepare shipping instructions—prepare the dealer invoice—and finally, order the inventory replacement—all automatically and in a matter of minutes.

This parts-orders system should be in operation in all zones by early fall.

The broader the business growth, the greater the need for this kind of technology as a basis for sound management decision-making.

Overseas Sales and Facilities

American Motors' international sales rose from 9,085 in 1958 to 59,450 in 1963 (see table 1). This expansion continued in 1964 and 1965, with sales reaching 72,348 in the former year and expected to surpass 80,000 in the latter. Although AMC produced 14 percent of the units exported from this country in 1963, its international vehicle sales represented 2.6 percent of the total U.S. international vehicle sales in 1963. American Motors manufactured a larger percentage of the cars it sold in international markets in this country, since it lacked the overseas manufacturing facilities of the Big Three.

TABLE 1.   U.S. International Vehicle Sales (thousands of units)

	GM	Ford	Chrysler	AMC	Total
1963	1,091.5	1,200.0	172.4	59.4	2,523.3
1962	853.2	1,116.0	137.4	52.6	2,159.2

Source: Data from *Steel,* February 10, 1964, 165.

During the 1962 to 1965 period, General Motors and Ford were making heavy capital investments abroad. For example, GM invested over $475 million in its foreign operations between 1962 and 1964. Ford spent $280 million overseas in 1964 alone. Chrysler, on the other hand, preferred to share its foreign buildup with distributions rather than investing as heavily in its own facilities abroad. American Motors followed a plan similar to Chrysler.[18]

According to *Ward's Automotive Reports:*

American Motors is involved in twelve assembly facilities on foreign soil. "Involved in" because each of the countries require particular and different degrees of participation by the American car builder.

The Canadian plant is the only foreign operation wholly owned by the company. In Argentina, Mexico and Venezuela, AM Corp. owns a minority interest. In Australia, Belgium, Chile, New Zealand, the Philippines, Uruguay and South Africa, the Rambler assembly plants are completely locally owned.

The general procedure in the foreign countries is for the local company to purchase the Rambler as Knock-Downs (just the basic body stampings) and to assemble, paint and sell them as a local operation. While the degree of local content varies greatly, in all countries the tires, batteries, glass and paint are locally procured.

In Argentina, where 90 percent of the finished automobile is locally manufactured, the Argentine company uses their own 6-cylinder engine and even produces some of the body stampings—the roof panel for instance.

In Belgium, the Rambler is sold as a luxury car, and a good percentage is built to be chauffeur driven. The Belgium company uses stitched velour fabric interior and sells the Rambler for $600 to $700 more than it costs here. In Mexico the automobile is 60 percent Mexican in content and uses a Mexican-built engine.

American Motors refers to their foreign assembly plants as evidence of their "partnership philosophy" and points out that it has a very favorable effect upon the oft-mentioned balance of payments.[19]

Mr. Pickett, president of American Motors International Corporation, commented on the partnership approach:

We decided on a partnership approach in setting up assembly facilities as the best way to sell our product and our American way of life at the same time. We believe that to be partners rather than bosses in foreign lands is not only the best practical way to operate, but the best moral way to operate as well.[20]

The *Journal of Commerce* continues:

In Venezuela, for example, Rambler announced that its cars would be made and sold there through a joint arrangement. For a total American Motors investment of $8,900, the Venezuelan operation was started. The rest of the funds were provided by local capital and banking arrangements.

The Market Ahead

In his article "The Auto Industry's Road Ahead," William Bower included some predictions about future developments in the car market:

"Common sense tells you it's too good to last," a Detroit automobile company executive said recently. He was talking about the auto boom that began in 1962, and it does indeed have a too-good-to-last look about it. . . . What lies down the road? The question divides into two interrelated, but distinguishable, questions: What is the short-term outlook through 1966? What is the larger-term trend to 1970 and beyond?

Paradoxically, these two questions require divergent answers. Almost everybody except makers and distributors of practical shoes can welcome the news that auto makers view the long-term trend with confidence and even exuberance. The executive who said, "Common sense tells you it's too good to last," went on: "but when you look at the underlying facts of the auto market they tell you it's for real."

The short-term outlook through 1966, however, is somewhat more sobering . . . the auto makers are wary of pinning themselves to formal forecasts of the 1966 market, but the informed, don't-quote-us estimates cluster within a range of 8,000,000 to 8,500,000.

But despite the clouds over 1966, the longer-term outlook is reassuringly sunny. For the years ahead, the auto industry projects a rising trend that by 1970 will make a nine-million-dollar year seem rather drab. Chrysler projects a ten-million norm in

1970. The official forecasts of the companies differ a bit, but they are all happy about the prospects. The industry's cheerful view of things to come is the more convincing because over the years the auto makers have tended to underestimate the future potentials of the market. . . . Detroit's current version of a well-paved road to 1970 and beyond is founded upon much of the same considerations that underlie *Fortune*'s projections in "Markets of the Sixties"—basic determinants such as old car scrappage and new household formation. . . . It is hard to imagine the next decade, at least, would keep the registration total from growing, and growing faster than population. . . . A Detroit executive recently said of the future: "To me it looks better than anybody in his right mind would want to be quoted as saying."

Within a decade or two beyond 1970, trends eroding demand for cars may set in. The population growth that enlarges demand for cars also produces crowding of both people and cars. Congestion will (1) make autos a less appealing mode of transportation; (2) bring steep and possibly prohibitive increases in the costs of producing highways; and (3) foster radical improvements in mass transportation. In the meantime, however, there is no reason to doubt the view expressed by Lynn A. Townsend, president of Chrysler, in a speech to the Economic Club of Detroit: "All the particulars are there to make the next ten years a golden age for our industry."[21]

However, according to *Fortune*, the golden age will not mean a revival of the "insolent chariots" and "gas-guzzling dinosaurs" of the fifties. Rather the proliferation of automobile styles started by the Rambler is likely to continue. As Roy Abernethy remarked at the Marlin introduction news conference: "The increasing amount and diversity of car use will lead to specialized types—cars specifically designed for short errands, recreational driving, long freeway trips, commuting, and so on. It is likely, on the other hand, that a strong demand will develop for the all-purpose, well-balanced car—equally at home and efficient on the turnpike or the village side street."

A pessimistic description of life in a large American city ten years from now was made by *Forbes*.

The scene is suburban Los Angeles. The time: 1975, a scant decade hence. A middle aged aircraft worker gulps his coffee, kisses his wife and jumps into one of the family's three cars. It is

7 a.m. Three frustrating hours later he reaches the plant. The parking lot is far bigger than the plant itself.

Since it is now 1975, our hero works a six-hour day. Finished at 4 p.m., he walks 20 minutes across the crowded lot to his car, climbs in, eventually gets to the nearby freeway. He drives home through traffic that alternately creeps and stops, stops and creeps. At 7 p.m. he arrives home, exhausted.[22]

This is not a too extreme example of what Frank McCulloch, former managing editor of the *Los Angeles Times,* calls "McCulloch's Law," namely, that "the more miles of freeway Los Angeles builds, the more automobiles it can put on them, and the more automobiles it puts on them, the more freeways it must build, and where it all ends, the Almighty only knows."

EXHIBIT 1.   Consolidated Statements of Profit and Loss ($000)

	1962	1963	1964	1965 (9 mos.)
Sales	1,135,190	1,217,932	1,077,144	
Less excise taxes	78,795	85,576	67,673	
Net sales	1,056,395	1,132,356	1,009,471	762,161
Other income				
Equity in net earnings of				
unconsolidated subsidiaries	2,568	5,308	6,333	
Interest and miscellaneous	6,475	6,823	6,085	
Total other income	8,944	12,131	12,418	
Total net revenue	1,065,439	1,144,487	1,021,889	
Costs and expenses				
Cost of product sold	870,701	942,056	833,410	
Depreciation				
Plant	9,744	10,709	12,498	
Tools and dies	19,876	19,277	31,680	
Cost of pensions	10,144	9,870	8,388	
Selling, advertising, and				
administration	81,731	80,018	94,085	
Refrigerator warranties	—	—	—	
Interest	120	—	—	
Sundry expenses	—	—	—	
Total costs and expenses	992,299	1,069,930	980,062	
Net profit or loss on operations	73,140	74,557	41,827	
Income tax	38,900	36,750	15,600	12,080
Net income after tax	34,240	37,807	26,227	18,241

EXHIBIT 2. Consolidated Balance Sheets ($000)

	1962	1963	1964
Assets			
Current assets			
Cash and government securities	87,059	95,382	45,105
Accounts receivable (net)	45,579	47,843	47,657
Accounts receivable from unconsolidated subsidiaries	4,816	5,329	10,575
Inventories — lower of cost (First-in First-out) or market	96,078	127,600	124,180
Miscellaneous items	3,916	4,078	4,996
Total current assets	237,448	279,992	232,513
Investments in unconsolidated subsidiaries	40,947	45,970	54,440
Miscellaneous assets	7,892	8,175	7,542
Property, plant and equipment (net)	88,789	106,235	126,203
Total assets	375,076	440,373	420,698
Liabilities and stockholders' equity			
Current liabilities			
Bank notes and amount due on long-term debt	0	0	0
Accounts payable	74,564	90,081	85,557
Salaries, wages, and amounts withheld from employees	12,436	13,927	13,776
Accrued expenses	28,207	30,017	29,493
Income taxes	5,761	27,100	9,034
Total current liabilities	120,968	161,125	137,859
Other liabilities	4,654	6,145	4,120
Long-term debt	0	0	0
Stockholders' equity			
Common stock	31,199	31,624	31,775
Additional paid — in capital	44,773	48,973	50,063
Retained earnings	173,482	192,507	196,881
Total stockholders' equity	249,454	273,104	278,719
Total liabilities and stockholders' equity	375,076	440,373	420,698

EXHIBIT 3. Total and Percentage Breakdown of New Car Production by Makes, Calendar Years 1962–65

	12 Months, 1962		12 Months, 1963		12 Months, 1964		6 Months, 1964		6 Months, 1965	
	Units	%Total	Units	%Total	Units	%Total	Units	%Total	Units	%Total
Chevrolet	1,495,466	21.56	1,625,920	21.29	1,440,185	18.61	917,728	20.71	1,039,021	20.14
Chevelle	—	—	113,780	1.49	320,938	4.15	191,574	4.32	198,258	3.84
Chevy II	369,245	5.32	312,118	4.09	157,798	2.04	116,049	2.62	78,884	1.53
Corvair	296,687	4.28	251,525	3.29	195,770	2.53	107,101	2.42	140,341	2.72
Total Chevrolet	2,161,398	31.16	2,303,343	30.16	2,114,691	27.33	1,332,452	30.07	1,456,504	28.23
Pontiac	401,674	5.79	481,652	6.31	443,306	5.73	283,075	6.39	298,715	5.79
Tempest	145,676	2.10	143,616	1.88	250,328	3.23	149,243	3.36	184,576	3.58
Total Pontiac	547,350	7.89	625,268	8.19	693,634	8.96	432,318	9.75	483,291	9.37
Oldsmobile	356,058	5.13	371,033	4.86	335,637	4.34	207,546	4.68	243,133	4.71
F-85	102,301	1.48	133,522	1.75	175,294	2.26	105,792	2.39	124,209	2.41
Total Oldsmobile	458,359	6.61	504,555	6.61	510,931	6.60	313,338	7.07	367,342	7.12
Buick	241,936	3.49	290,641	3.81	257,438	3.33	153,051	3.46	202,974	3.93
Riviera	14,830	0.21	36,532	0.48	36,313	0.47	24,503	0.55	21,490	0.42
Special	159,126	2.30	152,226	1.99	188,980	2.44	110,018	2.48	143,127	2.78
Total Buick	415,892	6.00	479,399	6.28	482,731	6.24	287,572	6.49	367,591	7.13
Cadillac	158,528	2.29	164,735	2.15	154,603	2.00	103,820	2.34	115,278	2.23
Total General Motors	3,741,527	53.95	4,077,300	53.39	3,956,590	51.13	2,439,500	55.72	2,790,006	54.08
Ford	722,647	10.42	911,496	11.94	881,054	11.38	523,662	11.81	599,500	11.62
Fairlane	386,192	5.57	318,018	4.16	233,718	3.02	143,086	3.23	126,313	2.45
Falcon	381,559	5.50	341,870	4.48	279,114	3.61	170,011	3.84	123,825	2.40

Mustang	—	—	—	—	303,407	3.92	84,269	1.90	310,513	6.02
Thunderbird	75,536	1.09	66,681	0.87	90,239	1.17	53,948	1.22	41,787	0.81
Total Ford	1,565,934	22.58	1,638,065	21.45	1,787,532	23.10	974,976	22.00	1,201,938	23.30
Mercury	109,346	1.58	118,815	1.55	125,431	1.62	58,313	1.31	109,173	2.12
Comet	144,886	2.09	150,694	1.97	195,229	2.52	112,876	2.55	82,144	1.59
Total Mercury	335,445	4.83	292,086	3.82	320,660	4.14	171,189	3.86	191,317	3.71
Lincoln	33,829	0.49	33,717	0.44	37,750	0.49	14,735	0.33	17,645	0.34
Total Ford Motor Co.	1,935,208	27.90	1,963,868	25.71	2,145,942	27.73	1,160,900	26.19	1,410,900	27.35
Fury	177,651	2.56	274,735	3.60	266,683	3.45	133,942	3.02	164,665	3.19
Belvedere	—	—	—	—	63,757	0.82	—	—	80,408	1.56
Barracuda	—	—	—	—	50,110	0.65	17,263	0.39	30,036	0.58
Valiant	153,428	2.22	221,677	2.90	190,789	2.46	107,079	2.42	72,837	1.41
Total Plymouth	331,079	4.78	496,412	6.50	571,339	7.38	258,284	5.83	347,946	6.74
Polara	167,869	2.42	246,425	3.23	215,896	2.79	143,590	3.24	67,777	1.31
Coronet	—	—	—	—	80,552	1.04	—	—	109,614	2.13
Dart	83,853	1.21	174,876	2.29	208,646	2.70	110,307	2.49	105,529	2.05
Total Dodge	251,722	3.63	421,301	5.52	505,094	6.53	253,897	5.73	282,920	5.49
Chrysler	119,221	1.72	111,958	1.47	145,338	1.88	80,897	1.81	117,028	2.27
Imperial	14,787	0.21	18,051	0.23	20,391	0.26	9,622	0.21	7,940	0.15
Total Chrysler Corp.	716,809	10.34	1,047,722	13.72	1,242,162	16.05	601,989	13.58	755,824	14.65
Rambler – American Motors	454,784	6.56	480,365	6.29	393,863	5.09	199,427	4.50	202,003	3.92
Studebaker Corp.	86,974	1.25	—	—	—	—	—	—	—	—
Total U.S. cars	6,935,302	100.00	7,637,630	100.00	7,738,557	100.00	4,432,293	100.00	5,158,743	100.00

Source: Ward's Automotive Reports, January 7, 1963, 8; January 11, 1965, 16; July 5, 1965, 216.

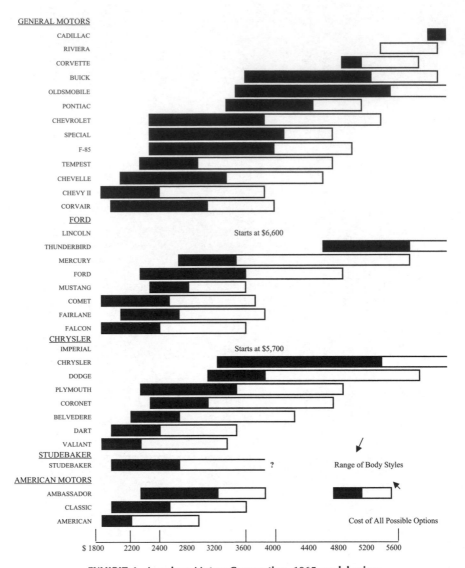

GENERAL MOTORS
CADILLAC
RIVIERA
CORVETTE
BUICK
OLDSMOBILE
PONTIAC
CHEVROLET
SPECIAL
F-85
TEMPEST
CHEVELLE
CHEVY II
CORVAIR
FORD
LINCOLN   Starts at $6,600
THUNDERBIRD
MERCURY
FORD
MUSTANG
COMET
FAIRLANE
FALCON
CHRYSLER
IMPERIAL   Starts at $5,700
CHRYSLER
DODGE
PLYMOUTH
CORONET
BELVEDERE
DART
VALIANT
STUDEBAKER
STUDEBAKER   ?
AMERICAN MOTORS
AMBASSADOR
CLASSIC
AMERICAN

Range of Body Styles

Cost of All Possible Options

$ 1800 2200 2400 2800 3200 3600 4000 4400 4800 5200 5600

EXHIBIT 4. American Motors Corporation, 1965 model prices

Source: Car Life, April 1965, pp. 18,19.
Note: The left end of the black bar represents the cost of the lowest price body style without options; the right end of the black bar represents the highest price body style without options; and the right end of the clear bar represents the highest price that can be paid for the car in question including all options which can be put on the car. Thus the clear bar approximately represents the cost of all options which can be put on the car.

EXHIBIT 5. Market Shares (%) Domestic-Make New Car Sales by Price Class
(January–July)

	GM		Ford		Chrysler		AMC		Studebaker	
	1964	1963	1964	1963	1964	1963	1964	1963	1964	1963
Luxury	61.9	71.5	32.6	24.9	5.5	3.6	—	—	—	—
Medium	80.1	81.4	8.2	8.1	11.7	10.5	—	—	—	—
Standard	52.3	55.3	30.1	29.7	17.6	15.0	—	—	—	—
Light	44.4	38.6	29.9	30.5	12.5	12.5	12.1	16.0	1.1	2.4
Total	54.4	54.5	26.3	25.8	13.9	12.8	4.9	6.0	0.5	0.9

Source: Ward's Automotive Reports, August 31, 1964, 274.

Note: Market shares each year horizontally add to 100%. Luxury cars: Imperial, Cadillac, Riviera, Corvette, Lincoln, Thunderbird. Medium cars: Chrysler, Dodge 880, Buick, Oldsmobile, Pontiac, Mercury. Standard cars: Dodge, Plymouth, Chevrolet, Ford. Light cars: Dart, Valiant, Special, F-85, Tempest, Corvair, Chevy II, Chevelle, Comet, Mustang, Falcon, Fairlane, Rambler, Studebaker. "Total" represents each producer's share of industry sales in all price fields.

EXHIBIT 6. Entire 1964 Model Year Passenger Car Production in the United States by $500 Groups (prices are suggested factory list pretax prices but include the heater cost)

	GM		Ford		Chrysler		AMC		Studebaker[a]		Industry	Total (%)
	Output	Share (%)	Output	Share (%)	Output	Share (%)	Output	Share (%)	Output	Share (%)		
1,801–2,000	92,416	14.3	216,060	33.6	212,065	32.9	116,549	18.1	7,295	1.1	644,385	8.17
2,001–2,500	1,552,536	48.8	866,726	27.2	493,362	15.5	249,828	7.9	20,183	0.6	3,182,635	40.33
2,501–3,000	1,915,442	62.2	796,145	25.9	334,089	10.8	27,482	0.9	4,861	0.2	3,078,019	39.00
3,001–3,500	325,866	77.5	61,138	14.6	32,994	7.9	—	—	—	—	419,998	5.32
3,501–4,000	164,850	85.0	—	—	29,055	15.0	—	—	—	—	193,905	2.46
4,001–4,500	43,666	36.2	83,267	61.8	1,836	1.4	—	—	811	0.6	134,580	1.70
4,501–5,000	75,913	87.6	9,198	10.6	1,574	1.8	—	—	—	—	86,685	1.10
5,001 and over	90,046	59.5	36,297	24.0	24,045	16.5	—	—	—	—	151,388	1.92
Total	4,265,735	54.1	2,068,831	26.2	1,130,020	14.3	393,859	5.0	33,150	0.4	7,891,595	100.00

Source: Ward's Automotive Reports, October 26, 1964, 338.

Note: "Share" represents percentage share of industry volume in indicated price group; hence, shares horizontally add to 100%. Totals represent actual cars built at the manufacturer's suggested factory list prices. Each V-8 or six-cylinder car produced is counted separately. Because the prices are "suggested factory list" they exclude federal excise and state and local taxes and optional equipment charges. However, all prices used include cost of the heater. Accordingly, this tabulation is not directly comparable with previous $100 price group tabulations presented by Ward's, which excluded the heater cost.

[a]Portions estimated.

EXHIBIT 7. 1965 Model U.S. Output to June 30

	V-8 Engines	Six-Cylinder Engines	Automatic Transmissions	Four-Speed Synchromesh Transmissions
GM	3,102,970	816,993	3,252,637	261,312
Ford	1,652,179	590,042	1,707,546	103,760
Chrysler	894,579	427,290	1,109,312	39,085
AMC	104,202	272,609	267,784	0
Total	5,753,930	2,106,934	6,337,279	404,157
Percentage of 1965s	73.2	26.8	80.6	5.1
Percentage of 1964s	69.0	31.0	77.7	4.6
Percentage of 1963s	62.3	36.5	75.6	3.9
Percentage of 1962s	56.0	41.5	74.2	2.9

Source: Ward's Automotive Reports, August 9, 1965, 250.
Note: 1965 percentage shares represent model year output through June 30 and prior year's entire model year.

EXHIBIT 8. Factory Installations: Air Conditioners (1964–61 models, by company)[a]

	1964 Models		1963 Models		1962 Models		1961 Models	
	Units	% Co.	Units	% Co.	Units	% Co.	Units	% Co.
GM	592,081	22.5	703,063	17.9	525,178	14.6	279,503	10.8
Ford	184,191	14.1	198,753	10.3	147,571	7.9	101,242	6.0
Chrysler	94,774	12.7	89,487	9.5	53,886	7.9	39,434	5.7
AM	24,932	8.7	38,058	8.2	28,752	6.5	17,383	4.6
Studebaker	1,160	3.5	2,437	3.2	1,800	1.9	718	1.1
Total industry	897,138	17.9	1,031,798	14.1	757,187	11.3	438,280	8.1

Source: Ward's Automotive Reports, April 27, 1964, 130.
Note: Figures for Chrysler Corp. are preliminary; figures for Studebaker Corp. are through end of U.S. output in January 1964.
[a]1964 models through March 31, 1964.

EXHIBIT 9. Factory Installations of Leading Equipment Items (includes optional and standard equipment entire 1964 model year)

Item Factory Installed	Cars Built with Item	All 1964 Cars Equipped with Item (%)
Automatic transmission	6,129,000	77.7
4-speed Synchromesh transmission	366,000	4.6
V-8 engine	5,445,000	69.0
Six-cylinder engine	2,445,000	31.0
Radio	5,178,000	65.6
Heater	7,726,000	97.9
Power steering	4,244,000	53.8
Power brakes	2,316,000	29.3
Power windows	509,000	6.4
Bucket seating	1,448,000	18.3
Movable-type steering	419,000	5.3
Whitewall tires	5,543,000	70.2
Windshield washers	4,961,000	62.9
Tinted glass (windshield only)	2,407,000	30.5
Tinted glass (windshield and other)	1,539,000	19.5
Backup lights	5,427,000	68.8
Air conditioning	1,412,000	17.9
Dual exhaust	942,000	11.9
Limited slip differential	526,000	6.7
Wheel covers	5,139,000	65.1

Source: *Ward's Automotive Reports,* October 5, 1964, 316.

EXHIBIT 10. Body Style Preference in the $2,001–$3,000 Market

	$2,001–$2,500 Market		$2,501–$3,000 Market	
	Number of Vehicles	%	Number of Vehicles	%
2-door sedan	608,920	19.1	3,933	0.1
4-door sedan	1,427,667	44.9	810,013	26.3
2-door hardtop	692,919	21.8	1,039,480	33.8
4-door hardtop	0	—	452,721	14.7
Convertible	111,947	3.5	255,758	8.3
Station wagon	341,182	10.7	516,114	16.8
Total	3,182,635	100.0	3,078,019	100.0

Source: *Ward's Automotive Reports,* November 2, 1964, 347.
Note: Based on entire 1964 model year car production.

EXHIBIT 11.   Body Style Preference for 1964 by Manufacturer

	2-Door Hardtop Most Popular V-8 Body Style[a]						
	GM	Ford	Chrysler	AMC	Studebaker	Total	% Total
2-door sedan	80,104	56,593	11,746	1,651	1,989	152,083	4.5
4-door sedan	484,466	326,753	172,915	27,882	11,596	1,023,612	30.0
2-door hardtop	647,662	333,023	107,830	14,653	3,305	1,106,473	32.4
4-door hardtop	414,492	63,832	55,735	0	0	534,059	15.6
Convertible	142,117	53,447	16,196	0	416	212,176	6.2
2-door, 2-seat wagon	799	491	0	0	0	1,290	—
4-door, 2-seat wagon	137,739	96,183	31,623	16,674	2,514	284,733	8.3
4-door, 3-seat wagon	43,715	34,290	19,186	0	0	97,191	2.9
5- and 6-door wagon	0	0	0	3,087	0	3,087	0.1
Total	1,951,094	964,612	415,231	63,947	19,280	3,414,704	100.0

	4-Door Sedan No. 1 Six-Cylinder Car[b]						
	GM	Ford	Chrysler	AMC	Studebaker	Total	% Total
2-door sedan	208,789	105,285	72,529	42,440	4,383	433,426	27.1
4-door sedan	295,791	139,812	166,124	91,127	6,981	699,835	43.8
2-door hardtop	61,342	30,849	47,756	33,417	224	173,588	10.9
4-door hardtop	10,706	528	0	0	0	11,234	0.7
Convertible	36,484	9,514	13,603	5,432	0	65,033	4.0
2-door, 2-station wagon	1,137	3,675	0	0	0	4,812	0.3
4-door, 2-station wagon	61,461	38,790	29,879	57,740	1,285	189,155	11.8
4-door, 3-station wagon	3,418	751	2,113	0	0	6,282	0.4
5- and 6-door station wagon	5,241	11,161	0	0	0	16,402	1.0
Total	684,369	340,365	332,004	230,156	12,873	1,599,767	100.0

Source: Ward's Automotive Reports, April 27, 1964, 130.
[a]Based on 1964 model car V-8 output through March 31, 1964.
[b]Based on 1964 model six-cylinder car output through March 31, 1964.

EXHIBIT 12.   U.S. Auto Company Floor Space Abroad (as of December 31, 1964)

Company	Floor Space (sq. ft. in thousands)
General Motors	62,355
Ford	48,630
Chrysler	16,060[a]
AMC	770[b]

Source: Ward's Automotive Reports, April 26, 1965, 130.
[a]Includes 2,088,000 sq. ft. that are leased.
[b]Does not include space partly owned in three countries or locally owned plants that assemble Rambler Knock-Downs in eight other countries.

Notes

Copyright © by Chuck Hofer. This case was first published as a Harvard Business School Case, 1960.

1. *Wall Street Journal,* August 3, 1965, 1.

2. Case Writer note: For comparative purposes, Chrysler spent $95 million and Ford spent $234 million for new model tooling in 1964.

3. *Business Week,* May 4, 1963, 33.

4. *The Changing Car Market: Phase II,* American Motors Corp., September 19, 1963, 1.

5. *Wall Street Journal,* November 17, 1964, 7.

6. *New York Times,* July 25, 1965, 1.

7. *Ward's Automotive Reports,* August 9, 1965, 253.

8. *New York Times,* July 25, 1965, 5.

9. Remarks by Roy Abernethy, Benton and Bowles Briefing, April 20, 1965.

10 *Wall Street Journal,* July 29, 1964, 1.

11. Engine displacement (cubic inches), not horsepower.

12. "The Challenge of 1965," remarks by Roy Abernethy, *1965 Product Review,* May 27, 1964.

13. "The Challenge of 1965," remarks by Roy Abernethy, *1965 Product Review,* May 27, 1964.

14. *New York Times,* July 25, 1965, 5.

15. Remarks by Roy Abernethy, Benton and Bowles Briefing, April 20, 1965.

16. *New York Times,* July 25, 1965, 1.

17. Edmund Faltermayer, "The Squeeze in American Motors' Road," *Fortune,* September 1964, 170.

18. *Ward's Automotive Reports,* April 24, 1965, 130.

19. *Ward's Automotive Reports,* April 24, 1965, 130.

20. *Journal of Commerce,* July 3, 1964, 9.

21. William Bower, "The Auto Industry's Road Ahead," *Fortune,* June 1965.

22. *Forbes,* July 15, 1965, 15.

Financial Issues

Restructuring

18. RCN: How to Invest in a Turnaround

Howard Zukin was the chief in-house analyst for Lazarus Partners, a hedge fund engaged in investing in the stocks and bonds of distressed companies. Lazarus had been founded in 1995 by a group of elite business school MBAs who had all worked for major mutual fund companies as research analysts and portfolio managers. In approaching the discipline of investing in troubled firms, Lazarus took the approach of passively buying or selling short securities as opposed to acquiring controlling positions and trying to influence the reorganization process of its investees. This approach to distressed securities investing necessitated a very high degree of diversification, which required a large amount of research. Howard had been with the company for a little over three years and had distinguished himself as a thorough and insightful analyst. While he was not the only analyst working for Lazarus, it was his job to form independent opinions of prospective portfolio companies that were not influenced by Wall Street research. The other analysts working for Lazarus regularly interfaced with analysts from major sell side firms. Frequently the sell side analysts would have different opinions about a particular company than Howard did. This was primarily due to the fact that the sell side analysts were oriented toward short-term trading as opposed to long-term investing. Therefore they spent much of their time analyzing the liquidity of prospective investees as opposed to determining their intrinsic value. Intrinsic value is a concept that was first developed by

---

This case was prepared by Henry Garelick.

Benjamin Graham and later used extremely successfully by Warren Buffett to acquire interests in companies that were effectively mispriced by the largely emotional gyrations of the stock market. As the true values of companies purchased on a bargain basis, or at less than their intrinsic values, were realized, the prices of their securities rose significantly. Applying the Graham-Buffett methodology to investing in troubled companies was Howard's mission as far as his professional life was concerned.

RCN was a company that Howard had been looking at for some time. RCN was a broadband communications company with networks in Boston; New York; Philadelphia; San Francisco; Los Angeles; and Washington, D.C. RCN's strategy was to develop significant market share in these prime markets at the expense of older, more established rivals, namely, Comcast and Cablevision. The way that RCN competed with these companies was to offer high-speed state-of-the-art broadband service encompassing basic cable, telephony, and Internet access in a bundled fashion where the customer would pay RCN every month rather than several different vendors. The company's strategy largely had been successful. In October 2002, having only been in business five years, the company had achieved over 30 percent penetration in the markets that it was attempting to serve. From a financial perspective RCN had become less of a success story and more of a poster child for "alternative" communications companies, many of which had failed and fallen into bankruptcy over the preceding twenty-four months. Its once high-flying stock was trading below a dollar on the NASDAQ and had been for quite some time, and its unsecured bonds were trading for less than thirty cents on the dollar.

Since 1999 Howard had made a practice of keeping track of RCN's performance by using what he called a cash flow mapping approach whereby he projected and then subsequently recorded RCN's earnings before interest, taxes, depreciation, and amortization (EBITDA) and its coverage of capital expenditures, interest, and taxes. The company's stated goal was to be EBITDA positive by late 2003 and capable of covering capital expenditures, interest, and taxes by the end of 2004. Looking at the numbers Howard noticed that the company was falling short of his projections from a revenue standpoint but was matching or exceeding his projections in other areas by aggressively reducing expenses and capital expenditures. The other way that the company was reaching or exceeding its projections was by reducing its interest burden by retiring debt at a discount. Although this seemed like a logical way for the company to use its capital, Howard had reservations about it in that it effectively shrank the window of opportunity for the company to turn the corner from an operations standpoint.

From where Howard sat, RCN was an interesting opportunity for the following reasons. First, RCN had built a subscriber base with over four hundred thousand basic cable subscribers, many of whom also used the company for telephone and Internet access. Therefore the average monthly revenue per customer was in excess of $70.00, nearly double that of conventional cable companies operating in the same area. Howard had spoken with RCN employees who had told him that the company regarded each customer as an asset worth $4,000. While Howard viewed this figure with some skepticism he could easily see how the subscriber base could be valued at $2,000 per customer, or $.8 billion. In addition to its subscriber base RCN had considerable cash and other assets. If Howard truly believed in his estimate of the subscriber base's value then RCN's bonds were conspicuously undervalued. Second, RCN seemed to have enough cash on hand and cash coming to it from asset sales that were subject to firm agreements to last at least another year and a half according to Howard's projections. In that amount of time the interest that would be paid to the bondholders would almost equal the value of the bonds at present trading levels. Third, RCN had relatively little bank debt ahead of its bonds. This meant that the likelihood that the company would be liquidated to satisfy secured creditors was very slim. If the company went into Chapter 11 chances were that the bondholders would wind up with most of the equity in a largely debt free enterprise. When Howard calculated what this would mean in terms of cash flows, he was pleasantly surprised at how good the company might look in a couple of years. Finally, there were several prominent and very wealthy investors who owned considerable amounts of common and preferred stock in RCN. These interests all ranked junior to the bonds from a priority standpoint, and in bankruptcy they would be severely impaired if not wiped out altogether. Although it had been Howard's observation that well-heeled investors that were involved in distressed companies were generally loath to put "good money after bad," there were some situations where it seemed to make sense for them to protect their investments by doing so. It occurred to Howard that it might be a good idea for

RCN's major investors to create availability for the company at the senior secured level in order for it to become profitable and perhaps access capital markets on its own. However his experience told him that the chances of this happening were slim.

All in all, Howard's research pointed toward a prepackaged bankruptcy filing for RCN, where the bondholders would wind up with most of the equity in a reorganized company. From his research and what he felt the intrinsic value of the company was likely to be in several years, he determined that at present levels the bonds represented an excellent opportunity, but there was still one major problem. Some of the other analysts at Lazarus had asked about RCN at the sell side firms that they were doing business with. As was frequently the case, some of the sell side analysts had problems agreeing with Howard's prognosis for the bonds. Their reservations were primarily those of questioning the quality of RCN's assets. According to these analysts, RCN's subscriber base was much less valuable than the subscriber base of a "conventional" cable operator due to the fact that RCN was always the second participant in the markets that it served as opposed to a monopoly franchise owner. Also the analysts questioned the viability of the company's promises regarding cash flow breakeven and future profitability. As far as they were concerned there was a distinct possibility that the company would never generate EBITDA and that it would go out of business altogether. This scenario would leave little or nothing for the bondholders.

Facing this skepticism Howard sought to address the one major issue regarding the company that he had not thoroughly investigated. Like any company that is trying to make inroads on an established competitor, RCN was faced with the task of acquiring customers if it wanted to grow. Howard wanted to know if the company knew what the costs associated with adding incremental customers were. Also Howard was curious as to how well the company handled service issues and retained customers. In order to accomplish this Howard employed the "scuttlebutt" method of talking to company employees, customers, and executives. What his informal survey told him was that customer acquisition costs were estimated by the company at less than $1,000 per new account. In addition all of the customers surveyed were extremely happy with the service. Finally the employees told him that the company was extremely service oriented and that a majority of new accounts were deeply dissatisfied with the service that they had received from prior vendors, who had all been entrenched monopolies before RCN arrived on the scene. RCN saw this as a major opportunity, and its workforce was specially screened to take advantage of this.

In talking with the CEO of Lazarus, Jorge Putalones, Howard stated his position as clearly as he could. "Jorge, I think that our only risk on the bonds occurs in the near term. I think that the company has intrinsic value in excess of the market value of the securities. All we need to do is acquire some of these bonds and wait for the situation to work out." "That's all well and good, Howard, but we do have to be concerned with the short run as well as the long run due to the fact that we have some institutional money that's tracking us on a quarterly basis," Jorge said. "This year we are down relative to the high-yield index, and I'm not sure that I want to take the risk of acquiring these bonds if they might wind up subject to a Chapter 11 filing in a couple of months."

This was not the first time that Howard had run up against the short-run versus long-run dilemma. In Howard's view the short run was something that couldn't be mastered. Only the long-term prospects of companies could be measured with any precision. It was Howard's view that Lazarus should avoid taking on money from myopic institutions. If the fund was smaller as a result then so be it. Talking to Dave Amsterdam, a fellow analyst, one day, Howard said, "We have to have the opportunity to load up on garbage, and then we need the time to let that garbage turn to gold." "Sure, Howard," Dave responded. "But do you really want to bite the hand that feeds you?"

Student Assignment

Answer the following questions.

1. How can Howard persuade Jorge and the other analysts that making long-term investments is in the best interests of Lazarus?
2. What are the strengths of Howard's argument, and what are its weaknesses? What kind of information could he add to the mix to make it more convincing?
3. What are the business concerns facing managers like Jorge in this situation? How should Jorge operate his business to create the best long-term results? How does all of this affect Howard?

4. RCN may find itself with $100 million in excess cash from asset sales in the near future. Should the company use the money to repurchase debt at a discount, or should it hold on to the money to prolong its window of survival?
5. Some of the company's preferred stockholders, namely, Paul Allen and also Hicks, Muse, Tate, and Furst, have approached you for a strategy whereby they would invest an additional $250 million in RCN. How would you advise them to go about this?
6. A client approaches you with the information that he has discovered three thousand shares of RCN common stock in his grandmother's portfolio. He asks you if the shares should be held or sold. As a point of information, a close friend of Warren Buffett has invested $50 million in RCN common stock at higher levels than it presently trades. This friend is a director of RCN, and he serves as vice chairman. In addition he is the chairman of the board of Level 3 Communications, a large, long-haul broadband company. How should you advise your client?
7. What is the significance of what Howard discovered in his informal survey? What percentage of Wall Street analysts do you think conduct similar surveys? Are such surveys valuable, or are they a waste of time? How does this agree or disagree with modern concepts of portfolio management such as the efficient market theory?

EXHIBIT 1. Selected Actual and Projected Financial Data, 2000–2003 ($ millions)

	3/31/2000	6/30/2000	9/30/2000	12/31/2000	12/31/00Y	3/31/2001	Projected 6/30/2001	Actual 6/30/2001	Projected 9/30/2001	Actual 9/30/2001	Projected 12/31/2001	Actual 12/31/2001	Projected 12/31/01Y	Actual 12/31/01Y	Projected 3/31/2002	Actual 3/31/2002
Revenues	71.3	78.9	88.3	95.0	333.5	105.9	116.5	110.9	128.1	116.3	141.0	122.7	491.5	455.8	135.0	124.5
Operating income	(111.9)	(141.5)	(166.2)	(198.0)	(617.6)	(176.0)	(160.2)	(145.5)	(145.7)	(113.7)	(132.6)	(109.1)	(614.5)	(544.3)	(102.0)	(103.1)
Depreciation	44.4	68.8	83.1	89.4	285.7	91.7	94.0	83.9	95.5	73.2	95.5	72.7	376.7	321.5	70.0	75.9
EBITDA	(67.5)	(72.7)	(83.1)	(108.6)	(331.9)	(84.3)	(66.2)	(61.6)	(50.2)	(40.5)	(37.1)	(36.4)	(237.8)	(222.8)	(32.0)	(27.2)
Capex	155.3	246.9	330.9	394.8	1,127.9	203.3	175.0	152.8	155.0	115.0	135.0	100.0	668.3	571.1	85.0	60.0
Interest	53.4	55.4	55.6	59.5	223.9	53.6	51.0	50.7	50.0	48.2	50.0	44.5	204.6	197.0	44.5	40.6
Taxes	(0.8)	(0.7)	(0.9)	(2.4)	(4.8)	(2.6)	(2.8)	(0.7)	(2.4)	0.1	(2.6)	(0.4)	(10.4)	(3.6)	(2.3)	(0.8)
Net EBITDA	(275.4)	(374.3)	(468.7)	(560.5)	(1,678.9)	(338.6)	(289.4)	(264.4)	(252.8)	(203.8)	(219.5)	(180.5)	(1,100.3)	(987.3)	(159.2)	(127.0)
Cash and securities	3,111.1	2,559.6	2,159.8	1,728.5	1,728.5	1,234.9	945.5	1,059.9	692.7	1,131.9	473.2	650.0	473.2	650.0	490.8	508.1
Bank debt	562.5															
Bonds	1,146.2															
Preferred stock	2,027.6															
Common shares	87.7															
Price/Share	1.2															
Market cap	107.9															
Enterprise value	3,281.7															

(continued)

EXHIBIT 1—Continued

	Projected 6/30/2002	Actual 6/30/2002	Projected 9/30/2002	Actual 9/30/2002	Projected 12/31/2002	Actual 12/31/2002	Projected 12/31/02Y	Actual 12/31/02Y	Projected 3/31/2003	Projected 6/30/2003	Projected 9/30/2003	Projected 12/31/2003	Projected 12/31/2003
Revenues	144.5	127.9	130.0	114.5	133.0	117.2	542.5	484.1	136.0	139.0	142.0	147.0	564
Operating income	(95.9)	(109.4)	(102.0)	(76.3)	(95.9)	(83.9)	(395.8)	(372.7)	(91.3)	(87.2)	(85.6)	(82.1)	(346.2)
Depreciation	70.0	87.6	90.2	55.7	93.1	64.4	323.3	283.6	94.5	96.0	98.0	100.0	388.5
EBITDA	(25.9)	(21.8)	(11.8)	(20.6)	(2.8)	(19.5)	(72.5)	(89.1)	3.2	8.8	12.4	17.9	42.3
Capex	65.0	41.2	55.0	35.0	45.0	29.9	250.0	166.1	37.0	35.0	33.0	30.0	135.0
Interest	44.5	38.9	44.5	47.1	44.5	40.9	178.0	167.5	36.0	32.0	32.0	32.0	132.0
Taxes	(2.5)	(0.1)	(2.7)	(0.1)	(2.4)	(0.1)	(9.9)	(1.1)	(2.0)	(1.9)	(1.7)	(1.5)	(7.1)
Net EBITDA	(132.9)	(101.8)	(108.6)	(102.6)	(89.9)	(90.2)	(490.6)	(421.6)	(67.8)	(56.3)	(50.9)	(42.6)	(217.6)
Cash and securities	357.9	415.4	249.3	390.0	159.4	277.0	159.4	277.0	91.6	35.3	(15.6)	(58.2)	53.3
Asset sale proceeds									245.0	245.0	245.0	245.0	245.0
Total availability									336.6	280.3	229.4	186.8	186.8

	12/31/00Y	12/31/01Y	12/31/02Y
Revenues	333.5	455.8	484.1
Operating income	(617.6)	(544.3)	(372.7)
Depreciation	285.7	321.5	283.6
EBITDA	(331.9)	(222.8)	(89.1)
Capex	1,127.9	571.1	166.1
Interest	223.9	197.0	167.5
Taxes	(4.8)	(3.6)	(1.1)
Net EBITDA	(1,678.9)	(987.3)	(421.6)
Cash and securities	1,728.5	650.0	277.0

EXHIBIT 2. Historic RCN Income Statement, 1999–2001

	Dec. 31, 2001	Dec. 31, 2000	Dec. 31, 1999
Total revenue	455,971,000	333,450,000	275,993,000
Cost of revenue	205,132,000		
Gross profit	250,839,000	333,450,000	275,993,000
Operating expenses			
Research and development			
Selling, general, and administrative expenses	536,632,000	706,646,000	407,960,000
Nonrecurring	470,880,000		
Other operating expenses	321,525,000	285,648,000	146,043,000
Operating income	(1,078,198,000)	(658,844,000)	(278,010,000)
Total other income and expenses net	97,723,000	119,202,000	(82,149,000)
Earnings before interest and taxes	(980,475,000)	(539,642,000)	(95,861,000)
Interest expense	196,910,000	223,868,000	158,139,000
Income before tax	(1,177,385,000)	(763,510,000)	(354,000,000)
Income tax expense	(3,682,000)	(4,778,000)	(5,094,000)
Equity earnings or loss unconsolidated subsidiary	(17,185,000)	(34,497,000)	(33,960,000)
Minority interest	22,088,000	24,515,000	28,262,000
Net income from continuing operations	(1,168,800,000)	(768,714,000)	(354,604,000)
Nonrecurring events			
Extraordinary items	484,011,000		(424,000)
Net income	(684,789,000)	(768,714,000)	(355,028,000)
Preferred stock and other adjustments	(151,663,000)	(122,752,000)	(13,542,000)
Net income applicable to common shares	(836,452,000)	(891,466,000)	(368,570,000)

EXHIBIT 3. Historic RCN Balance Sheets, 1999–2001

	Dec. 31, 2001	Dec. 31, 2000	Dec. 31, 1999
Current assets			
Cash and cash equivalents	476,220,000	356,377,000	391,412,000
Short-term investments	385,947,000	1,372,015,000	1,424,988,000
Total current assets	956,174,000	1,854,331,000	1,904,939,000
Long-term assets			
Property, plant and equipment	2,320,198,000	2,255,959,000	893,179,000
Goodwill	96,939,000	463,187,000	103,785,000
Total assets	3,603,131,000	4,775,552,000	3,192,114,000
Current liabilities			
Total current liabilities	357,430,000	530,889,000	249,445,000
Long-term debt	1,873,616,000	2,257,357,000	2,143,096,000
Total liabilities	4,435,273,000	2,889,461,000	2,546,373,000
Total stockholder equity	(832,142,000)	(104,522,000)	645,741,000
Net tangible assets	(929,081,000)	(567,709,000)	541,956,000

19. Ajax Electronics

In midsummer 2002, John Clark, a loan officer of the SaveMe Bank of Ipswich, Massachusetts, was reviewing a loan request for $100,000 from Bob Roberts, president of Ajax Electronics.

Products

Ajax Electronics had two product lines, industrial sensors and defibrillators. Revenue was split evenly between them.

Bob Roberts, who had an electrical engineering degree, had worked previously as a manufacturing engineer. Ajax had started out as a manufacturing process control consulting firm in 1985. In 1988, it began producing customized sensors for chemical, paper, and brewery companies for use in their manufacturing processes to measure flow volumes, temperatures, pressures, and so forth. Roberts did the selling to client manufacturers himself. He also did the design work and supervised the manufacturing of these sensors. His engineering staff for this end of the business consisted of an electrical engineer and a manufacturing engineer. Over the years, he had achieved a gross margin for these industrial sensors of about 40 percent. Roberts felt that he could do better.

In 1989, through discussions with his father (who was a retired cardiologist in his late eighties), Roberts became convinced that there was an opportunity to design a low-cost defibrillator for emergency medical applications. Health care was improving around the world. Also, inexpensive offshore manufacturing was becoming in-

This case was prepared by Marc Meyer and James F. Molloy, Jr.

creasingly available to small firms (Roberts was particularly interested in southern China). By late 1989, he had designed a low-cost defibrillator and had received FDA approval to sell it. His father had provided the limited clinical expertise needed for the product. He began manufacturing the product in one side of his existing facility in 1990. Ajax, located in rented space in northeastern Massachusetts, was fully equipped with the latest electrically driven machinery.

Defibrillators are used to apply electrical shock to the heart when it stops beating. The types of buyers of defibrillators are in-hospital users, that is, doctors (mainly cardiologists) and emergency room technicians; and out-of-hospital organizations, such as ambulance services. There are also three basic types of defibrillators: "low-end" defibrillators, which produce and deliver the required electrical shock at the hands of a trained operator; mid-range defibrillators, which have the capability to detect when a shock is required by the heart but require a trained operator to deliver the shock; and "high-end" defibrillators, which are programmable "computers" that detect the need for shock and target the delivery of the shock to a point in the heart rhythm.

Ajax made only low-end defibrillators and had achieved a gross margin in the 25 percent range. High-volume manufacturers of defibrillators were known to achieve gross margins of about 40 percent. There were many competitors in the low-end market. In the high-end market, two firms dominated the in-hospital applications, Hewlett Packard and Zoll, while the out-of-hospital emergency market was dominated by PhysioControl. Interestingly, PhysioControl's government permit to sell defibrillators was recently revoked by the FDA for product quality problems. Given the broad scope of the market for defibrillators, most firms, particularly the smaller ones, employed medical products distributors as the primary sales channel. Industry observers found that the U.S. defibrillator market was about $100 million in 1989. This market was projected to increase to approximately $700 million by 2000, fueled by high levels of growth in markets such as China and South America.

Financials

The company was owned 100 percent by Roberts. Sales volume grew steadily but always seemed to be higher than could be supported by available capital. In other words, Ajax always seemed starved for cash. Capital needs were usually furnished through short-term borrowing. Mr. Roberts, the company's only officer, was anxious to maintain Ajax's record of profitability, so he only drew a salary of $40,000 in recent years. He was fifty years old.

Mr. Roberts was thoroughly unhappy with the company's present loan arrangement with the Webster Bank, from which it had been borrowing between $45,000 and $60,000 at an annual interest rate of 11 percent. Mr. Roberts pledged accounts receivable as security. He thought that Mr. Schell, the loan officer at the Webster Bank who handled the Ajax account, was a hindrance. Mr. Schell seemed to constantly make suggestions that weren't appropriate for Ajax. In fact, the bank arbitrarily selected the receivables it would accept as collateral. This put pressure on Roberts because of the uncertainty of having adequate funds to keep creditors in line.

Mr. Roberts thought this attitude from the bank limited the company's ability to grow. The company had been unable to solicit new customers for fear of insufficient funds. Increased sales volume was financed internally and came from expansion of existing accounts. Since the plant was being operated at only 60 percent of capacity, Mr. Roberts was eager to increase sales. Operations were currently above the breakeven point, and since the general, selling, and administrative expenses should remain fixed, any further increase in sales volume would increase profits.

Mr. Roberts felt that pledging the company's accounts receivable or any other asset that the bank thought would be desirable security would be satisfactory. Of course the arrangement had to be fair and produce money when needed.

Mr. Clark, of SaveMe Bank, explained that money was tight at the moment but that it was always interested in sound loan proposals from companies that showed promise. Mr. Clark promised to look into Mr. Roberts's request and said he planned to visit the company in a few days. He suggested that Mr. Roberts prepare an estimate of his cash requirements, and the meeting was adjourned on an upbeat note. The Webster Bank was only a short distance from the plant, yet Mr. Schell had never visited Ajax.

Before going to Ajax, Mr. Clark phoned Mr. Schell to obtain his opinion of Ajax. Schell's experience with Ajax was thoroughly unsatisfactory. Mr. Schell reported that Ajax on several occasions had overdrawn its account. Also, the receivables pledged as security often did not meet the bank's collateral standards. He went on to say that Mr. Roberts was competent from a technical standpoint but he lacked financial and administrative skills. Mr. Roberts never had been able "to get his house in order." However, Mr. Schell believed that the company's products were well received by the trade. Ajax, he said, had a possibility of developing into a sound business if there was stronger management.

Accounts receivable on Ajax's books as of July 31, 2002, were aged as shown in table 1.

Of the $9,000 representing accounts over ninety days old, $6,000 was due from the General Service Administration, which was often slow in paying its account. The other $3,000 was owed by two hospitals. The remaining $34,000 in receivables over thirty days old was due from twelve medical products distributors and three distributors of sensors.

After visiting the Ajax plant, Mr. Clark noted that, although the production process included some fabricating for the custom work, it was primarily an assembly operation. The defibrillators were all standard models and were produced in small lots. There was an erratic flow of work, and there was excess inventory in storage awaiting further processing. It took eight to ten weeks to complete the processing of defibrillators. The sensors were manufactured and designed to meet the specific requirements of a customer. Since each order required specific engineering modification by Mr. Roberts, the company rarely completed these sensors in less than three months.

On July 31, 2002, Ajax's inventory was valued at $252,000. Finished goods inventory, which included only defibrillators, totaled $27,000; work in process was $51,000 for defibrillators and $48,000 for sensors; and raw material represented the remaining $126,000. Mr. Clark noted that the raw material inventory consisted of a large number of electronic and mechanical parts, ranging in value from a few cents each to several hundred dollars.

TABLE 1.   Ajax's Accounts Receivable, July 31, 2002

Shipment	Age	Outstanding Receivables ($)	Sales ($)
July	0–30 days	49,000	55,000
June	30–60 days	20,000	66,000
May	60–90 days	14,000	51,000
April	90–120 days	9,000	54,000
Total		92,000	

Mr. Roberts agreed that inventory probably should be reduced to $150,000. Most of this would result from a recently installed inventory control system. This system had already showed results since purchases had dropped from an average of $20,000 per month at the beginning of the year to under $10,000 in recent months despite a steady increase in sales volume. Terms of purchases ranged from COD to net 30.

In probing several disturbing aspects of the balance sheet, Mr. Clark learned that the accounts payable had a balance of $74,000 while total purchases were $100,000 during the first seven months of 2002. An aging of the trade debt on the company's books as of the middle of August 2002 was as shown in table 2.

Approximately $5,000 of payables was in dispute, and another $5,000 was to friendly creditors to whom payment could be postponed indefinitely.

As of August 15, delinquent withholding taxes totaled $30,000. Federal income taxes had been paid in March and June. Mr. Roberts said that the IRS had been pushing him to reduce his delinquency to $15,000 before the end of the month. The IRS further threatened to file a tax lien against Ajax on all delinquencies. This would put Ajax on a "pay as you collect" withholding tax basis. This would require an arrangement where Ajax would make weekly payments to the tax collector. According to Mr. Roberts, Webster Bank's negative attitude toward Ajax might be behind this.

An outside group of Mr. Roberts's friends had loaned Ajax $53,000 at 15 percent interest secured by a lien on the company's machinery and equipment. The note was payable on demand with no definite repayment schedule established.

Mr. Roberts estimated that sales for the remainder of 2002 would average between $60,000 and $65,000 per month and would

TABLE 2.   Ajax's Trade Debt, Mid-August 2002 ($)

Purchase Month	Purchases ($)	Trade Debt Payable ($)
August (1–15)	6,000	5,000
July	8,000	6,000
June	11,000	8,000
May	15,000	13,000
Prior		35,000
Total		67,000

increase to $75,000 per month for 2003. Mr. Roberts thought that with bank support there would be little difficulty in achieving these goals. This was because a number of medical wholesaling houses had expressed continued interest in carrying Ajax's instruments and because the company's sensor products were almost without competition. In this respect, he estimated his needs as shown in table 3.

Since the company had recently modernized its production facilities, no further expenditures were planned. Depreciation charges, using straight line depreciation, amounted to $1,000 per month.

When Mr. Clark returned to the bank, he sent out letters of inquiry to a random list of Ajax's suppliers. (Excerpts from the responses received from the bank are shown in exhibit 3.) He also obtained a copy of the Dun and Bradstreet report on the company. Since the report was almost a year old and related to financial statements prior to 2001, it contained no additional information that was helpful to Mr. Clark. However, he noted that Mr. Roberts had withheld from the Dun and Bradstreet reporter general financial information and in particular had declined to give information on payables and sales.

On September 1, Mr. Roberts returned to SaveMe Bank to discuss the loan proposal further. He reported that the accounts receivable balance on August 31 was approximately $100,000 (August sales totaled $62,000), of which $90,000 represented accounts less than sixty days old. Mr. Roberts said he had no additional personal funds to invest in the company. However, he would agree not to pay dividends, increase his salary, or take repayment of the personal loans he had made to the company until the bank debt had been paid in full. Finally, Mr. Roberts said he had discussed the lien on the machinery and felt that the group might be willing to subordinate to the bank loan. On September 1, the company's loan balance at the Webster Bank amounted to $39,000.

Mr. Clark agreed to consider this proposal further and promised to let Mr. Roberts know the bank's decision within a few days. Clark set to work considering three basic questions.

TABLE 3. Ajax's Financial Requirements ($)

Repayment of present bank loan	39,000
Additional working capital	61,000
Total requirement	100,000

1. What business is Roberts in? What are his strengths and weaknesses? What are the keys to success for running that business?
2. Should SaveMe Bank give Roberts the loan?
3. What advice might Clark give to Roberts with respect to Ajax's business strategy?

EXHIBIT 1. Ajax Electronics Balance Sheets for the Period Ending 1997–2002 ($000)

	12/31/97	12/31/98	12/31/99	12/31/00	12/31/01	7/31/02
Assets						
Cash	—	—	2	—	6	2
Accounts receivable	75	54	57	64	107	92
Inventory	113	108	150	195	246	252
Total current assets	188	162	209	266	359	346
Fixed assets, net	33	30	27	32	33	68
Deferred assets	11	9	9	11	21	21
Total assets	232	201	245	309	413	435
Liabilities and owners equity						
Overdraft — bank	6	6	—	—	—	—
Notes payable — bank	39	26	46	42	56	39
Notes payable — mortgage	11	—	—	—	27	53
Accounts payable	32	26	26	66	71	74
Taxes payable	11	11	24	20	37	33
Miscellaneous accruals	9	11	12	15	29	30
Total current liabilities	108	80	108	143	220	229
Subordinated loan from officers	38	30	18	28	39	39
Total liabilities	146	110	126	171	259	268
Common stock	51	51	51	51	51	51
Surplus	35	40	68	87	103	116
Total liabilities and owners' equity	232	201	245	309	413	435

EXHIBIT 2. Ajax Electronics, Income Statements 1997–2002 ($000)

	1997	1998	1999	2000	2001	Jan–July 2002
Net sales	309	334	389	558	594	354
Less cost of goods sold						
Material	101	107	116	180	190	112
Labor	46	48	54	88	95	61
Overhead	54	58	63	87	89	45
Depreciation	4	3	3	3	6	4
Total cost of goods sold	205	216	236	358	380	222
Gross profit	104	118	153	200	214	132
General, selling, and administrative	95	111	117	173	190	106
Net profit before taxes	9	7	36	27	24	26
Taxes	2	1	9	8	8	
Net profit after taxes	7	6	27	19	16	

EXHIBIT 3. Ajax Electronics: Excerpts from Responses to Letters of Credit Inquiry Sent out by Mr. Clark

The firm in question appears to have a good market for its products and always appears busy. Their available capital has always been small, resulting in slow payments to their suppliers. From time to time we have had to ship orders on a COD basis.

They are slow paying, but all amounts are eventually paid. They are pleasant people and one of our favorite customers.

Ajax owes us a four-figure amount. In the past, payments have all been met in approximately 60 to 90 days. The company appears to be a small, progressive, and expanding concern. We sell to them in the hope that they develop into a big customer.

Their payments were so slow we now sell them only on COD.

We have sold to the company for several years. Our credit line to them is a medium four-figure amount. Their payments have been continuously six months or more slow, and we are now contemplating withdrawing our line of credit and putting them on COD.

Negotiations

20. Jet Interiors Company Inc.: Negotiating to Restructure a Convertible Note

Julie Brooks sat at her desk in mid-November 1998 contemplating her options in an upcoming telephone call to Joseph Stimple Inc., a small merchant bank that had loaned $3 million just nine months before to her company, Jet Interiors Company Inc. (JIC). The bank expected her to call that evening to propose a plan to restructure its loan. JIC lacked the resources to repay the debt, nor did it have access to new financing sources. Unless she could find a way to restructure the issue, the bank would exercise its option and convert the debt into equity. However, the corporate treasury contained an insufficient number of shares to accommodate the conversion now that the price of the stock was $0.25 a share. The board of directors felt that the company was more valuable than its current market price indicated and wondered whether the merchant bank had contributed to the 80 percent decline in market price since the note was issued.

In preparation for the phone call Julie asked the CFO to prepare a cash report indicating how much cash was currently available and how that quantity would change over the next twelve months. He reported $400,000 of surplus cash currently available from cash holdings exceeding $1 million and estimated that $50,000–$75,000 more might be freed up over each of the next nine months. Julie debated the wisdom of contributing the company's modest cash hoard to a restructuring. She also asked the CFO to detail how much of the note

---

This case was prepared by Harlan D. Platt.

remained. He reported that $710,000 of the original $3 million issue had been converted into 1,750,000 common shares during the year and that $1,040,000 was bought back at face value on October 1. That cash came from friendly private investors in a term note raising $1.333 million. The remaining $1,300,000 of the convertible debt would convert into 5.2 million common shares or more depending on how the market responded to a conversion.

Julie reviewed her options. She could hand over the $400,000 and pledge to repay the residual over time, but that would leave the company cash poor. She could let the debt be converted into a controlling interest in the company provided that shareholders approved an increase in the number of common shares. Finally, the company could file for bankruptcy. None of the options appealed to her, but she knew that she would have to do something, possibly a mix of strategies.

History

Like other start-up high technology companies, Jet Interiors Company Inc. had greater success raising money than making it. During the company's ten-year history its accumulated losses equaled nearly $47 million, with only two quarters showing a profit. While these losses provided an ample tax loss carryforward opportunity should the company ever earn a profit, this frustrating history complicated the task of raising fresh capital. A recent management change brought superior leadership. Julie Brooks was hired as president and CEO after retiring as a senior vice president of a major airline.

Despite its ignoble financial history, investors remained loyal to the company because of its proprietary software that allowed crisp audio and video transmissions between in-flight aircraft and ground links. Seven patents protected JIC's software. Four related to audio transmission allowed satellite hookups that gave round-the-globe communications capabilities for multiple on-board users. Three patents linked video signals to audio transmissions. Depending on weather conditions, the video could look nearly as good as broadcast television.

JIC was a software company and a systems integrator, meaning a company that buys off-the-shelf parts from original equipment manufacturing (OEM) manufacturers and then combines them with its software, in this case to yield an improved aircraft communication system. JIC's primary customers were blue-chip corporations such as Gillette, Boeing, Bank of America, and MCI, who purchased JIC's equipment for corporate jets devoted to their top management teams. Follow-up sales extended the product's reach downward within these companies after their technology officers had experienced and benefited from the extra value added by this software. With arguably the best product in the world, JIC suffered from a paucity of companies able or willing to spend up to $100,000 on "flawless" aircraft communication. Less perfect systems were available from equipment manufacturers for $50,000 or less. As seen in table 1, JIC's aircraft business never exceeded $13.6 million a year. Company officials privately described the total aircraft communication market as being about $1 billion a year and growing by 20 percent per annum and the corporate jet market served by JIC as being about $100 million. JIC's market share of about 15 percent was falling. A prior attempt to bring its software into the $50,000 systems market failed because as an integrator JIC had a cost disadvantage versus OEM manufacturers with whom it competed for sales.

TABLE 1.   Consolidated Statements of Operation

	1998	1997	1996
Revenues			
Jet Interiors	13,574,213	12,168,107	11,159,943
ITE	5,863,198	7,451,686	1,549,281
Total revenues	19,437,411	19,619,793	12,709,224
Cost and expenses			
Cost of goods sold, Jet Interiors	12,242,823	9,686,633	9,115,556
Cost of goods sold, ITE	1,470,198	2,068,321	1,346,763
Selling, general, and administrative	13,023,732	13,503,540	8,256,087
Research and development	786,103	1,031,814	1,192,000
Impairment loss[a]	7,767,444	—	—
Total cost and expenses	35,290,300	26,290,308	19,910,406
Loss from operations	(15,852,889)	(6,670,515)	(7,201,182)
Loss on sale of investment	452,005	—	—
Finance charges	1,682,303	76,169	139,048
Net loss before tax	(17,987,197)	(6,746,684)	(7,340,230)
Income tax	—	193,241	—
Net loss	(17,987,197)	(6,939,925)	(7,340,230)
Weighted number of shares	47,724,928	43,606,480	35,476,932

[a]From goodwill of ITE.

Several acquisitions made in late 1997 strained the company's finances still further. Recent balance sheets and an abbreviated statement of cash flow are contained in tables 2 and 3. ITE, which provides ground maintenance services to corporate jet fleets, was purchased for $9 million. The concept was that its battalion of mechanics could uncover potential communication sales while servicing corporate jets. Somehow JIC failed to realize that ITE's mechanics never interacted with the personnel responsible for buying JIC's expensive aircraft equipment. Moreover, shortly after the purchase a large international airline began offering competing maintenance service. JIC's unit prices fell by 34 percent as it fought to hold on to its clients. Twelve months later a further 37 percent price reduction occurred when several other airlines joined the fray. ITE rapidly changed from being a cash cow with a potentially synergistic sales force to a cash drain. A second acquisition, SNI, was described as a wire-pulling company that physically installed Intranet and fiber-optic cables in modern office buildings. No potential synergies between the parent and SNI were ever described. SNI became a cash drain almost immediately. It was shut down at the end of 1998 after losing $2.43 million. Since it is a discontinued operation, SNI is excluded from the financial tables.

JIC was spun off from Sprint in 1988. Over the period 1990–99 its equity market price ranged between $1 and $6 per share. The $6 spike occurred after a major investment was made in JIC by a wealthy investor who later joined its board. However, continued losses soon had the price hovering in the $1 to $1.50 range. With 46 million shares outstanding, the value of the firm was about $70 million.

JIC's stock was listed on the NASDAQ Small Cap. After the price of the stock fell below $1.00 the company was in violation of the exchange's minimum stock price requirement of $1.00 share price. A letter from NASDAQ received at the beginning of December warned the company that it had sixty days in which to correct the problem or face delisting. After an equity conversion the company would be financially stronger, but a delisting would impede its ability to sell its primary product to blue-chip companies. Julie wondered what a conversion would do to stock price. Management believed that the price of the stock had fallen due to uncertainty associated with the conversion and thought that it would pop back if the debenture could be restructured. Giving management some power in its negotiations with the bondholder was the fact that after a conversion at the current

TABLE 2. Consolidated Balance Sheets, December 31

	1998	1997
Assets		
Current assets		
Cash and equivalents	1,134,231	859,684
Accounts receivable, less allowance for doubtful accounts of $1,141,091 and $415,989 in 1998 and 1997	5,975,254	5,703,560
Inventory, less obsolete inventory of $1,677,440 and $178,235 in 1998 and 1997	1,059,142	2,464,818
Demonstration inventory	136,883	990,054
Prepaid expense	164,088	404,181
Current assets of discontinued operations	334,022	557,125
Total current assets	8,803,620	10,979,422
Long-term assets		
Property, plant and equipment, net	1,048,983	1,071,381
Other assets of discontinued operations	—	131,912
Other assets		
Goodwill, net	955,688	9,020,715
Software development costs, net	75,349	658,052
Other	77,325	1,018,981
Total other assets	1,108,362	10,697,748
Total assets	10,960,965	22,880,459
Liabilities and stockholders' equity		
Current liabilities		
Current portion of short-term notes	1,737,948	1,142,012
Short-term borrowing	157,376	154,938
Accounts payable	2,235,852	3,036,587
Accrued expenses	1,463,536	878,813
Accrued commission	501,515	849,078
Deferred revenue	1,522,416	445,245
Current liabilities of discontinued operations	334,022	781,862
Total current liabilities	7,952,665	7,289,535
Notes payable, less current portion	1,105,655	—
Stockholder's equity		
Preferred stock, authorized 800,000 shares, none issued	—	—
Common stock, authorized 50,000,000 shares	12,300	11,566
Additional paid-in capital	48,209,039	45,976,291
Accumulated deficit	(46,877,847)	(29,941,875)
Cumulative comprehensive income	(340,847)	(455,038)
Total stockholders' equity	1,002,645	15,590,924
Total liabilities and stockholders' equity	10,060,965	22,880,459

price, or lower, the investor would be hard pressed to sell the acquired securities.

The Convertible Debenture

Early in 1998 JIC needed additional funds for working capital purposes. With virtually no debt on its books, a debenture offering was contemplated. The best offer came from a merchant bank that agreed to lend the company $3.0 million in the form of a convertible note. The note paid interest at a rate of 5 percent and allowed the investor to convert into common stock at the lesser of (i) $8.00 per share or (ii) 85 percent of the average closing bid price of the company's common stock. The board believed the contract specified a floor on the stock price at which the note could be converted, but in fact if there was one, it was only a glass floor. The indenture proscribed the holder from shorting the stock, but this activity would be hard to document and prove. With the equity priced at about $1.50 when the note was issued, 4 million shares of stock were reserved from the corporate treasury to handle any conversion, though management hoped to be able to buy back the note before it could be converted.

When it became clear that the company would not earn sufficient funds to repay the loan, an alternate approach was sought. Private investors were approached to raise new funds that would be used to partially repay the debenture holder and for additional working capital needs. The amount of $1.3 million was raised from twenty-seven investors with two individuals, both board members, accounting for nearly 50 percent of the total. These funds were secured by the potential future sale of ITE, which was put out for sale with a distressed company broker. Estimates at the time put the future sale

TABLE 3. Abbreviated Statement of Cash Flow

	1998	1997	1996
Cash flow from operating activities			
Net loss	(16,935,972)	(5,817,366)	(6,706,894)
Noncash charges	13,008,550	1,140,645	1,498,547
Balance sheet changes	(426,238)	1,488,123	1,848,129
Net cash used in operations	(4,353,660)	(3,188,598)	(3,360,218)
Net cash from funds	3,752,576	2,815,727	5,733,968

price at $3 million plus, but future events would show that not a single bid was received after three months. Buyers were skittish because of the rapid fall in unit price and the apparent lack of customer loyalty.

As of that morning, 47.7 million out of 50 million authorized shares were outstanding, so that at most 2.3 million shares were available to redeem the remaining debenture in a conversion. Continued losses and allegations of shorting by the debenture holder resulted in the price of common stock falling to about $0.25 per share. Partial repayment and some conversion reduced the size of the outstanding debenture to $1.3 million. At the low stock price 5.2 million shares would be needed to redeem the loan assuming the price did not fall further.

Joseph Stimple Inc.'s Objectives

The bank wanted to get its money back but of course also wanted to maximize its return on this investment. So far, the investment had paid off handsomely. The two options available to the bank, (i) converting to equity or (ii) accepting a new debt instrument, had various risks and rewards. If the bank converted its debt into equity, there was a risk that it would not be able to dispose of those shares for some time if the conversion upset the equity market and sent the stock price downward. On the other hand, an 11 percent or greater equity position in JIC might have extra value. Accepting a new debt instrument would lock the bank into a relationship with JIC at a time when the company's future seemed doubtful, while a new debt security would preserve the bank's relative ranking in a possible bankruptcy filing. The only valuable asset that JIC had that interested the bank was its patents, which might have potential in other commercial and industrial applications.

At this time, a private shareholder of JIC approached a major law firm about the possibility of suing the bank since the shareholder felt that the investor had shorted the stock, in violation of the agreement. Shorting would have lowered the price of the equity, thereby increasing the number of shares received in a conversion, but would potentially invalidate the agreement. Coincidentally, the law firm also represented the bank. Though it is not known whether the shareholder's inquiry was communicated to the bank, not long afterward the investor adopted a more conciliatory tone in discussions with the company.

21. We Hear a Symphony . . . Or Do We?

The case is prepared as a two-part role play because some of the issues to be addressed involve the power, personality, and perspective of the symphony's leadership in relation to the musicians. If the user wishes to highlight other issues presented in the case, one of the roles may be eliminated.

The Board's Position

The tension could be felt almost as soon as one entered the room. The negotiating committee for the Symphony Orchestra (union) had been locking horns with the negotiating committee of the Symphony Association (management) since their contract expired last August 31. It was now into the new year, and it seemed as if negotiations had gone from bad to worse. The winter season had been canceled, and the public was outraged at the financial chaos facing the Symphony Association and the problems associated with the viability of the orchestra, in particular.

In the fall of 1975, the Symphony Association began nine years of ambitious expansion under a succession of board presidents. In 1984 the board decided to purchase a downtown theater, restore it, rename it Symphony Hall, and establish it as a permanent home for the Symphony Orchestra. A capital fund-raising drive culminated with a gala opening of Symphony Hall a year later but fell nearly $2

This case was prepared by Miriam Rothman.

million short of its $6.5 million goal (i.e., $4.8 million was raised to acquire and restore the old theater as the symphony's new home).

In early 1986, symphony board president N. E. Morgan shocked the community by announcing the need to raise $2 million in order to eliminate a $1.8 million deficit that had accumulated over a ten-year period. Three days later he publicly stated that the symphony had ten days to raise the $2 million. If this amount was not raised, the organization would file for protection under Chapter 11 of the federal bankruptcy laws. In the interim, a consortium of four local banks declared the symphony in default on its $4.5 million loan for the renovation of Symphony Hall.

Local business and political leaders expressed concern over a history of financial mismanagement at the symphony. Nonetheless, the community responded. From contributions large and small, the emergency fund-raising drive netted $2.4 million, apparently staving off the need for a Chapter 11 bankruptcy filing. Hopes soared that the symphony would begin the 1986–87 season "in the black for the first time in 10 years," as Morgan put it.

Two weeks after the emergency fund-raising drive, more bad news emerged. The executive director of the symphony announced that, despite the fund-raising, the organization might end the year with an $820,000 deficit. The public was outraged. The executive director asked musicians to take a 10 percent pay cut in the middle of the last year of their contract. However, shortly thereafter management retracted its controversial request for a pay cut, noting opposition by the musicians and skepticism by the public. After eighteen months in office, the executive director resigned his position.

The summer of 1986 found major changes at Symphony Hall. Mel Brown was hired as the new symphony executive director. His reputation as a "turnaround man" for troubled orchestras held great promise for managing the turbulence at Symphony Hall. In addition, a new president of the symphony board was installed, and preparations were under way for negotiations with the musicians' union, whose contract was set to expire August 31, 1986.

Negotiations between the association and the American Federation of Musicians, which represented the symphony players, continued through September 15. On that date, symphony musicians received their last paycheck and announced that they were "locked out" of negotiations by the management. Management wanted a thirty-eight-week contract and no pay raises; musicians wanted forty-five weeks and a raise. The most volatile issue, however, involved artistic control of the orchestra by music director Kendall Adams. A month later, deadlocked in contract negotiations, management called off the first three weeks of the 1986–87 season.

Brown publicly confirmed the dire predictions of his predecessor, stating that the $877,000 deficit from 1985–86 was projected to grow to $1.8 million by the end of the 1986–87 season. There was also a $2.36 million shortfall in the capital fund.

Still deadlocked in bitter negotiations, the Symphony Association management canceled the second three weeks of the winter season and on November 11 canceled the entire 1986–87 season. Management promised full refunds within sixty days to subscribers who sought them, but two months later they acknowledged that the Symphony Association could not pay the $400,000 potential cost (over half the subscribers asked for refunds).

A state mediator was called in to help resolve the labor dispute. After several attempts, the musicians and the association could not agree on a new contract, and a deadline for scheduling a spring miniseason passed. On January 12, 1987, symphony management dissolved its relationship with the orchestra and formed a committee to pay off $6 million in debts. The community became the only city in the nation with a symphony association board of directors and a symphony hall but no symphony orchestra to play in that hall.

Representatives of both sides in the labor dispute agreed to negotiate a contract for 1987–88 and meet and confer in sixty days.

Role for Symphony Board Negotiators

The board of directors for the Symphony Association is facing rough times. The symphony's reputation, credibility, and financial viability are being questioned in the press every day and discussed on the streets by politicians and citizens alike. How this happened is not as important as what can be done to solve the crisis facing the symphony and the city. Negotiations must be held with the musicians' union because of overwhelming pressure from the community. The community wants a symphony orchestra and will not suffer this blow to its civic pride in silence.

Brown, the executive director, has worked overtime to overcome the financial problems besetting the association. Among the most notable changes will be a reduction of the annual budget from

$7.9 million in 1985–86 to $5.7 million in 1987–88 and a leaner office staff reduced from forty-five to twenty-four. Thanks to liberal donors who have agreed to provide $1.25 million in necessary start-up funds to pay off current debts, there will be no carryforward deficit for the first time in years.

As with orchestras nationwide, ticket sales provide only 50 percent of required income. About 18 percent of the orchestra's income is from government support and miscellaneous sources such as hall rental and concession sales. At least one-third of the symphony's budget must come from contributions to the sustaining fund; nationwide, the sustaining fund requirement of symphony orchestras averages about 45 percent.

In the meantime however, the Symphony Association will try to sustain itself by renting out Symphony Hall to local and out-of-town musical groups—performing as a presenter of concerts rather than as a producer.

Before negotiations broke down between the association and musicians' union, there seemed to be three main unresolved issues left on the table: artistic control, wages and terms and conditions of employment, and scheduling of rehearsals.

Artistic Control

The artistic direction of a symphony is the responsibility of the conductor/music director, who has the expertise to make decisions as he or she sees fit. About five years ago the symphony was delighted to get the highly respected and talented Kendall Adams to assume that position. The board and musicians were pleased to get a conductor of his quality and stature, and his most recent salary contract was set at $250,000-plus per year.

Because the purpose of a board of directors of a symphony association is fund-raising, artistic control is left to the discretion of the music director. The board, while appreciators of fine music, are not professional musicians, and therefore they fully support any decisions made by the person hired to lead and conduct—Kendall Adams. They have full confidence in his ability and understand that as with any leader, there will be individuals (musicians in this case) who will disagree with his decisions. Thus far, the board has been pleased with his decisions. For example, they enthusiastically endorsed Adams's decision to bring in entertainers to perform at the gala opening of

Symphony Hall and at the Christmas Pops Symphony. Both of these events received a great deal of media coverage and were considered very successful from a public relations/fund-raising perspective.

Adams wants greater artistic control over the audition and review procedures. With regard to the audition procedures, he wants the screen removed behind which aspiring symphony musicians perform during the preliminary and final phases of the audition process. The removal of the screen would allow observation of the performance of the musician, which otherwise is hidden from view. The performance of the musician is important because symphony musicians not only play music but perform on stage as well. The removal of the screen will allow better selection decisions.

The review process over which Adams wishes greater control is reseating. That is, a musical director can reseat (demote) a musician (e.g., from principal to associate or associate to assistant) if the musician is not measuring up to the standards of the symphony. As director, it is his responsibility to maintain the highest standards possible and to ensure that the musicians perform to the best of their ability at all levels within the orchestra. If a player is not meeting those expectations, then it is the musical director's responsibility to demote him or her and promote someone else who can. The musicians, however, demand that reseating decisions be subject to review and be made part of the collective bargaining contract. The board fully supports Adams in making reseating decisions without review by the musicians and does not want any review procedures included in the next contract.

Wages and Terms and Conditions of Employment

Given the financial difficulty of the symphony and loss of public confidence, the board would like to keep the length of the 1987–88 playing season to a minimum so as to (1) avoid the costs of putting on performances for small audiences, (2) give the symphony time to win back its supporters through some innovative programming, and (3) rent out Symphony Hall during the weeks when the symphony does not have a performance scheduled in order to gain some much-needed revenue.

The musicians had a forty-five-week playing season in their 1985–86 contract and earned a minimum of $470.00 per week. The board offered a thirty-eight-week playing season and no pay raises when negotiations stalled. The board is willing, however, to give pay raises in exchange for a reduction in the number of playing weeks. They are aware that the salaries of the musicians are not as high as elsewhere, and they want to be reasonable. They are offering up to a 25 percent pay increase with a commensurate reduction in the length of the playing season.

The musicians also want the Symphony Association to pay for a dental plan for the musicians and increase contributions to the pension plan from 5½ to 6 percent. The board is reluctant to take on any extra financial obligations.

Scheduling of Rehearsals

When Symphony Hall was acquired two years before, the sellers intended to build Symphony Towers, a $150 million hotel and office twin-tower project flanking Symphony Hall. As previously arranged, construction is scheduled to allow evening events in the hall. In order to accommodate the construction of the towers, the board would like the freedom to schedule symphony rehearsals around the construction schedule. That is, rehearsals could be scheduled on weekends or during the evening, if necessary, so as to avoid noise associated with construction. Currently the musicians have daytime rehearsals. Rehearsals are at 10 A.M. and 1:45 P.M. on days when the musicians don't perform, and there is one rehearsal on days when a concert is scheduled for that evening.

As members of the management negotiating team, you must prepare for your first meeting to negotiate what you hope to be a two-year contract with the musicians' union. Sixty days have passed since you terminated your relationship with the musicians.

The Musicians' Position

The tension could be felt almost as soon as one entered the room. The negotiating committee for the Symphony Orchestra (union) had been locking horns with the negotiating committee of the Symphony Association (management) since their contract expired last August 31. It was now into the new year, and it seemed as if negotiations had gone from bad to worse. The winter season had been canceled, and the public was outraged at the financial chaos facing the Symphony Association and the problems associated with the viability of the orchestra, in particular.

In the fall of 1975, the Symphony Association began nine years of ambitious expansion under a succession of board presidents. In 1984 the board decided to purchase a downtown theater, restore it, rename it Symphony Hall, and establish it as a permanent home for the Symphony Orchestra. A capital fund-raising drive culminated with a gala opening of Symphony Hall a year later but fell nearly $2 million short of its $6.5 million goal (i.e., $4.8 million was raised to acquire and restore the old theater as the symphony's new home).

In early 1986, symphony board president N. E. Morgan shocked the community by announcing the need to raise $2 million in order to eliminate a $1.8 million deficit that had accumulated over a ten-year period. Three days later he publicly stated that the symphony had ten days to raise the $2 million. If this amount was not raised, the organization would file for protection under Chapter 11 of the federal bankruptcy laws. In the interim, a consortium of four local banks declared the symphony in default on its $4.5 million loan for the renovation of Symphony Hall.

Local business and political leaders expressed concern over a history of financial mismanagement at the symphony. Nonetheless, the community responded. From contributions large and small, the emergency fund-raising drive netted $2.4 million, apparently staving off the need for a Chapter 11 bankruptcy filing. Hopes soared that the symphony would begin the 1986–87 season "in the black for the first time in 10 years," as Morgan put it.

Two weeks after the emergency fund-raising drive, more bad news emerged. The executive director of the symphony announced that, despite the fund-raising, the organization might end the year with an $820,000 deficit. The public was outraged. The executive director asked musicians to take a 10 percent pay cut in the middle of the last year of their contract. However, shortly thereafter management retracted its controversial request for a pay cut, noting opposition by the musicians and skepticism by the public. After eighteen months in office, the executive director resigned his position.

The summer of 1986 found major changes at Symphony Hall. Mel Brown was hired as the new symphony executive director. His reputation as a "turnaround man" for troubled orchestras held great promise for managing the turbulence at Symphony Hall. In addition, a new president of the symphony board was installed, and preparations were under way for negotiations with the musicians' union, whose contract was set to expire August 31, 1986.

Negotiations between the association and the American Federation of Musicians, which represented the symphony players, continued through September 15. On that date, symphony musicians received their last paycheck and announced that they were "locked out" of negotiations by the management. Management wanted a thirty-eight-week contract and no pay raises; musicians wanted forty-five weeks and a raise. The most volatile issue, however, involved artistic control of the orchestra by music director Kendall Adams. A month later, deadlocked in contract negotiations, management called off the first three weeks of the 1986–87 season.

Brown publicly confirmed the dire predictions of his predecessor, stating that the $877,000 deficit from 1985–86 was projected to grow to $1.8 million by the end of the 1986–87 season. There was also a $2.36 million shortfall in the capital fund.

Still deadlocked in bitter negotiations, the Symphony Association management canceled the second three weeks of the winter season and on November 11 canceled the entire 1986–87 season. Management promised full refunds within sixty days to subscribers who sought them, but two months later they acknowledged that the Symphony Association could not pay the $400,000 potential cost (over half the subscribers asked for refunds).

A state mediator was called in to help resolve the labor dispute. After several attempts, the musicians and the association could not agree on a new contract, and a deadline for scheduling a spring miniseason passed. On January 12, 1987, symphony management dissolved its relationship with the orchestra and formed a committee to pay off $6 million in debts. The community became the only city in the nation with a symphony association board of directors and a symphony hall but no symphony orchestra to play in that hall.

Representatives of both sides in the labor dispute agreed to negotiate a contract for 1987–88 and meet and confer in sixty days.

Role for Symphony Musician Negotiators

Over time, the quality of the relationship between the symphony board of directors and musicians had deteriorated, yet no one ever anticipated these serious consequences. The formal dissolution of the board's relationship with the symphony orchestra stunned and angered the musicians.

From the musicians' point of view, there are three main areas of concern to be addressed in the collective bargaining negotiations.

First and foremost is the struggle with Kendall Adams, the conductor, over artistic control issues. Second is the dispute over wages and terms and conditions of employment. Third is the underlying disharmony between the board and musicians concerning lack of respect.

Relationship between the Board and Musicians

In 1980, the symphony was named a major orchestra by the American Symphony Orchestra League. As such, they consider themselves a first-rate professional ensemble, with a full contingent of eighty-one players, and not a part-time orchestra. Yet given this stature, on a percentage basis, less of the symphony's total budget goes to musician salaries than anywhere else. That is, when compared to major city symphonies with budgets of comparable size, this orchestra's members receive less money as a percentage of the budget than colleagues elsewhere. In addition, the board's use of discretionary monies to lure high-priced guest conductors and soloists at what the musicians perceive to be their expense (i.e., citing their minimum salaries) has created resentment among the players.

A case in point was the gala opening of Symphony Hall. For the event, movie stars and famous musicians were flown in and highly paid by the Symphony Association while the musicians were greeted with warm sodas and packaged cookies in the basement of Symphony Hall before the performance. Moreover, although many pre- and postopening parties were held in honor of the event, musicians claimed they did not receive invitations to any of them. The general feeling among the musicians about the association is that it is grandiose in everything except its respect and support for the players. The musicians believe the board members are too involved in the day-to-day operations of the symphony and not involved enough with fund-raising, which is typically the backbone of the board member function.

Artistic Control

The board is, and has been, 100 percent behind Kendall Adams, who receives an annual salary of $250,000-plus as music director and conductor of the symphony. When Adams came to the symphony about five years ago, the musicians were pleased to get a conductor of his quality and stature. As time went on, however, a division in the symphony occurred.

The essence of the conflict concerned the way Adams treated people. Musicians stated that he had a short fuse and a poor temperament and would berate musicians in front of their colleagues and embarrass them in public. He was described as a "tyrant" by many of the musicians, and his constant demands for greater artistic control over the musicians resulted in low morale among the orchestra players.

Two areas over which Adams wanted greater artistic control were the audition and the review procedures. When auditioning an aspiring symphony musician, it was customary to have the musician perform behind a screen, thus shielding his or her identity from the auditioning committee in both the preliminary and final phases of the audition process. This allowed a decision to be made solely on artistic talent without personal bias. Adams, however, wanted the screen removed in both phases, and he was supported in this decision by the board. The musicians were against the removal of the screen, claiming they could not trust Adams to make selection decisions based on merit rather than on favoritism.

The review process that concerned the musicians was the matter of reseating. That is, the musical director could reseat (demote) a musician (e.g., from principal to associate or associate to assistant) if he subjectively perceived that the musician did not measure up to the musical director's standards. These decisions often led to division among the ranks of the orchestra members. There was no mechanism in the contract by which musicians could challenge a demotion if they did not agree with the musical director's subjective view. During negotiations, the musicians requested that reseating decisions be subject to review and therefore be made part of the collective bargaining contract.

Although there was division among the symphony players over the audition and review procedures, the straw that broke the camel's back and united the players against the conductor was an alleged love affair he was having with the wife of one of the musicians. The affair traumatized the musician and lowered morale among the orchestra members. Consequently, the relationship between the musicians and Adams is at an all time low.

Wages and Terms and Conditions of Employment

The musicians had a forty-five-week playing season in their 1985–86 contract and earned a minimum of $470.00 per week. They want at least a forty-five-week playing season in their next contract and a 50 percent salary increase in minimum wage (i.e., to approximately $700.00 per week) because they believe they are being seriously underpaid. After all, the board initiated a $2 million fund-raising drive and has the money. There are strong feelings about salaries, partially because musicians are still chafing after the last Christmas Pops Symphony, where the board (at Adams's request) brought in twenty-one guest soloists/performers from outside the orchestra and paid eighteen of them over scale, while the musicians continue to receive what they believe to be minimum scale wages.

The musicians are also reluctant to cut back on the length of the playing season because they do not want to be perceived as a "part-time orchestra," playing a shortened season. The potential cost of being perceived as a part-time orchestra is thought to be twofold: (1) theoretically, the more an orchestra performs the better it will be, and (2) due to the lockout, the orchestra lost about ten of its musicians to other orchestras or jobs, compounding the difficulty of recruiting top-notch musicians with a short playing season.

In addition to a wage increase, the musicians want the board to pay for dental care and to increase contributions to the pension plan from 5½ to 6 percent. They have four weeks paid vacation and do not request more, particularly if they have a forty-five-week season.

The board wants carte blanche in scheduling rehearsals. Currently, musicians rehearse twice a day, at 10 A.M. and 1:45 P.M., when no evening concerts are scheduled and once a day when they perform that night. However, due to current construction around Symphony Hall, the board wants to be able to schedule rehearsals at any time, including weekends and evenings, to work around construction noise. From the musicians' perspective, this would significantly interfere with their personal lives, (e.g., baby-sitting; being with children and spouse in the evenings and on weekends when home from school and work; the scheduling of private music lessons or other teaching, performances, etc.). The players want to stick to the regular rehearsal schedule so they can have some control over their personal lives.

As members of the musicians' negotiating team, you must prepare for your first meeting to negotiate what you hope to be a three-year contract with the board. Sixty days have passed since the symphony management terminated its relationship with the union.

Need for Cash

22. P. A. Bergner & Co.

In late July 1991, Michael MacDonald, executive vice president finance and management information system (MIS) of P. A. Bergner & Co (Bergner), a large midwestern U.S.-based department store retailer, received word that Bank One had pulled its $32.1 million letter of credit. The letter of credit had been earmarked to finance the import of goods through AMC, the firm's largest supplier (see exhibit 1), in time for the busy back-to-school fall fashion season and to rebuild inventories during the run-up to Christmas.

It was a difficult time for Bergner. The company's buyout of the Carson Pirie Scott (CPS) chain in 1989 had left the firm highly leveraged, and the sudden downturn in the economy at almost the same time had severely depressed earnings, leaving the firm in critical condition.

Richard Ivey School of Business
The University of Western Ontario **IVEY**

Will Matthews and Chris Lane prepared this case under the supervision of Professors Mark Griffiths and Robert W. White solely to provide material for class discussion. The authors do not intend to illustrate either effective or ineffective handling of a managerial situation. The authors may have disguised certain names and other identifying information to protect confidentiality.

Early in 1991, with the help of outside consultants, management had formulated an aggressive five-year plan to exit non–department store related businesses, close unprofitable stores, and refocus operations on categories of merchandise generating high contribution. With the implementation of many of the elements of the plan already under way, MacDonald was confident in the long-run retail sales viability of Bergner. However, in the short term the company's operating line was nearing its limit, accounts payable were stretched, and a few key suppliers had started demanding cash on delivery terms. He realized that he would have to work quickly to formulate a strategy to appease the bank and trade creditors, raise new funds for capital expenditures, and cover any expected shortfalls on debt service and working capital needs. He was to present his recommendations to Stanton Bluestone, president of Bergner, in the last week of July 1991.

The U.S. Economy

Beginning in 1987, after five years of solid economic expansion, the Federal Reserve began a policy of tightening monetary policy in an effort to counter increasing inflationary pressures and engineer a soft landing for the U.S. economy. By 1990, there was a perceived general slowdown in the economy, and many believed the soft landing had been achieved. The outbreak of the Gulf War later in the year led to an immediate doubling of the price of oil and dampened consumer confidence, leading the economy officially into a recession in early 1991.

By midyear, the stock markets had rebounded from lows in late 1990 with the NYSE up 12.7 percent, the AMEX up 16.2 percent, and the NASDAQ up 27.3 percent over their closing positions in December 1990. Consumer confidence had jumped with the end of the Gulf War and despite having fallen back somewhat was still up over the previous year. The Federal Reserve, responding to a perception of a "credit crunch," began loosening interest rates, resulting in the prime rate falling 1.5 percent during the first six months of the year.

The U.S. Retail Industry

The 1980s were a prosperous time for U.S. retailers. A combination of steady underlying economic growth, high consumer confidence, and favorable demographic trends culminated in a compound average annual growth rate for sales of total general merchandise, apparel, furniture and appliance, and miscellaneous categories (known collectively as GAF sales) of 7.2 percent over the decade.

This high overall growth rate masked somewhat a fundamental restructuring occurring in the industry driven by discounters, warehouse clubs, and category specialists. These new retail formats were competing with department stores and other traditional retailers through superior merchandising, sophisticated information systems, higher levels of customer service, and lower prices. They were providing customers with greater value and, as a result, were growing quickly. Specialty retailers, the Gap, the Limited, Nordstrom, and Toys 'R' Us, which in 1985 had a combined market share of less than 1.6 percent of total GAF sales, had grown to 12.4 percent by 1991. Wal-Mart, a discount chain, became the largest U.S. retailer in 1990 with total sales of $32.6 billion, and sales were forecast to continue growing at an annual rate of 20 percent.

State-of-the-art information systems were a key component of many of these new retailers. Data regarding sales by product line were available daily, allowing restocking of fast moving merchandising and quick discounting of slower moving products. The more successful specialty retailers had been able to reduce the time required from purchasing to stocking on the shelves to two weeks. In contrast, direct importers, ordering name brand merchandise produced overseas, generally operated on a five-month cycle; department stores could reorder more quickly from domestic suppliers. This allowed the specialty retailers the flexibility to react quickly to changing market conditions or fashions and keep inventory turns high. On average, these new retail formats were outperforming traditional retailers, averaging, in 1990, sales of $243 per square foot of selling area versus $173 for department stores.

In late 1989, with consumer debt levels near all time highs and the economy beginning to falter, consumer confidence started to stall, and real GAF sales contracted slightly (see exhibit 2). In July 1991, industry analysts were forecasting overall real GAF sales growth in the 1 to 2 percent range through the remainder of the decade.

Department Stores

Department stores are retail outlets selling a combination of furniture, home furnishings, appliances, apparel for the family, household linens, and dry goods. They have been the backbone of American retailing for over a hundred years and are the cornerstones of another American retail tradition, the shopping mall. Sales are correlated with the business cycle and are highly seasonal. Approximately one-third of total sales and one-half of annual profits are earned in the quarter ended January 31. In 1990, total department store sales amounting to $171 billion accounted for 36.6 percent of GAF sales, down from 38.9 percent in 1981.

Many department stores responded to the challenge presented by the new retail formats through takeovers and mergers to gain economies of scale. Consolidation of head office functions was seen as a way of reducing operating costs and increasing purchasing clout. Undervalued real estate holdings, strong name recognition, and stable cash flows through the 1980s had made department stores attractive candidates for leveraged buyouts (LBOs). By 1991, four of the eight department stores forming the S&P retail department store index in 1986 had been acquired or taken private, and a fifth was undergoing a major restructuring.

When the economic slowdown began in late 1989, many traditional department store shoppers started defecting to discount stores. This forced department stores to compete through expensive promotions and merchandise markdowns, which in turn cut severely into operating margins.

In January 1990, Federated Holdings, the holding company of Federated Department Stores and Allied Stores Corporation, filed for Chapter 11 protection. It was the second-largest nonbank bankruptcy in U.S. history and the largest ever in the retail sector. A total of 67 separate companies were involved, representing 101,000 employees, 15,000 vendors, and 200,000 creditors. The legal proceedings were expected to take years. Federated Holdings had been assembled by Robert Campeau, a Canadian real estate developer, through a $3.6 billion LBO of Allied Stores in 1986 followed by a $6.6 billion LBO of Federated Stores in 1988.

With the Chapter 11 filing, the firm had been able to quickly secure over $700 million in new financing, and by April most suppliers were back shipping product. While accounts payable owed prior to the Chapter 11 filing would not be received until the resolution of the proceedings, payments on any shipment were virtually guaranteed due to the refinancing of the firm and the freeze on interest payments on all prior debt. The firm executed an extensive internal communications program in an effort to educate their employees about Chapter 11 and to generally keep up morale. While many industry analysts had predicted that Chapter 11 would be the death of the firm, customers continued to shop at the stores and seemed generally unaffected by the proceedings.

Company Background

Bergner was acquired as a single store operation by Maus Freres in 1938. Over the years, Bergner grew through small acquisitions and new store openings and by 1985 had grown to seventeen stores located primarily in central Illinois. In 1985, the firm made its first large-scale acquisition with the purchase of the Boston Store chain. The Boston Store acquisition doubled Bergner's size to $400 million in annual sales and thirty-two department stores. Within two years, the two chains were completely merged and in 1988 had a record year with revenues of $468 million and an earnings before interest, taxes, depreciation, and amortization (EBITDA) margin of 11.4 percent, which ranked it in the top quarter of department stores nationally.

With the acquisition of the Boston Store, Bergner became a major midwest department store. Confident from the success of its latest acquisition, Bergner sought another target that would solidify its regional market position and allow it to take advantage of additional operating synergies. At the time, Bergner was very strong in central Illinois and southern Wisconsin but weak in the Chicago market. In contrast, CPS's stores were concentrated in the Chicago area, making CPS the logical choice (exhibit 3) as an acquisition target.

By 1991, Bergner was operating sixty-seven stores in the U.S. midwest under the nameplates of Bergner's, Carson Pirie Scott, and Boston Store. Sales for the fiscal year ended February 2 were $1,215 million, which meant that Bergner was the eleventh largest department store chain in the United States. Estimated shares of total department store sales in key markets were 15 percent in Milwaukee, 12 percent in Chicago, and 8 percent in Minneapolis–St. Paul. In total, approximately 50 percent of sales came from the Chicago area, with the remaining 50 percent split between stores in Wisconsin, Minnesota, and central Illinois. The company remained privately owned by Maus Freres S.A. of Switzerland.

Maus Freres is a large European retailer with operations in Switzerland and France. It is controlled by the Maus and Nordmann families, who are considered to be among the wealthiest in Europe. Bergner was Maus Freres's only North American operation.

The Acquisition of Carson Pirie Scott & Company

CPS was acquired in a hostile takeover in May 1989 for $753 million ($453 million for equity and the assumption of $300 million of debt). The acquisition was funded primarily with debt. In addition to department stores, CPS operated a catalog retailer, a casual clothing chain known as County Seat, and several other small businesses.

The department store chain targeted middle- to upper-middle-income consumers. Estimated sales and operating profit for 1989 were $560 million and $16 million, respectively.

County Seat was repositioning itself from a traditional jeans retailer to a contemporary apparel retailer, targeting a younger, more fashion-forward group than the Gap. Estimated 1989 sales and operating profit were $330 million and $25 million, respectively.

Financial Impact of the Acquisition

The financial results since the CPS acquisition had been less than desirable (see exhibit 4). Several factors contributed to these results. The assimilation of the larger company, CPS, into Bergner proved difficult. Integration of the promotions and marketing efforts for both chains was problematic. Bergner's advertising focused on moderate prices and good values, whereas CPS's professed a fashion flair. The cancellation of CPS's high fashion "image" television advertisements and the new down-market look of its print ads prompted industry analysts to wonder if Milwaukee-based Bergner really appreciated the competitive realities of the Chicago market. Difficulties were also encountered in combining the two companies' information systems. These systems are used to monitor what items are selling well in which stores, which items should be reordered, and which should be marked down. These problems were further exacerbated by the general slowdown in the retail sector.

In addition, proceeds from the sale of CPS's non–department store operations, including County Seat, took longer than expected, and the proceeds were $100 million below estimates. As a result, in late 1990, Maus Freres had to make a $150 million equity infusion into Bergner.

In May 1991, Bergner's chairman, Alan Anderson, resigned and as of July had still not been replaced. The remaining management team had an average of twenty-six years of experience in the industry. Director and president, Stanton Bluestone, had been with the firm in that capacity since 1985. Prior to joining Bergner, Bluestone had extensive specialty store experience, serving in the senior merchant role at both Lane Bryant (division of the Limited) and Paul Harris. His prior experience included a variety of merchandising positions with Howland-Steinbach and a seventeen-year career with Shillito's (division of Federated Department Stores). Both the vice presidents of finance and MIS and merchandising had joined in 1990. MacDonald was enticed to join the company in September 1990, leaving a position as senior vice president and chief financial officer of Marshall Fields (1985–90), another U.S.-based department store retailer. Prior to his position at Marshall Fields, he was chief financial officer of Dayton Hudson Department Stores. John Fruenthal, executive vice president, merchandising, brought to Bergner fourteen years of senior level experience with the May Company. The remainder of the senior management team had long tenures with the company.

In order to help identify and evaluate the options available to the company to restore its margins, Bergner's management team hired a prominent consulting firm. The consulting firm identified several potential areas for reducing operating expenses and capital expenditures over the short term (see exhibit 5).

Over the medium term, the consulting firm identified the need to integrate and focus the promotions and marketing efforts and to deliver the proper corresponding merchandise. The consulting firm also noted that over the long term, Begner would have to address further its strategy and cost structure to resist continued onslaughts from expanding discounters and specialists.

Options Available to Bergner

Bergner had a number of options available to it for raising cash. In general, it could raise additional cash through the issuance of new securities or the sale of assets, renegotiate with existing banks or its owner for additional cash, or seek bankruptcy protection, as detailed below. Bergner's balance sheet is included in exhibit 6, and its expected capital requirements and loan principal repayments are shown in exhibit 7 for reference.

- *Renegotiate the lines of credit.* Bergner's lines of credit were near their limits. Bergner could try to renegotiate these lines of credit to extend maturities and increase the amounts available under them. Alternatively, Bergner could approach new lenders for additional credit.
- *Sell land.* CPS owned some of its real estate, including its Chicago flagship store, as well as a mall in suburban Chicago. These properties had an estimated value of $70 million. In addition, it was estimated that by downsizing its existing stores and selling the excess space, $15 million could be realized. This estimate assumed that these values could be realized without altering the cash flows of the company.
- *Issue equity.* Other U.S. publicly traded department stores traded on average multiples of approximately 14.3 times latest twelve months earnings before interest and taxes (EBIT). While Bergner's investment bankers felt that an equity offering was possible, it would be difficult to obtain an EBIT multiple as high as 14.3 due to the recent poor operating performance of the company. Some statistics of comparable companies and valuations are included in exhibit 8.
- *Dispose of operating assets.* Most of the non–department store assets with immediate realizable values had been sold. Management could sell some or all of the department stores or the entire business.
- *Negotiate with Maus Freres for more money.* Maus Freres had invested $100 million in Bergner at the time of the acquisition of CPS. A further $150 million had been made available earlier in 1990. Based on the consultant's analysis of the business, Maus Freres had determined that a further substantial cash infusion would be required to turn the operation around. While Maus Freres had recently sold its interest in the supermarket chain Euromarche in France for $330 million, its willingness to make another investment in Bergner was not certain. Maus Freres had loan guarantees of $300 million that would become due in the event of a Chapter 11 filing. Satisfying these claims would require the sale of additional assets in France.
- *Seek bankruptcy protection.* Another option available to the company was to file for protection from its creditors under the United States Bankruptcy Reform Act of 1978 (the act).

The two parts of the act that concern corporations are Chapter 11 (reorganizations) and Chapter 7 (liquidations).

Bankruptcy Protection

When a company files for bankruptcy, each of the interested parties (stakeholders) should determine what course of action will maximize the value of the firm and, hence, the recovery of its claim against the company. Each party has to ask itself, should the company be liquidated through an asset sale or sale of its various operating entities, or should it be rehabilitated? Each analysis must consider the risks and costs associated with each alternative. These costs and risks include the outlook for the industry; the market for the firm's assets; liabilities associated with closure of the business, including those related to environment and pension funds; and any additional capital that may be required to fund losses or to provide for asset acquisitions.

Under a Chapter 7 filing, the business is liquidated in an orderly manner either through a sale of assets, in whole or in part, or a sale of the business. In this scenario, an interim trustee may be appointed to operate the business to avoid any additional operating losses and to conduct an orderly sale. The proceeds of the liquidation are then applied to each creditor in order of priority (determined by the type of claim a creditor has on the assets of the company) with the remainder (if any) distributed to the equity holders of the business.

Under a Chapter 11 filing, the act maintains the company as an ongoing entity with current management continuing in their roles (as opposed to appointing a trustee) until a plan of reorganization can be agreed to. The act prevents any creditor from seizing the assets of the company in order to repay its claim. The act provides that no interest or principal will be paid (interest continues to accrue only on fully secured debt) on the company's debt until the reorganization is complete. The act allows the company to grant lenders who make loans to the company for ongoing operations priority status over existing insolvent loans. Committees of creditors (usually the seven largest creditors are chosen) with similar claims are formed to represent each class's interest in the reorganization proceeding.

Under a Chapter 11 filing, the company is or will be, in the near future, insolvent, and its liabilities exceed its assets or ability to generate cash flow. A plan of reorganization proposes to reduce and reschedule fairly the outstanding claims in such a manner that they feasibly can be met by the company. In general, "feasibly" means that the company will have sufficient earnings to cover its fixed charge obligations. "Fairness" means that claims must be recognized in the order of their legal and contractual priority. A plan of reorganization can incorporate operational details such as the closure of loss making divisions, the modernizing of plant and equipment, or the recruitment of new management, so long as it supports the projections on which the feasibility and fairness are based.

Management has a high degree of control during the bankruptcy proceedings as it continues to control and operate the firm, and it has an advantage for proposing a plan of reorganization. To continue to operate the business, management can arrange for additional debt financing called debtor-in-possession (DIP) financing. This financing must be approved by the bankruptcy court but is generally agreed to, provided it is used in the normal course of business. Lenders are apt to participate in DIP financing as the act allows these loans to supersede any existing loans to the company and, unlike the other distressed loans, DIP loans pay current interest.

Management has a 120-day "exclusivity" period in which to propose a reorganization plan; that is, exclusivity is a period specifically reserved for management action. Typically, management will use this time to discuss with all the parties involved management's outlook and obtain the creditors' respective positions in order to put together an initial plan of reorganization. Beyond the 120 days, other interested parties can begin to propose alternative plans. If management's plan is proceeding to the satisfaction of the creditors, then the exclusivity can be extended from 60 to 90 days at a time; that is, there is no need to come out of exclusivity. In addition, the act gives management the ability to cancel and renegotiate collective bargaining agreements and other agreements, including leases.

While entering Chapter 11 gives management increased flexibility to continue to operate the business, there are risks. While customers may not notice or care about bankruptcy, they will notice any changes in the quality of the product and/or service resulting from the switching of suppliers or wage-related disagreements with employees. As a result, revenues can be affected dramatically if management is unable to control these aspects of the business. The threat of loss of business is highest in industries where competition is high and switching costs of the customer are low. The ability of management to continue to focus on the business is reduced by the effort it must spend on the reorganization process. Bankruptcy proceedings typically take on average two years but can stretch into longer periods.

The Decision

Michael MacDonald knew that he would have to act quickly to address both the short- and long-term financing requirements of the company. Alternative financing was urgently required to replace the $32.1 million letter of credit no longer available from Bank One. This financial crisis raised the question of how Bergner should deal with its suppliers. There were also several outstanding issues that needed to be resolved. These included the amount and timing of cash requirements and the identification of options for sourcing these funds. He was also concerned with how the ongoing operating value of the company compared to its current liquidation value; ranges for EBITDA multiples for public sale, LBO, and merger were 5–5.6×, 5–6.3×, and 4.5–6×, respectively. He knew that any strategy would have to be approved by Maus Freres, the longtime owner of the company, but he was also concerned about the potential impact on other stakeholders, including management, trade creditors, and employees.

EXHIBIT 1. Top Twenty Vendors, Purchases per Annum (dollars in thousands)

Vendor	Account Size
AMC	165,643
Liz Claiborne	41,064
Levi Strauss	34,759
Estée Lauder	21,686
Bernard Chaus	19,362
London Fog	17,900
Clinique Laboratories	15,333
Arrow Company	15,157
Esprit de Corp	14,033
Alfred Dunner	13,828
Jockey International	12,118
Liz Petites	11,120
Lancome	10,337
Hartwell	9,465
Hanes Hosiery	8,571
Haggar	7,960
Norton McNaughton	7,451
Leslie Fay	7,423
Bonaventure	7,418
Warners	7,289

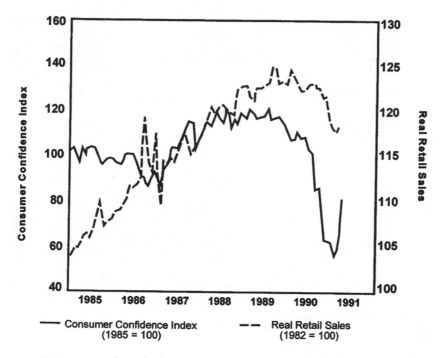

EXHIBIT 2. Real retail sales and consumer confidence (seasonally adjusted), 1985–91

EXHIBIT 3. Location of Bergner's, Carson, and Boston store outlets

EXHIBIT 4. Statement of Operations[a] Fiscal Periods Ending 1991–94 (dollars in thousands)

	Actual 2/2/91	Forecast 2/1/92	Forecast 1/30/93	Forecast 1/29/94
Total net sales	1,214,691	1,112,045	1,108,311	1,025,831
Less leased depts. and service depts.	121,865	112,088	117,693	109,548
Owned sales	1,092,826	999,957	990,619	916,282
Cost of merchandise sold	674,441	624,691	613,493	562,127
Owned department margin	418,385	375,267	377,126	354,155
Leased department margin	18,271	16,415	17,654	16,432
Total gross margin	436,656	391,681	394,780	370,587
Selling, general, and administrative	401,559	383,258	385,298	351,794
Service charge income	(41,187)	(39,724)	(37,767)	(35,803)
Other income	(3,388)	(530)	(614)	(568)
Total selling, general, and administrative	356,984	343,003	346,917	315,423
Income (loss) before interest, taxes, depreciation, amortization, and nonretail operations	79,672	48,678	47,863	55,164
Noncash deductions and nonretail operations Depreciation and amortization	36,401	32,530	36,066	39,341
Provision for last-in first-out	3,393	3,267	3,600	3,900
Other	4,788	16,497	12,000	6,000
Income (loss) before interest and taxes	35,090	(3,616)	(3,803)	5,924
Less interest expense	(88,467)	(72,550)	(59,387)	(64,929)
Income (loss) before taxes	(53,377)	(76,166)	(63,190)	(59,006)
Income tax provision	10,500	—	—	—
Net income (loss)	$ (42,877)	$ (76,166)	$ (63,190)	$ (59,006)

[a]Excludes consultants' suggested improvements.

EXHIBIT 5. Potential Cost Savings Identified by Consultants ($ millions)

	Amount of Benefit in Fiscal Years			
	1991	1992	1993	1994
Exit markets and stores	3	(5)	12	(3)
Exit certain merchandising categories	9	3	3	3
Adjust store layouts	(7)	(10)	0	16
Improve merchandising	0	0	3	5
Reduce costs	0	6	7	7
Exit real estate operation	(1)	(1)	2	2
Total	4	(7)	27	30

EXHIBIT 6. Consolidated Balance Sheet (dollars in thousands)

	Actual February 2, 1991
Assets	
Current assets	
Cash and cash equivalents	21,625
Receivables, net	10,690
Inventories	214,275
Last-in first-out reserve on inventory	(7,000)
Prepaid expenses and other current assets	30,746
Net assets held for sale	25,573
Total current assets	295,909
Property and equipment, net	337,984
Investments and other assets	
Intangible assets, less applicable amortization	465,757
Other assets, net	65,805
Total investments and other assets	531,562
Total assets	1,165,455
Liabilities and stockholders' equity	
Current liabilities	
Merchandise accounts payable	29,805
Expense accounts payable	25,911
Accrued liabilities	66,893
Accrued interest	27,993
Total current liabilities	150,602
Other long-term liabilities	107,442
Long-term debt	699,989
Total liabilities	958,032
Stockholders' equity	
Common stock and paid-in-capital	189,263
Retained earnings	18,160
Total stockholders' equity	207,423
Total liabilities and stockholders' equity	1,165,455

EXHIBIT 7. Cash Requirements, Principal Repayments and Forecasted Capital Expenditures ($ millions)

	Actual 1990	1991	1992	1993	1994
Principal repayments[a]	72	22	27	32	39
Forecasted capital expenditures	—	25	29	34	39

[a]Based on current capital structure. See exhibit 6, Consolidated Balance Sheet.

EXHIBIT 8. Financial Information on Comparable Companies ($ millions)

Company	Sales	Five-Year Cash Sales to Gross Revenue (%)	Net Income	Net Margin (%)	Average Return on Assets (%)[a]	LTD/LTD + Common Equity (%)[b,c]
Dayton-Hudson Corp.	14,739	12.3	410.0	2.6	5.4	64.0
Dillard Dept. Stores	3,734	18.1	182.8	4.9	6.6	38.9
May Dept. Stores	10,066	7.9	500.0	5.0	6.2	55.5
Mercantile Stores Co.	2,367	3.9	123.6	5.2	7.9	15.0
Nordstrom Inc.	2,894	15.4	115.8	4.6	6.4	36.7
J. C. Penney	17,410	2.4	577.0	3.3	4.6	41.6
P. A. Bergner	1,215	33.0	(42.9)		(3.5)	82.0

Market Valuation

Company	Total Market[d] to Tangible Book Value (%)[e,f]	LTM EBIT Multiple[g]	LTM Sale Multiple[h]	Current Year Estimated PE Ratio[i]	Next Year Estimated PE Ratio
Dayton-Hudson Corp.	239	9.0×	0.6×	12.4×	10.5×
Dillard Dept. Stores	334	14.9	1.5	20.4	17.1
May Dept. Stores	364		1.1	13.4	11.7
Mercantile Stores Co.	122	9.5	0.7	11.1	10.1
Nordstrom Inc.	438	29.0	1.5	23.9	20.1
J. C. Penney	152	9.1	0.6	11.1	9.1

Source: Goldman Sachs, July 1991.

Note: LTD = long-term debt; EBIT = earnings before interest and taxes; PE = Price/Earnings; LTM = latest twelve month.

[a]Most recent fiscal year's net income divided by the average of total assets at the last two fiscal year ends.

[b]Total stockholders' equity less carrying value of preferred stock.

[c]All indebtedness for borrowed money including capitalized lease obligations but excluding current maturities of long-term debt.

[d]Average number of shares outstanding for most recent interim period used in calculating primary earnings per share multiplied by most recent common stock price.

[e]Common equity divided by common shares outstanding, at capitalization table date.

[f]Common equity less intangibles divided by common shares outstanding at capitalization date of table.

[g]Market Capitalization + Preferred Equity + Long-Term Debt + Short-Term Debt − Cash and Equivalents (as of latest quarter) divided by latest four quarters Operating Income.

[h]Market Capitalization + Preferred Equity + Long-Term Debt + Short-Term Debt − Cash and Equivalents (as of latest quarter) divided by latest 12 Net Sales.

[i]Historical value is based upon market price per share and earnings per shares for the corresponding calendar year; earnings per share are split adjusted but not restated.

Breakeven Analysis

23. Investing in BN.com: Can Breakeven Be Achieved?

"I am not sure whether the portfolio managers will agree with me that barnesandnoble.com Inc. is a good buy. It may be a great opportunity for us, but I still have some nagging doubts," said Jason Leigh, a relatively new research analyst.

"Yeah, I had the same problem when I presented the case for OMI Corporation last year," replied Leah Rosen, another junior analyst. "What I did then, and my advice to you now, is to go in with several scenarios: a best and worst case and something in between. That way, fund managers can decide where they fit in terms of the company's risk and make their decision accordingly."

Jason Leigh had recently graduated from business school and was now employed at a large mutual fund family located in Connecticut where he worked as an analyst at a distressed securities mutual fund. The fund purchased equity and debt securities of companies in severe financial distress whose security prices were extremely low and, in the words of Jason's superior, "were priced based on fear not value." Jason's principal duty was to monitor several companies in the fund's portfolio, but he also had a mandate (which he had not yet exercised) to scout out new possible investments for the fund. As the year 2000 drew to a close, his attention was drawn to the Internet sector because of the steep decline in prices of web-based companies. Many Internet companies had folded. Others had experienced dramatic price erosion. For example, CMGI Inc. fell from $151 to $2.50;

This case was prepared by Harlan D. Platt and Marjorie B. Platt.

Inktomi from $241 to $5.75; and theGlobe.com from $40 to $0.05. Jason knew, of course, that many of these remaining companies were likely to go bankrupt, with their security holders receiving little return if anything at all. A few companies, the survivors, would likely experience a price rebound to a level between their original high and their current low.

An avid reader, Jason enjoyed the convenience and selection afforded by purchasing reading materials over the Internet. Subscribing to Peter Lynch's wisdom to buy stock in companies that you know, Jason had the equity of barnesandnoble.com Inc. (BN.com) on his radar screen since it went public in June 1999. The stock had reached $25 per share at the offering but had performed poorly since then. At the end of 1999, the price fell to $15, reaching $5 per share in August 2000, $1.20 at the end of the year, and $0.75 by mid-September 2001. Jason's fund had never purchased any shares of BN.com because of its high valuation, but now at little more than $1 per share, his interest was piqued.

BN.com

BN.com is a spin-off from Barnes & Noble Inc., an established brick and mortar bookseller with over nine hundred stores nationwide. The parent company and Bertelsmann AG own a majority of the company, with just 27.6 percent of the equity in public hands. Barnes & Noble Inc. had been criticized for delaying its entry into the Internet market space, thereby allowing Amazon.com, the best known of the Internet retailers, to capture the market. Yet, despite the delay BN.com has over 5 million unique visitors each month. By the end of 2000, Amazon had achieved profitability in bookselling though it suffered losses in its newer market segments such as music, furniture, and toys. On February 2, 2001, Amazon announced a 15 percent employee layoff and that it would drop unprofitable items from its web site. BN.com responded with a job cut of its own on February 8 when it cut 350 employees representing 16 percent of its workforce. At the same time, an analyst at Lehman Brothers forecast that Amazon would have negative working capital by the third quarter of 2001 that might trigger a credit squeeze.

Competitive Analysis

Jason knew that BN.com had a plethora of Internet-based bookselling competition that included Amazon, Powell, 1BookStreet, Borders, allbooks4less, BookCloseOuts, Books-A-Million, Fatbrain, half.com, LaissezFaire, textbooks@costs, TradersLib, and Wal-Mart. There is little actual difference between any of these companies since they all access the same book databases and product distributors, though consumer loyalty seems to have benefited Amazon and BN.com to some extent. In addition, traditional brick-and-mortar stores were omnipresent, expanding, and stubbornly attempting to hold on to their customers. The economics of the bookselling business did not seem to favor small Internet stores either. It was estimated that Amazon.com spent nearly $100 million a year to maintain its web site while the one time cost of opening up a new Barnes & Noble Inc. store was just $5 million (Ip 2001). Smaller Internet booksellers presumably spent less than Amazon on their sites, but the costs were still substantial. Moreover, for its $5 million investment in a traditional store, Barnes & Noble Inc. soon began earning a profit.

The market for books, videos, and music exceeded $300 billion in 2000. Less than 3 percent of those sales occurred on the Internet. Jason believed that long term the industry would continue to grow and that as much as 25 percent of sales would be Internet based. He believed that whichever company survived the early tumultuous years would be profitable. He hypothesized that BN.com's two healthy and rich parents would not allow their infant venture to fail and would inject further capital should the need arise. On the other hand, Amazon stood alone without a rich parent; however, Amazon's size and substantial market recognition might induce a healthy company such as Wal-Mart or Sears to either acquire it or make a substantial investment in it.

Compounding his confusion, Jason discovered that Books-A-Million (BAMM) had adopted a hybrid strategy between the pure Internet approach of BN.com on the one hand and the storefront model of Barnes & Noble Inc. on the other hand.[1] In addition, BAMM employs a subscription model like that used by Costco Inc.; BAMM's club membership, called the Millionaire's Club, costs $5 per year but reduces cost to the customer by 10 percent on each purchase. BAMM is the third largest bookstore chain in America. Its operations are based in the South with headquarters in Alabama. In addition to its chain of bookstores, BAMM owns and operates Books-A-Million .Com, an Internet web site which operates similarly to BN.com. BAMM's annual financial results for the last five years are reproduced in exhibit 1.

Jason thought he could gain some insight into the costs inherent in running an Internet web site dedicated to selling books by comparing BN.com to BAMM (BN.com's financial statements are reproduced in exhibits 2 and 3) even though BAMM's figures combined Internet and bricks-and-mortar operations and although BAMM is a great deal smaller than its rivals in terms of sales. BAMM's profitability is in stark contrast to the financial results of the other "dot.com" booksellers. Further, when examining Books-A-Million.Com's web site, it does not appear to suffer from the out-of-stock problems evident at other sites.

Financial Results

Like Amazon, BN.com believed that it could benefit by expanding the number of products sold on its web site to include nonbook material such as magazines, computer software, music CDs and tapes, and posters. The strategy relied in part on an incremental or variable cost analysis which argued that customers attracted to the site to buy one type of product could be induced to purchase other products while there at no additional cost. The strategy had several downsides. First, product expansion increased fixed costs. Adding computer software as a product offering, for example, would require marketing expenditures to publicize its presence in the sector, programming expenditures to expand the web site, and inventory costs from buying and holding new products. Second, it was necessary to offer substantial product discounts to induce consumer purchases for these new products.

During the first two quarters of 2001, BN.com reported a loss of nearly $40.0 million per quarter. For the year 2000, it lost $275.7 million, which included a $75 million impairment charge and a $30 million write-down on equity investments in other companies. Despite these losses, sales had grown. Second quarter 2001 sales of $83.7 million exceeded sales in the like quarter in 2000 by 24 percent. Likewise, sales in the first quarter 2001 were 39 percent above those in the prior year. Full year sales of $320 million in 2000 were 65 percent above those in 1999. Also on the plus side, the company's gross margin, the difference between revenue and the cost of sales, in the first quarter of 2001 increased to 24.5 percent from 15.5 percent in the prior year. The company explained that the increase had come from lower promotional spending, reduced discounting by BN.com in response to tempered competitive pressure, and a new state-of-the-art distribution center that reduced buying costs. Moreover, the company added nearly 1 million new customers in the fourth quarter of 2000, bringing the cumulative customers count for the year to 7.3 million. Jason noted that the company reported having a $225 million hoard of cash and marketable securities at the end of 2000, down from $286 million three months earlier. Not only were its cash holdings substantial, but also its debt position was zero as of December 31, 2000. In contrast, Amazon has over $2 billion in long-term debt, some of which had a near term maturity.

Preparing for the Meeting

Jason lobbied to put BN.com on the discussion agenda for the upcoming Monday morning equity conference at the firm. At these meetings analysts present new stock recommendations to a committee comprised of portfolio managers representing all of the individual funds run by the mutual fund family. Three outcomes were possible from the meeting: a universal endorsement, a partial endorsement, or a rejection. If a universal endorsement were received BN.com could be purchased by any of the individual funds in the fund family. With a partial endorsement Jason's fund would be allowed to purchase it. After a rejection, BN.com could not be purchased by any of the funds.

Jason's reputation was at stake in the meeting. As a relatively new employee he did not want to present a company that received anything but a universal endorsement.

In preparation for the meeting, Jason worked on developing a report that would be submitted to fund managers. He followed the checklist of analytical steps, detailed in exhibit 4, that his fund manager had recommended to him. He knew that companies like BN.com, which had cash but suffered from major losses, were racing against the clock to achieve a breakeven state in which cash outflows and inflows were equal. Jason felt that for BN.com, the breakeven calculation was probably the most important item on the list.

Jason recalled the formula shown in equation (1) for breakeven analysis from graduate school:

$$Q^* = FC/CMR \tag{1}$$

where Q^* is breakeven revenue, FC is total fixed cost, and CMR is the company's contribution margin ratio, which is found by relating the contribution margin (net sales $-$ total variable costs) to net sales.

However, he had not had an opportunity to use this formula since his professor had assigned several problems from a chapter in a finance book. Examining BN.com's financial statements (exhibits 2 and 3), Jason did not see fixed and variable costs as separate categories as they were needed to fit into the formula. Then he remembered his accounting professor's directions for overcoming the differences between the artificial world in a textbook and actual company income statement reports: "Guesstimate fixed and variable costs to determine breakeven. Start by making assumptions and then modify them when the answer you come up with does not make sense."

Jason relied on BN.com's third quarter report since detailed reports for the fourth quarter and the year were still unavailable. He knew that fixed costs might include parts of cost of sales (COS), marketing, technology, general and administrative (G&A), and depreciation charges. But he didn't know what portion of those items belonged in variable costs. Making a simple start, he assumed that marketing expenses were one-third variable and two-thirds fixed and that COSs were entirely variable. All other costs were assumed to be fixed. Total fixed costs equaled the aggregate of all the separate pieces as seen in equation (2), with the data coming from exhibit 2. The derivation of variable costs is seen in equation (3).

$$FC = 59{,}221 \times (0) + 31{,}048 \times (2/3) + 10{,}723 + 5{,}598 + 9{,}236$$

$$FC = 46{,}234.97 \tag{2}$$

$$VC = 59{,}221 \times (1) + 31{,}048 \times (1/3)$$

$$VC = 69{,}559.98 \tag{3}$$

The contribution margin ratio (CMR) is calculated by subtracting variable costs from sales $(74{,}073 - 69{,}559.98)$ and then dividing the remainder by sales, which in this case gives a value of 0.061.[2] Jason was now ready to find breakeven output by solving equation (1) using results from equations (2) and (3) as seen in equation (4).

$$Q^* = FC/CMR$$

$$Q^* = \$46{,}234.97/0.061 = \$757{,}950.32 \tag{4}$$

After running the numbers, Jason doubted that breakeven quarterly sales were $757 million, as derived in equation (4), while actual sales were only $74 million. The difference between the two figures was too large. If true, the business plan for BN.com was implausible, and the company was not merely highly distressed as reflected in the $1.20 stock price but was significantly overvalued.

Jason decided that the problem lay in his assumptions regarding variable and fixed costs. Clearly, the assumption that all COSs were variable was too simplistic. In addition, Jason wanted to modify his assumption about the breakdown between fixed and variable marketing costs. He was even willing to rethink the other cost assumptions. Fortunately, he had downloaded some information from BN.com's quarterly report (see exhibit 3 and app. A) to help him conduct his analysis. Often the management discussion section gives clues to how costs tend to behave or are treated by management. In any case, he realized that subjective assumptions regarding cost behavior must be explicitly stated in order for others to understand his analysis and ultimately be persuaded to buy BN.com

Another issue that Jason thought about was operating changes that might be implemented at BN.com. Advertising, a large component of total costs, could be viewed in terms of its costs relative to the marginal number of customers gained by that expenditure. Jason tried several estimates of advertising cost per marginal customer versus average revenue and gross profit per customer. This gave him several ideas on how to renew the firm. Moreover, with the declining demand for Internet advertising, future costs of advertising over the Internet would probably decline. Jason thought that he should bring some of these numbers to the meeting.

EXHIBIT 1.   Books-A-Million Inc. Annual Results (millions of dollars)

	For the Period Ending				
	2/3/01	1/29/00	1/30/99	1/31/98	2/1/97
Sales[a]	418.6	404.1	347.8	324.8	278.6
Gross profit	109.2	107.7	91.1	86.4	72.3
Operating income	9.7	13.8	12.9	11.6	9.5
Net income	3.1	5.9	4.5	6.9	5.8

[a]Results are not available by sector.

EXHIBIT 2. barnesandnoble.com Inc. Quarterly Consolidated Statements of Operations (thousands of dollars, except per share data, unaudited)[a]

	Q2: 2001	Q1: 2001	Q4: 2000	Q3: 2000	Q2: 2000	Q1: 2000	Q4: 1999	Q3:1999
Net sales[b]	83,684	105,041	100,370	74,073	67,428	78,244	76,236	46,999
Cost of sales	63,195	82,914	82,563	59,221	56,966	63,051	65,479	38,959
Gross profit	20,489	22,127	17,807	14,852	10,462	15,193	10,757	8,040
Operating expenses								
Customer fulfillment	9,929	12,370			11,804	9,154		
Marketing and sales[b]	14,930	17,434	37,657[c]	31,048[c]	19,770	23,050	37,044[c]	24,050[c]
Technology and web site development	10,843	13,947	13,711	10,723	9,593	6,364	8,187	5,251
General and administrative	7,453	8,353	13,274	5,598	7,125	5,296	6,596	4,749
Depreciation and amortization	10,404	9,953	12,108	9,236	8,425	6,319	5,264	3,780
Stock-based compensation					(175)	11,915		
Equity in net loss of equity investments including amortization of intangibles	7,051	6,157	8,857	1,090	5,575	5,206		
Impairment			75,051					
Total operating expenses	60,610	68,214	100,768	67,695	62,117	67,304	57,091	37,830
Operating loss	(40,121)	(43,087)	(126,669)	(52,843)	(51,655)	(52,111)	(46,344)	(29,790)
Interest income, net	1,719	3,246	4,727	4,814	6,289	7,907	7,979	7,913
Net loss	(38,402)	(39,841)	(121,942)	(48,029)	(45,366)	(44,204)	(38,365)	(21,877)
Basic and diluted loss per common share	(0.24)	(0.25)	(1.08)	(0.33)	(0.31)	(0.30)	(0.27)	(0.15)
Average shares (diluted — if converted)[d]	158,787	158,787	146,118	146,118	145,783	145,176	143,972	143,972

[a]Pro forma consolidated statement of operations includes the consolidated results of barnesandnoble.com Inc. and barnesandnoble.com LLC as if the two companies were consolidated as of the earliest period presented.

[b]In accordance with the Emerging Issues Task Force Issue No. 00-14, "Accounting for Certain Sales Incentives" ("EITF 00-14"), expenses related to coupon redemptions, formerly classified as marketing and sales expense, are now recorded as a reduction of sales. EITF 00-14 requires the implementation of this change effective within all reporting periods beginning in the first fiscal quarter beginning after May 18, 2000, and also requires all prior periods to be reclassified to reflect this modification.

[c]For reasons unknown, third and fourth quarter reports combine order fulfillment and marketing expenses.

[d]Includes the conversion of outstanding membership units of barnesandnoble.com LLC converted into outstanding shares of barnesandnoble.com Inc. for all periods presented.

EXHIBIT 3. barnesandnoble.com Inc. Third Quarter Consolidated Balance Sheets (thousands of dollars, except share and per share data)

	December 31, 2000	December 31, 1999
Assets (unaudited)		
Current assets		
Cash and cash equivalents	$179,609	$247,403
Marketable securities	32,695	230,644
Receivables, net	26,129	15,520
Merchandise inventories	48,220	3,886
Prepaid expenses and other current assets	5,983	8,161
Total current assets	292,636	505,614
Fixed assets, net	150,500	97,854
Long-term marketable securities	5,000	71,852
Other noncurrent assets	80,799	4,198
Total assets	$528,935	$679,518
Liabilities and stockholders' equity		
Current liabilities		
Accounts payable	$ 19,066	$ 19,204
Accrued liabilities	89,820	39,627
Due to affiliate	27,101	17,109
Total current liabilities	135,987	75,940
Minority interest	284,494	482,896
Stockholders' equity		
Common stock Series A; 0.001 par value; 750,000,000 shares authorized; 31,268,591 and 29,347,067 shares issued and outstanding, respectively	44	29
Paid-in capital	187,612	134,452
Accumulated deficit[a]	(79,202)	(13,799)
Total stockholders' equity	108,454	120,682
Total liabilities and stockholders' equity	$528,935	$679,518

[a]Represents accumulated deficit of barnesandnoble.com Inc. since the company's initial public offering on May 25, 1999.

EXHIBIT 4. Critical Analytical Measures for Company Analysis

(1) Breakeven analysis
    (a) Cash breakeven
    (b) Profit breakeven
(2) Early warning model (failure risk)
    (a) Altman Z
    (b) Platt and Platt industry relative model
(3) Sustainable growth rate
    (a) Sources of new funds
    (b) Capital expenditure requirements
(4) Critical growth rates
    (a) Sales
    (b) Employment
    (c) Customers
    (d) CEO compensation
    (e) Market share

Appendix A. Information from barnesandnoble.com Inc. Quarterly Report

Net sales are composed of sales of books, music, software, prints & posters and related products, net of returns, as well as outbound shipping and handling charges. Sales of BN.com's products are recognized, net of estimated returns, at the time the products are shipped to customers.

The cost of sales . . . consist[s] of the cost of merchandise sold to customers and outbound and inbound shipping costs.

Marketing and sales expenses consist primarily of advertising and promotional expenditures, as well as payroll and related expenses for personnel engaged in marketing, selling, editorial, fulfillment and customer service activities. Fulfillment activities include receiving of goods, picking of goods for shipment and assembly for shipment. All fulfillment costs, including the cost of operating and staffing distribution centers and customer service, are included in marketing and sales.

Accounting standard setters are currently reviewing financial statements of internet companies in order to achieve a consensus with respect to the financial statement presentation of certain items. Included in this review is the current practice of including certain warehouse and fulfillment costs in marketing and sales expense instead of in cost of sales. Also being reviewed by accounting standard setters is the practice of classifying certain coupon redemption costs as marketing and sales expense instead of as a reduction to sales. BN.com has included in marketing expenses approximately $6 million, or 3% of sales, of coupon redemptions for the full year ended 1999. No coupons were redeemed in 1998. Had BN.com treated coupon redemptions as a reduction to sales and marketing expense in 1999, gross margin would have decreased from 21.0% to 18.6% and marketing and sales expense as a percentage of sales would have decreased from 55.1% to 53.7%. In addition, the accounting standard setters are reviewing Web site development costs. The Company's accounting for the features, content and functionality of BN.com's online stores, transaction-processing systems, telecommunications infrastructure and network operations is described in Note 2 to the financial statements as follows.

> Technology and Web site development expenses consist principally of payroll and related expenses for web page production, editorial and network operations personnel and consultants, and infrastructure related to systems and telecommunications. Development expenses included in the accompanying statements of operations consist principally of indirect development costs and all costs associated with the maintenance of the features, content and functionality of BN.com's online stores, transaction-processing systems, telecommunications infrastructure and network operations.

> General and administrative expenses consist of payroll and related expenses for executive, finance and administrative personnel, recruiting, professional fees and other general corporate expenses including costs to process credit card transactions.

Notes

1. We thank Henry Garelick for his analysis of BAMM.
2. The use of sales instead of price multiplied by quantity assumes that price is constant over the entire period. While this assumption is obviously false it does allow contribution margin to be calculated from publicly released data.

Reference

Ip, G. "Blame the Profit Dive on a Marked Change in Companies' Costs." *Wall Street Journal,* May 16, 2001, 1.

Operating Issues

Bank/Lender Liability

24. Crane Manufacturing Company

Walter Workout was sitting at his desk when he received a call from Steve Boswell, a longtime business acquaintance. Steve was head of lending at Augusta National Bank (ANB), a midsized commercial bank in Augusta, Georgia. Proud of his roots at an Atlanta money center bank, Steve had been able to bring more sophisticated lending practices to ANB. This had resulted in more creative structures than standard lines of credit.

Walter had gotten to know Steve during a workout involving his former bank. Steve had been the lending officer on that deal and was pleased with the manner in which Walter was able to assist the borrower in developing and implementing a turnaround plan. Steve had had some bad experiences with the workout officers at his former employer. It seemed that when a borrower got into trouble, their first concern was how much they could receive in liquidation. "Cut your losses and run" was the favorite saying of the head of workout at that bank.

ANB did not have a workout department per se. Each lender was responsible for handling his or her own problem loans. At the first sign of trouble, Steve and his lender would visit the borrower to assess the seriousness of the problem. They would then usually alert Dan Sharp, the bank's senior credit officer. If it was a really serious problem, Joan Sitter, the bank's CEO, would sit in on many of the strategy discussions.

Steve had a problem. One of his largest exposures was to Crane Manufacturing Company (CMC, or the company), a manufacturer of construction cranes. Steve was proud of this deal because he had

---

This case was prepared by James Ebbert.

worked so hard to get it done. The deal was about eighteen months old. Unfortunately, the company was not performing as well as projected and several months ago had begun falling behind in its trade payments. Now it was falling behind in its debt service payments. Management did not seem to have a good grip on the problems, plus it bothered him that the two owners drove around in nice company cars when he knew they were behind in their payments to the trade and the bank.

The outcome of Steve's call to Walter was the scheduling of a meeting in Augusta in two days. The call had lasted about an hour, and Walter had taken notes.

Crane Manufacturing Company

Crane Manufacturing Company was founded by John P. Grandslam (JPG) during the mid-1970s. Beginning with some experimental models built in his basement, John had been successful in developing a flexible crane that could lift heavy loads from almost any position. He had several patents on the crane. Although some models were freestanding, he had also developed a smaller but just as flexible model for piggyback mounting on the backs of excavators. By mounting the crane on an excavator, the user could transport the crane with the excavator as opposed to incurring the expense of moving a separate, freestanding crane. The user could also save substantial investment dollars by buying the combination machine as opposed to two separate machines.

In order to help sell his cranes, John became close to the excavator dealers for the various American and foreign manufacturers in the surrounding six-state area. When a customer visited these dealers to purchase an excavator, the dealers would tell them about the crane and refer them to CMC for additional information. The excavator dealers knew CMC's price structure for the cranes and would work out a package deal with the customer for both the excavator and the crane. The excavators would be delivered to CMC for installation of the crane, and CMC would then ship it to the customer's designated site.

As highway and commercial construction began to accelerate in the early 1980s, John saw the demand for the piggyback crane jump significantly. Augusta was also close to coal country, and the coal companies liked his crane as well. Not having a high school diploma, John ran the company using his instincts. He hated owing people money, and he paid COD for all his supplies and parts. John did not want to worry about some big debt jumping up and staring him in the face. He also kept expenses low, working out of a rundown building on the outskirts of Augusta. He paid his employees well, in fact, too well, in that many of them were being compensated through both salary and liberal expense accounts.

Over the years John discovered that the market for the piggyback crane was more of a short-term lease market than a sales market. The construction business was cyclical, and many users did not want the fixed overhead in bad times. Leases were also available on excavators through the manufacturers' dealer networks. John had even been able to convince some of the excavator manufacturers' captive finance companies to finance the crane as well as the excavator. Business was good, and all John knew was that there was always more money coming in than going out. He had a bookkeeper working for him who kept the money straight. His revenues were approximately $6 million when he decided to sell the company.

John hired a local accounting firm to put some information together on the company. The accounting firm produced an attractive book, with projections extending out for several years into the future. The projections utilized a common multiple on earnings approach and suggested that a fair price would be between $10 and $12 million.

After CMC was on the market for several months, John was introduced to George Small, a wealthy individual in his early seventies George was a very successful entrepreneur who had had many ups and downs in his career. His big fortune came from mining when he sold several mines to one of the large mining companies. That had occurred almost ten years before, and George had been living a very comfortable life since that time. Since then, he had become involved in several companies, both as an investor and as a member of the boards of directors. He even held a directorship on one of the Fortune 500 boards.

One of the several investments George had made was in a crane manufacturer located in Texas. The investment was made in good economic times, and that company's sales kept growing and growing. It was eventually purchased by a foreign crane manufacturer. His involvement with that company had allowed him to meet Tom Snyder, its president. Over the years he became close friends with Tom. When Tom was not offered a job by the acquiring company, George started

Dig Deep, Inc. (DDI), a specialty crane fabrication company, and installed Tom as its president. DDI did not fare so well and had manufactured several units that were not very reliable. DDI ceased operations, leaving a lot of debts in its wake. In addition to the normal bank and trade debt, several customers owned faulty cranes and had warranty claims. This had cast a questionable reputation over DDI, Tom, and George in the marketplace. Fort Worth Machinery Company, one of DDI's largest customers, was owed over $500,000 and was threatening to sue George personally.

George was proud of his success, especially since he had only a seventh grade education. His fortune had been earned through long days of hands-on experience in the mines. He had been close to bankruptcy on several occasions but had always managed to pull a rabbit out of the hat. Indeed, most businesspeople who knew George marveled at how he had been able to turn a bankrupt situation into a fortune by selling out to the large mining company. Many, on the other hand, called it dumb luck made possible by a stupid big company.

George loved the crane business. CMC had an excellent reputation. The price John was asking was steep, but George had an idea on how he could grow CMC well beyond anyone's expectations. George reasoned that a large untapped market existed for CMC's products, a market untouched by John because he had no interest in expanding the business beyond the regional business that it was. He also lacked the working capital. George's years of operating mines had brought him into contact with some of the largest heavy equipment manufacturers in the world. He had some good contacts and within a month was able to strike a deal with Yellow Equipment Company (YEC), one of the world's largest and best known heavy equipment manufacturers, to distribute the cranes through its dealer network. CMC's prices would even be listed in YEC's price book. Parts, a very lucrative business, would be sold through YEC's dealer network. The only drawback was that CMC could not deal directly with dealers of excavators manufactured by others. However, YEC agreed to stock CMC's yard with various models of excavators and not charge the company any financing costs.

With the YEC contract in hand, George began looking for financing. While he had a mid-seven-figure fortune comprised of cash, real estate, and securities, he did not want to liquidate most of his investments. He was used to high leverage. Unfortunately, most of the lending sources he contacted were concerned over what appeared to be a steep purchase price and George's desire to highly leverage the acquisition. They had learned their lessons in the go-go eighties.

John really wanted to sell CMC. George really wanted to buy CMC. As George kept meeting resistance on the financing, John approached ANB, his bank since CMC's founding. He had built a good working relationship with Steve Boswell. He appealed to Steve to find a way to finance George's acquisition of CMC. Steve told John that the asking price was too high and that if the deal was to get done either the price would have to be lowered, real equity would have to be invested, or John would have to personally finance some of the purchase price.

During the ensuing six weeks, Steve structured a deal that seemed to suit both George and John. The purchase price approximated $9.6 million. The deal was structured as shown in table 1.

ANB's notes would be secured by a first secured lien on all of the company's assets. All of the debt for the transaction, including the JPG notes, was to be personally guaranteed by George Small. In order to provide more comfort to ANB, George was to deposit $2 million of collateral in an escrow account at ANB. All of the ANB debt was cross-collateralized and cross-defaulted. In addition, the ANB and JPG obligations were cross-defaulted.

An asset purchase reflecting the structure just described was documented and closed shortly thereafter. George installed Tom as president. Steve felt very comfortable with the deal he had structured. In addition, the bank had satisfied a longtime customer. Other departments of the bank were benefiting from the deal. John retained ANB's trust department to manage the money, establishing trusts for his four children with ANB as the trustees.

TABLE 1.   CMC Acquisition Deal

Transaction	Amount ($)
Purchase price	9,600,000
ANB note 1	1,260,150
ANB note 2	4,250,000
ANB note 3	165,000
ANB note 4	988,000
JPG note 1	1,000,000
JPG note 1	1,000,000
JPG note 1	666,170
ANB structuring fee	250,000
George Small equity	guarantees all debt

Subsequent Developments

Twelve months into the deal CMC's performance began to slip. Steve first heard about the problems during lunch with another good customer of his. This customer owned a steel fabricator and mentioned that his receivables from CMC were beginning to approach ninety days in age. He asked Steve what was happening at CMC. Steve had also heard through the grapevine that CMC had agreed to assume DDI's $500,000+ warranty obligation to Fort Worth Machinery.

Steve spoke to John, who assured him that everything was fine; sales had been a little slow during the previous month, which had caused the company's payables to age longer than normal. Annual sales were running at a rate of $6.5 million as opposed to the projected $8+ million. Trade payables totaled almost $1.5 million. Tom was communicating with the vendors, who were working with the company during this slow period.

Over the next several months Steve noticed that CMC's loan payments were beginning to be paid later in the month. John and Tom denied there were any serious fundamental problems with the business. However, they did admit that the dip in sales was lasting longer than expected and that the costs of selling through YEC were greater than anticipated. YEC was a huge company and wanted CMC to bend over backward for its dealer network.

What prompted Steve's phone call to Walter were the results of an emergency meeting requested by John and Tom the day before. During the meeting they informed Steve that it would be difficult for the company to make the upcoming payroll. While they assured Steve that the long-term fundamentals of CMC were fine, they admitted to some short-term difficulties and asked that several of the term notes be restructured over longer periods of time. They also requested a $500,000 increase in the working capital line. This was needed because they had fallen behind with several of their key vendors, whose refusal to ship could cause production to cease. Furthermore, their South American salesman was on the verge of an order for five units.

When Steve indicated a reluctance to meet their requests, they suggested that ANB did not sufficiently understand their business. This stirred Steve's memory about some of the things he had learned while working with Walter on a case many years before. One of Walter's favorite sayings was "They always tell you they need more money and that you do not understand their business. If you give them more money, they will just blow that too." Walter also had told him that another solution often mentioned was a big order just around the corner. On the other hand, Steve was worried about the vendors' shutting down the company because he sensed that ANB might not recover all of its money in a liquidation.

Just before Walter Workout was ready to leave for the airport, he became ill. You are now sitting on the plane headed toward Augusta. You have a meeting in the morning with Steve, John, and Tom. Steve has told you that his intention, notwithstanding lender liability problems, is to have you retained initially as a consultant and then probably as interim CEO.

Activity-Based Costing

25. Turning around the South Dakota Microbrewery

In 1992, two former Anheuser-Busch employees started their own brewery, South Dakota Microbrewery (SDM). Sandy Bennett and Dave Goldstone developed a business plan and obtained a business start-up loan from a local commercial bank. The loan proceeds, combined with their own savings, were sufficient capital to purchase a small manufacturing facility and equipment. To save money, they purchased most of the stainless steel equipment at a dairy farm auction and then converted the equipment to suit their needs. Other supplies and equipment were purchased from a brewers' supply house in Wisconsin. South Dakota Microbrewery has grown steadily and now (December 1997) produces three labels of specialty beers. The company posted its first profit in December 1995.

The Brewing Process

Brewing is essentially a four-stage process, as shown in exhibit 1. Direct labor is incurred primarily in stages one, two, and four. The first stage requires mixing various malts, sugar, hops, and water and "cooking" the mixture. At this point the mixture is referred to as *wort*. SDM uses a 350 liter copper kettle with a natural gas burner for this part of the process. Preparing wort takes four to seven hours, depending on the particular brew produced.

The second stage of the brewing process requires siphoning the

---

This case was prepared by Marjorie B. Platt and James Weisel.

wort through a *wort chiller* into one of eight fermentation tanks owned by SDM. The wort chiller is a double copper tube in which cold water is forced one direction in the outer tube and the wort is pumped the other direction (into the fermentation tank) through the inner tube. This action is required to chill the wort as rapidly as possible from boiling temperature to approximately 21 °C, or 70 °F. Rapid chilling is necessary to minimize the possibility of contamination and bacterial growth in the wort. This stage of the process takes about one-half hour per batch, as the chiller can process about ten liters per minute.

Fermentation is the third step in brewing. Brewer's yeast is added after the wort has been properly chilled and collected in the fermentation tank. The tank is then sealed, and a *fermentation lock* is placed on the tank. Yeast, malt, and sugar combine to form two products: carbon dioxide and alcohol. The carbon dioxide is allowed to escape through the fermentation lock, which prevents air from entering the tank. The fermentation process takes from three to fourteen days, again dependent on the product being brewed. Several samples are taken from the brew during the fermentation process. Some samples are taken for taste testing. Others are used to determine the status of the fermentation process using a hydrometer.

After this first fermentation is completed, flat beer has been produced. The final stage of the brewing process consists of carbonating the brew and siphoning it from the fermentation tank through a filter into bottles. The filter is used to prevent *wild yeast* from entering the bottles and to help the beer "clear" properly. Wild yeast can result in bacterial growth and cause the beer to have a cloudy appearance. SDM utilizes the injection method of carbonation. Essentially, carbon dioxide is injected into the bottle simultaneously with the beer. The bottles are then capped, labeled, and put into cool storage for several days. After three to five days of aging, the brew is ready to be sold and delivered to the local pubs that sell South Dakota beer.

SDM Brews

South Dakota Microbrewery produces three different types of beer: Buffalo Ale, Four Heads Stout, and Bismark Bock. Buffalo Ale is a medium-colored amber ale with a slightly sweet taste. SDM's Four Heads Stout is similar to the rich, bitter stouts from well-known Irish breweries. For both of these brews, the production process is fairly straightforward. By contrast, Bismark Bock requires more attention in order to obtain the thick, rich, full-flavored aromatic taste characteristic of bock beers. The ale is sold primarily to bars in college towns that order large shipments. SDM is planning to brew 250 batches of ale in the 1998 fiscal year. The stout and bock beers are more specialty-type products that are shipped to upscale restaurants and hotels that order smaller quantities. Consequently, SDM plans to brew 120 batches of both their stout and their bock beers. Distribution logistics is an important factor in maintaining a stable customer base and opening up new opportunities for SDM. After covering all of their manufacturing costs and distribution costs, Sandy and Dave split the remaining profits after paying their interest costs and taxes and setting aside a reasonable amount to fund unforeseen expenses.

Company Prospects

Between them, Sandy and Dave have fifteen years of experience in the brewing industry. However, neither was experienced in management until they formed SDM. Local competition has been intense, causing some beer prices to fluctuate substantially. Ale prices have been falling throughout the market, and SDM has followed recently with price declines over the last year. However, SDM recently raised its bock beer price 10 percent with no apparent market response to the price increase. Sandy attributes this to steady demand and no local competition for this particular product offering. She is concerned, however, that ale prices have fallen such that the ale's gross margin has eroded far below the targeted 30 percent that she and Dave have established as a goal for each brew label. Sandy is convinced that extended sales of Buffalo Ale at low margins are causing SDM's declining profitability. In fact, the company's gross margin has fallen for three consecutive years. Both Sandy and Dave are uncomfortable about the future viability of the firm if the gross margin declines any further, despite increasing sales volume. Currently, SDM is charging $1.05 per 0.5 liter bottle for Buffalo Ale, $1.50 for Bismark Bock, and $1.40 for Four Heads Stout.

Sandy and Dave mentioned their concerns about Buffalo Ale's declining gross margin to the company's accountant, Tom Hawkins. After some discussion, Tom suggested that he talk to people he knew at a turnaround management consulting firm in Chicago, Allison Partners (AP), about SDM's problems. Tom arranged a meeting between AP and SDM during which there was a free-ranging discussion of the business, the current competitive environment, and SDM's recent financial performance. Dave argued that the real problem for SDM was Buffalo Ale. Its gross margin had slipped to 19 percent, which was far below the target set by management. At that gross margin, the product could not cover the other operating expenses, interest expense, and other nonoperating expenses that might be incurred. Sandy wondered whether SDM would be better off if they dropped Buffalo Ale and concentrated their efforts on the more profitable brews. She reiterated SDM's relatively strong market position for the other beers, especially Bismark Bock. After spending some time with Sandy, Dave, and Tom as well as touring the plant and talking to key workers there, the AP team departed for Chicago, promising to send a proposal to SDM that would help turn the company around. They took with them some financial cost analyses that Tom had prepared for them (see exhibit 2).

AP's Turnaround Proposal

Ten days after their meeting, SDM received a proposal from AP to fix the business (see exhibits 3–5). Sandy, Dave, and Tom sat down to discuss it. They weighed the options presented in the proposal.

Student Assignment

Answer the following questions.

1. If SDM continues to use the plantwide cost system to allocate overhead to products, should SDM drop Buffalo Ale? Explain your results. Justify your answer with appropriate financial analysis.
2. If SDM uses activity based costing (ABC) to allocate overhead to products, what are the estimated manufacturing costs by product?
3. Compare the two cost systems using gross margin and gross margin percentage per bottle. Why is there a difference?
4. What action(s) should SDM take to correct its problems? Make a recommendation to management based on your analyses.

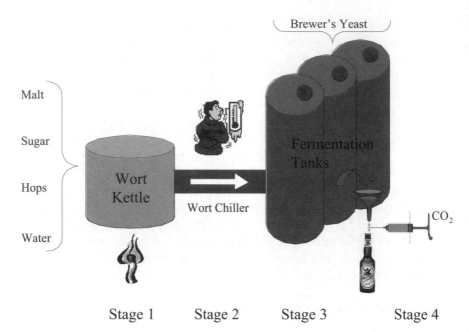

Stage 1   Stage 2   Stage 3   Stage 4

EXHIBIT 1. The brewing process

EXHIBIT 2. Product Cost Analysis for a Single Batch of Each Beer Label

Direct Materials (DM)	Quantity	Cost per Unit ($)	Total Cost ($)
Buffalo Ale (expected yield = 22 cases)			
Coopers Amber Malt	50 kg	0.60	30.00
Northumberland Malt	50 kg	0.30	15.00
Corn sugar	5 kg	0.25	1.25
Geleany hops	1.75 kg	1.00	1.75
Filtered water	220 ltr	0.03	6.60
Brewer's yeast	100 gm	0.08	8.00
Total DM cost			62.60
Direct labor	18 hr	6.00	108.00
Overhead costs	18 hr	15.57	280.20
Total product cost per batch			450.80
Four Heads Stout (expected yield = 18 cases)			
Irish Stout Malt	40 kg	1.02	40.80
Strong Export Bitter Malt	14 kg	2.40	33.66
East Kent Goldings hops	1.32 kg	2.80	3.69

EXHIBIT 2—Continued

Direct Materials (DM)	Quantity	Cost per Unit ($)	Total Cost ($)
Filtered water	180 ltr	0.03	5.40
Brewer's yeast	75 gm	0.08	6.00
Total DM cost			89.55
Direct labor	13 hr	6.00	78.00
Overhead costs	13 hr	15.57	202.37
Total product cost per batch			369.92

Bismark Bock (expected yield = 16 cases)

John Bull Dark Malt	55 kg	1.08	59.25
Newquay Brown Malt	20 kg	0.75	15.00
Perle hops	2.87 kg	1.50	4.30
Filtered water	160 ltr	0.03	4.80
Brewer's yeast	70 gm	0.08	5.60
Total DM cost			88.95
Direct labor	12 hr	6.00	72.00
Overhead costs	12 hr	15.57	186.80
Total product cost per batch			347.75

EXHIBIT 3. Budgeted Overhead Costs for the 1998 Fiscal Year

Activity	Estimated Cost ($)	Cost Driver
Maintenance and sterilization	30,000	fermentation days
Mixing and cooking	8,000	fermentation days
Chilling and siphoning	7,500	direct labor hours
Equipment depreciation	5,500	machine hours
Quality control	10,500	number of quality control inspections
Bottling and labeling	21,000	number of bottles
Storage	3,000	number of bottles
Shipping	31,250	number of orders
Total	116,750	

EXHIBIT 4.   Estimated Activities for the 1998 Fiscal Year

Cost Drivers	Estimated Annual Volume	
		Total
Fermentation days[a]		2,910
Direct labor hours		7,500
Machine hours		82,700
Number of orders		3,740
Number of quality control inspections		4,850
Number of bottles produced[b]		229,920

	Estimated Requirements per Batch by Beer Label		
Cost Drivers	Buffalo Ale	Bismark Bock	Four Heads Stout
Fermentation days	3	14	4
Direct labor hours	18	12	13
Machine hours	110	325	135
Number of orders	2	18	9
Number of quality control inspections	5	22	8
Number of bottles per batch	528	384	432

[a]A fermentation day is one 24-hour period in which wort occupies a fermentation tank. South Dakota Microbrewery owns eight fermentation tanks. Thus, eight tanks occupied 365 days per year result in 2,910 fermentation days when time is allowed for cleaning (about 1 hour/tank/year).
[b]There are 24 bottles to one case.

EXHIBIT 5.   Excerpts from Allison Partners, PLC, Proposal to South Dakota Microbrewery

It is clear that SDM management used a plantwide costing system based on direct labor hours to allocate overhead for the purposes of developing the total product manufacturing cost for the three brews. If this cost system is appropriate, pursuing the course suggested by management, that is, dropping Buffalo Ale, might cause a scale problem and put pressure on the remaining products. If SDM deems that dropping ale is the best course of action, AP strongly recommends that SDM take steps to reduce manufacturing costs.

An alternative course of action for SDM at this time is to develop product cost estimates based on an activity based costing system. For that purpose, we have analyzed the brewing process used by SDM. We have identified eight different key activities based on last year's records and anticipated cost increases, as shown in exhibit 3. Also shown in exhibit 3 are the cost drivers that we determined were associated with each activity. Exhibit 4 contains the estimated total volume for each cost driver for the coming fiscal year and cost driver volume broken down by product. Note that depreciation and storage are primarily fixed costs, while the maintenance and sterilization cost is half variable and half fixed. The remaining cost pools are substantially variable in nature.

Developing a Layoff Plan

26. Intelligent Signals, Inc.

Thursday was nearly over, and Mike Morgan knew that he needed to produce a workforce reduction plan by 5:00 P.M. the next day. Intelligent Signals, Inc. (ISI), where Mike was the CEO, was in terrible shape; the high-technology slump that had begun in 2000 had dragged on, leaving its sales in 2003 at less than 15 percent of their peak. Plans to rapidly expand its switch and router businesses had substantially increased ISI's capacity in 1999 and 2000 but had nearly drained its liquid resources and its credit line. When new business failed to develop and sales plunged, a cash crisis ensued.

ISI was not the first company in its industry to hit the wall. No manufacturer escaped the crash. Consequently, ISI's lenders were unforgiving and demanding. The bank group was doubtful that ISI could recover and recommended a merger or sale. Mike Morgan had started ISI in 1994 when he left a large firm that dominated the router business. That year he received a high-technology MBA from Northeastern University and felt ready to take on the world. The business was a success from the get-go. By the last quarter in 1995 sales had reached $10 million. From then on until 2000, ISI seemed to be a golden goose, with sales and profits growing by 50 percent or more annually. With this history, Mike was reluctant to heed the bank's advice. Instead, he proposed a radical restructuring that would bring the firm to breakeven.

This would not be ISI's first layoff. The company had reduced its workforce by 10 percent in 2001, 2002, and 2003. But those layoffs had not been designed to achieve breakeven. Instead, ISI had used

This case was prepared by Harlan D. Platt.

them primarily to balance out the employee count (table 1) after years of having hired more workers than were needed because of the extreme difficulty in hiring in the high-tech sector. The lack of concern for breakeven was a result of ISI having a substantial cash balance following the successful completion in 2000 of a major stock offering that raised over $240 million. Mike and ISI's board were uniformly of the opinion that the telecom slump would end soon. They repeated that phrase each quarter almost like a sacred mantra. Meanwhile ISI's cash hoard was rapidly depleted. By the end of 2003, it was down to $70 million in cash (table 2). Of four manufacturing facilities, the company needed less than one as a consequence of its sales having fallen from roughly $65 million a quarter to $5 million.

At the board of directors meeting that Thursday, Mike noticed a watershed change. The board was now resigned to the permanence of the business slump. Discussions with the chief salesperson of poten-

TABLE 1.   Employee Count

	1997	1998	1999	2000	2001	2002	2003
R&D engineers	95	110	136	160	140	120	110
R&D support	33	43	48	51	41	31	30
Manufacturing	234	314	411	477	400	375	310
Manufacturing support	38	50	52	60	55	50	45
Quality control	17	22	25	29	29	20	15
Shipping	22	27	29	34	34	27	21
Sales	16	22	24	28	28	28	25
Sales support	26	35	33	39	39	39	33
Marketing	21	22	26	30	30	30	30
Marketing support	16	21	26	31	31	31	31
Legal	6	11	13	15	15	15	15
Administrative	9	14	19	22	22	22	22
Human relations	3	5	7	8	8	8	8
Investor relations	2	3	4	6	6	6	6
Executive	11	15	19	22	22	22	22
Total	549	714	872	1,012	900	824	723

TABLE 2.   Assorted Financials ($ millions)

	1997	1998	1999	2000	2001	2002	2003
Revenues	82.42	128.58	193.12	258.78	188.91	100.12	42.05
Liquid assets	14.00	23.00	32.00	278.00	230.74	168.44	70.00
Bank line	2.00	3.00	3.00	5.00	12.00	25.00	30.00

tial sales to two major new customers, a Spanish utility and a baby Bell, were met with guffaws of disbelief from the board. One director even went so far as to say, "Don't tell me about any more of these transactions. Every meeting I hear about new prospects, but at the next meeting they're gone." It was true that ISI had not booked a new account in over eighteen months and that its order backlog was down to virtually zero. What sales were taking place were mainly system repairs and reworks. The bankruptcies of the telecom companies like Global Crossing and WorldCom had left the entire supplier industry in turmoil.

The board of directors debated a motion to simply liquidate the firm in an orderly manner. This followed Mike's statement that discreet efforts by an investment banker to find a buyer or a merger partner had turned up no leads. The lending bank was owed about $30 million. Like most high-technology companies, ISI had few hard assets. Its buildings were leased, as was most of its equipment. Mike estimated that a liquidation sale plus cash on hand could pay off the bank and settle with landlords and leave about $40 million for shareholders. With 60 million shares outstanding that meant that each share would receive about 66 cents after the liquidation. The stock was then trading at about 30 cents, suggesting that the market did not believe that the company would liquidate and that it believed that further losses would continue to erode the cash position.

Several directors and Mike combined to own nearly 20 million shares. Most of the board was inclined to favor the liquidation option until Mike made a counterproposal. He said, "What if I were to reduce the personnel count enough so that after renegotiating with the landlord I got us to cash breakeven? That way if we stayed in business for a bit we could either liquidate next year or if the market picked up actually make a profit." The other directors were dubious. First of all, they didn't think that the landlord would budge despite the fact that the commercial real estate market in Boston had collapsed. Second, they didn't think that Mike could reduce the workforce to the cash breakeven point and still have a viable company remaining. They agreed to meet with Mike at 5:00 P.M. on Friday and instructed him to produce a layoff plan. The meeting ended with no conversation, no directors' dinner, and Mike alone in the building.

Wage and benefit payments varied widely across job functions. A top research engineer could easily earn $250,000, while a shipping clerk might only receive $30,000. Fixed-cost benefits such as health and dental insurance cost about $7,500 per employee, while variable benefits such as bonuses were as high as 100 percent of salary for executives and as low as 10 percent of wages for junior engineers. The fully loaded cost per employee in 2003 averaged approximately $68,000.

People and Incentives

27. Berkshire Industries PLC

We had to do something different. The company was doing great according to all the performance indicators we monitored, and our managers were earning nice bonuses, but the shareowners weren't benefiting.

— *William Embleton*

William Embleton, managing director of Berkshire Industries PLC, explained why his company had implemented a new incentive system based on an "economic profit" measure of performance starting in the year 2000. In 2002, however, Berkshire managers were questioning whether their new system had had its desired effects. The new economic profit measure did not seem to be any better in reflecting shareowner returns than did the old measure—accounting earnings—on which Berkshire managers had previously focused. And the new system was causing some management confusion and a perceived unfairness issue. Mr. Embleton had to decide whether to modify the new system—and, if so, how—or to replace it with something else.

The Company

Berkshire Industries PLC (Berkshire) was founded in 1852 as a brewery serving local pubs. Over the years it had grown, both internally and by acquisition. In 2002, Berkshire was a medium-sized, publicly held corporation focused on the beverage and snack foods industry. It had annual turnover of about £500 million, and it employed nearly thirty-five hundred people in six countries. Berkshire was listed on the London Stock Exchange. The company headquarters were still located in Manchester, England, where the company was founded.

This case was prepared by Kenneth Merchant and Wim A. Van der Stede.

Berkshire had four operating divisions: beer, spirits, soft drinks, and snack foods. The managing directors of each of these divisions had considerable autonomy because Berkshire operated in a decentralized fashion. The small headquarters staff was primarily responsible for coordinating the finance, human resources, and various administrative functions (e.g., legal, information systems).

Measurement and Incentive Systems

Since the company had gone public, the primary performance emphasis at Berkshire had been on corporate earnings per share (EPS). The company's long-term EPS growth target was 8 percent, but the target was modified each year based on anticipated market conditions and pending acquisitions, if any.

The company's annual planning process was a bottom-up process that first involved the operating divisions proposing their earnings targets for the year and their means of achieving them. The divisions' draft plans were consolidated and compared with Berkshire's corporate EPS growth target. Typically the difference between the divisions' plans and the corporate target was material. This "planning gap" was eliminated in a series of discussions among corporate and division managers, typically by increases in the targets of some or all divisions.

Because top management considered it so important to meet analysts' EPS expectations, they also established a corporate "profit reserve" of approximately 10 percent of planned earnings. This reserve was established to ensure that the corporation would achieve its targets even if one, or perhaps even two, of its divisions failed to achieve their targets. If, later in the year, management determined that the company would achieve its targets, they would release this reserve to the Investments Committee for spending on discretionary projects, most of which had relatively long-term payoffs. But in 2000 and 2001, none of this reserve was released to the Investments Committee. All of it was turned in to meet the corporate EPS targets.

Senior managers at Berkshire, a group of about forty people, participated in an annual incentive compensation plan. Performance was evaluated based on achievement of earnings targets in the entity to which the manager was assigned: a division in the case of division-level personnel or the entire corporation in the case of corporate-level personnel. The target bonuses ranged from 20 percent to 90 percent of base salary, depending on the manager's level of seniority. The plan allowed for subjective overrides if superiors, or the compensation committee of the board of directors in the case of top management, felt that performance shortfalls were caused by factors beyond the manager's control.

The Motivation for a New Incentive Plan

In 1999, Berkshire's board of directors asked William Embleton to explore the desirability of a new performance measurement and incentive system based on an "economic profit" measure of performance, a concept that had received many popular reviews in the management press.

The board's motivation for a new plan stemmed from two concerns. First, they were concerned that managers' interests were not aligned with those of shareowners. They were particularly concerned that EPS was not a good measure of performance in the new era, where the management mantra had become "maximization of shareowner value." They noted that while Berkshire's EPS had been improving steadily, at an average annual growth rate of 9 percent in the last decade, the company's shareowners had not benefited. The company's share price had increased only slightly over that period of time.

Second, the board wanted to force more objectivity into the performance evaluation and reward system. Some board members believed that too many subjective bonus awards were being made, giving managers bonuses even in years where their entity did not perform well. One effect of allowing subjective judgments was that bonus awards were only loosely correlated with the realized operating performances. Another effect was a lot of misspent time as managers engaged in "politicking." They tried to convince their evaluators that they had performed well, even though the results were disappointing. The board members in favor of change thought that a new incentive system should place sharp limits on the use of subjectivity in granting bonus awards, if not eliminate it entirely.

The New System

In response to the board's request, William Embleton asked three consulting firms to submit proposals for an engagement to design a new measurement and incentive system. After a series of meetings, the Berkshire management team and board selected the large New York–headquartered firm of Corey, Langfeldt and Associates (CLA). The consulting engagement was staffed by CLA associates based in London.

The CLA approach was based on the firm's proprietary economic profit measure of performance. The CLA formula for economic profit was

Economic profit = Adjusted net operating profit after taxes
− [Capital × Cost of capital].

Net operating profit after taxes (NOPAT) excluded all nonoperating noncash charges, such as depreciation, amortization, asset write-offs and write-downs, and reserves. Cost of capital was determined annually for each business unit based on the yield on long-term government obligations plus a risk premium calculated based on an assumed capital structure and risk factor (β value) for comparable peer firms. Since Berkshire's business units were all seen as being in relatively stable industries, all were given the same cost-of-capital rate—10 percent.

In each of their engagements, CLA would propose a specific combination of adjustments to NOPAT to make the economic profit measure "better," to better match costs and benefits and, hence, to improve the relationship between economic profits and share prices. The CLA system designers had identified well over a hundred adjustments that might be used in certain situations. But in Berkshire's case, the consultants proposed only two adjustments because they wanted "to keep the model simple." First, they suggested that the company's consumer advertising expenses should be capitalized and amortized on a straight-line basis over three years. The current year's expense was added back to operating profits, and the capitalized amount was added to net operating assets. Exhibit 1 shows an example.

Second, the CLA consultants suggested that the goodwill that had arisen from the company's acquisitions should not be amortized.[1] Hence, they suggested that cumulative goodwill that had been amortized to date should be added back to net operating assets and that all goodwill amortization expense should be added back to operating earnings.

In their presentations, the CLA consultants explained that their economic profit measure was superior to all other measures, particularly accounting earnings, that Berkshire could use. The consultants presented charts showing that their measure of economic profits was highly correlated with returns to shareowners in a broad range of corporations. Thus, they claimed, it is the one measure that provides "the right signals to management all the time." Motivating managers to maximize their entities' economic profit would induce them to invest in their entities' futures. They would make all investments promising returns greater than the corporation's cost of capital. It would also motivate them to recognize the full cost of tying up the company's capital and, hence, to reduce their employed assets where the returns are inadequate.

Knowing their competition, the CLA consultants also directed some of their critique at systems that tried to link management incentives to elaborate combinations of measures. The multiple-measurement systems, they explained, were usually hopelessly complex. The systems typically incorporated measures that were not directly linked with shareowner value. They included performance concepts that were vague (e.g., personnel development) and supported by weak measures. And they rarely made the trade-offs among the multiple measures clear. The overall effects were diffusion of management attention and loss of understandability and accountability.

The CLA consultants also recommended against the implementation of a stock-based incentive program. They pointed out that stock prices are affected by many external factors and are highly volatile in the short term. They further explained that stock-based incentives are not an effective tool for motivating division-level and lower level managers, who can have, at best, a modest impact on share prices.

The measurement focus of the CLA presentation was highly convincing to some of the board members. One remarked: "This is what we need, one simple measure that goes up when shareowner value is created and that goes down when value is destroyed. If we get our managers focused on this measure, they will be working in the best interest of our shareowners. With earnings, we just don't know what we're getting."

A second element of the CLA system involved the automatic ratcheting of performance targets. In the CLA system, managers were compensated directly for improving their entities' economic profits. In the first year, the performance targets were set based on a projection of the unit's historical economic profit growth rate, if that growth rate was deemed to be good performance, multiplied by 75 percent. Thereafter, performance targets were set automatically based on improvements from the actual performance of the prior year. Each business unit's performance target was ratcheted up (down) by 75 percent of the amount by which actual performance exceeded (fell short of) the unit's prior year's performance. The CLA consultants explained that this method of setting targets avoided the need to renegotiate performance targets each year and, hence, the politics and game playing that were almost inevitably associated with these negotiations. It also incorporated the desired management philosophy of continuous improvement.

A third element of the system was the explicit elimination of payout thresholds and caps. Managers were assigned a target bonus, a fixed percentage of base pay, that would be earned if their units just achieved their performance targets. These targets were increased slightly from the bonus levels that were earned under Berkshire's old system to encourage managers' acceptance of change. The target bonuses ranged from 20 percent of base salary for functional managers within a division to 100 percent for Berkshire's managing director. If the units exceeded their performance targets, managers would earn larger bonuses. The slope of the line connecting the prior year's actual economic profit and the forthcoming year's target determined the slope of the payoff line (see exhibit 2).[2] The maximum bonus that could be earned was unlimited.

The fourth element of the system was a "bonus bank" that was intended to reduce manager risk by smoothing out the bonus awards, to reduce managers' short-term gaming behaviors, and to improve manager retention. If a unit's economic profit performance exceeded the performance target, the "excess" bonus earned (calculated as the slope of the payoff function times the amount by which the actual economic profit exceeds the target) was credited to the bonus bank. Managers were then paid their target bonus plus one-fourth of the amount in the bonus bank. If economic profit fell below the target amount, a negative entry (obtained as the slope of the payoff function times the amount by which the actual economic profit fell short of the target) was made to the bonus bank. If managers changed divisions, their bonus bank amounts would follow them. Managers who left Berkshire voluntarily forfeited the amounts in their bonus bank accounts.

Problems and Concerns

While Berkshire's board members' and managers' hopes were high after the company's introduction of the new economic profit system in 2000, early experiences with the system were disappointing. The new system had caused several problems and concerns. The board and the top management team were considering whether the system needed fixing. Some even questioned whether the new system should be continued.

One problem was that the new system had created considerable management confusion, which persisted even after all the operating managers had attended a series of training sessions. Corporate managers thought that the operating managers would quickly learn how the economic profit measure worked, since their bonuses now depended on it. But a number of the managers seemed not to understand how the economic profit measure was computed, and some of them continued to manage their entities based on their old earnings-based management reports.

A second problem was discouragement and demotivation in the Spirits Division (Spirits). In both 2000 and 2001, economic profits in Spirits were poor. In the recessionary times, consumers were drinking less spirits. With consumer demand down, some of the Spirits Division's competitors cut prices significantly, and Spirits had to match their reductions. This had a disastrous effect on margins. Spirits failed to achieve both its 2000 performance target and its ratcheted-down 2001 target by wide margins. As a consequence, bonus awards for Spirits managers were significantly below target levels, and all Spirits managers had sizable negative balances in their bonus bank accounts.

Ian Dent, Spirits' managing director, asked William Embleton for some special adjustments. He requested that the Spirits Division performance targets be adjusted retroactively to reflect the economic conditions that were actually faced. He did not think it was fair for his managers to suffer the negative effects of factors over which they had no control. He explained that his team had worked very hard in the trying conditions they had faced and they had made the hard decisions that were called for, including layoffs and cutbacks in discretionary expenses. He also requested that the economic profit system not be applied to his division because it was not responsive to changing market conditions. Ian was worried that his division would suffer some significant management losses because of his managers' negative bonus bank balances.

A third problem was a widely shared perception of a basic failure of the economic profit measure itself. Overall, Berkshire's performance, as measured in terms of economic profit, seemed excellent. Economic profit had improved since 2000, but the company's stock price had actually declined over this period (see exhibit 3). The CLA consultants had sold the new system based on a promise of a high correlation between the company's economic profit numbers and returns to shareowners, but to date, at least, the economic profits did not seem to be moving in parallel with the stock price. The shareowners had not benefited.

EXHIBIT 1. Example Showing Effect of Capitalization and Amortization of Consumer Advertising Expenditures (£000)

	1998	1999	2000[a]	2001
Advertising expense as reported on income statement	900	1,200	1,800	2,400
Amortization for economic profit report				
1998	300	300	300	
1999		400	400	400
2000			600	600
2001				800
Advertising expense on economic profit report			1,300	1,800
Cumulative advertising expense (on income statement)	900	2,100	3,900	6,300
Less cumulative amortization (economic profit report)	300	1,000	2,300	4,100
Capitalized advertising for economic profit calculation of capital for economic profit report			1,600	2,200

[a]2000 was the first year of use of the new system.

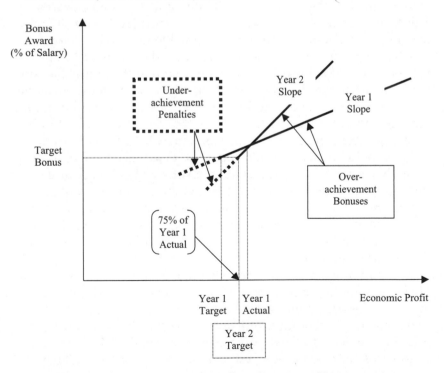

EXHIBIT 2. Link between economic profit performance and bonus awards

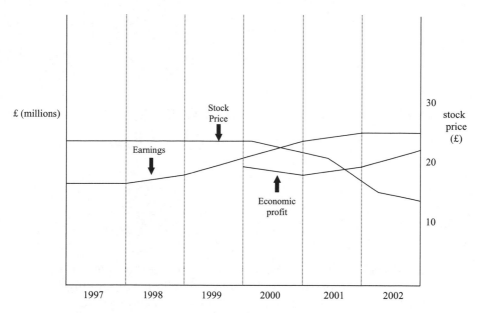

EXHIBIT 3. Berkshire Industries' earnings, economic profit, and stock price, 1997–2002

Notes

Copyright © 2004 by Kenneth Merchant and Wim A. Van der Stede.

1. In the United Kingdom, companies can disclose goodwill amortization charges on the income statement, and they can also present goodwill-adjusted earnings per share figures.

2. For the initial year of implementation, the slope of the payoff function was set such that a historically reasonable overachievement of the target (110%) would earn slightly higher bonuses compared to the same level of overachievement in the old bonus system.

28. Titeflex Corporation: The Turnaround Challenge

On December 1, 1988, Jon H. Simpson, forty-one, became president of Titeflex Corporation, a firm that sold $45 million worth of high performance hoses to the aerospace, industrial, and automotive sectors. Simpson had worked for many years in the R&D Department of the 3M Company and, more recently, as VP (Operations) in CHR Industries, which, like Titeflex, was a part of the Bundy Group of companies. In January 1988, when Bundy brought in the Boston Consulting Group (BCG) to study Titeflex's operations, Jon Simpson was asked to get involved with the project. Within a year, two important events occurred: first, the British engineering conglomerate Tube Investments (TI) acquired the Bundy Group; second, TI assigned Jon Simpson to manage the Titeflex subsidiary.

The promotion transformed Simpson's life. Suddenly, he found himself in Springfield, Massachusetts, managing a new division under a new set of (British) bosses. Simpson noted that it felt good to have been promoted but admitted that the task before him in Titeflex was daunting: To be sure, the company was profitable and its sales were growing, but competitors were nibbling away at Titeflex's market share, production was slow, deliveries were more often late than on time, and relations between management and Titeflex's union were abysmal.

Sir Christopher Lewinton, the CEO of Tube Investments, had divested nearly 70 percent of the group's assets and bought nearly a bil-

---

This case was prepared by Ravi Ramamurti.

lion dollars worth of new companies since becoming TI's head in 1985. He wanted TI's seventy companies to be worldwide leaders in technology and market share in their respective niches. Lewinton believed in giving his companies a great deal of autonomy but expected their sales and profits to grow at 15 percent per annum while yielding at least a 15 percent return on sales and a 30 percent return on net assets before interest and taxes.

As CEO, Simpson said he felt sandwiched between irate customers, warring employees, and demanding superiors. How should he deal with his customers? What could he do to improve Titeflex's operations and relations with the union? Would he be able to change the culture within Titeflex? How should he handle his bosses in England? It seemed there was so much to do and so little time. Simpson wondered what his priorities ought to be, where he ought to begin, and how he ought to proceed.

Brief History

Titeflex was founded in 1916 by Westinghouse Corporation. At that time, flexible hoses were made either from metal or natural rubber. Titeflex introduced a hose made from interlocking brass strips tacked with string. These early hoses were used in industrial and automotive applications as well as in World War I aircraft engines. With the advent in the 1930s of synthetic rubber and plastics that could withstand the corrosive effects of fuels and oils, Titeflex shifted its emphasis to shielded metal conduits. During World War II, every B-17 and B-24 was equipped with a Titeflex ignition harness. In the late 1950s, Titeflex began developing metal hose products with inner cores made of Teflon for use in fuel and oil systems in jet engines. In 1971, Titeflex re-entered the industrial hose market and, in 1978, the automotive market. In 1978, Bundy Corporation added Titeflex to its Performance Plastics Group.

Marketing and Sales

According to customers that Simpson met in his first few days in the company, Titeflex had a reputation for producing "pricey" products of excellent quality. A total of 100,000 different hoses varying in size, shape, fittings, and type of protective sleeving was offered by Titeflex. Customers for these hoses were concentrated in three market segments: aerospace (50 percent of sales), industrial (30 percent of sales), and automotive (20 percent of sales).

Aerospace

Titeflex's Marketing Department estimated that with 35 percent of the market in the early 1980s, Titeflex ranked second in market share in the aerospace segment. Its customers included all aircraft engine and airframe manufacturers worldwide. Titeflex and other two firms accounted for 90 percent of all sales, with the remainder shared by several smaller competitors. Few competitors existed in this segment because of the long time required to demonstrate effectiveness in usage and the need to get certified as a qualified supplier. While the number of pieces sold was small (ten units per day), the parts were highly customized for each client and involved large margins. Some complex hoses went through all forty-four manufacturing departments, traveling 2½ miles from start to finish. In recent years, Titeflex's market share had declined to approximately 25 percent; in 1988, sales to this segment were expected to be 10 percent below the 1987 level. Indeed, two of Titeflex's largest customers told Simpson that they were seriously considering dropping Titeflex as a supplier.

While products for the aerospace segment were highly engineered, the rate of technological change was small until a new series of aircraft was announced. Then, the technological change was substantial. Continued success in the market depended both on delivery and price for existing products and on technological advances for future products.

Demand in this market had boomed in the 1980s, thanks to the defense buildup in the United States and the growth of the commercial airline industry. However, the outlook for the future was somewhat bleak due to the thaw in East-West relations and the shakeout occurring in the airline industry.

Industrial

Industrial application of hoses ranged from oil field equipment to refrigeration equipment. Half of all sales were to equipment OEMs (original equipment manufacturers) and the other half to distributors. Many firms participated in this segment, including a number that competed primarily on price. Titeflex held only 1 to 2 percent of the overall market for industrial hoses but as much as 20 percent of the market for the high pressure/high temperature segment, where price was less important than quality and reliability.

A key feature in the replacement portion of this market was rapid response to customer requests. In contrast, in the OEM segment meeting delivery schedules, rather than immediate response, was crucial. Product customization was not as critical as in the aerospace market, and unit demand was roughly twice as large. Titeflex's Marketing Department estimated that demand would grow in line with the general economy.

Automotive

As automobiles and their engines became smaller, engine temperatures and vibration effects increased dramatically. Titeflex had a technological advantage when entering this market because these problems had been solved ten years earlier in aerospace applications. Demand was somewhat seasonal, according to the automotive companies' production schedules, as well as cyclical, according to overall economic performance nationwide.

Price competition was intense. Margins were low in contrast to those in the other two markets, but there was little variety in products. A customer might expect two thousand hoses to be shipped per day. Late deliveries could shut down an engine assembly or components plant, and customers would not accept early delivery. Technological change was continuous, although changes were small when compared to those encountered in aerospace. Of the three markets served by Titeflex, the automotive segment was expected to grow the fastest.

Sales and Marketing Organization

Titeflex had separate sales and marketing departments for the aerospace segment and the industrial and automotive segments, both based in Springfield (see exhibit 1 for Titeflex's organization structure in 1988). Salespersons were paid a base salary plus commission. The Sales Department was the principal contact point with customers, and other forms of contact between customers and Titeflex employees were strongly discouraged. For instance, when customers visited the company to follow up on orders, they were whisked away to a small room in the Sales Department and not permitted to wander around the offices or on the shop floor.

Competitors

Titeflex's strongest competitor in high performance hoses was Aero-quip Corporation, based in Jackson, Michigan, which was also the leading supplier to the aerospace segment. The other major competitor, Stratoflex, was based in Dallas, Texas. Stratoflex had become increasingly aggressive after it was acquired by Parker Hannifin, which invested heavily in the firm's modernization. Both companies were reducing their costs and improving customer service at a brisk pace. As of 1988, no foreign competitor of any significance had emerged.

Organization and Operations at Springfield

In 1988, Titeflex employed about 750 people. Nearly 600 worked in its largest facility in Springfield, and the rest were employed in plants and offices located in Canada and France. About half the employees at Springfield were shop-floor workers, while the rest worked in "front offices": operations planning, engineering, quality control, sales, finance/MIS (management information system), R&D, and human resource management (see exhibit 1). Bundy had invested significant sums to expand and modernize the Springfield plant and strengthen the MIS system. However, Bundy had not tampered with Titeflex's organization or management methods.

The Sales Department took three to five weeks for order entry and processing, while Operations took about seven to ten weeks to manufacture a standard, "made to stock" product, for a total of ten to fifteen weeks from order receipt to shipment—provided all went according to plan. In the Operations function, there were five to six levels in the hierarchy from the head of the department to the shop-floor employee. A purchase order for a bearing to fix a machine might require seven or eight signatures. Departmental loyalties were strong, and interdepartmental coordination was achieved primarily through formal meetings. Said one busy executive: "We have morning meetings, afternoon meetings, quality review meetings, engineering review meetings, purchasing meetings, make-buy meetings, and meetings to schedule meetings!"

The production process for an average hose began with the Plant Engineering Department, which developed the drawings required for manufacture—unless the customer supplied drawings with the order. The basic hose was manufactured in the Hose Fabrication Department, while parts and fittings were manufactured in the Machining Department. Each of these departments had a handful of very expensive pieces of equipment that were common to the manufacture of all parts. In the Assembly Department, hoses and fittings made by Hose Fabrication and Machining were assembled with outside parts to make finished products for the aerospace, industrial, and automotive markets.

In all departments, workers and equipment were organized by type of activity rather than type of hose or type of customer. For instance, the same machine or worker might be used to fabricate a $10,000 hose for a jet engine as well as a $50 exhaust-recovery hose for a car. Most machine operators—direct workers—were paid on a piecework basis. Material handlers moved work from one location to the next; the company had designed special carts to minimize damage during such transportation. Indirect workers of this sort accounted for about 20 percent of the shop-floor workforce. Most direct workers were paid on a piecework basis.

Shipments were frequently held up for want of outside parts or internal production bottlenecks, leading in some cases to delays of several weeks and infuriated customers. To alleviate this problem, Titeflex built up inventories of parts and work-in-process at all stages; by 1988, inventories had risen to four months of sales. A computerized materials requirement planning (MRP) system introduced in the mid-1980s at a cost of nearly $1 million generated very detailed reports on schedules, inventories, and manufacturing costs (by order, by department, etc.). In addition, Production Planning and Control (PPC) held periodic meetings to review the status of various jobs. When all else failed, the "sales action" group in the PPC Department shepherded high priority orders through the production maze to placate angry customers. Despite this, in 1988, only a fourth of all industrial orders and a tenth of all aerospace orders were delivered on time.

Titeflex had the reputation of shipping high quality products. A large Quality Department, which reported to the Engineering Department rather than the operations manager, inspected parts and subassemblies at every stage of the production process, sending anything that fell short of specifications for rework. Typically, 25 percent of the output had to be reworked. A competent fifteen-person New Products Engineering Department was engaged in R&D. This department had recently been downsized and was quite heavily focused on new products for the automotive industry.

Several of the seniormost executives were included in an incentive plan that awarded bonuses at the end of the year based on the company's overall performance. The accounting system yielded cost data on individual departments and generated profit numbers for the company as a whole. Titeflex had no scheme for employee stock ownership, although a few senior executives were believed to own Bundy stock. John Makis, who headed Titeflex from 1980 to 1988, had been with the company for more than thirty years and was described by a colleague as "conservative and cautious."

Management-Union Relations at Springfield

Ralph Galarneau (an imposing 6 feet 1 inch tall and 265 pounds) was chief steward of Titeflex's Springfield union. Galarneau had joined Titeflex at age nineteen, following in the footsteps of his father, who was himself a union leader in Titeflex. Although workers voted (over his objections) in 1976 to join the Teamsters Union rather than remain an independent union, Galarneau remained an influential member of the union, eventually becoming its head. Like Galarneau, who was forty-two, the average Titeflex worker was about forty years old, had been with the organization twenty years, and had at least a few relatives working in the company.

Historically, union contracts had been negotiated annually, usually through a contentious process that involved a one- or two-week strike. In addition, workers went on wildcat strikes from time to time. The contract stiuplated work rules in detail, including who could perform which tasks: for instance, only welders could weld, and only material handlers could move materials. In 1987, management and the union signed a three-year contract for the first time, one that would expire in April 1990. Although Ralph Galarneau represented workers at contract negotiations, it was the local Teamsters Union's business agent that formally signed the contract.

Kevin Roberts, head of Operations, represented management in contract negotiations. A subordinate described him as "brilliant," while another noted that Roberts had a large following among the supervisory staff within Operations. According to one employee: "Kevin and Ralph play cat and mouse day in and day out." Roberts expected his foremen to take disciplinary action against troublemakers on a regular basis; in turn, Galarneau filed grievances with Kevin Roberts at the rate of at least one per day and often pursued individual cases for as long as possible. Workers were subject to "progressive discipline"; that is, they could be fired only after a long series of prior warnings and hearings. Typically, only one or two workers were fired every year. However, when demand slackened, layoffs were permitted on a reverse seniority basis. Reflecting on the work environment, Chris Ward, a supervisor, said: "It's unfortunate, but true, that in this company to get work out of your guys and to keep your bosses happy you've got to be an s.o.b.!"

Once signed, the contract became the primary basis for union-management relations. As one employee put it: "Both management and union walk around with copies of the contract in their back pockets." There was minimal interaction between front office people, such as engineers and salespersons, and shop-floor workers. Although in the 1960s and 1970s management and workers had celebrated special times like Christmas together, in recent years each had organized its own holiday parties.

Jon Simpson

Jon Simpson earned degrees in polymer chemistry from Duke University and the University of Arizona before joining the 3M Company in 1969 as a bench chemist. Eleven years later, he had become supervisor of an R&D lab employing seventy scientists. In 1980, he left 3M to become vice president of R&D at CHR Industries, a Bundy company within the Performance Plastics Group based in New Haven, Connecticut. CHR made high performance pressure-sensitive tapes and silicone rubber products for the aerospace and electronics industries. Like Titeflex, CHR worked with Teflon technology and served some of the same end users. In 1982, Simpson became VP (Operations) of CHR, with continued responsibility for R&D. CHR workers were members of the United Rubber Workers Union. Describing his stint as VP (Operations) at CHR, Jon Simpson said:

At 3M, I was used to managing professionals doing R&D. It was always very gentlemanly. At CHR, they ate me alive when I tried managing in that style. So, I turned into a Genghis Khan. At the end of the day, my blood pressure was high, theirs was high, and we all went home with knots in our stomach. But I fought and I won every goddamn battle with the unions. And I won it bloody and I won it dirty, but I won every battle. I wouldn't even let 'em win the small ones!

In 1988, when Bundy brought in the Boston Consulting Group to study Titeflex's operations, Jon Simpson was asked to get involved with the project. Over a period of nine months, he spent two days a week in Springfield serving as an internal consultant to the BCG team, whose mission was to flow-chart organizational processes in every area to identify how efficiency and speed of response could be improved. In August 1988, Bundy transferred Simpson to Titeflex with the intention of making him head of Titeflex's industrial and automotive businesses, leaving the aerospace/marine business under the charge of another general manager. This plan went astray when Tube Investments (TI) bought Bundy and announced its decision to divest all four subsidiaries in Bundy's Performance Plastics Group, including CHR Industries and Titeflex. After further study, however, TI pulled Titeflex out of the divestment package because its technology was seen as having value for Bundy's automotive business as well as for TI's flourishing aerospace business. Christopher Lewinton then made Jon Simpson president of all of Titeflex.

The Task Ahead

In 1988, Titeflex earned a 5 percent margin on $45 million in sales and a return on net assets (gross fixed assets less accumulated depreciation) before interest and taxes of 20 percent. (See exhibit 2 for the trend in several performance indicators in the two years prior to Simpson's arrival at Titeflex.) In recent years, sales had grown at 6 to 7 percent per year, with growth in the automotive segment offsetting sluggish growth in the industrial sector and negative growth in the aerospace market. Meanwhile, Titeflex's costs were rising faster than sales. Customers were also beginning to expect their suppliers to provide more and better service for less money.

Simpson estimated that Titeflex had a 15 to 20 percent cost disadvantage relative to its major competitors on account of its location in Massachusetts, where taxes and wages were higher than other parts of the country. At the same time, moving to a different location could be an expensive proposition; among other things, a new facility would have to be recertified before it could supply the aerospace industry. In addition, Simpson believed the workforce in western Massachusetts was highly skilled and had a strong work ethic.

Simpson wondered what course of action he ought to take in the coming weeks and months.

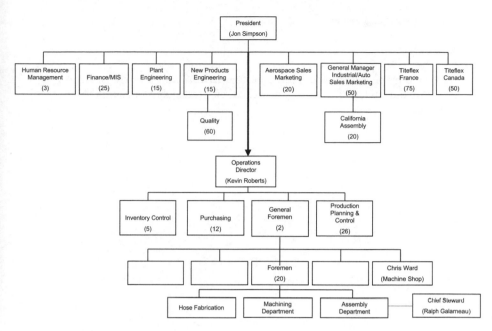

EXHIBIT 1. Titeflex organization structure and staffing, December 1988

EXHIBIT 2. Trends in Performance Indicators, 1988 vs. 1987 (1987 = 100)[a]

	1987	1988[b]
Sales		
Aerospace	100	89.5
Industrial	100	113.1
Automotive	100	146.3
Total	100	107.4
Quality		
Returns	100	102.3
Rework	100	105.4
Inventory	100	116.5
Overhead/Sales ratio	100	110
Pretax return on net assets before interest (earnings before interest and taxes/net assets)[c]	100	94.6
Return on sales	100	87.3

[a]As Titeflex did not report divisional financial results, the actual amounts are not shown in this table; only changes in each item in 1988 relative to 1987 (base year) are shown. Thus, the table gives some idea of the trends in performance at the time Simpson took over as head of Titeflex (December 1988).

[b]Estimates as of December 1988.

[c]Net assets equal gross fixed assets less accumulated depreciation.

Note

29. Gillette Metal Fabrication

Walt Gillette

Walt Gillette took over Gillette Metal Fabrication from his father, William, seven years ago. The company was founded in 1947 to do subcontracting work for firms supplying parts to the automobile industry. Durable goods sales boomed in the post–World War II period as consumers made up for the shortages of the war years, and Gillette Metal Fabrication grew significantly during this period. The company continued to prosper over the next two decades as automobile sales soared in direct proportion to the wealth of the American consumer. The company never grew beyond approximately two hundred employees, but the margins in the business were good. As a result, the Gillettes amassed enough of a fortune to be comfortable but not ostentatious.

The company began to encounter difficulties with the first oil shock. As the automobile industry's fortunes waned under the combined effects of model downsizing and foreign automobile imports, Gillette Metal Fabrication fell on hard times. The company managed to survive largely because William Gillette was willing to operate the company without drawing a salary. And he had long-established relationships in the industry that kept sufficient work flowing his way to keep the company alive, although just barely.

Now, Walt had seven hard years behind him and was beginning to wonder if there was any point keeping the company going. Japanese suppliers and subcontractors had become a significant presence in the industry, and it did not look like Gillette could compete with

This case was prepared by Jack Brittain.

them. For reasons that were not apparent to Walt, Gillette's Japanese competitors were selling at prices well below Gillette's production costs. Walt did not see how they could make any money at the prices they were charging. They had the same basic labor costs that Gillette had, the same materials costs, and they bought their equipment from the same manufacturers. But they were beating Gillette's prices by a significant amount on every contract that came up for bid. Walt figured he could keep the company open for another year the way things were going. But if profits did not improve, he was going to close down. There were no other options.

"The Project"

Walt had gone to high school and college with Dennis Gordon. Dennis had continued his education right through to a Ph.D. in anthropology. He now worked as a professor at Midwestern University in Chicago. He and Walt were lifelong friends, so no favor seemed too big. When Dennis asked if he could send one of his Ph.D. students—a young man named David Wade—down to do a yearlong field study inside Gillette's machine shop, Walt was not thrilled. But it was Dennis. After meeting the kid and finding out that he had prior experience as a machine operator, Walt okayed the project, figuring at worst he was getting a motivated employee for a year and was helping the university.

The kid had finished up his work late last year, but Walt had never heard anything about the dissertation. Walt and Dennis were talking one day on the phone, and Walt was bemoaning the fragile state of Gillette's finances. Dennis paused and then said, "Walt, you need to take a look at Wade's dissertation. Things are not working the way you think they are in that plant of yours." Walt was shocked to hear Dennis express any opinion on a business matter. Dennis refused to discuss the matter over the phone, so the next day Walt was on his way to Chicago.

"Walt, you are not going to like what I am about to show you, but you need to see it. Wade's dissertation research shows your workforce is not working half the time." Dennis was serious.

Walt was stunned by what he saw in David Wade's field notes. He knew that the people that worked for him goofed off every now and then, but what Wade reported was systematic cheating. Workers were having their friends clock them out and going home for the afternoon. Workers were finishing their work for the day by noon and spending their afternoon in the warehouse talking and hatching practical jokes. And a long coffee break was not five extra minutes, it was three extra hours. If Wade's estimates were right, the shop employees at Gillette Metal Fabrication spent much of their time *not* working.

The Compensation System

The employees in the machine shop where Wade had worked were paid a piece rate, a common practice in the industry. Every job had a per piece compensation rate (e.g., machining a transmission shaft paid $8 per shaft, so a machine operator that could finish two an hour was paid $16 per hour for the job). The rates were set by the firm's three industrial engineers. They based the rate on a timing study conducted the first time a job was run for a customer. Times were updated whenever material changes were requested, the part was modified by the customer, or industrial engineering came up with improved processing techniques. The engineers set the rate by watching a trained employee perform the job and then estimated the percentage effort the employee was putting out during the timing period to come up with the final "realistic" rate for the job based on the company's compensation philosophy.

The piece rate system was designed to provide an incentive for Gillette's employees to work harder. The system design called for a mean rate slightly higher than the average hourly rate for machine shop workers locally. In addition, Gillette had a guaranteed base rate of $12 per hour to protect workers from timing errors. This base rate was also the hourly rate used when workers were doing rework, conducting timing studies, and working on jobs that had not yet been timed or were one-time, special order work. The basic design of the compensation system is shown in figure 1. Workers always were paid a minimum of $12 per hour, even when working on jobs where their actual production was less than $12 per hour on the piece rate.

The firm's cost accounting data indicated that the system worked as designed. Figure 2 shows the most recent numbers that Walt had on the distribution of hourly pay for the employees in the machine shop. As expected, the employees were working at the guaranteed rate less than half the time. The rest of the time, they were receiving a bonus based on superior output. The firm's average hourly cost of labor was $15.43, which was consistent with historical performance net inflation adjustments.

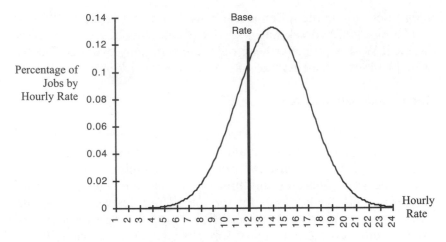

Fig. 1. Piece rate system

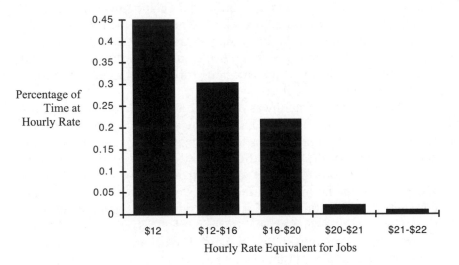

Fig. 2. Cost accounting data on earnings rate frequency for machine shop employees

Bimodal Output Pattern

Although the accounting data were consistent with management's expectations, David Wade's study indicated that the employees' actual output was distributed in a bimodal pattern, not the bell-shaped pattern of the expected normal distribution. The pattern observed by

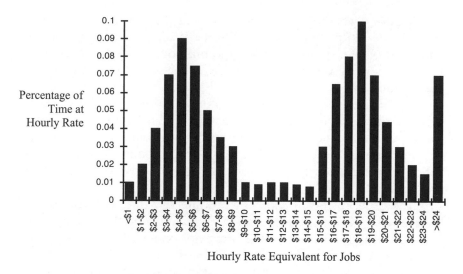

Fig. 3. David Wade's data on output frequency by hourly rate

Wade is shown in Figure 3. Based on Wade's data, the employees were only producing at an average rate of $8.18 per hour, considerably below what was expected. Since labor costs were 50 percent of Gillette's cost of goods sold, this explained a great deal of the firm's cost disadvantage in recent years.

Wade's research indicated that the bimodal pattern of output reflected two distinct responses to the piece rate system. First, the machine shop workers engaged in goldbricking (i.e., they took it easy) when the piece rate was close to or below the guaranteed rate. Even if the worker could do the job for $11.50 per hour on the piece rate, the typical response was to work slowly and take the guaranteed $12 per hour. Based on Wade's data, the employees were only working at $5.22 per hour on jobs where they were earning $12 per hour. In addition, Wade's data indicated that the machine shop employees even goldbricked on jobs where they could earn as much as $15 per hour. The logic for this completely escaped Walt.

The second response to the piece rate system was a "quota restriction" developed by and policed by the employees. According to Wade's observations, the employees enforced a maximum work rate of $20 per hour on the piece rate. The cost accounting information that Walt had indicated that workers were turning in work in excess of the $20 quota, but only 3 percent of the jobs turned in were above quota, well below the 18 percent of the jobs completed at a rate above $20 per hour. According to Wade's description of the shop, more often than not, once the employees produced enough pieces to achieve $20 per hour for the day, they quit working for the rest of the day.

Given Wade's observations as graphed in figure 3, the workers were sacrificing an average of $21.65 a day in earnings on quota jobs. Walt found this especially baffling, because in some cases the workers were giving up more than $32 a day—representing 20 percent additional earnings per day—in order to do nothing. Why? Walt had no explanation.

The costs to the firm of lost productivity due to goldbricking were obvious. But the quota restriction was costing the firm as well. The firm bid jobs on a per piece price, not on an hourly rate. So, for instance, a job with a piece rate of $16 *per piece,* a materials cost of $10 *per piece,* and $6 *per hour* fixed cost might be bid at $40 *per piece.* If an employee produced eight pieces in an eight-hour shift, the firm's earnings would be $64 per worker day on the job. If the employee produced ten pieces in an eight-hour shift, the firm's earnings would be $92 per worker day on the job, even though the employee's hourly earnings increased to $20 per hour. This was the beauty of the piece rate for the firm and its employees; both gained from increased productivity. The employee's gain was increased earnings per hour based on acquired skills. And the firm's earnings increased with workforce productivity because fixed costs per piece went down as productivity increased. So if the workers were producing at $24 per hour on a $16 job (twelve pieces per day)—a rate of production they were not claiming because of the quota restriction—the firm's earnings would be $120 per worker day, almost double the earnings from a 50 percent increase in productivity.

The same productivity logic applied to the jobs where the workers goldbricked, which made this behavior doubly distressing. The workers were not only drawing $12 per hour and working at a much lower rate, they also were eating up any earnings the firm might make by being unproductive.

Because Gillette was being hammered by foreign competition, an increase in productivity would allow the firm to bid lower and still make money. The firm was barely breaking even and steadily losing work. A 50 percent increase in productivity could make the firm competitive and profitable, the two conditions that Walt needed to meet to keep the firm in business. And Wade's data indicated a 50 percent productivity increase could be achieved if the employees just worked an eight-hour day.

Machine Shop Workforce

The pattern of work behavior uncovered by Wade was not apparent in the cost accounting data for two reasons. First, the accounting information only indicated what the workers were paid, so the lower hump was summed as work at the guaranteed rate. Second, Wade's analysis indicated that the workers managed their "turn-in" rate to conform to the quota restriction, which resulted in a pattern of payment that appeared more in compliance with the expected pattern than was in fact the case. There was no way the cost accounting system could identify the bimodal pattern Wade had discovered, because the accounting system could only capture work turned in, not actual work behavior. Walt Gillette depended on his shop foreman to motivate and control his employees' work behavior.

The machine shop was the domain of Fred "Pappy" Mitchell. Pappy had worked for Gillette Metal Fabrication for over thirty years and had been machine shop foreman for eighteen years. Pappy assigned all the jobs, deciding who would work on what job based on job difficulty, the employees' skills, and customer service considerations. Walt had always believed Pappy was a good man and could be trusted to run the shop in the best interests of the company. Sure he was a little coarse, sloppy in following company reporting rules, and not always completely cooperative with industrial engineering, but the men in the machine shop seemed to love him and would do anything he asked to get an emergency order out to a customer.

The employees in the machine shop were all graduates of trade schools and had all completed some kind of apprenticeship period before Gillette hired them. Times were too tough for Gillette to train anyone on the job. All the employees were highly qualified and had significant experience. They had the skills to be productive. The question that Walt had to wrestle with was, "Why aren't they producing as expected?" The incentives were in place, but the workers were working contrary to the rewards of the compensation system. It just did not make sense.

What Next?

Walt was deeply disturbed by what he had seen in David Wade's field notes. If the information was correct, most of the firm's productivity disadvantages were due to goldbricking and quota restriction by the employees. Walt tossed and turned that night in bed, wondering what he was going to do next.

Jon Ball

Jon Ball had worked for Gillette Metal Fabrication for ten years. He was thirty-six; had a wife, three kids, a mortgage, and a car payment; and had feared losing his job for ten years. The company seemed constantly about to go under. Many of Gillette's competitors had already failed, developments all Gillette's employees followed closely. Everybody in the plant knew that if they lost their jobs at Gillette, it was very unlikely that they would ever find similar high-paying production work.

All things considered, Jon liked working at Gillette. The work was often challenging, he had the freedom to develop and use his own procedures for getting the job done, and he liked his co-workers. The downsides were the insecurity of the job and the constant pressure of the Methods Department looking over your shoulder.

Machine Shop

Gillette's machine shop worked on the piece rate system. You got paid for what you produced, which was sometimes fair, sometimes not. If a job was timed wrong, you had to work for the guaranteed day rate of $12 an hour, hardly enough to make ends meet. When a job was timed right, you could earn a bonus of up to $8 an hour without alerting Methods that you were actually making some money for a change. But if you went over $20 per hour, Methods would be on you like flies on a cow pile. And you would end up working for day rate.

All the workers in the shop were well trained and experienced hands. Jon was no exception. He had trained as a machinist in a vocational program at community college before joining Lockheed as a machinist. He had worked at Lockheed for four years and then made the move to Gillette. He was attracted to the job at Gillette because of the work variety, the opportunity to expand his skills, and the possibility of making more money working with a piece rate. He was a better machinist now than he ever could have become at Lockheed, and he was making better money. Not a lot better, but better.

There was a strict pecking order in the machine shop. Vern and Bud were the two most respected workers in the place. Both were in their late fifties and had been working at Gillette since the dawn of time, at least as far as Jon could tell. They had worked every machine and job in the place. They knew more about machining than anyone walking the planet. And as a result, the machine shop was their domain.

Pappy Mitchell was the shop foreman. Pappy had been around a long time, was a good friend of the Gillettes, and was in charge of job assignments. If you crossed Pappy, you would be working day rate for the rest of your life. So everyone gave Pappy a lot of room. He was a grouch but lovable in his own way. If you did not make problems for Pappy, Pappy would not make trouble for you.

Gravy and Stinker Jobs

The jobs in the machine shop fell into two categories, gravy and stinker. A gravy job was any job where you could make a significant bonus above the $12 an hour guaranteed rate, which the workers called the "day rate." Most of the guys would not bust ass unless they could make at least $16 an hour on a job. Jon felt this was a good rule of thumb. Given the choice between cruising through the day at $12 an hour and being stressed out for $14 an hour, Jon preferred the $12 an hour. And by not killing himself for a measly $2 an hour, he had the energy he needed to crank when he hit a real gravy job.

Jon was to the point on some jobs that he could work at rates that approached $30 an hour. Of course, because of the quota maintained by the workers to avoid retiming by Methods, he could only turn in $20 an hour for the day. On days when he was finished early, Jon either worked on projects for the shop he had at home or left early. It seemed ridiculous to him that he was forced to not work a good portion of the time, but it was the way the shop ran.

The day rate was paid on jobs that were not timed, rework, jobs that were one-time work and would not be timed, and jobs that were in the process of being timed by Methods. The "timing" process was a joke. Some young, green industrial engineer from Methods would come down and watch one of the guys run the job, and then he would divine a piece rate. It was all hocus-pocus guesstimation as far as Jon could tell. The guys doing the timing could not run the machines if their lives depended on it, and the guys being timed were dogging it to try to get a good time. If Methods wanted to know the right time, all they had to do was ask Vern. When Vern said a rate should be X, it should be X. You could count on it. And if a rate was below X, it was a stinker job.

Anything that did not pay a bonus was a stinker job. And there were more stinkers in this place than anybody liked. When you worked a stinker, you settled for the day rate. By working to the rules, you could run the job at an easy pace and take time to have some coffee, talk to the other guys, and maybe even catch an afternoon nap out in the warehouse. The warehouse stayed cool in the summer, and it was sometimes hard to find a spot to curl up on hot summer afternoons.

David Wade's Project

Jon had been good friends with David Wade, who had worked in the shop for a year some time back. It turned out that David had been doing a study of the behavior in the shop for a Ph.D. in anthropology at Midwestern University. Jon had thought David was quick, but he did not come across as a real brainy type. He was—all things considered—a pretty mediocre machinist. It was a good thing he had something else to fall back on.

David had finally told Jon about the project he was doing after he left. He apologized for the secrecy but said he had to be "one of the guys" to get honest observations. Jon was a little miffed at first, but David was his friend and had been straight with him otherwise. They still got together for beers on occasion and were going on a fishing trip over the summer. And now that David was no longer undercover—at least not to Jon—Jon was getting some interesting information from David.

David had mapped the pattern of productivity in the machine shop. Jon found this pretty interesting. Judging from his data, there was a lot of wasted time in the shop. "How in the hell does this relate to the company's problems?" Jon wondered. If the company did not come down so hard on productivity, it seemed like output levels could go up. And Jon sure would like to know that he was going to have a job in a year.

Appendix A. Excerpts from David Wade's Field Notes

Day 1. I started the day with an orientation session with Nick Whitman, director of personnel. As per the agreement between Dennis, Walt Gillette, and myself, no one is supposed to know I am studying the machine shop. Whitman did not seem to give me any special treatment. In fact, he was abrupt and hurried. I think my status as "employee" is secure.

Whitman indicated that I was hired because I had excellent experience. I asked him about pay. I know the shop is on piece rate, but with no experience, it is difficult to know how I will do. Whitman told me I should average about $20 per hour working under the piece rate. Sounds pretty good, especially given my job last summer only paid $14 an hour.

After going over the company's health and benefits package, Whitman walked me down to the shop and introduced me to Pappy Mitchell, the shop foreman. Pappy is a piece of work. His office is an unbelievable mess of papers, tooling, bits, and scrapped parts. Whitman scurried back to his office after Pappy growled, "What the hell you hangin' around for?" at him.

Pappy talked to me for about an hour after Whitman left, asking me questions about by previous experience, what jobs I had run at my last job, and all the training I had from high school on. Although he did not come out and say it, his line of questioning let me know that I was neither as experienced nor as trained as he would have liked. Our conversation ended with "You've got some things to learn" and my assignment as a drill press operator, the lowest run on the machine shop ladder.

Today was slow. I did not have any work assigned. I spent most of the day wandering around and getting acquainted, figuring out the procedures for checking tools out of the tool crib, for requisitioning materials, filling out job slips, and meeting the guys in the shop. Things must have been slow for everyone, because I spent two hours in the afternoon with Vern and Bud sitting in the warehouse, talking about the Skyhawks, and drinking coffee.

Day 2. I was assigned a housing with four holes at four different angles when I arrived this morning. Pappy told me to pick up the jig from the tool crib and get to work. The job looked simple enough and had a piece rate of $1.50. I was figuring I should be able to do a hole a minute, which would translate into $22.50 an hour. I was expecting a good day.

An hour into the job, I realized I was in Fantasyland when I calculated my potential earnings. I had only finished 4 pieces, was cursing the malevolent sinner that had designed the jig I was using, and had attracted the attention of several of my co-workers. Bud, who appears to be one of the "personalities" in the shop, decided to give a play-by-play of my work to those gathered around. I glared at him initially and made a remark about work piling up over on his bench, but my reaction only encouraged him. And not a lot of encouragement was needed judging from the laughter that followed my repeated efforts to loosen the jig and remount it to drill the next hole. The group broke up when Pappy walked up and yelled at everyone to "Get the hell back to work!" Then he turned to me and offered the closest thing to encouragement I had heard yet: "Just don't turn all those parts into scrap. That's all I ask."

I got a lot of ribbing over lunch. Bud was still on me about my inability to handle "the sweetest of all gravy jobs." As best I can figure, the job I have has been performed at a rate generating tremendous bonuses by every man in the shop at some point in time. And they were all greatly amused by my inability to even make the guaranteed pay rate. I could feel myself getting angry, but I had to admit that I was not a productivity wizard. Even though I had experience, I had never had to crank out volume work with tight tolerances, and that was the name of the game in this shop.

After I got going again after lunch, Vern came over to take a look at what I was doing. After watching me run through a mounting cycle, he stepped up and said "Watch me run this." He drilled the first hole according to procedure, but then he took a small clamp out of his pocket and remounted the piece without adjusting the jig. He did the same thing after each of the next two holes, finishing the piece in 3 minutes maximum. He then handed me the clamp he had and said, "Hang onto this. Be good to this job and it will be good to you."

I asked Vern why he did not use the jig as it was designed, and he gave the obvious answer: "I'll start using the jigs when the jigs are designed by someone that knows something about running these damn machines." It turns out that Vern had designed the clamp himself and used it for several years while he was still being given an occasional drill press job.

I was not a whiz, even with Vern's help. But I did do better this afternoon, producing at close to $15 per hour by the end of the day. I finished the job with an hour to work, but Pappy did not offer me anything else. "Just be thankful for day rate while you are learning the ropes," was all he said. I took this comment, plus his admonishment to "Get the hell out of my office," as an indicator that I was done for the day.

Day 7. Halfway through my second week and I have finally figured out what is "gravy" and what a "stinker" is. Gravy jobs are what I thought they were: jobs where it is easy to make a premium above "day rate," which is shop lingo for the $12 per hour guarantee. Stinker jobs—as in "this job stinks"—are jobs where no one can make a premium, even the very experienced guys like Vern.

Everybody dogs it on the stinker jobs. At first I thought it might be a good idea to try to get the stinker jobs over with so I could move onto something else, but Bud laid it out for me. "Why bust your hump for day rate? If you try to work through a stinker job, you are playing right into management's hands. Why do you think the rates on some of these jobs are so lousy? It is because management expects us to scurry around for the few crumbs they throw our way. Well, I am not willing to play their game, and neither are the rest of the guys. If management wants us to work a job, they are going to have to raise the rate to make it worth our while."

The basic logic everybody follows on the stinker jobs is to punish management into changing the rate. Bud, for instance, went out to the warehouse for some material in the middle of his stinker job, returning two hours later looking like he had just gotten up. He assured me my perception was accurate. Bud only got his job half run by mid afternoon; then he split at 2:00 PM to go to softball practice for his city league team. He said Ronny would punch him out.

Pappy came around looking for Bud about 3:30, but Vern covered for him. Pappy ranted and raved for about 20 seconds, then walked off cursing. It scared the hell out of me, but Vern was unconcerned. "It is okay to go home early if you finish up a gravy job early, but only Bud has the balls to leave with a stinker job in the queue. But that is because Pappy knows that he can count on Bud when there is rush work to be done. And the secret to getting along with Pappy is to make sure you always make him look good. Never, and I mean never, make Pappy look bad to a customer or management. If you do, you will find out just how many stinker jobs actually exist in this shop."

Day 18. There was an argument this morning between Vern and Bud over whether a valve body grinding job was a stinker or gravy. Bud said it was a stinker, and Vern said he thought it might be gravy. Vern was not as adamant as Bud and decided to put the part to a test. I asked Ronny about the argument, and he indicated that "if Vern says it's a stinker, it's a stinker. If Bud says it's a stinker, it probably is a stinker. Unless Vern proves that it is not. But then sometimes Vern is the only guy that can make gravy on it." It was clear to him.

The word came down on coffee break. The job was a stinker. Vern had tried it and could do no better than $14 per hour. I expressed the opinion that $14 sounded pretty good to me, but Vern set me straight. "Do you mean to tell me that you are willing to bust your hump for an extra $16 a day?" Actually, at this point I was. But I could tell yes was not the right answer. "Kid, life is too short to kill yourself for $2 an hour when you can use the energy the next day to do a job that will get you $8 an hour gravy. You got a lot of years working in front of you. Put your effort into something with some returns. You cannot bust hump every day in here and stay human."

Day 43. Jon Ball and I went out last night after work and killed a few million gray cells. I am feeling it today. He and I are becoming pretty good friends. He is a stand-back guy, but he has been a big help the past two months. I have picked up a lot of pointers from him. If I make gravy anytime soon, it will be because of his help.

An interesting thing happened today. The timing men were down riding Vern on the valve body that he and Bud had the argument over awhile back. They were trying to persuade him that the milling operation could be done faster than he said it could be done. He told us about it later. "Those Methods guys got their heads up their ass. They do not know what they are talking about. They want a rate of $15 to mill those valve bodies. They are out of their mind. It is going to take 2 hours minimum to run that job right. Every step on that thing is a stinker. Somebody bid the price on that thing too low a year ago, and now Methods wants to take it out of my ass. Well, I can tell you right now that they are not getting any more than a piece every three hours out of me."

When Vern was doing the Methods study, there was little doubt that he was "doing it right." The job has very precise tolerances, and Vern was playing them for all they were worth, adjusting his machine after every step and double-checking every procedure. The Methods guys knew he was dogging it, but what are they going to do? Vern is the only guy in the shop that can do this job with any kind of productivity at all.

Day 45. We got the rate on the valve body today, and we were floored. $18 a piece! Bud lit up the lunchroom. "What do those Methods assholes think we are, a charity shop? They might as well ask us to work for free! Did you see Vern working on that job? Three hours per piece! If they are going to keep setting rates like this, we may as well pack it in. My kids are going to go hungry if this is what I am getting paid. What the hell do I care if the company folds if my family is going hungry because I am working here?"

I asked Jon about it later. "If Vern says it's a stinker, it's a stinker." I pointed out that Vern was really dogging it when they timed him, something the industrial engineers couldn't help but notice. "Yeah," Jon said, "but they should have listened to Vern in the first place. If it is a two-hour job, then the rate should be $30. It is the most complex piece in the shop. It has very precise tolerances and a lot of steps. They are lucky Vern can do it at all."

All the guys in the shop were bent out of shape over the valve body, even though most of us would never work the job. It was an interesting kind of anger, not really directed at anybody. One of the things that I have noticed here is that relations with the industrial engineers from Methods are pretty good. They are generally okay guys, willing to joke around, and helpful most of the time. But "Methods" is the enemy around the shop. The guys in the shop do not blame the individual engineers when they get screwed on a rate, but there is a lot of anger with the system here.

Day 68. I "made out" big for the first time today! I was cranking out pieces all morning, when Vern came over to see how I was doing. When I showed him, he became concerned. "Hey, you're doing great. But be careful. You are going to have to quit at noon at this rate. You might want to stretch it out a little. If you do this all day, we are going to have Methods down here tomorrow resetting the rate on this. Milk it a little. If you stretch it out until after lunch, Pappy will be too busy to notice you finished up with it. Then you can take your time cleaning your machine and get out of here. I will punch you out."

I wanted to crank parts all afternoon to build a kitty, but they are too big to store in my locker. Jon has a job he does all the time, and he can usually store up enough of a kitty that he does not have to work the job every third or fourth time. He uses the extra time to work on the bench he is building for his garage at home. It is a thing of beauty. He should have it finished in another month; then he can come in on Saturday when no ties are around and pick it up from the warehouse.

The quota really impacts what people do around here. But you have to respect it. If you don't, Methods will cut all the rates, and we'll all end up working for day rate. It sure would be nice to bring home $24 an hour for a change, however. But the company won't let it happen. Bud told me how Ronny and Vern got in a competition a couple of years back "to see who was champ on the milling machine. They had a big job that they worked on for a week, cranking out the pieces at $30 an hour by the end. Methods was down here the next week retiming that job so that we could not make more than $10 an hour on it. Now nobody will work it. We make Ronny and Vern deal with that stinker. It's their fault that we lost a gravy job. You got to respect the quota, because otherwise we will all be working day rate."

Day 74. I screwed up big time today. I was not watching my piece count very closely and ended up turning in $22 an hour for the day. Pappy seemed surprised but did not say anything. If the job gets retimed, the guys will be pissed. When Jon has the job, he can run it at $32 an hour. If it comes back with the rate halved, he is going to be pissed. And the job will be mine for life.

Day 92. Methods was back today, working on Vern and the valve body again. Vern and Ronny have been running the job at 2–3 hours per piece and are none too happy about it. Apparently Methods is not either. All three engineers were down working with Vern, trying to get him to try some new procedures and discussing tolerances. They spent the whole day on the part, and Vern was pissed. "A whole day on day rate because those Methods bastards got a problem. I will be running that stinker all day tomorrow because they screwed up the price to the customer. The only way they are getting any output on that job is if they set the rate at $30 a piece. It is a two-hour job! There is no getting around it."

Day 93. The job I busted quota on came back around again today. Thank heaven Methods did not retime it. I got lucky this time. I am going to be more careful. I cannot afford to screw things up for the rest of the guys.

Day 145. The saga of the valve body continues. They have retimed the job 5 times in the last six months. Vern finally got a $24 piece rate out of them two weeks ago. Then he got 30 pieces to do this week. "I am going to spend the rest of my life working this stinker" was his comment on Monday. Well, he finished the job today. After a day of dogging it, he got fed up and started working the job. By Thursday, he was doing a piece an hour.

I asked him about it when we were having afternoon coffee. He said, "I guess this is some real gravy after all. I am glad Methods finally set a reasonable rate. If they had set a decent rate in the first place, I would not have been working day rate a third of the time for the past three months."

Note

This case was inspired by Donald Roy's classic anthropological study "Quota Restriction and Goldbricking in a Machine Shop," *American Journal of Sociology* 57 (1952): 427–42.

Products and Pricing

30. Bouvet Springs, Inc.

When Ennis Green, the president of Bouvet Springs, picked up the chairman's memo from the secretary announcing the impending meeting with the other senior executives, he knew that he and the business were at the beginning of a critical stage in the firm's California bottled water business. Green, Martin Winters (the chairman), and Sarah Hopkins (the VP of finance) were meeting prior to the board of directors meeting to finalize plans for the next twelve to eighteen months.

One issue on the agenda for the board was a decision on building a conference center on the California property of the bottled water company. A second, more pressing issue was the desirability of expanding into private label water sales.

The board knew from the beginning of the venture three years ago in 1992 that the first three years would be difficult from a financial and marketing viewpoint. The pro forma numbers in the original plan projected rather large but diminishing losses for the first three years up to the period ending in December 1994.

In 1993, the firm had projected that the bottled water business would begin to show a modest profit for 1995 of about $500,000, with the range up to $2,000,000 in 1996. At that point, it was expected that the firm would go public with a potential price-earnings multiple of fifteen times, which would put a value on the firm of about $30,000,000. The returns on the investors' $10,000,000 would have generated a handsome profit for a five- to six-year holding period.

This case was prepared by John Dunkelberg and Thomas Goho.

Current Problem

However, the problem facing Ennis and the small group of senior management is that the forecasted sales and profits for 1995 look anything but encouraging. Green, along with his sales manager, Lawrence Troup, estimates case volume at nine hundred thousand cases for 1995, with an expected price per case of bottled water of $6.50. The operating costs are estimated at $4.50, with 80 percent being variable and 20 percent fixed. In addition, Green projects general and administrative expenses at $1,500,000, freight at $750,000, and advertising of $750,000. Overall, Green expects the firm to lose about $1,250,000 on an operating basis.

This latter figure does not include a sizable interest expense projected to be about $700,000.

No one in senior management is happy with the current situation, and the board of directors has not been prepared for this news. Green's pitch to Martin Winters and Sarah Hopkins is that the firm can dramatically shrink operating losses by moving into the private label water business. Private label sales would be made to hotel chains, grocery stores, and convenience stores, among other customers. The benefit to Bouvet Springs, according to Green, is that each case sold would generate a contribution margin of about $1.75 per case. The purchaser pays the freight expense, and the private label purchaser incurs any advertising costs. Ennis believes that the private label sales could add approximately seven hundred thousand cases in 1995. Given that the springs and the bottling operation can handle 3 million cases per year, the firm has more than enough available capacity to accommodate the private label sales.

In an earlier meeting, Hopkins, the finance VP, questioned the wisdom of the private label business. She pointed out that from an accounting viewpoint, these sales would generate a loss and therefore were not worth doing.

The accounting loss that would be reported to the board of directors would end up being larger than the current forecast of $1,250,000. She also pointed out that private label sales were never part of the strategic plan. It was felt originally that such sales would divert the small company from "rolling out" Bouvet Springs Water along the West Coast (California, Oregon, and Washington), and then east to Arizona, New Mexico, Colorado, and Texas, and then ultimately as far east as Florida.

Green argued that the financial situation of the firm was anything but robust and any incremental sales that generated a positive cash flow should be undertaken. He estimated that the firm might run out of cash as early as December 1995. Unless the original investors or new investors were willing to kick in additional financing, the firm might not make it to 1996.

In the background of the discussion was a somewhat vague offer presented to Martin Winters by a business broker. The broker indicated that a foreign buyer might be interested in investing about $5,000,000 conditioned on receiving a 51 percent stake in the business and three of the five seats on the board of directors. Winters, as the chairman of the board and the major shareholder, categorically rejected the informal entreaty. He continued to reiterate his long-held position that the business is worth $30,000,000 and an initial public offering (IPO) could net the investors that much when the company becomes profitable in the next several years. The IPO market has been hot, and he remains optimistic about the IPO value of the Bouvet Springs partnership.

Background on the Industry

The executives of Bouvet Springs were drawn to the bottled water business by the potential growth and positive demographic characteristics.

In 1992, 9.9 gallons of bottled water were consumed on a per capita basis, a figure three times greater than in 1982. In addition, bottled water sales grew 21 percent in 1993 over 1992.

Also, it was estimated that per capita consumption would grow to twenty gallons by the year 2001. It was estimated that "New Age" beverage consumption would grow at an 11 percent annual rate between 1995 and 1997. Bottled water was included in that category, which also included bottled tea, flavored water, and similar products.

This growth in consumption was fueled by three factors (based on marketing research data).

- The preferred taste of bottled water relative to tap water
- Water safety concerns in light of contamination in some public water supplies
- Health concerns

In 1990, bottled water was the main source of drinking water for one in six households in the United States.

In the 1990s, consumers of bottled water in the United States had a wide range of products available, with six hundred domestic brands and seventy-five imported brands of bottled water.

Bouvet Springs Key Executives

The three key executives for Bouvet Springs are Winters, Hopkins, and Green. Their background and experience are as follows.

Martin Winters—chairman (age 70)

- B.A. in English from Stanford
- Substantial top level executive experience culminating in chairmanship of a major West Coast consumer packaged goods company. Experiences primarily on the marketing side of the business (retired).

Sarah Hopkins—vice president of accounting and finance (age 53)

- B.S. in accounting from U.C. Berkeley
- M.B.A.—UCLA
- CPA—big six tax experience for seven years. Vice president of finance for a midsized consumer packaged goods company (retired).

Ennis Green—chief executive, president (age 55)

- B.S. in journalism, California State University at Chico
- Many positions in marketing, advertising, and public relations. Vice president of marketing for a large consumer packaged goods company (retired).

As a result of downsizing, all three of the key players had been terminated from the company where they had worked for many years. Each retired with a golden parachute and adequate financial resources for a very adequate standard of living even if they never worked again.

Notwithstanding their financial security, they each decided they wanted to get back into the business world. When Winters contacted his former employees, both Hopkins and Green expressed an interest in the job and investment opportunities at Bouvet Springs. Hopkins contributed 2 percent of the invested capital, and Green's contribution was 4 percent. Winters was the largest partner, with a 40 percent share of partnership contribution. Winters received a salary of $100,000 per year, and Hopkins and Green each earned $50,000. All these salaries were a small fraction of what they earned prior to retirement.

Since the business was organized as a partnership, any losses would flow through to the partners, who could reduce their taxable income by the pro rata amount of the loss at Bouvet. The remaining 54 percent of the partnership equity was provided by a disparate group of high asset investors known to Winters through social and business contacts. Several of these investors sat on the board of directors, although none of them had the range of packaged goods business experience of Winters, Hopkins, and Green.

Winters's View of the Business

Winters believes that Bouvet Springs has five major strengths that should leave the business in a strong position for a profitable IPO.

1. Water Supply. The water source for Bouvet Springs is a natural flowing spring in the Sierra Nevada Mountains near Bouvet, California. The quality of the water is recognized to be very high by any objective standard. In addition, the springs have a flow rate that could support sales of 5 million cases per year. The water is very low in bacteria and particulants. The volcanic rock in the area of the springs serves as a natural filtration system. As Winters has noted on many occasions, some of its competitors get their water from underground wells that are subject to possible contamination. Other competitors are simply bottling tap water and selling it at a premium. "When customers understand the purity of our water, they will be impressed," Winters has stated frequently.

2. Production Facilities. The firm has state-of-the-state bottling equipment, purchased in 1991. The plant can produce 3 million cases per year. An incremental investment of about $7,500,000 could raise the output to 5 million cases.

3. Experienced Management. If a firm is to be successful in the bottled water business, it needs strong marketing, advertising, and brand management skills. Winters and Green together have fifty-five years of experience in consumer packaged goods businesses. In addition, the plant manager worked for a major soft drink bottler in southern California for twenty-five years. Winters has substantial confidence in Sarah Hopkins's financial and accounting acumen. Last, Winters and Green hired Lawrence Troup to be Bouvet's national sales director in 1993. He has more than eighteen years experience working for a well-known international bottled water company. In order to lure Troup to Bouvet Springs, he was awarded a 2 percent equity position in the partnership with an investment of only $20,000.

4. Geographic Strength. Winters believes that Bouvet benefits from being in a very strong market for bottled water. The marketing research studies indicate that West Coast consumers are very health conscious compared to the rest of the country. As a result, these consumers are the highest per capita purchasers of bottled water. In addition, the market still has substantial growth prospects according to *Beverage World,* a trade magazine for the beverage industry.

Since freight costs are an important element in the firm's cost structure, Winters believes he has a substantial cost advantage relative to Bouvet's East Coast and Canadian competitors.

5. Debt Restructuring. Bouvet's bank debt was restructured to permit a more secure source of long-term financing as opposed to the previous revolving line of credit, which could have been terminated.

Overall, Winters believes that Bouvet Springs has a very promising future and it is only a matter of time until the firm is able to go public and the original investors will be able to "liquefy" their investment in the partnership.

Ennis Green's View of the Business

Green knows and respects Winters's business skills. He originally invested $400,000 in the business based on his confidence in Winters's business acumen. The original business plan seemed to be thoughtful and well reasoned. The firm would develop and market a high quality bottled water that would be rolled out in California and then to Oregon and Washington. The emphasis would be on sales to upscale restaurants, hotels, and specialty food and beverage operations. With Winters's contacts in these businesses, it should have been relatively easy to build an image of quality for Bouvet Springs. Also, with Winters's contacts, Bouvet Springs did have some early success in building the franchise. Bouvet Springs was able to sign an agreement to be the sole provider of bottled water for one of the most prestigious hotel chains in the world. The contract was expected to generate sales of seventy-five thousand cases per year. In reality the sales were closer to forty thousand cases per year. In addition, Bouvet only generated a profit of about $.25 per case after paying freight charges. The company is currently in the process of negotiating a similar contract with a second hotel chain. Both contracts were an outgrowth of contacts that Winters had through business and social activities.

In addition, through Winters's contacts Bouvet was able to sign an exclusive contract with a major California cola bottler to distribute Bouvet Springs Water through its distribution channels. This agreement assured Bouvet of mass distribution to grocery stores, convenience stores, and other outlets in northern California. The estimate was that the cola bottler would sell about two hundred thousand cases per year in the relevant market. However, sales for 1994 were only a hundred thousand cases, and the net margin (after freight and advertising allowance) was less than $.50 per case.

On a longer term basis, Winters plans to use the high quality water for a basic ingredient in beer production. He thinks that after the completion of the conference center (which is discussed in more detail subsequently) a microbrewery would be a logical extension of the business. This development would be implemented in two or three years.

In brief, Green sees that Winters's contacts have been invaluable in helping to develop the business in its early stages. However, the attendant sales are not translating into a sustained level of profit that would permit the brand and company to prosper. Green thinks that the company is approaching a perilous financial condition. He has reiterated to Winters and others that even though he isn't a financial person he thinks that drastic steps need to be taken to strengthen the firm financially. Winters seems to be somewhat indifferent to these financial matters. In fact, Winters thinks that it would be a good idea to develop the firm's beautiful mountain property (including a hundred-acre lake) into a tourist attraction and conference center. "If we can get tourists, day-trippers, and others up here, they will see for themselves the purity of the environment. That image will carry over to our water business." Winters's long-term plan is to spend $2,250,000 on a conference center and camping facility.

Even though Green has great respect for Winters, he questions the wisdom of diverting that amount of money from the core business, bottled water. Green feels that the executives' attention needs to be focused on financial solvency and brand development. Green's desire to do private label bottling is an outgrowth of his concerns about the financial vulnerability of the firm at the present time. He thinks that the incremental cash flow from the private label business could permit the firm to deploy those assets to building the core brand for the firm.

Green has continued to reiterate his position as a nonfinance person that any sales that would more than cover their out-of-pocket expenses should be considered. Sarah Hopkins, the accountant, is less than enthusiastic about this incremental business because it would potentially cause the firm to report a larger loss from operations even though it might enhance cash flow in the short run. This might postpone the IPO even further into the future. Winters seems to be ambivalent on the issue.

Nevertheless, the executive group needs to come up with a unified position when they meet with the board of directors for the quarterly meeting. Should Bouvet expand in the private label water business? How will the decision enhance the long-term success of the firm?

EXHIBIT 1.   Bouvet Springs Statement of Operations and Partners' Equity ($)

	1994[a]	1993[a]
Revenue	4,742,176	2,468,776
Cost of sales	4,091,917	2,609,668
Gross profit (loss)	650,259	(140,892)
Selling, general, and administrative expenses	3,212,159	(2,498,468)
Interest expense	583,361	(395,022)
Net loss	(3,145,261)	(3,034,382)
Partners' equity at the beginning of the period	2,899,184	2,889,966
Capital contributions	1,101,011	3,043,600
Partners' equity at the end of the period	854,934	2,899,184

Source: Audited partnership records.
[a]For the year ended December 31.

EXHIBIT 2. Bouvet Springs Balance Sheet ($)

	1994[a]	1993[a]
Assets		
Cash	767,418	85,322
Accounts receivable, trade	276,488	236,090
Inventories	401,545	271,138
Prepaid expenses	470,823	467,664
Total current assets	1,916,274	1,060,214
Property, plant and equipment, net	8,399,853	8,687,338
Total assets	10,316,127	9,747,552
Liabilities and partners' equity		
Notes payable	200,000	20,000
Short-term borrowings	500,000	
Current portion of long-term debt	8,096	7,492
Accounts payable	406,651	550,557
Other accrued liabilities	209,294	148,592
Advances from general partner	—	176,174
Total current liabilities	1,324,041	902,815
Long-term debt	8,137,152	5,945,553
Total liabilities	9,461,193	6,848,368
Partners' equity	854,934	2,899,184
Total liabilities and partners' equity	10,316,127	9,747,552

Source: Audited partnership records.
[a]For the year ended December 31.

EXHIBIT 3. Bouvet Springs Statement of Cash Flows ($)

	1994[a]	1993[a]
Operating activities		
Net loss	(3,145,261)	(3,034,382)
Adjustments to reconcile net loss to net cash used by operating activities		
Depreciation	460,195	441,036
Amortization of intangibles	—	—
Increase (decrease) in cash from changes in assets and liabilities, net of the partnership acquisition		
Accounts receivable — trade	(37,793)	(231,135)
Accounts receivable — other	(2,605)	109,880
Inventories	(130,407)	(486,308)
Prepaid expenses	(3,159)	37,455
Accounts payable	(143,906)	411,273
Other accrued liabilities	60,702	74,198
Net cash used in operating activities	(2,942,234)	(2,677,983)

EXHIBIT 3—Continued

	1994[a]	1993[a]
Investing activities		
Additions to property, plant and equipment	(173,312)	(426,700)
Book value of disposed property, plant and equipment	602	16,188
Net cash used in investing activities	(172,710)	(410,512)
Financing activities		
Proceeds from issuance of long-term debt	10,817,950	198,370
Advances from general partner	—	176,174
Repayment of debt to Bayview Corporation	(176,174)	—
Repayment of bank debt	(8,445,747)	(21,517)
Proceeds from short-term borrowings	500,000	—
Cash contributions from partners	1,101,011	2,793,600
Net cash provided by financing activities	3,797,040	3,146,627
Net increase in cash and cash equivalents	682,096	58,132
Cash at beginning of period	85,322	27,190
Cash at end of period	767,418	85,322
Supplemental cash flow information		
Noncash investing and financing activities		
Conversion of notes payable to partners to equity	—	250,000
Inventory traded for advertising credits	—	406,068
Cash paid during the year for interest	587,161	408,435

Source: Audited partnership records.
[a]For the year ended December 31.

EXHIBIT 4. Competitor Profile, Publicly Traded Companies Only (in thousands)

	Saratoga Beverage[a]		Aqua1 Beverage		Canadian Glacier Beverage		Clearly Canadian Beverage	
	Sales	Net Income	Sales	Net Income	Sales	Net Income	Sales	Net Income
1994	6,235	(1,928)	602	(2,087)	413	(1,858)	88,733	(5,630)
1993	3,643	(2,437)	503	(200)	416	(2,441)	120,310	387
1992	1,411	(850)	374	(641)	74	(1,102)	187,579	2,346
1991	N/A	N/A	294	(215)	186	—	173,663	2,919

Saratoga Brands	Aqua1 Brands	Canadian Glacier Brands	Clearly Canadian Brands
Saratoga (NE U.S.)	Aqua1, Regain (U.S., Asia)	Canadian Glacier and Selkirk Springs (N. CA, AZ)	Clearly Canadian Natural Artesian Water, Clearly Canadian Quenchers (U.S., Canada, Japan, UK, Caribbean, etc.)

[a]Saratoga was acquired by Evian from Anheuser Bush for $8,000,000 in 1988, and Evian invested another $3,000,000 and then closed the business in 1991. In April 1992, Evian sold to the Prever Group for $2.3 million.

EXHIBIT 5.   Other Competitors

Divisions of Large Companies — No Financial Information Available by Division

Perrier — division of Nestlé's
McKesson Water Products — division of large U.S. company
(McKesson Corp.) — sells Sparkletts in southern California;
Nevada; Texas
Alhambra in northern California; Crystal in Arizona

Private Companies — No Financial Information Available Other than Sales ($000)

Arrowhead Mountain Springwater, Monterrey Park, California	460,000
Crystal Geyser Water, Calistoga, California	31,000
Black Mountain Spring Water, San Carlos, California	25,000
Crystal Rock Water, Watertown, Connecticut	10,000
Cloister Spring Water, Lancaster, Pennsylvania	10,000

Plus dozens of smaller companies

Plant Issues and Productivity Improvement

31. CUP Corp.: Measuring the Customer Care Center

The CUP Vorstand (board of directors) decided to create a customer care center (CCC) to stem the increasing defection of customers resulting in part from dissatisfaction with the firm's services. The central idea was to provide private customers with one telephone number to be used for all of their questions and problems and for all types of insurance offered by CUP. The CCC would be staffed twenty-four hours a day seven days a week to make sure someone was always available for the customer. The CUP personnel would be able to address all inquiries and handle customer problems 90 percent of the time on the first call. The remaining 10 percent of the problems would be resolved in one day with a follow-up call.

Derrick Westmuller was assigned as the project manager responsible for the creation and development of the CCC. In developing this center he was tasked to display the kind of entrepreneurial behavior the chairman of CUP was seeking to develop. Mr. Kirk, the energetic and dynamic chairman, was seeking to change the CUP insurance company from a stiff bureaucracy to a nimble entrepreneurial driven firm. The design was to have the center function as a central services profit center supporting the separate insurance business units of CUP.

Derrick, a seasoned manager, saw this assignment as a real career opportunity. He began to think about meaningful indicators and measures for success of the center. He was politically savvy and wanted the performance of this center to stand on its true accomplishments.

This case was prepared by Lawrence P. Carr.

Product Lines Responding to Declining Growth Rates

CUP is one of the largest insurance firms based in Europe. It has a worldwide operation and was recently acquired by another major insurance company. CUP has enjoyed remarkable growth of more than 25 percent each year over the past ten years. The firm has used a series of acquisitions to broaden the type of insurance offerings and has also grown internally to meet the expanding needs of its served market. It sells various forms of insurance in the health, life, casualty, property, and automotive areas.

Over the last couple of years the growth of premium income in the German insurance industry has leveled off. In 1993 and 1994, the industry still enjoyed high growth rates and grew at 10.3 percent and 9.5 percent, respectively. By 1995, however, the growth rate had decreased to only 4.8 percent. By 1996 and 1997, growth was flat instead of the planned 3 percent, and the expectation is that "growth will only be moderate, if any growth is recorded at all."

The declining growth rates resulted from a set of reinforcing trends.

(i)   The economic climate was worsening, with increasing economic downsizing, increasing unemployment, and stagnating real income.

(ii) In part due to the reunification of Germany, taxes and social welfare levies were higher.

(iii) There was increasing competition resulting from the deregulation of the European market, which was "fully noticeable for the first time" in 1995.

(iv) The basic demand for insurance in Germany, an area of sustained growth up to 1994, had been extensively satisfied.

Despite these worsening market conditions, the operating divisions of CUP were often able to gain market share. However, the squeeze of increasing competition and increasing client price sensitivity led in the private insurance market to shorter contracts and more cancellation of existing contracts. This effect varied in intensity by product line.

In response, product lines and the branch offices began to pay more attention to providing better service as a way to keep agents, brokers, and existing clients satisfied. There was a range of ideas and responses to the problem, varying from remaking newsletters for customers to creating a "calling center." The latter idea was in response to the complaints of many customers, agents, and brokers about the difficulties of reaching clerks and about the level of service they received if and when they could reach them.

Within the decentralized structure of CUP, in which product lines operated rather independently, a number of "calling centers" had been created. The more concentrated product lines, such as life and health, created their own central telephone centers. Some branch offices also created "telephone centers" for those product lines that had decentralized much of their clerical work to the branches.

Re-forming the "Lapse Rate" Problem as a Customer Loyalty Problem

Traditionally the firm, through its two brand names, CUP and Southern, has focused on the lower middle segment of the market that was not very price sensitive. Exclusive agents handled 70 percent of this business. The increasing defection rate began to draw the attention of some senior executives. They ordered a study by an international management consultant.

In March 1996, this management consulting firm reported that the "lapse rate"—the number of customers canceling contracts compared to the total number of contracts—had reached DM 800M in 1995 (DM 900M in 1996), which was around 10 percent of total premium revenue. The lapse rate percentage was comparable to that of other German insurance firms. In some products, such as car insurance, the figures were much higher (20 percent) and had passed a pain threshold.

The management consulting firm also reported that the commissions of the agents was almost exclusively tied to generating new contracts. The agents were spending 70 percent of their time just generating enough new business to keep up with cancellations. If this trend were to continue, they would have to spend 100 percent of their time by the year 2000 just on finding new business to keep up with cancellations.

In-depth interviews with defected customers, or "root cause interviews," indicated that 58.7 percent of the defections could be influenced by CUP (without changes in the contracts), indicating that 5.8 percent of the customer base of the firm was lost through the firm's own fault. Dissatisfied customers mentioned (apart from price,

33.3 percent) problems with agents (34.7 percent), bad claims processing (13.3 percent), slow and bureaucratic responses (9.3 percent), and too little information (4.0 percent). When customers mentioned high price, it would often not be an issue as such but rather in combination with other problems such as dissatisfaction about the agent.

Finally, the management consulting firm found the following.

(i)   Customers who had more than one insurance contract were less likely to defect.

(ii) Trigger events (e.g., exasperation about being passed from one clerk to another without getting any help) seemed to precipitate cancellation.

(iii) If a customer with several policies canceled one, it was likely that he or she would not continue when other contracts came up for renewal.

The traditional market research techniques used by CUP, the consultant maintained, were not able to detect these kinds of problems because they were geared toward customer satisfaction with a (new) product and were not event/action related.

The lapse rate problem of CUP was summarized with the image of a leaking bucket: new customers would flow into the bucket while at the same time many leaked out through big holes. The focus of product lines was on increasing the inflow rather than intelligently addressing the outflow. This was the case not only within CUP but also throughout the German insurance industry.

Instead of focusing on the lapse rate or "customer defection rate" of individual product lines, the problem was restated as a customer loyalty problem that cut across product lines and was considered a corporate problem.

A Corporate Problem: From Vicious to Virtual Cycles

Customers look at the firm as a whole, not as a product line with which they have one contract. It turned out that the more contracts customers have, the longer they remain loyal to CUP. The longer they remain with the firm, the lower the commissions for new products and the lower the damage rate. If this virtual cycle were to lead to small improvements in customer retention, profitability would be significantly improved.

Conversely, if customers have only one contract, they cancel much more frequently. Replacement then leads to a commission for the agent. And when this process gains enough momentum—as it does—all insurance firms suffer from high lapse rates and pay high commissions. Hence a vicious cycle.

To induce a virtual cycle, customer retention would have to become a strategic target. There were many positive ideas and responses in CUP's product lines and branch offices at the time. There were also managers who thought quite differently. They felt the responses were often geared to symptoms and would have little positive effect on the business. With regard to the telephone centers, a senior manager from one of the product lines mentioned that they lacked critical mass. There would be insufficient sophisticated technology and training of personnel, and not enough would be learned from the customer.

The customer needed to be viewed as a person, a family, or even as extended family going through a life cycle with critical events (such as getting a driver's license, getting married, having children, buying a house, setting up a retirement fund, etc.), each creating new insurance needs. The firm was a collection of product lines. In anticipation of future business, CUP should try to satisfy the customer needs in all of these stages.

Moreover, rather than the company treating the risk associated with each customer as part of a large pool with certain statistical averages, customers could and should be segmented into highly profitable groups, unprofitable groups, and loss-generating groups. The firm as a whole should proactively pick and target the most profitable group and learn more about the customers. At the same time, it should defend its existing customer base through (i) becoming sensitive to early signals of defection, (ii) carefully monitoring trigger events, and (iii) trying to recover "lost" contracts/customers.

While the efforts of individual product lines clearly would be important, some executives at the corporate level felt that there was a need for a comprehensive and integrated approach. However, such an approach should be taken in incremental steps.

The First Step: "Quick Hits" and New Discoveries

The data suggested that CUP could benefit from using a number of ideas for customer retention derived from the practices of leading

U.S. insurance firms and banks as well as new ideas from internal managers. The CUP Vorstand ordered a specific study of customer loyalty to CUP between May 1996 and October 1996. It was anticipated that this would create ideas for "quick hits" and begin to close the "holes in the bucket."

But the project also led to new discoveries about the prevailing thinking in the firm concerning the customers. According to one of the consultants:

1. A customer typically calls because his or her agent is either unreachable (either a part-timer or trying to generate new business) or cannot effectively address a question. When a customer calls one product line, say, health, and then has a question about life insurance, the health clerk will say, "I don't know." On average, it takes a client four contacts to get to the right person, and even then, in 30 percent of the cases, the questions are not resolved. Customers tend to cancel when a specific question or problem is dealt with in the wrong way.
2. A clerk working in one product line only has one screen (related to the contract that line has with the client) and has little access to information about other contracts the customer may have. However, if a customer with multiple policies cancels one policy because he or she is dissatisfied with the service in one product line, this person is likely to cancel the other policies as well. The clerks often do not sense that the business is at risk because, quite literally, and also figuratively speaking, it is "not on their screen" and therefore the pattern of defections remains hidden to them.
3. Car insurance plays a critical role in binding clients because it is often the first contract. It appears that most people buy a car on the weekend, when insurance firms are closed. In addition, it was difficult to create a team to help clients because, in general, customers could not reach a clerk after 5:00 and trade unions do not allow work after 6:00. Therefore, the response to the idea was often "Yes, but it can't be done."
4. Most CUP people talk about the customer but don't do anything about improving customer service. The firm has a strong analytical culture. When confronted with the figures, they would say, "This is true for health but not for life" or "It is worse with other insurance firms."

5. When customer focus groups were organized in June 1997, the Vorstand members were invited to attend. Only one showed up apart from the manager of the study. The others maintained that "we know the customer."

The Customer Care Center

In October 1996, when the results of the customer loyalty studies were in, the CUP Vorstand ordered a feasibility study for a CCC reaching far beyond specific product lines. The key idea was to provide customers with one telephone number and professionally trained people who could answer a variety of questions effectively and thereby increase the service dramatically. In addition, a center would be able to eliminate process steps in the future and eliminate sources of errors. Finally, it was believed that the center would be a cheaper and more efficient way of processing information.

By January 1997, an outline for the center design was ready and specified the following goals.

1. CUP's private customers will have one and only one telephone number for all their questions and problems. This service will be available to them in addition to the agents.
2. The center will be open twenty-four hours per day and seven days per week. It will be able to finalize 90 percent of all customer inquiries in one telephone call. It will lead to a significant increase in service quality and efficiency.
3. CUP will benefit from a reduction in the lapse rate, specifically in cases where, in the past, the client's inquiry was not addressed or the service was unsatisfactory.
4. Additional goals of CUP are (i) becoming a service leader in the insurance industry and (ii) increasing the number of customers with multiple policies.

Concerns and Inventing Solutions

The proposal generated a number of concerns. For instance, the agents saw the center as a threat to their relationship with the client. In response, it was decided that agents would be informed of any communication between the center and their clients. Moreover the center could act as a backup for the agent in case he or she was inaccessible to the client (e.g., at night and on weekends). Finally, the center could help agents by contacting prospective clients. Typically, an agent may get one out of ten potential insurance contracts. The center can provide a first screen by telephone and improve this ratio.

The product lines had a different concern. They thought that it was impossible that a "generalist" could address questions related to their specialized business and that it would take "at least ten years" of experience to learn to do this. However, it was discovered that product line clerks got caught in a vicious cycle. Typically, the clerks intended to provide the highest possible quality when talking to customers but in doing so tended to become too technical. Their response was "overengineered," and they tended to waste their time while the client became exasperated.

In addition, many customers had the same kinds of questions. An expert might become annoyed when having to repeat the answers or might forget to mention part of the answers. Less specialized persons with additional skills, however, might quite easily answer questions based on scripts that provide "good answers."

Finally, it turned out that at least 70 percent to 80 percent of the questions (depending on the product lines) were rather mundane and did not need a specialist answer because the customer asked about the status of his or her claim or gave a change of address, and so on. Again, an expert might become exasperated with such questions. However, a special team with extended product knowledge could still address the remaining 20 percent to 30 percent of the questions that were more technical.

A final set of concerns had to do with the fact that calling centers were already established in some product lines and branch offices. For instance, a product line would argue that a change of address couldn't be dealt with by a center because a change of address might have implications for insurance related to the house. Or, some product lines would say, "We are learning from the market through our own calling center, and now we lose our ear"; or "Why break up a winning team?"

At the time that a central center was discussed, some of the branch offices had just installed their own telephone centers as a way to screen calls to the back office. Branch office managers had received employee acceptance by claiming that "this was their future." Dismantling their unit would undermine trustworthiness. The first two concerns could be dealt with through agreements about making information in the center readily accessible to the product lines. The latter concern might be dealt with, in part, by a promise that the center would be in or around the two branch offices with telephone centers. This would make it easy for employees to apply for jobs in the central center.

By April 1997, the Vorstand agreed on the following critical aspects for the center's design.

1. The CCC will be a "Greenfield" (new) solution, and it will be the only center within the CUP. Other newly established calling centers in branches and some product lines will be closed down.
2. It will centralize all customer inquiries, be available 100 percent of the time, and be able to address effectively 90 percent of all questions and problems.
3. The center will be established outside the existing organizational structure of CUP; that is, it will not be part of any of the product lines or operating divisions. This will also make it possible to sign more flexible employment contracts (flexible working hours and compensation).
4. The center will be a profit center and be paid on a telephone call basis by the product lines rather than a cost center supported by corporate or the operating divisions' overhead.
5. The center will be a stand-alone central service business unit with a mission to support the product lines.
6. The product lines will supply technical insurance know-how and competent personnel, and interface with the product lines will be clearly organized.

During the first year, the center will focus on "inquiry" initiated by the client. In addition, it will also initiate inquiries on behalf of product lines in case a customer cancels a contract. This initial setup will require an electronic data processing (EDP) system with the least possible integration into the rest of the information technology (IT) infrastructure of the CUP, allowing for an autonomous EDP center for the CCC with only a relatively small link to the central EDP.

However, as soon as the center operates effectively (expected within half a year of its opening), new tasks can be added. For instance, the center could become involved in claims processing, in correcting errors, or in changing information such as addresses, and so on. It may also carry out marketing research at the request of the product lines. And finally, it may become the care center for agents and brokers as well.

The customers (depending on the product line) expect the center to address 70 percent to 80 percent of their inquiries through its generalists, and 20 percent to 30 percent of their questions will be passed on to specialized teams with extended product knowledge in the center. Not only will the processing within the center be "transparent and traceable," thereby reducing errors, the links to the product lines will be transparent and traceable as well.

Indicators and Measurement of Success

The center will have to be up and running within one year, in May 1998. The effort will be widely watched within the firm and within the German insurance industry. If successful, CUP will have a first-mover advantage and will be instrumental in reshaping the industry.

But what are meaningful indicators of success of the CCC, and how should that success be measured? Should Derrick, the project manager for the new center, focus on one indicator, or should he focus on a set of indicators reflecting a wider sense of performance? How many indicators should he focus on, and which are really critical? Which indicators can he really influence and how?

When asked how he will measure success with the clients, Derrick initially mentions "a decreasing lapse rate—that part of the lapse rate connected to the service quality of the CUP should decrease." However, other executives differ about what constitutes a "balanced scorecard." For instance, a senior executive suggested: "speed of processing, efficiency in terms of cutting out process steps, quality in terms of fewer errors, accessible all the time, and friendliness of the telephone operators."

Another senior executive responsible for sales through the agent channel said that the critial question is "whether we lose fewer clients." At the moment, the firm loses and adds 12 percent per year of its customer base. If the center could stem losses to 11 percent that would be success. However, 50 percent of the agents grow more than the market." If the agents' sales force is trimmed, then more professional and entrepreneurial agents with greater numbers of clients can be created. If the commission structure is adjusted, agents will remain a formidable sales force.

One consultant draws a more complex picture for measuring success with clients: "How can we measure defection if we have two channels to the customer: the center and the agents?" Some customers will call; others will not. The first group calls because the agent channel does not work for them. But what is the situation with the second group of customers? Are they satisfied with the agent? Are they indifferent? One measure could be as follows: if an existing customer has recommended CUP to a new customer who complained about having to work through an agent (of a competitor), did he or she mention the center? Also, the picture of what led people to defect should change. The percentages for "bad claim processing," "slow and bureaucratic responses," and "too little information" should significantly decrease.

For shareholder value, this consultant suggests a look at a decreasing defection rate and selling more contracts. Finally, for innovation and learning, he thinks that the center will generate information that is at present with the agents and inaccessible to the firm. For instance, if the total number of calls is twenty thousand per week and fifteen hundred are about a new topic, and increasing, this factor could be a trend to be monitored. Finally, he was surprised that the product lines did not realize the opportunity created for them. Rather than thinking about the drawbacks, they should consider what the center could do for them.

During a final meeting with Derrick, the consultant repeated that "the hard figure" for success is the following rate: the number of cancellations (attributable to poor service) after the center has made an effort to "recover" them versus the total amount of cancellation. If customers blame the product lines or the agents, the question remains, "Can we get them back?"

Derrick, politically astute and considered a competent manager, wants to insure the success of the CCC. The key in his mind is getting the measures right. These measures have to work for all the stakeholders: the CCC workers, the product lines, the corporate managers, the customers, and finally himself.

Student Assignment

Answer the following questions.

1. As an adviser to the project manager, Derrick Westmuller, what set of measures would you advice them to adopt?
2. Develop a balanced measurement system showing how the measures and measurements link to what you believe are the key success factors of the CCC.

Process Issues

32. Lucent Technologies: Shared Financial Services—Balanced Scorecard Implementation

We have made some real progress with our balanced scorecard, but it just doesn't seem to have the effect on performance I thought we could achieve. Now that corporate is talking about a Lucent-wide rollout of the balanced scorecard, our people might take our leading edge effort a little more seriously.
— Tom Francesconi, financial planning and quality manager

Tom, as the manager for quality and process improvement at the Lucent Global Financial Services[1] (GFS) group, was constantly in search of tools and techniques to assist in the process improvement of financial services. He was trained in the principles of quality and was given the assignment of implementing a continuous improvement program at the GFS facility in Alpharetta, Georgia.

The Company

Lucent Technologies, a $30 billion global equipment and service telecommunication firm, was spun off from AT&T in 1996. Lucent designs, builds, and delivers public and private networks, communication systems and software, data networking systems, business telephone systems, and microelectronics components. They have approximately 140,000 employees in more than ninety countries, with headquarters in Murray Hill, New Jersey.

Management quickly established a new and aggressive entrepreneurial culture. Lucent was competing in a fast paced and extremely

---

This case was prepared by Lawrence P. Carr.

competitive market, and management's strategic plan and commitment to the stockholders was to achieve double digit top and bottom line growth, double return on assets (ROA) from 5 percent to 10 percent, and reduce sales, general, and administrative expenses (SG&A) by 4 percent to 8 percent. The finance leadership team established objectives called "conditions of satisfaction" for the central financial organization (CFO) as a way to link finance to the aggressive corporate performance commitments, or the "strategic intent," and to support the new entrepreneurial culture. The conditions are as follows.

- 100 percent of our business partners acknowledge Team CFO as a strategic business partner in achieving Lucent objectives.
- 100 percent of Team CFO agrees that we live our values and purpose.
- Total CFO budget is less than 1 percent of Lucent revenue.
- Financial modules of SAP (a computing system) implemented Lucent-wide.

Lucent uses a central shared service model for their financial organization. The transaction-intensive activities such as invoicing, accounts payable, payroll, cost accounting, accounts receivable, and inventory accounting are done by Global Financial Services. The CFO organization called "Team CFO" consists of three basic groups: (1) Business Support for transactions, Global Financial Services, (2) Policy and Corporate Center Support, Treasury, Tax, Auditing, Controller, and (3) Business Analysis and Decision Support, the Business Unit CFOs. The manager of GFS report directly to the corporate controller, Jim Lusk. Over nine hundred people work to provide these transaction services. Most are based in Georgia, with global satellite operations currently under development.

The Lucent chief financial officer, Don Peterson, joined the company during the spin-off from AT&T in late 1996. He led the drive to make the CFO world class and a real strategic business partner. Don's concept was for the CFO to focus on participating in, planning, and executing the corporate vision, not merely reporting the financial state of the business. He wanted Team CFO to "add value" to decision making at the best cost to the firm. Don stated that he wouldn't rest until 100 percent of Lucent viewed 100 percent of his CFO team as invaluable strategic business partners. The CFO mission and conditions of satisfaction were clear for the GFS group, especially the challenge to revamp systems and process so that the total cost of CFO to the corporation was no more than 1 percent of revenue. For GFS this drive translated into being an "Incredibly Awesome Partner Service ... Delivered by Incredibly Awesome People." This meant delivering the financial services at the lowest cost, on time, with quality and customer satisfaction ahead of the competition.

GFS Process Improvement

With the mandate to cut costs and improve the level of service, GFS needed to take a very hard look at all of their processes. The timing was appropriate, as they were also in the midst of implementing an enterprise-wide computing system, SAP. They started the quality improvement process by benchmarking and researching best practices and developing specific programs to improve each process. The primary processes they performed organized the GFS group: Accounts Payable, Payroll, Accounts Receivable, Treasury Operations, and Inventory. Each process leader developed a plan for improvement. Tom's group, Financial Planning and Continuous Improvement, was assigned the task of supporting and helping GFS process owners with their improvement efforts.

Accounts Payable was striving to be a paperless process. They wanted to improve the 60 percent current electronic payments. Payroll was consolidating the many different systems under one SAP system. This involved simplifying payroll practices and increasing the use of electronic funds transfer. Accounts Receivable was mechanizing subledger reconciliation using SAP tools and increasing the speed of matching payments with the appropriate invoices for customers with multiple purchases. Treasury was implementing software packages to identify check fraud and encoding errors online before checks were cleared. Inventory was improving their processes to obtain greater accuracy and speed in inventory accounting.

In order to monitor the progress of these improvement efforts, each process owner developed a set of internal measures that captured progress. Tom reported to the GFS director and provided quality improvement support to each of the process managers. His continuous improvement group helped the process owners find the appropriate measures and developed ways to collect the information. Through this quality operation he became aware of the balanced scorecard system. He thought this simple integrative technique fit the current measurement efforts and was consistent with the Lucent GFS quality improvement efforts. He saw it as an umbrella to cover all of the new measurement efforts and to pull together the various process owners' self-measurement efforts. Using the scorecard they could clearly communicate process improvement.

Implementation

Tom and his team, known as continuous improvement analysts, began an intensive reading and training effort on balanced scorecard (BSC) principles. They attended seminars and a weeklong professional training program. Given their experience in quality and process improvement measures, they felt they could build on the measurement efforts already under way at GFS and develop a scorecard for each business process. There was no need to involve an expensive consulting firm or to purchase an available BSC software package. Grounded in quality process principles, they felt they had enough knowledge and the spreadsheet skill to pull together a scorecard system. "The concept is quite simple. The difficulty is proper implementation."

They met with each of the business process managers to help them develop their scorecards They explained the principles and demonstrated how they could use this as a tool to measure their process improvement efforts as well as the effectiveness of their strategic plans. Stressing the fact that this was not an official document, they eased fears that yet another corporate measurement system was about to be introduced. The scorecard was strictly an internal tool to generate information the managers could use to run their business. Tom saw the BSC as a rich set of data that the process owners would actively use on a day-to-day basis. There were no plans to develop reports for circulation outside GFS. The vice president of GFS, Danny Lanier, encouraged this effort. He believed in open communication and supported the concept of full disclosure. Sharing the progress on the achievement of the targeted measures during the monthly review meetings would help keep the GFS team focused.

The intent was to link the balanced scorecard to the operating budget with the target of achieving a 15 percent productivity improvement. Each process department was operating under the mandate to cut costs and show productivity improvement. In reality, with Lucent's 25 percent sustained annual growth rate, this did not mean job cuts but rather process improvements. Managers had to do more with fewer people. They had to find innovative ways to process the ever-increasing volume of accounting transactions. The old habit of just putting more people to the task would not work in the new team CFO environment. The emphasis was on faster customer response time, reduced cycle times, and improved customer and employee satisfaction. As shared service operators they wanted to be viewed by their Lucent customers as the best provider with the best price.

There was an additional dividend to using the balanced scorecard measurement system. Each process owner was expanding operations on a global basis, with regional hub operations in Asia, Europe, and Latin America. They planned to use the same scorecard for each of these operations so management could have a real comparison and benchmark of productivity performance. Scorecards would provide a global measure of the total shared service performance.

In order to get the various metrics in a balanced format, Tom's group put together a conceptual illustration of what a balanced scorecard would look like using the available information. They used the generic scorecard categories as suggested by Robert Kaplan and David Norton in their writings and seminars (financial, internal business, learning and growth, and business partner). These seem to be inclusive and offered "boxes" to put measures in and a good way to start the organization of the measurements.

Tom's group set two conditions; first, the process must be well documented, and second, the management needed to be personally involved with and committed to the project. They started with the value chain or flow of each process, ignoring department boundaries. This set the tone for a better understanding of the process flow itself. It was important that each scorecard have a link to the GFS objectives (conditions of satisfaction) that were defined by Lucent's strategic intent. Once the scorecard outline and form were agreed upon, the business process teams determined the content, measures, and measurements of their scorecards.

The teams agreed on a two-dimensional scorecard (fig. 1) based on the Lucent conditions of satisfaction and the specific GFS process. There was a clear blend of finance and operational measures, and the frequency of the measures varied by the nature of the metric. Each process team was responsible for determining the appropriate measures and finding an efficient method to obtain the data. The team agreed to baseline the scorecard before they rolled it out as a management tool. It was important to have a solid starting point. Tom's group served as coach and facilitator, providing guidance and advice to the process owners.

Data for the scorecards was obtained from a variety of sources. The existing data from the various computer systems provided the budget and financial information. Other IT systems provided the various counts of the numbers of transactions or events that took place over a period of time. The emphasis was on data that was simple and easy to obtain. Other data such as customer and employee satisfaction information was obtained by creating a web-based survey to capture the opinions of these two important stakeholders. The process managers were responsible for gathering the data and "normalizing" it for the scorecard. Tom's team served as consultants and coaches for the development of the scorecard data.

Part of the GFS initial quality effort and continued with the "Team CFO" program was the focus on obtaining customer feedback. Most of the GFS customers, known as business partners, were internal Lucent individuals and departments that use the GFS services. GFS created a Lucent web site and sought customer and GFS employee feedback. There were specific questions to be answered on a periodic basis, and there was always the opportunity for any individual to give immediate feedback through their web-based data collection system. This data collection program was easily incorporated into the balanced scorecard data management system.

The GFS-level scorecard in figure 1 provided the key summary data for all of the processes. Each process owner could drill down further in each of the categories to see the process-level scorecard. For example, the process-level scorecard, depicted in figure 2, contained more detailed information and served as an operational guide for the payroll process owner. The payroll process leaders still need to incorporate their specific objectives along with the appropriate metrics to complete their balanced scorecard template. A further drill down (fig. 3) links to the process owners' (payroll) strategic plan and commitment to achievement. Finally, figure 4 shows how the balanced scorecard was linked to the process value chain.

Tom's group worked very diligently with the process teams to make sure their measures linked to Lucent's strategic intent and conditions of satisfaction. To facilitate this process, the continuous improvement analysts developed a tool to ensure that the metrics were in alignment with the strategic objectives. They designed a form that illustrates the strategic objectives and their associated metrics. The

Process / Condition of Satisfaction	Hubs						
	Financial Process					Financial Reporting	
	LFS Overall	AP and T&E	AR and Billing	Cost Acctg.	Payroll	Book Close	Mgmt. Rptg.
Business Solutions/ Partner Satisfaction - 100% of our business partners acknowledge that LFS provides business solutions. - Deliver real-time knowledge to optimize business performance. *(from Strategic Intent II)*	1) # of times you meet with a client to obtain feedback	1) % of invoices paid on time	1) Internal customer survey index – Overall rating		1) Paycheck resolution in 24 hours 2) Overall client satisfaction with the pay process	1) Internal Client survey index – Overall rating 2) # of days until flash OI is available	1) Reporting cycle time 2) Ad hoc request cycle time 3) % of expense $ defaulted to other or misc.
Operations, Processes and Quality - LFS is the recognized leader in Global Shared Services creating a competitive advantage for Lucent.		2) % of inv. paid electronically 3) % exp. vouchers processed electronically 4) # of FTEs using XMS software	2) Ship to invoice cycle time 3) % of invoices processed electronically 4) % payments processed electronically		3) % of active employees on EFT – *Reach Award Best Practice*	3) % of LEs migrated to SAP 4) # of days to close the books – *Reach Award metric* 5) Value of unreconciled amts. 6) # of MJEs – *Reach Award Best Practice* 7) # of assessments	4) Timeliness of data in the warehouse 5) Consistency of data in the warehouse
Colleague Excellence - 100% of LFS Colleagues acknowledge that LFS is a talented and enthusiastic Global Workteam. - People together and individually accountable for a work force of high performance leaders. *(from Strategic Intent II)*	2) # of CFO awards won by LFS employees (e.g. Key Cup, Spot and Turbo Charge Awards) 3) Progress on winning Reach Awards 4) Employee satisfaction rate 5) Employee turnover rate		5) Employee satisfaction rate 6) Employee turnover rate		4) # of client recognition letters ("kudograms")	8) # of internal (to Lucent) applicants looking for positions in LFS 9) # of LFS employees up for transfers who opt to take another position within LFS	
Financial Performance *(not a condition of satisfaction)*		5) Cost/ invoice processed – *Reach Award metric* 6) Cost/ T&E voucher	7) % of unapplied cash 8) YTD results/Budget 9) Cost/ invoice processed – *Reach Award metric* 10) Cost/ payment processed – *Reach Award metric* 11) Cost/ Bank account reconciled		5) Process cost/ pay distribution – *Reach Award metric* 6) Support cost/ paycheck 7) Payroll cost/ employee paid	10) Closing cost/ revenue – *Reach Award metric* 11) Value of annualized cost reductions – *Reach Award metric*	

Fig. 1. LFS balanced scorecard, revised draft

basic principle behind this tool is that strategy must be cascaded down to metrics to ensure that the right metrics are being used. The initial effort found process managers selecting almost at random measures for each of the four categories. They selected measures that they were good at or for which there was readily available data. It took considerable coaching to get a reasonable set of measures that corresponded to the strategic intent and had meaning to the operation. Payroll is still working to find the appropriate measures.

Usage

The process managers, their direct reports, and the VP of GFS review GFS and process scorecards once a month. This review includes a discussion point of productivity and process improvement efforts. This is a supplemental reporting and review process, which is in addition to the monthly operational budget and performance review. The meetings have resulted in a very rich process discussion and

Critical Success Factors	Financial Perspective	Internal Business Perspective	Learning and Growth Perspective
	How should we appear to our Shareholders?	What business processes must we excel at?	How can we sustain our ability to change and improve?
Strategic Intent II Conditions of Satisfaction	Finance experts providing business leadership throughout Lucent		People together and individually accountable for a work force of high performance leaders…setting the benchmark for GROWS
Conditions of Satisfaction By December 2000	Technology - LFS contributes $5M in revenue growth by being a technology showcase featuring Lucent's products and services	Operations & Processes - LFS is the recognized leader in Global Shared Services creating a competitive advantage for Lucent	Workplace Equation…Formula for Success - 100% of LFS Colleagues acknowledge that LFS is a talented and enthusiastic Global Workteam thriving in a career enhancing values-based environment contributing to Lucent's Success
Process Leader Objectives			
Process Leader Strategy			
Metrics			
	Payroll Cost/Employee Paid	% of Active Colleagues on EFT # of Active Colleagues Paid per FTE	# of Colleague Recognition Letters Received
Process Initiatives			

1999 Commitment Statement from the Process Leader
Some of the metrics will be considered as candidates for the Reach Award.

Fig. 2. LFS strategic objectives, balanced scorecard process: Payroll

We will measure our progress using these metrics for Payroll…

Global Process

	Baseline	1998	1999	2000	Benchmark TopQ/BIC
Payroll					
Manual Check Volume	120/10K	120/10K	100/10K	4/10K	7/10K/ 14/10K
% Error Free Payments	96%	98%	99%	100%	99%/100%
# of Employees Supported Per Payroll FTE	800	850	1200	1700	NA/1700
Cost Per Employee Paid	$100	$100	$90	$ < 70	$74/NA
% Paperless Paystub	0%	10%	50%	100%	NA 100%
EFT Usage	83%	85%	100%	100%	79%/100%

Note: Metrics are "directional"

Fig. 3. Balanced scorecard metrics for Payroll

Partner/Supplier
  Business Units
  Benefits
  Administrators
  HR
  CIO

Partner/Customer
  Business Units
  Employees
  Federal & State Agencies

------------*Payroll Process* ------------

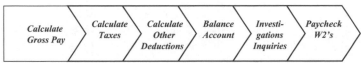

Input
  Payroll Data
  Benefits
  Savings Plan

Primary Customers: Domestic Colleagues &
International Expatriate Colleagues

Output
  Employee Payments
  Tax Statements
  Tax Data &
  Remittances

Note: Value Chain Diagrams illustrate the Key Value-Added activities in a process.
03/23/99

Fig. 4. Value chain, LFS transaction processing, Payroll

often lead to a request for more analysis of trends and the reasoning behind the numbers.

Most recently Lucent has started a corporate financial services initiative to introduce a balanced measurement system throughout the organization. They are starting slowly with very loose headquarters guidelines. One of the benchmark examples for the organization is the progress GFS has made in their scorecard efforts at Alpharetta, Georgia. It was very clear to corporate GFS that the balanced scorecard system was an excellent way to measure the performance and contribution of a shared services group. They felt that if they could show real progress in a BSC system their business partners would feel that the shared service center was making a real effort to deliver value.

Frustration

Tom and his team are frustrated with the fact that the balanced scorecard data is used principally to support the achievement of process improvement goals. The data can also support and supplement process efficiency claims. He feels the data works well when communicated upward and external to GFS but has little effect as a management tool to help improve processes or motivate people. Wasn't this one of the key attributes of adopting a balanced measurement system? To further complicate matters, the GFS director and supporter of the balanced scorecards recently retired. The new manager, Barry Kydd, came from outside Lucent, and Tom is very curious to meet with him to discuss this project and his frustration.

Another troubling issue is the concern over the measurements themselves. Tom wonders, "Are we measuring the right things? How can we determine that the measures are critical to the business process goals? Is there a better way to link the business process key success factors to their set of performance measures?"

Note

1. The group was formerly known as Lucent Financial Services (LFS) and only recently changed the name to "Global" to reflect their worldwide mission.

Special Topics

Small Business Liquidation/Fraud

33. Cabriole

This is just plain crazy. The endless pressure with no rewards but huge risks is demoralizing. I find that owning and managing a small business during difficult times is infinitely more complex than people realize.

There were different alternatives that I had considered prior to my decision to close the company. I set a number of different deadlines to check our progress.

Susan White, sole owner of a custom fitness wear/body wear company, was reflecting upon her decision to close Cabriole (the French word *cabriole* means "leap" and refers to a ballet step), the business she had founded and run for thirteen years. In some ways it really didn't seem to make sense. Ever since she had announced her decision to close the company, sales had picked up. Loyal customers had been coming in or calling in orders to stock up with merchandise because they didn't know where they would be able to find a comparable product once Cabriole closed its doors. In fact, sales in November 1991 had been over $45,000, the best in four months. (See exhibits 1–3 for financial statements.) It was true she had been discounting her merchandise 35 to 40 percent, but everyone loved the product and claimed there was no substitute. Could she really turn her back on them when the industry was perceived to be booming? On the other hand, Susan had started the business to sell a good product and do something she enjoyed. She loved to design body wear and then see how it really complemented the body. However, the constant financial pressures and eighteen-hour days had taken their toll. White commented on starting the business:

I had two disadvantages when I started Cabriole. I started it as a custom leotard business with no organized business plan, no

---

This case was prepared by R. M. Kinnunen and James F. Molloy, Jr.

organization chart, and no organized financial plan. The second disadvantage that I had was that I brought 150 percent effort to every job. That is so innate in me that it took a while for me to realize that the trait is certainly not universal.

I didn't even realize that I was really starting a company, much less one that at one point would reach a million dollars in sales. For me, that was pretty awesome to take it from zero to a million dollars. I just started it because whenever I made anything, it just plain worked well. So I just kept selling it, making it, and selling it.

The History of Cabriole

In 1978 Susan White started Cabriole as a custom leotard manufacturer, designing leotards and body wear primarily for theater and dance clientele. Originally, the company catered to a niche within the body-wear market—that of professional performers who demanded style, functionality, and quality. Initially, Cabriole's product proved to be superior to anything on the market for two reasons. First, it was designed to move with the body. The fabrics were excellent in quality and retained their shape despite rigorous exercise or washing. Second, the designs sculpted the body and were flattering to the wearer. Patterns were made to accommodate a variety of body sizes. The Cabriole designs seemed to have the optimal combination of style and functionality. Tights retailed in the $26 to $32 range and leotards from $32 to $40, and it was not uncommon for a buyer to spend between $75 and $100. Through referrals and word of mouth, the product quickly gained acceptance, and sales began to accelerate.

In 1980 Susan moved operations from her home to a 2,500-square-foot retail store located in a town just outside of the city of Boston. She had been using a studio in her home and renting the basement of the house next door. The volume of sales seemed to justify the move. Cabriole used the front of the store to merchandise body wear, while the back was used for production. At the time that the enterprise moved to the new location, five employees assisted Sue with the cutting of fabric, sewing, and sales. By 1985, sales exceeded $698,000, and Cabriole employed twenty people. Sales grew to the extent that more space was needed, and Sue decided to look for a larger facility.

In 1985, the "Massachusetts Miracle" was at its height: real estate values in New England were rapidly escalating, high-tech start-ups in electronics and computer science were mushrooming on Route 128 just outside of Boston, college enrollments were at an all-time high, and jobs for graduates were plentiful. Susan found an excellent building with 14,500 square feet of space only a short distance from her rented facility. The building was acquired by Susan and her husband for $840,000, and they spent an additional $110,000 for necessary improvements. The business only needed a third of the space, but Susan was confident that she could find tenants to fill the space and that Cabriole plus the renters would be able to pay the mortgage. With the encouragement of her banker Susan made the investment, and in September of 1985, Cabriole moved to its new warehouse. Susan used a small portion of the space to open an outlet store; the majority of the space, approximately 5,000 square feet, was devoted to production.

Susan commented on the purchase of the building:

> As it turned out, leasing the building was a huge responsibility and huge distraction from running Cabriole. At the time I moved over to that building it took another year to lease out the space. I had to manage a whole building, find tenants, do all of the managing of the lease, etc. It was a whole other business which also ate up a lot of capital.

Up to that point in time, Susan was the only member of management. After consultation with her banker and accountant, she decided to hire a few more professionals to help with the workload. In October of 1985 she found an experienced production manager through an advertisement in the *Boston Globe*. Susan interviewed Jim with the help of an industry consultant; she received glowing reports from references contacted by telephone, and the banker and accountant agreed that Jim seemed ideal for the new position. The following March, Susan hired a production assistant, Tommi, at Jim's recommendation. They had worked with each other in the past. Concurrent with the move to the new building, operations were being computerized, Tommi took over coordinating the installation of the computer system. From 1985 to 1987, revenues continued to climb, but overall profits and margins declined.

Shortly after he was hired, Jim suggested that to ease the problems associated with growth, the fabric cutting be partially subcontracted to a local firm which he knew. Also, after reviewing Cabriole's records, he noted that the waste on the nylon/Lycra fabric had been only 3 percent in the past. The industry norm was 8 percent, and Jim suggested that Cabriole was probably now experiencing levels of shrinkage closer to the industry average, which would account for the lower margins. To compensate for this he recommended that Cabriole adjust its price to improve margins.

About the same time Susan noted increasing delays in obtaining accurate and timely reports. For example, Susan was not receiving timely reports of gross profits per month. Investigation showed that the record-keeping system was more than adequate. When asked, Jim and Tommi explained that computer breakdowns and slowness in inputting data were causing the reporting delays. In late 1987, the bookkeeper gave notice, and Susan had to take direct control of the records in order to get the much-needed management information. She was forced now to monitor every bill and especially those of the contractor.

Marketing at Cabriole

Initially, sales had come in through referrals and networking. As Susan realized how popular her products were becoming, she was confident she had a hit. She knew she had a good product, but she needed more stores to carry the product. In 1980, Susan simply started calling department stores and convinced the better ones to offer her line. Cabriole's relationship with the department store chains was very unbalanced. Small manufacturers were very dependent on the large stores and often had to acquiesce to outrageous terms to guarantee floor space for the product. The stores typically placed large orders and frequently returned half for full refund. Fed up with this treatment, Cabriole dropped the department store accounts in 1983.

Sue was eager to pursue other distribution outlets but faced a major hurdle. The fitness industry was so young that little if any information was available. Until 1987, the industry didn't have a trade show. Fitness was included as part of tennis trade shows but was relegated to a corner, next to information on racket stringing and tanning beds. Not surprisingly, data on competitors was hard to get. Body wear, as a category of clothing, was classified in the athletic gear category, which included everything from sweatpants and T-shirts to baseball caps. Publicly traded companies such as Danskin might release sales figures in annual reports, but the published figures were usually vague and/or inconsistent.

Despite these barriers, Cabriole established five hundred to eight hundred accounts nationwide by exhibiting in regional and national trade show. These included elite spas, dance and fitness wear stores, and health clubs. Several collegiate athletic teams, including Princeton, wore Cabriole items. Cabriole also developed a mail-order catalog and built its mailing list over the years from loyal clients. In Susan's view, once someone tried a Cabriole product, they were hooked. The product lasted much longer and retained its shape better than anything offered by competitors. Although Cabriole had a strong following with individual consumers, retailers were much more fickle. With so many manufacturers to choose from, customers often played one manufacturer against another to get the best prices and terms.

Despite the trend toward body wear as "street" clothes and the increased competition, Cabriole resolved to keep its product marketed to the upscale, fashion-oriented consumer who was concerned with both form and function. Susan was convinced that the quality of the product would sell itself and justify the higher price.

The Fitness Craze

During the eighties—at the same time that Cabriole was establishing itself—Americans became more and more concerned with appearance and health. One manifestation of this concern was a huge expansion in the number of health clubs. One of the most popular forms of exercise was aerobics. According to a survey conducted by the NPD Group, Inc., for the National Sporting Goods Association, the total United States market for clothing for aerobic exercising was $831 million in 1990 and $1 billion in 1991, and continued growth was forecast for 1992. The attire de rigueur for the sport was leotard and tights. Research played a role too, as new fabrics were developed and tested to determine the optimal covering for the moving body. Fashion—for both men and women—was entering the weight room and athletic field. Since working out was often synonymous with socializing, having a fitness wardrobe was essential. No longer would a T-shirt and baggy sweats do.

As the public worked out, Lycra and spandex moved from the gym and onto the street. Tights, leggings, and cycling shorts could even be found on the fashion runways. The customers of body wear became more sensitive to the colors and prints available. The growth in demand was met by a jump in the number of body-wear manufacturers. With increased competition, prices were put under greater pressure. Many manufacturers moved their operations offshore to Taiwan, China, and Mexico, where labor costs were lower. Some manufacturers also sold their clothing under private labels to outlets such as Sears, Kmart, and J. C. Penney.

White commented on the competition in 1991:

Just in body wear and fitness alone, I'd say there must be a minimum of fifty competitors in the United States. I am not counting the ones that make special Halloween costumes. When I started in this business there were probably six. The number of small manufacturers who have already ceased operation is large.

Tights or leggings or pants are also now fashion. Because of that a number of people have said to me, "Wow, you must be doing fabulously now that it's fashion." That is not true, because now you have all of 7th Avenue manufacturing it very cheaply. The quality on most of it is poor. It doesn't stretch, and it is not made for performance function wear like Cabriole's. It just means that now there are more manufacturers doing more "nickel and diming" who can cut a better deal.

I manufacture a high-quality line that is classical in appearance and also performs well. So much of what is being manufactured is by my standards ugly, and it doesn't work for exercise.

Problems Arise

In late 1987, Susan became concerned about the business. Sales had been growing, but the company remained unprofitable. Susan recognized that competition had increased, but she thought Cabriole's positioning as an upscale manufacturer of body wear was somewhat sheltered from market swings. She was forced to lay off some of her staff. Then in 1988, Susan began to hear complaints about the quality of Cabriole's products. This she just could not understand. At the urging of the production manager, all fabric cutting had been contracted out. Stitching was still done in-house. Susan had a direct hand in buying the fabric. White commented:

In the spring of 1988 I began to hear complaints about our quality. I heard that our sizing was erratic and that our garments did not fit as they had before. I went to Texas to listen to and see some examples of problems. I became aware that our fabric was not stretching as well as it had. At about the same time Jim, my production manager, went into the hospital for a month.

I took over running production and shipping while Jim was in the hospital. I totally reorganized the systems and the tracking records and hired a new person to manage the computer system. I also set up a tracking record on the contractor cuts in relation to receiving and billings. Jim and his assistant had been handling this before. I made it clear that no bills would be paid when the figures did not totally reconcile.

In April of 1988 Tommi left, supposedly to be committed to a hospital for manic-depressive disorder. Jim returned in June 1988 only to get sick again in September. It was agreed that Jim would take a medical leave of absence without pay. Susan and a new assistant she had hired continued to manage production, using the new system to monitor contractor cuts and deliveries.

At this point Susan became aware of some irregularities involving Jim; his assistant, Tommi; and the cutting contractor. Apparently they had been skimping on the fabric used for her patterns (known in the trade as "shrinking the marker"), stealing the fabric, using it to make their own products, and selling the product under another name. Cabriole not only had been paying for fabric that was put into another firm's products, but even worse, the quality of Cabriole's body wear had suffered. Susan elaborated:

> I realized immediately that we had a big problem; I also began to understand what was behind the problem. I called my lawyer, and we started an investigation that lasted twelve nightmarish days. We arrived unannounced at the business where Cabriole was sending fabric to be cut, and everyone went running. We saw piles of tights stitched in our exclusive colors that had another brand name on them.

Thoughts of closing the business were not new to Susan; when the margins had first started to deteriorate, she had contemplated such a move. Now that this white-collar crime against Cabriole had been unearthed, Susan again considered shutting down. Instead, she terminated the director of sales and saw others leave the business.

Susan was never able to find out exactly who was involved or when the diversions had started. When asked to estimate the loss, she figured that about $250,000 worth of material had been stolen and that about $40,000 would be needed to replace substandard product with acceptable product. In addition, there were costs that were difficult to quantify: poor public relations; damage to reputation because of shoddy product; and the need to redo all patterns, restaff, and acquire new material. She consulted with lawyers about pursuing charges against Jim and Tommi but was advised against it. She had hard evidence but not enough time, money (lawyers estimated that it would cost \$80,000 to \$100,000 to pursue the case in court), or will. There was indirect evidence that Jim had some shady connections. Too much had happened during the move to the new building and the conversion to the new computer system to believe that Jim and Tommi had engineered the crime by themselves.

From 1988 to 1990, Susan also had problems with the excess space at her new warehouse. She had to find tenants, write a lease, and manage the space. One tenant couldn't keep up with payments. Then in the late 1980s, the real estate market started to soften, and Susan couldn't find another tenant. The building which had once been worth \$1.4 million was now valued at less than \$900,000.

Susan continued to have confidence in her product and felt the business still had a future. Cabriole concentrated more on signing with sporting goods stores, since that was the direction the industry was moving. Cutting of fabric was once again performed in-house. Closer controls were placed on production so that quality could be ensured. Cabriole worked to rebuild its relationship and reputation with accounts. Susan took complete control into her own hands, cut expenses by laying off more employees, and personally watched the finances very closely.

The best months for Cabriole had been September 1990 through March 1991. In the spring of 1991 Susan felt that if profits could continue through July, Cabriole could offset many of the recent losses. Survival required that the company be profitable during this period.

Calie, Susan's daughter, had joined the company in January of 1989 as director of sales. She had graduated from Connecticut College, completed an executive training program at a large regional retailer, and managed several departments in that chain for three years. She had been instrumental in keeping Cabriole in business during some very tough times. Sue explained their thinking as the fall of 1991 approached:

> Through the summer of 1991 Calie felt the same way that I did—that sales would grow and we would be able to turn things around. Something happened in late September. I went down to New York to look at new patterns and prints of materials. I observed that a number of my vendors were in real trouble. Then, as I walked the stores, I realized that the merchandise I was looking at was truly ugly. I also noted that vendors were increasing the prices and increasing the yardage you had to buy, and yet the quality of the goods was inferior.

Calie was at a Texas show of sporting goods dealers, an area that had been building for us. It turned out to be a very poor show. The vendor next to her had sold $100,000 worth of goods in 1990, and $30,000 in the March 1991 show, but at this September show she only wrote $7,000 worth of orders. Calie had written $35,000 at the show in March but only $6,000 in September. When she got home from the September show, even that buyer turned around and canceled half of the order.

Calie was beginning to reach the same conclusion that I had: we weren't doing anything wrong so it was hard to think of what we could do differently. It seemed to us that our line was complete, and we catered to an appropriate number of different types of stores. In addition, we had brought in very good-looking prints. Nothing was lacking.

In September of 1991, the recession was still impacting retailers. Susan had not seen the upturn she hoped for. In October of 1991 she decided to close the company. She commented on that decision:

Part of why I finally reached the decision to close was that I couldn't see anything more that I could do. There was no one area that I could see that was wrong. That has been the most difficult part of the last nine months. I am somebody that loves to see some kind of activity in what I do. We had gotten to a point where I could no longer see that, and it just was not feasible to go on any longer given our continued losses.

I found that there were two very important levels to go through in starting a business. One was figuring out if Cabriole was a viable business. Plus Cabriole was something I had started and operated for thirteen years. It was a very important part of me and an important part of what I have done in my life. I found it took a lot to really step back and look at where Cabriole stood and how I had changed in the thirteen years since I have started the company.

White's decision to close Cabriole had not been an easy one to make. Now she had to develop a viable liquidation plan. Her goal was to liquidate Cabriole in a manner which would satisfy customers, creditors, bankers, and employees without placing herself in complete financial disarray. The major question facing her was how to accomplish that task. At the same time she was considering whether or not to undertake another business venture.

EXHIBIT 1. Cabriole, Inc., Balance Sheet, December 31

	1991	1990	1989	1988	1987	1986	1985	1984	1983	1979
Current assets										
Cash	3.0	0.1	0.1	2.5	15.2	29.4	8.5	5.4	1.4	0.6
Accounts receivable	64.2	88.3	70.0	76.7	91.3	119.0	121.4	118.9	103.2	1.9
Merchandise inventory	76.2	255.0	322.0	229.1	142.9	177.5	215.2	152.9	114.5	17.6
Prepaid expenses	10.1	93.8	55.1	31.4	8.3	59.8	21.7	4.3	3.2	1.3
Total current assets	153.5	473.2	447.2	339.7	257.7	385.7	366.8	281.5	222.3	21.4
Property and equipment										
Manufacturing equipment	14.7	14.7	14.7	14.3	13.6	13.6	13.6	9.3	8.2	1.2
Other equipment	119.1	104.0	102.0	97.4	83.3	80.4	47.9	24.3	13.9	0.0
Other assets	15.0	36.6	28.6	31.9	33.7	31.8	17.9	35.6	36.5	0.0
	148.8	155.3	145.3	143.6	130.6	125.8	79.4	69.2	58.6	1.2
Less accumulated depreciation	119.8	114.0	112.5	93.6	73.2	53.2	40.0	41.8	26.9	0.0
Total property and equipment	29.0	41.3	32.8	50.0	57.4	72.6	39.4	27.4	31.7	1.2
Total assets	182.5	478.5	480.0	389.7	315.1	458.3	406.2	308.9	254.0	22.6

Current liabilities										
Notes payable	383.7	419.0	460.1	365.9	330.7	209.1	138.0	144.4	111.6	2.1
Capital lease obligations	0.0	3.6	3.0	2.5	3.7	3.2	3.2	0.0	0.0	0.0
Accounts payable	13.3	98.0	109.0	114.9	41.5	153.4	101.3	58.9	55.9	2.9
Accrued expenses	14.2	6.3	19.3	13.7	21.5	16.0	15.9	8.2	17.2	1.2
Total current liabilities	411.2	526.9	591.4	497.0	397.4	381.7	258.4	211.5	184.7	6.2
Long-term debt										
Notes payable	0.0	22.0	0.0	0.0	28.1	36.8	1.8	13.8	24.7	3.6
Capital lease obligations	0.0	3.7	1.7	1.3	4.0	7.7	10.0	0.0	0.0	0.0
Notes payable — shareholders	292.6	290.0	276.0	153.4	56.1	27.7	124.7	80.9	25.2	11.5
Total long-term debt	292.6	29.5	277.7	154.7	88.2	72.2	136.5	94.7	49.9	15.1
Total liabilities	703.8	556.4	869.1	651.7	485.6	453.9	394.9	306.2	234.6	21.3
Shareholders' equity										
Capital stock	47.4	1.3	1.3	1.3	1.3	1.3	1.3	1.3	1.3	1.3
Additional paid-in capital	459.2	468.0	236.2	236.2	236.2	236.2	106.2	46.2	46.2	0.0
Deficit	(1,027.9)	(833.4)	(626.6)	(499.5)	(408.0)	(233.1)	(96.2)	(44.8)	(28.1)	0.0
Total shareholders' equity	(521.3)	(77.9)	(389.1)	(262.0)	(170.5)	4.4	11.3	2.7	19.4	1.3
Total liabilities and shareholders' equity	182.5	478.5	480.0	389.7	315.1	458.3	406.2	308.9	254.0	22.6

EXHIBIT 2. Cabriole, Inc., Income Statement for the Year Ended December 31

	1991	1990	1989	1988	1987	1986	1985	1984	1983	1979
Sales	515.3	829.4	799.2	756.6	999.4	745.3	881.6	698.7	591.6	19.1
Costs of goods sold	398.1	523.8	475.2	435.7	633.0	476.9	511.4	403.0	349.4	11.2
Gross profit on wholesale	117.2	305.6	324.0	320.9	366.4	268.4	370.2	295.7	242.2	7.9
Income from retail operation	5.9	(16.7)	2.8	2.6	3.7	(7.1)	0.0	0.0	0.0	0.0
Gross profit	123.1	288.9	326.8	323.5	370.1	261.3	370.2	295.7	242.2	7.9
Operating expenses										
Design	1.3	2.9	0.0	0.7	19.1	27.1	0.0	0.0	0.0	0.0
Selling	123.4	222.6	176.7	159.6	246.9	171.7	182.6	167.8	121.9	1.3
Shipping	0.9	0.4	11.9	26.6	26.4	28.0	0.0	0.0	0.0	0.0
Administrative	103.5	178.4	179.2	161.2	179.9	132.4	141.7	96.0	84.7	4.5
Retail	0.0	0.0	0.0	0.0	0.0	0.0	9.4	17.9	11.1	0.0
Total operating expenses	229.1	404.3	367.8	348.1	472.3	359.2	333.7	281.7	217.7	5.8
Operating income (loss)	(106.0)	(115.4)	(41.0)	(24.6)	(102.2)	(97.9)	36.5	14.0	24.5	2.1
Other income										
Miscellaneous	1.6	3.6	0.5	3.5	(25.7)	0.1	0.9	1.0	1.0	0.0
Interest	(80.4)	(75.2)	(76.6)	(55.4)	(45.8)	(32.1)	(33.5)	0.0	(19.5)	(0.4)
Loss on bad debts	(2.6)	(1.1)	(5.5)	(7.5)	(6.5)	(7.0)	(7.0)	(26.1)	(4.2)	0.0
Abandonment of assets	0.0	0.1	(2.0)	0.0	0.0	0.0	(4.8)	(5.2)	0.0	0.0
Net rental income (loss)	(6.3)	(19.0)	(2.5)	(7.5)	5.3	0.0	0.0	0.0	0.0	0.0
Relocation expense	0.0	0.0	0.0	0.0	0.0	0.0	(43.3)	0.0	0.0	0.0
Total other income (loss)	(87.7)	(91.6)	(86.1)	(66.9)	(72.7)	(39.0)	(87.7)	(30.3)	(22.7)	(0.4)
Net income (loss)	(193.7)	(207.0)	(127.1)	(91.5)	(174.9)	(136.9)	(51.2)	(16.3)	1.8	1.7

Note: In years 1980–86, the fiscal year ended March 31. Figures for 1979 are for the seven-month period ending October. Figures for 1991 include amounts through November 30.

EXHIBIT 3.　Cabriole, Inc., Schedule of Retail Operations for the Year Ended December 30

	1991	1990	1989	1988	1987
Sales	36.2	39.8	31.8	34.8	65.1
Cost of goods sold					
Merchandise inventory	13.0	12.0	9.6	17.1	24.5
Transfers from wholesale	18.3	26.5	19.2	13.2	35.7
Total available	31.3	38.5	28.8	30.3	60.2
Less merchandise inventory	8.9	13.0	12.1	9.6	17.1
Total cost of goods sold	22.4	25.5	16.7	20.7	43.1
Gross profit	13.8	14.3	15.1	14.1	22.0
Operating expenses					
Payroll	0.2	17.5	4.1	4.6	7.6
Commissions	0.0	1.3	0.3	0.6	2.1
Advertising	0.3	0.7	1.1	0.5	0.1
Credit card charges	1.4	1.2	1.3	1.0	1.0
Depreciation	0.0	0.2	0.4	0.4	0.4
Factory overhead applied	5.4	5.6	4.1	3.2	5.8
Medical insurance	0.0	1.2	0.3	0.0	0.0
Payroll taxes	0.0	2.4	0.5	0.6	0.7
Postage	0.5	0.6	0.0	0.0	0.0
Store expenses	0.1	0.3	0.0	0.3	0.6
Total operating expenses	7.9	31.0	12.1	11.4	18.3
Operating income	5.9	(16.7)	3.0	2.7	3.7

Note

Reprinted by permission from the *Case Research Journal.* Copyright © 1994 by R. M. Kinnunen and James F. Molloy, Jr., and the North American Case Research Association. All rights reserved.

34. Sidethrusters, Inc. (A)

I wanted to do something on my own. I wasn't sure what that was or how to do it. I had a little money put away so I started talking to people about a business to buy or become part owner of.

I saw a lot of crappy businesses. Then the President of the South Shore Chamber of Commerce said, "I know an inventor who has a neat new product. You might want to meet him."

Michael Bardlow described how he got into the business of producing and installing auxiliary motors for pleasure boats. His company, Sidethrusters, Inc., produced and installed devices (often called "bow thrusters") that helped large pleasure craft maneuver safely while approaching or leaving the dock.

Excited by his meeting with the inventor, Bardlow began investigating the prospects for starting a business. He called the Boston Coast Guard Center and learned that data were available:

> I got a list of every registered vessel longer than forty feet in the United States, not just in Boston. There were a ton of them, many more than I'd thought. I lose track of the zeros—it was thirty thousand.
>
> To get technical expertise, I called every major boat builder in the country, and every naval architect I could find the name of. They were clearly in camps, which was not surprising. Nearly all the sail people were interested; they said, "Go for it." Power boat people often said they didn't need the product, because their big boats had twin engines and were naturally maneuverable. And that's true, certainly, if you have a professional crew.

This case was prepared by R. M. Kinnunen, John Seeger, and Robert Goldberg.

So opinion was mixed, but I said, "All right. I'm going for it." I called a friend, a lawyer who's done this before, and we drafted an offering circular. He told me the rules, and we touched all the bases—product description, markets, competition, management, technical, financial. I was ready to go out and sell the idea.

During the three months after meeting the inventor, Michael Bardlow drafted a business plan and raised $200,000 initial capital. The plan projected $357,000 total revenues for the first year, with after-tax profits of $36,000. The total new boat market was estimated at approximately seventeen thousand vessels that might qualify for the product. After three years, the plan projected annual sales of more than $2 million, with after-tax profits exceeding $350,000. (Exhibits 1 and 2 show the three-year projected financial statements taken from Bardlow's plan.)

The Product

The side thruster was a motor-driven propeller mounted in a tunnel that ran sideways through the hull of a boat—usually at the bow. The propeller could apply a sideways force on the hull, below the water-line, either to the right or to the left. The idea itself was not new; for decades, bow thrusters had been standard equipment on large craft such as ferryboats and tugs, which had to maneuver in constrained spaces. The application to small boats had not been practical until the inventor, Al Carella, adapted a hydraulic motor for the purpose. Michael Bardlow described the need for his product:

> Say you've got a man 55 or 60 years old, coming into the town pilings at Edgartown with his wife. He's got a new $400,000 boat and he's petrified. To him, this is like parking a truck at twenty miles per hour without brakes. Unless there's somebody on the dock, he goes back out and comes in again until there's some-body there he can yell to, "Catch us as we're coming in." This man is not a lifelong sailor, and he needs help.

Bardlow, in his patent and trademark applications and literature, had named the product the "side thruster," to draw attention to the advantages of having total side-motion power. He conceived the product as appropriate for both bow and stern installation, especially for longer pleasure craft and most assuredly for commercial fishing vessels, to provide the ultimate in safety and maneuverability. In vessels of greater tonnage, the installation of the side thruster in the bow, stern, and amidships would be highly feasible and desirable, he thought.

Sidethrusters, Inc., set out to establish its line of six-, eight-, and ten-inch side thrusters in the marketplace. The experience acquired through manufacturing, marketing, and selling these units would help the research and development of new products, Bardlow thought. The units were priced at $5,000 for the smallest unit, up to $15,000 for the largest. Additional installation costs varied depending on whether the work was done on a new boat during the manufacturing process or on an existing boat in dry dock. The business plan allowed for one trip to train each installing boatyard on the procedures to be followed.

Financing

Having completed his plan, Bardlow contacted a group of friends and associates who were interested in boating—doctors, lawyers, dentists, and other potential investors who might contribute start-up capital. They, in turn, called their associates and soon developed a network of potential investors.

Very quickly, $200,000 was raised from sixteen investors. Two of the investors contributed $20,000, and one invested $30,000. Bardlow retained 35 percent of the company stock, his inventor/partner had 20 percent, and the investors had 45 percent ownership in the firm.

Management

Michael Bardlow was a CPA and the controller of Hayden Street Research and Management Company, an investment advisory firm. He had spent six years with Price Waterhouse before joining Hayden Street. He owned a twenty-five-foot sailboat and was knowledgeable about the general marine industry. He intended to continue his work at Hayden Street during the start-up and to become the full-time president when Sidethrusters reached annual sales of 120 units. The CEO of Hayden Street Research supported Bardlow's plan, although he declined to become an investor in the new firm.

Bardlow's partner, Al Carella, became the company's vice president and only full-time employee. Carella had worked on propulsion systems with the navy and Coast Guard over the past twenty years.

He was the inventor of the side thruster and assisted Bardlow in the sales effort. Carella had total responsibility for manufacturing, assembly, and shipping.

The first sale was to the Shannon Boat Company, which installed a unit in a fifty-foot yacht at their Rhode Island boatyard. Bardlow recalled:

> One of the most nervous days in my life was watching a brand-new $350,000 boat sitting at the dock, with the president of Shannon next to me and my engineer standing in the cockpit saying, "OK, I'm ready." I'm saying to myself, "Please work. Please, please work." Al kicked it on.
>
> The bow went right away from the dock. The president said, "Wonderful. This is just what I want." The inventor is standing there smiling like a Cheshire cat. And I'm trying to remain cool and calm, as if I knew all along it would work. But we had never tested the thing. We assumed it would work but we weren't sure. I was ecstatic. Shannon makes three to five fifty-foot boats per year, and they gave us a blanket order.

In the first two years of company operations, approximately 110 sailboats in excess of fifty feet were built all over the world; side thrusters were installed in 70 of those boats. Mike Bardlow recognized early on, however, that the growth he wanted called for more than just installations in new sailboats. It called for more than a part-time effort, as well. He left Hayden Street Research and decided to go to the aftermarket, retrofitting existing pleasure boats. "We decided to go after the power boat market, because the ratio of power to sail is 25 boats to 1," said Bardlow. (Exhibit 3 shows approximate U.S. fleet sizes.)

An aggressive ad campaign featured quarter-page ads in two industry magazines—*Yachting* and a new publication called *Power and Motor Yacht.* "New Sidethruster maneuvers boats in tight spots!" shouted the headline, over a picture of a motor yacht swinging in to a crowded dock. "The first small thruster designed for boats 40 feet to 100 feet long!" The ads went on:

> Sidethruster's new hyraulic thruster delivers big moving power in a small package. Installed in the bow, the 6-inch model (less than half the size of a conventional thruster) can turn a 40-foot

yacht nearly within its own length. A unique direct drive 7-hp motor delivers 260 pounds of thrust in the 8-inch model and 230 pounds for the 6-inch model.

Side thrusters can be installed in one day. For more information on how to put some maneuvering power on your side, contact . . .

The Retrofit Market

In the retrofit market, side thrusters were installed on site at the boat owner's dry dock. Two oval holes were drilled on opposing sides of the fore section of the boat below the waterline. Pressure hoses, a power takeoff unit, and a precision-machined brass pump unit were installed while the boat was in dry dock. All the materials were purchased from subcontractors; they were mostly assembled from readily available components.

To install the side thruster, management had to hire its own work crew. Michael Bardlow explained:

> No boatyard would touch it. If a boatyard cuts two big holes in the hull and the boat happens to sink instead of moving sideways, that yard is liable to the tune of $250,000 to $500,000 (whatever the price of the boat was). I had to hire my own guys. We had never drilled a hole in the side of a boat—any boat.
>
> The very first power boat we did was a Grand Banks 36, owned by a doctor in New York. I personally led the three-man installation crew to the customer's yard. The guy doing the installation says, "I've worked on boats all of my life, this is no problem." So we arrive and there's this gorgeous fiberglass boat waiting for us. To mark the site for the holes we ran tape from the bow along the side to locate the right height and length. Fortunately, we're doing this at nine o'clock at night with flashlights, so no one can see us.
>
> We drilled one hole. It is a six-inch unit, but a hull is shaped at an angle, so elliptically the hole comes out about fourteen inches high. As my crew leader is doing this thing I am saying, "Are you crazy? Look at the size of this thing." We drilled a little bit, then a little bigger. We finished the holes at two o'clock in the morning.
>
> The boat owner came down the next morning at nine o'clock,

walked around the boat, and the color drained from his face. No tunnel. Just two huge holes, one on either side of the hull, and fiberglass dust all over everything. We hadn't realized how much dust we created. The owner said, "You guys have this thing in my boat by this afternoon, or tomorrow morning you're going to get sued!"

The next day they put the boat in the water. There was no leakage! It was perfectly dry, and it worked. It worked really well!

Sidethrusters' installation crew flew to boatyards in Maryland, Florida, Texas, California, and Alaska to install units in owners' boats. Bardlow knew the whole company would be at risk if anything went wrong, because insurance coverage for product liability was prohibitively expensive.

The retrofit market presented a great problem because every boat was different. No one boat in the powerboat market was standard. Even the same model boats were customized for individual buyers. Sidethrusters had installation agreements for half a dozen Grand Banks forty-two-foot cruisers, but Grand Banks offered three different engine configurations for their boats. Bardlow explained:

> We did the first one, and we died putting it in, but we put it in. We get the second order, we say to ourselves, "We've already done one of these; it should be a layup." So we cut all the hydraulic hoses based on our previous experience, went down to do the project, and the engines were in a different location. All our hoses were cut wrong. We had to airfreight new hoses in to complete the job.
>
> I couldn't legitimately and accurately estimate how long it would take us to install a unit. Not even once.

Bardlow believed the market potential for the side thruster was very large. During the first two years of operations they had sold over eighty side thrusters; a number of those had been retrofits. Company revenues reached nearly $500,000, but Sidethrusters had not made a profit. Bardlow had not foreseen the travel expense for the installation crews as a factor when he put together the financial projections in his business plan. Because of the large potential market, however, he was confident the company would succeed.

EXHIBIT 1. Pro Forma Year-End Balance Sheet

	Year 1	Year 2	Year 3
Assets ($)			
Cash, including short-term investments	232,060	463,604	856,010
Inventory	27,000	72,000	81,000
Patent	5,000	5,000	5,000
Total assets	264,060	540,604	942,010
Liabilities and capital ($)			
Accrued expenses	22,580	87,046	127,341
Capital stock, 1,000 shares outstanding	1,000	1,000	1,000
Capital surplus	199,550	199,550	199,550
Retained earnings	40,930	253,008	614,119
Total liabilities and capital	264,060	540,604	942,010

Source: Company financial records.

EXHIBIT 2. Pro Forma Income and Cash Flow Statement, Years 1–3 ($)

Month of Year 1	1	2	3	4	5	6	7	8	9	10	11	12	Totals:
Units Sold in Year 1			2	4	6	8	8	9	10	10	14	16	87
Sales	0	0	8,000	17,000	25,000	33,000	33,000	36,500	41,000	41,000	57,000	66,000	357,500
Less cost of goods sold	2,317	2,317	6,117	9,917	13,717	17,517	17,517	19,417	21,317	21,317	28,917	32,717	193,104
Gross margin	(2,317)	(2,317)	1,883	7,083	11,283	15,483	15,483	17,083	19,683	19,683	28,083	33,283	164,396
Other expenses													
MFB salary	867	867	867	867	867	867	867	867	867	867	867	867	10,404
Secretarial	160	320	320	480	480	480	480	480	480	480	480	480	5,120
Advertising	1,000	1,000	1,000	1,000	1,000	1,000	1,000	1,000	1,000	1,000	1,000	1,000	12,000
Travel	0	0	560	1,190	3,750	4,810	2,310	6,055	2,870	2,870	7,490	4,620	36,525
Postage	200	200	200	300	300	300	300	300	300	300	400	400	3,500
Telephone	200	200	200	300	300	350	400	400	400	400	600	600	4,350
Operating supplies	200	200	200	200	200	200	200	200	200	200	200	200	2,400
Accounting	420	420	420	420	420	420	420	420	420	420	420	420	5,040
Legal	4,000	0	0	0	0	0	0	0	0	0	0	0	4,000
Payroll taxes	224	224	234	245	245	245	245	245	245	245	245	245	2,887
Miscellaneous expenses	1,000	1,000	1,200	1,200	1,500	1,800	2,000	2,000	2,000	2,000	2,000	2,000	19,700
R&D	5,000	0	0	0	0	0	0	0	0	0	0	0	5,000
Total other expenses	13,271	4,431	5,201	6,202	9,062	10,472	8,222	11,967	8,782	8,782	13,702	10,832	110,926
Net income before taxes	(15,588)	(6,748)	(3,318)	881	2,221	5,011	7,261	5,116	10,901	10,901	14,381	22,451	53,470
State tax	0	0	0	0	0	0	0	0	1,074	1,090	1,438	2,245	5,847
Federal tax	0	0	0	0	0	0	0	0	2,147	2,180	2,876	4,490	11,693
Net income	(15,588)	(6,748)	(3,318)	881	2,221	5,011	7,261	5,116	7,680	7,631	10,067	15,716	35,930
Cumulative													
Add back noncash items	420	420	420	420	420	420	420	420	3,641	3,690	4,734	7,155	
Net cash before inventory	(15,168)	(6,328)	(2,898)	1,301	2,641	5,431	7,681	5,536	11,321	11,321	14,801	22,871	
Additions to inventory	(27,000)	0	(3,600)	(7,200)	(10,800)	(14,400)	(14,400)	(16,200)	(18,000)	(18,000)	(25,200)	(28,800)	
Relief from inventory	0	0	3,600	7,200	10,800	14,400	14,400	16,200	18,000	18,000	25,200	28,800	
Cash payments of accruals	0	0	0	0	0	0	0	0	0	0	0	0	
Net cash monthly	(42,168)	(6,328)	(2,898)	1,301	2,641	5,431	7,681	5,536	11,321	11,321	14,801	22,871	
Cumulative	47,832	41,504	38,606	39,907	42,548	47,979	55,660	61,196	72,517	83,838	98,639	121,510	
Noncash items													

Earnings per share (1,000 shares outstanding)   35.93

(continued)

EXHIBIT 2—Continued

Month of Year 2	1	2	3	4	5	6	7	8	9	10	11	12	Totals:
Units Sold in This Month	20	22	24	26	28	30	30	32	32	34	36	40	354
Sales	82,000	90,000	98,000	107,000	115,000	123,000	123,000	131,000	131,000	139,000	148,000	164,000	1,451,000
Less cost of goods sold	41,183	44,983	48,783	52,583	56,383	60,183	60,183	63,983	63,983	67,783	71,583	79,183	710,796
Gross margin	40,817	45,017	49,217	54,417	58,617	62,817	62,817	67,017	67,017	71,217	76,417	84,817	740,204
Other expenses													
MFB salary	5,000	5,000	5,000	5,000	5,000	5,000	5,000	5,000	5,000	5,000	5,000	5,000	60,000
Secretarial	1,000	1,000	1,000	1,000	1,000	1,000	1,000	1,000	1,000	1,000	1,000	1,000	12,000
Advertising	1,000	1,000	1,000	1,000	1,000	1,000	1,000	1,000	1,000	1,000	1,000	1,000	12,000
Travel	5,740	6,300	6,860	7,490	10,050	11,110	8,610	12,670	9,170	9,730	13,860	11,480	113,070
Postage	450	500	500	500	600	600	700	700	750	800	850	900	7,850
Telephone	700	800	800	850	1,000	1,000	1,050	1,100	1,200	1,200	1,300	1,300	12,300
Operating supplies	300	400	400	450	500	600	600	600	650	700	700	700	6,600
Accounting	500	500	500	500	500	500	500	500	500	500	500	500	6,000
Legal	0	0	0	0	0	0	0	0	0	0	0	0	0
Payroll taxes	632	632	632	632	632	632	632	632	632	632	632	632	7,584
Miscellaneous expenses	2,200	2,200	2,400	2,400	2,600	2,600	2,600	2,700	2,800	2,000	3,000	3,000	30,500
Total other expenses	17,522	18,332	19,092	19,822	22,882	24,042	21,692	25,902	22,702	23,562	27,842	25,512	268,904
Net income before taxes	23,295	26,685	30,125	34,595	35,735	38,775	41,125	41,115	44,315	47,655	48,575	59,305	471,300
State tax	2,330	2,669	3,013	3,450	3,574	3,878	4,113	4,112	4,432	4,766	4,858	5,931	47,136
Federal tax	10,483	12,008	13,556	15,568	16,081	17,449	18,506	18,502	19,942	21,445	21,859	26,687	212,086
Net income	10,482	12,008	13,556	15,567	16,080	17,448	18,506	18,501	19,941	21,444	21,858	26,687	212,078
Cumulative		22,490	36,046	51,613	67,693	85,141	103,647	122,148	142,089	163,533	185,391	212,078	
Add back noncash items	13,313	15,177	17,069	19,528	20,155	21,827	23,119	23,114	24,874	26,711	27,217	33,118	
Net cash before inventory	23,795	27,185	30,625	35,095	36,235	39,275	41,625	41,615	44,815	48,155	49,075	59,805	
Additions to inventory	(45,000)	(39,600)	(43,200)	(46,800)	(50,400)	(54,000)	(90,000)	(57,600)	(57,600)	(61,200)	(64,800)	(72,000)	
Relief from inventory	36,000	39,600	43,200	46,800	50,400	54,000	54,000	57,600	57,600	61,200	64,800	72,000	
Cash payments of accruals	(22,580)			(45,559)			(61,510)			(71,107)			
Net cash monthly	(7,785)	27,185	30,625	(10,464)	36,235	39,275	(55,885)	41,615	44,815	(22,952)	49,075	59,805	
Cumulative	113,725	140,910	171,535	161,071	197,306	236,581	180,696	222,311	267,126	244,174	293,249	353,054	
Noncash items													

Earnings per share (1,000 shares outstanding)   212.08

Month of Year 3	1	2	3	4	5	6	7	8	9	10	11	12	Totals
Units Sold in This Month	40	40	42	44	46	50	50	50	50	50	50	50	562
Sales	164,000	164,000	172,000	180,000	189,000	205,000	215,000	215,000	215,000	215,000	215,000	215,000	2,364,000
Less cost of goods sold	81,567	81,567	85,367	89,167	92,967	100,567	105,067	105,067	105,067	105,067	105,067	105,067	1,161,604
Gross margin	82,433	82,433	86,633	90,833	96,033	104,433	109,933	109,933	109,933	109,933	109,933	109,933	1,202,396
Other expenses													
MFB salary	5,417	5,417	5,417	5,417	5,417	5,417	5,417	5,417	5,417	5,417	5,417	5,417	65,004
Secretarial	1,125	1,125	1,125	1,125	1,125	1,125	1,125	1,125	1,125	1,125	1,125	1,125	13,500
Advertising	1,000	1,000	1,000	1,000	1,000	1,000	2,000	2,000	2,000	2,000	2,000	2,000	18,000
Travel	11,480	11,480	12,040	12,600	15,230	16,850	15,050	18,550	15,050	15,050	18,550	15,050	176,980
Postage	1,000	1,050	1,100	1,200	1,200	1,300	1,300	1,400	1,400	1,500	1,500	1,500	15,450
Telephone	1,350	1,400	1,400	1,500	1,500	1,500	1,550	1,600	1,600	1,700	1,700	1,700	18,500
Operating supplies	750	800	800	850	900	900	950	1,000	1,000	1,000	1,000	1,000	10,950
Accounting	700	700	700	700	700	700	700	700	700	700	700	700	8,400
Legal	0	0	0	0	0	5,000	0	0	0	0	0	0	5,000
Payroll taxes	837	837	837	837	837	837	837	837	837	837	837	837	10,044
Miscellaneous expenses	3,000	3,100	3,200	3,200	3,300	3,400	3,400	3,450	3,450	3,500	3,500	3,600	40,100
Research and development	3,000	3,000	3,000	3,000	3,000	3,000	0	0	0	0	0	0	18,000
Total other expenses	29,659	29,909	30,619	31,429	34,209	41,029	32,329	36,079	32,579	32,829	36,329	32,929	399,928
Net income before taxes	52,774	52,524	56,014	59,404	61,824	63,404	77,604	73,854	77,354	77,104	73,604	77,004	802,468
State tax	5,277	5,252	5,601	5,940	6,182	6,340	7,760	7,385	7,735	7,710	7,360	7,700	80,242
Federal tax	23,749	23,636	25,207	26,732	27,821	28,532	34,922	33,235	34,810	34,697	33,122	34,652	361,115
Net income	23,748	23,636	25,206	26,732	27,821	28,532	34,922	33,234	34,809	34,697	33,122	34,652	361,111
Cumulative		47,384	72,590	99,322	127,143	155,675	190,597	223,831	258,640	293,337	326,459	361,111	
Add back noncash items	29,726	29,588	31,508	33,372	34,703	35,572	43,382	41,320	43,245	43,107	41,182	43,052	
Net cash before inventory	53,474	53,224	56,714	60,104	62,524	64,104	78,304	74,554	78,054	77,804	74,304	77,704	
Additions to inventory	(72,000)	(72,000)	(75,600)	(79,200)	(82,800)	(90,000)	(103,500)	(94,500)	(94,500)	(94,500)	(94,500)	(94,500)	
Relief from inventory	72,000	72,000	75,600	79,200	82,800	90,000	94,500	94,500	94,500	94,500	94,500	94,500	
Cash payments of accruals	(87,046)			(90,822)			(103,647)			(127,947)			
Net cash monthly	(33,572)	53,224	56,714	(30,718)	62,524	64,104	(34,343)	74,554	78,054	(50,143)	74,304	77,704	
Cumulative	319,482	372,706	429,420	398,702	461,226	525,330	490,987	565,541	643,595	593,452	667,756	745,460	
Noncash items													361.11

Earnings per share (1,000 shares outstanding) 361.11

Note: MFB = Michael Bardlow.

EXHIBIT 3. Approximate U.S. Fleet Sizes, 1987–88

Category	Number	Totals
1987 new boat sales		
Inboard boats (cruisers)	13,100	
Sailboats (auxiliary powered)		
30 feet and under	1,100	
Over 30 feet	2,900	17,100
1987 industry estimate of inboard boats owned		
(includes powered sailboats)		481,000
1988 registration		
Over 65 feet		
Inboard	1,855	
Outboard	1,257	3,112
40–65 feet		
Inboard	33,942	
Outboard	5,735	39,677
26–40 feet		
Inboard	245,835	
Outboard	54,921	300,756
		343,545

Note

Nonprofit Business/Fraud

35. The National Financial Planners Association (A)

Dan Crosby, executive secretary of the National Financial Planners Association (NFPA), shook his head. It was clear he'd been taken for at least $100,000—maybe for two or three times that amount. The question was what to do about it.

Dan was assessing what he had learned about potentially incriminating practices by the management company that had served as "the office" of NFPA for over a decade. Twelve years earlier, as volunteer president of the then-fledgling trade association, Crosby had hired Pamela Gardner, president and co-owner of Program Management, Inc. (PMI), to handle some of the administrative details of running NFPA. Looking back, Crosby commented:

> All the members and officers of the association held full time jobs; we all contributed time to NFPA on a volunteer basis. Nobody had time to negotiate with hotels and suppliers to arrange meetings outside New York.
>
> If NFPA was to grow into a meaningful organization, as all the officers wanted it to, it had to have professional administrative help. Somebody knew of Pam Gardner. I talked with the other associations she was arranging meetings for, and they were delighted with her work. So we found the help we needed. Now I wonder how much help it's been.

This case was prepared by R. M. Kinnunen, James F. Molloy, Jr., and John Seeger.

NFPA Profile

NFPA, the National Financial Planners Association, was founded in New York in 1962 by a handful of sales executives associated with the insurance industry. In the beginning, NFPA was a small organization which was run informally by several members as a means of exchanging ideas and information. There were a president, a vice president, and a secretary-treasurer who had all the records in cardboard boxes at his office. They did not meet frequently but communicated with each other over the telephone. NFPA's secretary arranged all the meetings, including the meals, the guest speaker, the hotel, promoting attendance, and collecting the registration fees.

The mission of the association was to facilitate and promote leadership and innovation within the operations sector of the financial planning industry by

1. Encouraging a free exchange of ideas among companies.
2. Developing improved methods and practices to meet current and future needs.
3. Advocating uniform procedures and standard practices that take advantage of telecommunications and applications technologies.
4. Providing a medium through which members can confer, consult, and cooperate with government, the public, and other industry groups.
5. Maintaining a high standard of ethical conduct while providing service to our members.

During small, informal dinner meetings, these charter NFPA members shared information and developed solutions to common operational problems. People from the mutual fund industry and financial planners began to join the original insurance industry members as word of their periodic meetings spread. The association grew slowly and in the 1970s began to organize regional meetings, where industry experts and leaders would gather to talk about current issues. As many as 100 people would attend a Boston meeting, while 250 might attend one in New York.

Association annual dues at the beginning were $25 per company regardless of the company size. The only membership rule was that the members be employed as financial planners. People with only partial or tangential involvement in the industry could become an associate (nonvoting) member by paying $15. As the financial industry began to grow, bringing with it new members, dues rose. By the mid 1980s dues for full membership had increased to $350 per year. At the same time, the rules for becoming a full member were relaxed, and companies in other industries became involved. By 1992, with membership in NFPA approaching 250 member companies, dues reached $1,000 per year. The association's evolution was typical of many not-for-profit trade groups.

The Association Industry

According to *National Trade and Professional Associations of the United States*,[1] a trade association was defined by the late C. Jay Judkins, chief of the Trade Association Division of the United States Department of Commerce, as

> a nonprofit, cooperative, voluntarily joined organization of business competitors designed to assist its members and its industry in dealing with mutual business problems in several of the following areas: accounting practice, business ethics, commercial and industrial research, standardization, statistics, trade promotion, and relations with Government, employees and the general public.

There have been three periods of pronounced growth in the number of U.S. national trade associations. The first occurred during World War I, as the number grew from about 100 associations in 1900 to over 1,000 in 1920. The second period of growth occurred during the depression in the 1930s, when the National Industrial Recovery Act of 1933 encouraged the formation of trade unions to help stimulate the economy. Some 800 new associations were formed under this law, although many disappeared when the Supreme Court in 1935 declared the law unconstitutional. The third period of growth occurred during World War I as companies had to share information in order to produce at peak efficiency. By 1943 there were about 1,900 trade groups; some closed in the years just after the war, but the total has risen gradually ever since.

Trade associations were formed by individuals who came together to solve, through concerted action, a problem they could not solve acting alone. An example was the standardization of time zones, which resulted from joint action by the nation's railroads. Trade associations promoted research on new products, new uses for by-products, and improved methods of manufacturing. They also provided training seminars, collected market or cost data in order to compile industry statistics, and published quality and certification standards. They often sponsored exhibits, contests, awards, and cooperative advertising.

Perhaps the most important function of trade associations was keeping members informed of governmental developments which might impact the industry and representing the industry viewpoint to governmental agencies. Virtually no major law passed through Congress or the state legislatures without some lobby or trade association having had a hand in the process.

In 1990, there were 3,400 national trade associations in the United States. The total number of national offices, their local chapters, and independent local or regional groups was estimated at around 40,000. According to the United States Commerce Department, over 35 percent of those were retail trade groups, about 20 percent represented services, and about 15 percent were in manufacturing. An example from the service sector was the American Society of Association Executives, with a membership of 20,000 paid employees of associations and societies. Founded in 1920 and renamed in 1956, by 1990 the association had a budget of $14.5 million. A 1984 survey of 170 not-for-profit groups in the District of Columbia/Maryland/Virginia area showed an average salary for top officers of associations at $98,500; the range was from $25,500 to $258,000. Staff size for associations varied from one person to several hundred. The usual staff size was six to ten people.

A growing number of management companies handled operations for trade associations on a contract basis. In 1990 there were 264 such management firms operating in the United States, serving over 500 national and 1,000 local or regional organizations. The typical large firm handled administrative work for a number of associations, providing a range of skills and services beyond the means of most small trade groups. To the volunteer officers of many trade associations, management companies presented a very attractive option for conducting their business.

Association revenues were derived primarily through members' dues. In most cases dues were based upon a percentage of annual sales of the member company (usually ranging from .01 to .1 percent) or based on a flat fee. Associations typically had several classes of memberships, with different dues and privileges for each class. Associate members were vendors or suppliers of goods and services, with no voting rights. In most cases, only full members had the right to vote and hold office.

NFPA Growth

In the 1980s, the president and the board of directors had decided that in order to bring in more members, NFPA would have to expand the services it offered. They decided that the association should offer an annual conference in San Francisco in the month of February. The conference would offer panel discussions and workshops to all NFPA members, spread over an entire week.

President Dan Crosby realized that neither he nor any other officer had the time to put together all the details of a major out-of-town conference. He decided to hire an outside management company to run the event. After investigation, the board decided to retain the services of Program Management, Inc.

PMI employed three full time staff, headed by Pamela Gardner, to take care of the records and organize the meetings for its eight other clients. Gardner, a poised and sophisticated Smith College graduate, had twelve years of experience managing other associations. NFPA agreed to pay PMI $5,000 per month or $60,000 a year plus expenses (copying, mailing, etc.) to organize and handle all the details of the annual meetings (hotels, meals, accommodations, audiovisual equipment, etc.); to set up regional conferences and seminars and arrange board meetings; to create and send out notices to NFPA members about meetings and upcoming events and put together an annual membership directory; and to collect member dues for deposit into NFPA's account. PMI negotiated terms for all meetings, conferences, and seminars and paid all the bills after being reimbursed by the association.

With a sigh of relief, Crosby and the NFPA secretary-treasurer carried their seven cartons of records into PMI's office. Henceforth, this would be the headquarters address of the National Financial Planners Association.

The first annual meeting under PMI's management took place in San Francisco in February 1982. Approximately 200 people—evenly split between exhibitors and members—attended, and the administrative details went smoothly. While this first conference was not seen as a huge success by NFPA's leaders, it showed that the association had a strong base for national expansion.

Between 1982 and 1988 NFPA's membership grew steadily, and annual meetings and conferences had greatly increased in attendance. Seeing great potential for growth, NFPA leaders recognized that the association needed to become more formal and better controlled. The association needed to ensure professionalism yet retain management control as it grew.

In 1988, Al Dugan, an officer of a large bank, became NFPA's president. As the first president who was not himself in the financial planning industry, Dugan brought a new perspective to the association's leadership. He was less concerned with the control of daily operations than prior presidents had been. Dugan focused instead on a long term strategy for the association. He decided to convene a two-day strategic planning seminar for NFPA leadership in 1991. (see exhibit 1.)

The president invited approximately thirty members he thought would be active participants and contributors during the seminar and would be most likely to play an active role in implementing any changes. The seminar was conducted in a group format with the facilitators. The two days resulted in consensus on a wide range of strategic issues and the commitment of many key people to specific actions.

At that point, the only people familiar with NFPA's inner workings were Pamela Gardner and the employees of PMI, who were responsible for ensuring that the association ran smoothly and professionally and was financially sound. Throughout PMI's tenure, NFPA officers had been highly satisfied with conference arrangements, including meals, meeting rooms, lodging, and so on. PMI provided a monthly statement to the NFPA board of directors that included revenues, expenses, and the balance in the checking account. There was little detail in the reports, but NFPA's leaders could see the organization was struggling financially to provide its promised services. When asked about the apparent problem with cash flow, however, Gardner responded "Not to worry—everything will be fine. Compared to most trade associations, NFPA is in great shape."

Professional Management for NFPA

One result of the 1991 seminar was a decision to hire an executive secretary, who would be paid to work part time for the association to ensure that the association was being run in the best long term interest of the members. Dan Crosby, past president of NFPA and still a regular (although nonvoting) participant at board meetings, was hired to fill this position.

Crosby, formerly a line manager of Metropolitan Life Insurance Company, was considered to be a hard-nosed leader and seemed ideal for the position of executive secretary. He had served NFPA continuously for fifteen years and still consulted on the annual renewal of the PMI management contract. He held an MBA degree and taught courses in strategic management at a local university. Looking back at his decision to accept the job, Crosby commented on the time required for doing it:

> I told the board I would spend at the most six hours a day working; everybody knew that was all NFPA could afford. Actually, I would be there for ten, maybe twelve hours, but I'd only charge them for six. The board would say, "Don't charge us a lot." But at the same time, they would call and say, "Dan, will you do this? Would you do that?" Suddenly my hours were escalating because at the same time the association was growing, the board's involvement became greater and greater.

A Growing Suspicion

One of Crosby's initial undertakings was to review the way PMI was managing the association's business. He watched all aspects of the 1992 conference in San Francisco. Because of his prior relationship with association members and Pamela Gardner, Dan could see how things were run at the conference without attracting attention. He saw some things that made him wonder but nothing he could pinpoint. After returning from the 1992 conference, Dan learned from PMI's statement that the event had produced $300,000 of revenue from registration fees. This was offset by $298,000 in expenses. He commented,

> It just didn't make sense that our annual conference, with that kind of revenue, only had a surplus of $2,000. After spending a considerable amount of time probing and analyzing the situation, I could understand how the system worked. But that still didn't explain why it was so close to breakeven.

The limited profitability, if true, meant that NFPA needed to revise its policies, procedures, and records in order to improve cash levels. This led Dan to examine receipts and billings of recent New York meetings. For the big meetings in New York, the association would collect revenues of $30,000 to $35,000 and lose money. Those meetings attracted 300 to 400 people at $80 per person for a one-day meeting. Dan asked Pamela for a meeting to review expenses. It proved difficult, however, to schedule a meeting with her. Her other work interfered with efforts to prepare the special expense reports Dan asked for. "Our office is set up to produce the routine reports automatically," Pamela said. "But special reports are something else. It's not ready yet but will be soon."

When Crosby asked Pamela for a specific receipt, she responded, "It's around somewhere." When he sought assurance that PMI was bonded, she gave positive sounding answers. When asked again, Pamela said they "couldn't find the certificate and we're all looking for it." NFPA's annual audits, performed since the organization's inception by a "Big Six" firm whose managing partner had once served as association president, shed little light on the situation. As with most small business and not-for-profit audits, the annual CPA letter included the passage

> All information included in these financial statements is the representation of the management of the National Financial Planners Association.
>
> A review consists principally of inquiries of company personnel and analytical procedures applied to financial data. It is substantially less in scope than an audit in accordance with generally accepted auditing standards, the objective of which is the expression of an opinion regarding the financial statements taken as a whole. Accordingly, I do not express such an opinion.

Dan received the routine March reports from PMI and still didn't like what he saw. His instincts told him something was wrong. "I am seeing numbers that don't make sense," he said, "and I am dealing with a woman who appears not in touch with reality." Even though Al Dugan, president of the association, was a close friend, Dan felt it was premature to convey his suspicions to Al.

In April 1992, Pamela visited Crosby and requested an advance check for $5,000 for expenses for the New York Hilton, in connection with the association's May meeting. Dan was perplexed because he was quite sure that advances had never been required in the past. He asked why she needed it. Pamela responded, "We have to give them [the Hilton] an advance. I tried to get around it. They may be in trouble. They told me that they need the advance within three days." Dan asked if she had spoken to the hotel's general manager. She said, "Yes." Dan described his reaction:

> I said, "fine." After the meeting, I picked up the phone and spoke to the president of Hilton Hotels, in Seattle, Washington. I said, "I need your assistance with a problem. Either the Hilton Corporation must be in serious trouble, or you are trying to blow customers away." He said, "Neither. We are in great shape and we want customers." I told him what had happened. He said, "That's strange. We don't normally require advances from good customers." He inquired how long NFPA had used Hilton. When I said six or seven years, he said, "Stranger still. I'll call you back."

From Suspicion to Conviction

That night, while sitting in his office at the local university, Dan received a telephone call from the president of the Hilton. He had looked into the matter and said that the NFPA problem was not unusual. He asked Dan if a management company handled the association's business and went on to say the hotel had asked for an advance because the association's last bill had not been paid for 120 days and even then the check bounced. Dan couldn't believe what he was hearing. "I sign the checks myself. We pay in ten days. I sometimes pay within a week because when a supplier performs a service for us I want them to get their money. I want NFPA to be known as a choice customer—one vendors will fight to keep." The Hilton president said, "This is not all that unusual, Mr. Crosby. We've been through cases like this before. Let me do this for you. Whatever you need, you let me know and I'll find it for you. My New York people are alerted to help; if there's anything more you need, call me."

After hanging up, Dan was on a mission. He pulled out all the PMI bills, to search again for an answer.

> It's 11:30 at night, and I become an obsessed animal. I'm doing all kinds of reviews—looking and looking, and suddenly I realize these are Xerox copies of the bills. Where are the original copies of the bills? Why am I looking at Xeroxes? I approved a Xerox copy of a bill. We had all approved Xerox copies of bills, for

twelve years. I said, "Wait a minute. Wrong!" I called the Hilton at 11:30 at night and said I wanted to speak to accounting. The accounting manager wasn't in, of course, but the night manager told me he usually arrived by 7:00 A.M. and I should call back then.

The next morning at 7:00 A.M., Dan called the New York Hilton's accounting manager. Dan discussed his problem and said he needed to see the original bills. The accounting manager told Dan, "Come on in. I'll even validate your parking. Sounds like you're in a rush."

During the meeting with the hotel accountant, Crosby found that the original invoice requested an advance of $2,000; Pamela Gardner asked him for $5,000. Crosby decided to investigate further by reviewing three years worth of bills for regional one-day meetings. At the Hilton he compared his checks to the original hotel bills. He found $35,000 in NFPA payment overcharges in the New York Hilton invoices alone. Back at home, working by telephone with the San Francisco Hilton on the 1992 annual meeting, he found $40,000 extra had been paid to PMI.

Crosby consulted the law firm that occasionally helped the NFPA and learned that any accusations against Pamela Gardner or her firm would have to be handled with caution: a countersuit for defamation of character would be a likely response. Gardner herself might claim ignorance of any malfeasance: perhaps some one of her employees was fiddling with the books. Filing suit against PMI would probably cost $50,000 to $75,000 in legal fees, and it might take several years to get a judgment. Even if they did win a judgment in court, they would still need to get the money back from Gardner and PMI.

Crosby felt the prospects of actually collecting anything from PMI were doubtful at best, since the firm had few apparent assets. He also felt that if PMI were siphoning money, they would not have left the funds in PMI itself. This meant personal charges would have to be made against individuals, although it was likely to be difficult to prove them. For example, if Pamela Gardner was charged she could claim she knew nothing, that it was the accountant who had taken the money, without her knowledge.

Another concern for Crosby was the other trade associations that were being or had been serviced and perhaps victimized by PMI and Pamela Gardner. Crosby considered contacting organizations privately and suggesting that they be alert to potential fraud. He was unsure, however, of the risks associated with this option. It was very possible that this course of action might open NFPA and himself to a countersuit for defamation of character. On the other hand, if he did nothing PMI could continue to practice fraud.

Criminal charges were also a possibility, of course. The state's attorney general, or the city police, or the U.S. Postal Service mail fraud investigators might prosecute if they saw it as an attractive case. They, not NFPA, would be the accusers.

A fraud audit would also have to be conducted by an outside auditing firm, which would require studying every invoice received by NFPA over the past three to five years, identifying where it came from, what was done with it, and how it was paid by NFPA, and also contracting the vendor to verify the original bill amount and what actually had been received from PMI. Estimates of the accounting costs alone were between $25,000 and $35,000. Crosby estimated that PMI had diverted $100,000 to $200,000 from the association.

Armed with this information Crosby pondered the ramifications of his discovery. It was time to involve Al Dugan and the board of directors, but Dan was unsure what to recommend. He shook his head again. This was not what he'd expected when he took the NFPA job.

EXHIBIT 1.   NFPA Long Range Planning Workshop, January 19–20, 1991

Objective

To identify strategic issues that will face NFPA in the early 1990s and to plan appropriate actions that will enable NFPA to reach its full potential in membership benefits.

Process

1. Examine the mission of NFPA in light of its stakeholders and specify modifications.
2. Recognize the opportunities and threats that will become manifest in the early 1990s.
3. In the context of item 2, identify the current strengths and weaknesses of NFPA.
4. Clarify the strategic issues of the early 1990s that must be addressed by NFPA.
5. Identify and evaluate alternative actions that address the strategic issues and then decide on an action plan.
6. Specify what resources are necessary, who has responsibility for specific actions, when those actions will be taken, what results will be seen, and how accountability will be established.

Notes

    1. Data in this section were drawn from *National Trade and Professional Associations of the United States* (New York: Columbia Books, 1990).

Role Playing Exercise

36. U.S. Auto Parts Inc.: Insolvency Simulation Exercise

U.S. Auto Parts Inc. (UAP) is incorporated pursuant to the laws of Delaware, with plants, premises, inventory, and equipment in Chicago. UAP's head office is located in New York.

UAP carries on business as a manufacturing facility and is principally engaged in the manufacture of metal-stamped automotive parts for tier 1 and tier 2 automotive manufacturers. UAP's largest clients are Gonzo Auto (GA) and Daco Voitures (DV), which are located in New York and Detroit. UAP provides parts for 20 percent of the new GA "Excluso" passenger vehicle and 40 percent of the parts for the DV "Dingo" truck.

Under the terms of the business relationships UAP has with its principal contractors, UAP must supply parts on a *just in time* delivery system that allows both GA and DV to avoid the necessity of having to stockpile large inventories of parts. This practice places a heavy onus on parts suppliers such as UAP to produce and deliver automobile parts to manufacturers within an extremely short time span under threat of cancellation of the contract or under penalty. It is also standard in the industry that automobile manufacturers pay their accounts to parts suppliers on a timely basis that would generally

This exercise was prepared by Justin Fogerty.

average forty-five days from the date of shipment. The shares of UAP are 100 percent owned by Mr. John Capone Carpo (Carpo).

UAP employs approximately six hundred people, the majority of whom are unionized. UAP also has a small subsidiary, UAP Texas, located in Dallas (UAP Dallas), which employs approximately two hundred people, the majority of whom are also unionized. The chief executive officer and directing mind of both UAP and UAP Dallas is Carpo.

Lending History

The Bank of Chicago (BC) began its lending relationship with UAP in 1995. The latter's credit with BC is a demand facility credit, and it has been based on term sheets executed by BC, Carpo, and both UAP and UAP Dallas from time to time beginning in 1995. Chronic losses by UAP resulted in an increase in the aggregate credit facility the bank granted in 1995 of $70 million to the current amount of $130 million. BC has taken security against all of the real and personal property of UAP, and it has guarantees from Carpo personally.

The Lone Star Bank advanced a line of credit to UAP Dallas totaling $10 million. It is in first position on receivables for UAP Dallas but in second position to BC on equipment and machinery.

In addition, Lone Star Bank was granted collateral security over the parent UAP. However, it is in second position to BC on the receivables, inventory, and equipment with respect to the parent.

From a review of the December 31, 2002, financial statements, the secured debt owed to BC represents 76 percent of total liabilities of UAP. Total liabilities include approximately $27 million of accounts payable. In addition, the review of the December 31, 2002, statements demonstrated that the debt owed by UAP to BC was $95 million, whereas, in fact, the debt was approximately $130 million.

In February 2003, BC and Lone Star Bank received a copy of UAP's management-prepared financial statements reporting a net loss to February 29, 2003, of approximately $1.8 million. On or about March 15, 2003, a draft statement prepared by UAP accountants indicated a net loss of approximately $10.9 million.

The financial statements of UAP Dallas also dated December 31, 2002, indicated that the nonbank liabilities owed are $2,000,000, EBITDA is $4,000,000, and bank indebtedness $10,000,000.

Following receipt of the draft statement, BC and Lone Star Bank engaged in a series of meetings and discussions with Carpo and representatives of UAP to ascertain whether the banks should continue to grant credit facilities. In an effort to demonstrate his commitment to restructuring to the banks, Carpo retained the National Accounting Firm (NAF) to assist him in turning his company around.

Notwithstanding significant requests received from NAF, UAP did not respond to each and every one of these information requests, and the information was provided on a piecemeal basis.

In addition, UAP continued generally to be in default of its reporting requirements and its August 3, 2002, term sheet.

In addition to what appeared to be poor management of UAP, the accounting systems were grossly inadequate to deal with the volume of transactions.

After various site visits, NAF made the following determinations.

- A company that was owned directly by Carpo was contracting with UAP to provide services to UAP at a higher price than that which would otherwise have been competitive in the marketplace. Some $8.5 million was overcharged by the related company owned by Carpo to UAP for provision of services than easily could have been provided by a more cost-effective and efficient contractor.
- Carpo also had recently entered into a long-term lease for a storage facility located in Chicago. Carpo subsequently subleased that building to UAP for a 15-year term with a net profit to him in excess of $2.2 million.
- Just prior to the banks' receiving the December 31, 2002, financial statements of UAP and UAP Dallas, Carpo entered into an employment agreement with UAP providing him with a base salary in the amount of $750,000 per year as chief executive officer, an annual bonus of $100,000, and a no-cut hundred-year term with an extraordinarily generous severance package.
- In 2002, UAP had entered into two five-year contracts, one with GA and one with DV, to supply auto parts for both the Excluso and the Dingo at less than a competitive price point. The management of UAP hoped that it would be able to significantly reduce costs to make the production of these two major components profitable. GA and DV subsequently gave other smaller parts runs for unrelated products to UAP. Management at the time believed that they would be able to make their production lines profitable by use of good management of resources. Notwithstanding the intention that was expressed by management, each and every part that has been produced

by UAP over the last year and a half has resulted in a net loss. In other words, there is a negative gross margin on the production of each part. Every month that UAP stays in business results in a net "burn rate" of cash in excess of the revenues of $3.0 million. However, UAP Dallas has a positive cash flow that effectively makes the burn rate $2 million companywide.

- NAF was able to ascertain that the books and records of UAP were not accurate with respect to receivables. GA and DV disputed the production quality of approximately $10 million worth of parts produced by UAP and are holding back a setoff against receivables in those amounts. The GA holdback is approximately $7.5 million; DV's holdback is $2.5 million. GA and DV together account for 80 percent of the $100 million in sales generated by UAP, and they account for $30 million of the sales generated by UAP Dallas.

- Finally, NAF was able to determine from the term sheet that the Texas subsidiary of UAP is being drained in order to fund the parent operations. Consequently, UAP Dallas cannot meet its obligations, and its payables have been stretched. Furthermore, the cross-collateral default clauses have been triggered by the parent's default.

- UAP losses total $9 million to December 31, 2002, and the Texas operations have a total debt owed of $10 million. However, UAP Dallas is more credible than its parent, and its income statements are showing a positive income of $2 million and accounts payable of $6 million. However, every month $1 million of UAP Dallas's positive cash flow is burned off by the parent.

- NAF computed various ratios, including margins, current ratio, EBITDA to total assets, and the Z-score for UAP over the last few years. Financial distress became clearly evident in 2001 and early last year, and the Z has steadily drifted down from moderately distressed and now is deep in the default zone as a result of UAP's growing losses.

BC and Lone Star Bank's Reactions to UAP's Financial Difficulties

BC's Reaction

The term sheet provided by BC to UAP in 2002 set its credit limit at $70 million, but the bank had allowed it to temporarily bulge to $130 million. BC expressed its concern to UAP in a letter dated March 30, 2003, and advised it would not extend further credit. Accordingly, UAP's ability to meet its current payables, which are already stretched to 120 days, is at risk. The April 30, 2003, payroll of $2.1 million is due. In addition, because of the significant problems caused by the various setoffs from GA and DV, the frequency of receipt of payment from GA and DV has been extended from 45 days to 60–70 days.

GA and DV are also concerned that a failure of UAP and UAP Dallas would have a devastating impact on the production of the Excluso and Dingo, given that they do not have a sufficient stockpile of parts that would allow them to outsource the manufacture of these parts in less than 120 days.

Lone Star Bank's Reaction

Lone Star Bank was concerned when it learned that UAP was in financial difficulty. It reacted by applying pressure to UAP Dallas and by being forceful in guiding the subsidiaries' decisions.

The manager of Lone Star Bank also took advantage of his close relationship with Carpo, who effectively entered into a new loan agreement with the bank. The agreement granted the bank additional security in the form of intellectual property rights to a new and promising computer program developed in-house that will increase parts production. The agreement was set out on the back of a napkin at a golf course and accompanied by the bank manager's encouraging words: "Don't worry, we are in this together." It should also be noted that the relationship between the bank manager and Carpo is so close that the former is a de facto director of the business.

Contributors

Thomas Allison is Chief Operating Officer, Corporate Advisory Services, Huron Consulting Group.

Mark Blumling is Director, Burrill & Company.

Jack Brittain is Dean and Professor of Management, University of Utah.

Howard Brownstein is Principal, NachmanHaysBrownstein, Inc.

Lawrence P. Carr is Professor of Accounting, Babson College.

Tom Cook is Associate Professor of Accountancy, University of Denver.

Paul Croke is Principal and Founder, Deep Customer Connections, Inc.

Suzanne Cummins is Faculty Fellow, Department of Management and Policy, University of Arizona.

John Dunkelberg is Emeritus Professor of Finance, Wake Forest University.

James Ebbert is Managing Director, McShane Group.

Lawrence M. Fisher covered technology for the *New York Times* for fifteen years. He has written for many publications.

Justin Fogerty is a Partner at Bennett Jones LLP.

Kevin A. Frick is Associate Principal, McKinsey & Company, Inc.

Henry Garelick is with New Generation Advisors, Inc.

Thomas Goho is Associate Professor of Finance, Wake Forest University.

Robert Goldberg is Lecturer, Northeastern University.

Jon Goodwin is Managing Director, Barra Partners, LLC.

Hugh Grove is Professor of Accountancy, University of Denver.

James F. Hart is with Taylor Consulting, Inc.

Thomas Hays is Principal, NachmanHaysBrownstein, Inc.

Chuck Hofer is Regents Professor of Strategic Management and Entrepreneurship, University of Georgia.

Ray M. Kinnunen is Associate Professor of General Management, Northeastern University.

Henry W. Lane is Darla and Frederick Brodsky Trustee Professor in International Business, Northeastern University.

Daniel McCarthy is Professor of General Management, Northeastern University.

William F. Meehan III is Director, McKinsey & Company, Inc.

Kenneth Merchant is Deloitte & Touche LLP Chair of Accountancy, University of Southern California.

Marc Meyer is Professor of General Management, Northeastern University.

James F. Molloy, Jr., is Professor of General Management, Northeastern University.

Grant Newton is Professor of Accounting, Pepperdine University.

Harlan D. Platt is Professor of Finance, Northeastern University.

Marjorie B. Platt is Professor of Accounting, Northeastern University.

Ravi Ramamurti is Professor of General Management, Northeastern University.

Ramesh K. S. Rao is McDermott Professor of Banking and Finance, University of Texas.

Miriam Rothman is Professor of Management, University of San Diego.

Alison Sauve is Research Assistant, Northeastern University.

John Seeger is Professor of Management, Bentley College.

Paul N. Shields is a Partner at Neilson Elggren LLP.

Wim A. Van der Stede is Assistant Professor of Accounting, University of Southern California.

Andrew Watson is Assistant Professor of General Management, Northeastern University.

James Weisel is Associate Professor of Accounting, Mercer University.

David Wesley is Research Program Manager, Northeastern University.

Robert W. White is Professor of Finance, University of Western Ontario.

Susan White is Teaching Professor of Finance, University of Maryland.

Index of Cases

Teaching notes are available upon request to instructors who adopt the book for classroom use. Please send request on department or corporate letterhead to Professor Harlan Platt, Northeastern University, 413 Hayden Hall, Boston, MA 02115.